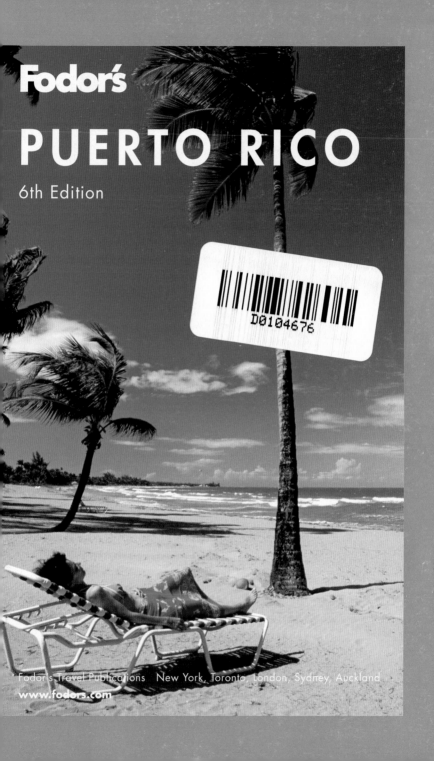

Fodor's

PUERTO RICO

6th Edition

Fodor's Travel Publications New York, Toronto, London, Sydney, Auckland
www.fodors.com

AMBROS
PUERTOR

Be a Fodor's Correspondent

Your opinion matters. It matters to us. It matters to your fellow Fodor's travelers, too. And we'd like to hear it. In fact, we need to hear it.

When you share your experiences and opinions, you become an active member of the Fodor's community. That means we'll not only use your feedback to make our books better, but we'll publish your names and comments whenever possible. Throughout our guides, look for "Word of Mouth," excerpts of your unvarnished feedback.

Here's how you can help improve Fodor's for all of us.

Tell us when we're right. We rely on local writers to give you an insider's perspective. But our writers and staff editors—who are the best in the business—depend on you. Your positive feedback is a vote to renew our recommendations for the next edition.

Tell us when we're wrong. We're proud that we update most of our guides every year. But we're not perfect. Things change. Hotels cut services. Museums change hours. Charming cafés lose charm. If our writer didn't quite capture the essence of a place, tell us how you'd do it differently. If any of our descriptions are inaccurate or inadequate, we'll incorporate your changes in the next edition and will correct factual errors at fodors.com immediately.

Tell us what to include. You probably have had fantastic travel experiences that aren't yet in Fodor's. Why not share them with a community of like-minded travelers? Maybe you chanced upon a beach or bistro or B&B that you don't want to keep to yourself. Tell us why we should include it. And share your discoveries and experiences with everyone directly at fodors.com. Your input may lead us to add a new listing or highlight a place we cover with a "Highly Recommended" star or with our highest rating, "Fodor's Choice."

Give us your opinion instantly at our feedback center at www.fodors.com/feedback. You may also e-mail editors@fodors.com with the subject line "Puerto Rico Editor." Or send your nominations, comments, and complaints by mail to Puerto Rico Editor, Fodor's, 1745 Broadway, New York, NY 10019.

You and travelers like you are the heart of the Fodor's community. Make our community richer by sharing your experiences. Be a Fodor's correspondent.

Happy Traveling!

Tim Jarrell, Publisher

FODOR'S PUERTO RICO

Editor: Eric B.Wechter

Writers: Christopher P. Baker, Julie Schwietert Collazo, Nicholas Gill, Marlise Kast, Charyn Pfeuffer, Heather Rodino
Editorial Contributors: Francesca Drago, Alexis Kelly, Mark Sullivan

Production Editor: Evangelos Vasilakis
Maps & Illustrations: Henry Colomb and Mark Stroud, Moon Street Cartography; David Lindroth, Inc., *cartographers;* Bob Blake, Rebecca Baer, *map editors;* William Wu, *information graphics*
Design: Fabrizio La Rocca, *creative director*; Guido Caroti, Siobhan O'Hare, *art directors*; Tina Malaney, Chie Ushio, Ann McBride, Jessica Walsh, *designers*; Melanie Marin, *senior picture editor*
Cover Photo: (Old San Juan): Shuttervision/Shutterstock
Production Manager: Angela L. McLean

COPYRIGHT

6th Edition

ISBN 978-1-4000-0452-2

ISSN 1531–0396

SPECIAL SALES

This book is available at special discounts for bulk purchases for sales promotions or premiums. Special editions, including personalized covers, excerpts of existing books, and corporate imprints, can be created in large quantities for special needs. For more information, write to Special Markets/Premium Sales, 1745 Broadway, MD 6-2, New York, New York 10019, or e-mail specialmarkets@randomhouse.com.

AN IMPORTANT TIP & AN INVITATION

Although all prices, opening times, and other details in this book are based on information supplied to us at press time, changes occur all the time in the travel world, and Fodor's cannot accept responsibility for facts that become outdated or for inadvertent errors or omissions. So **always confirm information when it matters,** especially if you're making a detour to visit a specific place. Your experiences—positive and negative—matter to us. If we have missed or misstated something, **please write to us.** We follow up on all suggestions. Contact the Puerto Rico editor at editors@fodors.com or c/o Fodor's at 1745 Broadway, New York, NY 10019.

PRINTED IN CHINA

10 9 8 7 6 5 4 3 2 1

CONTENTS

Fodor's Features

MAPS

ABOUT THIS BOOK

Our Ratings

Sometimes you find terrific travel experiences and sometimes they just find you. But usually the burden is on you to select the right combination of experiences. That's where our ratings come in.

As travelers we've all discovered a place so wonderful that its worthiness is obvious. And sometimes that place is so unique that superlatives don't do it justice: you just have to be there to know. These sights, properties, and experiences get our highest rating, **Fodor's Choice**, indicated by orange stars throughout this book.

Black stars highlight sights and properties we deem **Highly Recommended**, places that our writers, editors, and readers praise again and again for consistency and excellence.

By default, there's another category: Any place we include in this book is by definition worth your time, unless we say otherwise. And we will.

Disagree with any of our choices? Care to nominate a place or suggest that we rate one more highly? Visit our feedback center at *www.fodors.com/feedback*.

Budget Well

Hotel and restaurant price categories from ¢ to $$$$ are defined in the opening pages of each chapter. For attractions, we always give standard adult admission fees; reductions are usually available for children, students, and senior citizens. Want to pay with plastic? **AE, D, DC, MC, V** following restaurant and hotel listings indicate whether American Express, Discover, Diner's Club, MasterCard, and Visa are accepted.

Restaurants

Unless we state otherwise, restaurants are open for lunch and dinner daily. We mention dress only when there's a specific requirement and reservations only when they're essential or not accepted—it's always best to book ahead.

Hotels

Hotels have private bath, phone, TV, and air-conditioning and operate on the European Plan (aka EP, meaning without meals), unless we specify that they use the Continental Plan (CP, with a Continental breakfast), Breakfast Plan (BP, with a full breakfast), or Modified American Plan (MAP, with breakfast and dinner) or are all-inclusive (AI, including all meals and most activities). We always list facilities but not whether you'll be charged an extra fee to use them, so when pricing accommodations, find out what's included.

Listings

- ★ Fodor's Choice
- ★ Highly recommended
- ✉ Physical address
- ✣ Directions or Map coordinates
- Mailing address
- ☎ Telephone
- Fax
- 🌐 On the Web
- E-mail
- Admission fee
- ⏲ Open/closed times
- Ⓜ Metro stations
- Credit cards

Hotels & Restaurants

- Hotel
- Number of rooms
- Facilities
- Meal plans
- ✕ Restaurant
- Reservations
- Dress code
- Smoking
- BYOB

Outdoors

- Golf
- Camping

Other

- Family-friendly
- ⇨ See also
- Branch address
- ☞ Take note

1

Experience Puerto Rico

WHAT'S WHERE

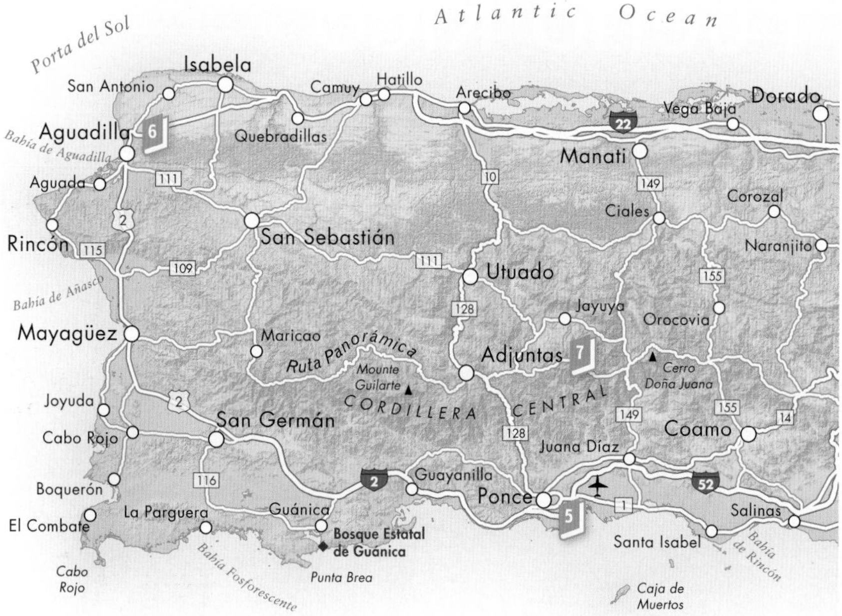

Atlantic Ocean
Porta del Sol
Isabela
San Antonio
Camuy
Hatillo
Arecibo
Dorado
Vega Baja
Quebradillas
Aguadilla
Bahía de Aguadilla
Manati
Aguada
111
22
10
149
Corozal
Ciales
Rincón
115
2
San Sebastián
Naranjito
109
111
Utuado
155
Bahía de Añasco
128
Jayuya
Orocovia
Mayagüez
Maricao
Ruta Panorámica
Adjuntas
Mounte Guilarte
Cerro Doña Juana
Joyuda
CORDILLERA CENTRAL
2
149
155
14
Cabo Rojo
San Germán
128
Coamo
Juana Díaz
116
Guayanilla
Boquerón
2
52
Ponce
El Combate
La Parguera
Guánica
1
Salinas
Bosque Estatal de Guánica
Santa Isabel
Bahía de Rincón
Cabo Rojo
Bahía Fosforescente
Punta Brea
Caja de Muertos
6
7
5

The following numbers refer to chapters.

2 San Juan. Old San Juan's a visual delight of cobbled streets, cathedrals, castles, and convents dating back centuries. Hotels concentrate in the beach-lined Condado and Isla Grande districts, where the nightlife sizzles. San Juan has tremendous museums, a vivacious bar scene, restaurants from earthy to trendy, plus fabulous boutiques and galleries.

3 El Yunque and the Northeast. El Yunque is the most popular day trip from San Juan: Hiking trails that snake through this tropical rain forest lead to hidden pools and mountaintop miradores (lookouts). Luquillo has one of the island's best-known beaches, Playa Luquillo. Westward, Reserva Natural Las Cabezas de San Juan teems with wildlife in mangrove lagoons. Fajardo is a base for exploring the Islas Palominos—exquisite offshore cays.

4 Vieques and Culebra. Once used by the U.S. military for target practice, this pair of sand-fringed isles is now famous for their jaw-dropping beaches. Boutique hotels and trendy eateries have popped up alongside earthy bars. And ecotourism is big, highlighted by snorkeling, diving, and kayaking.

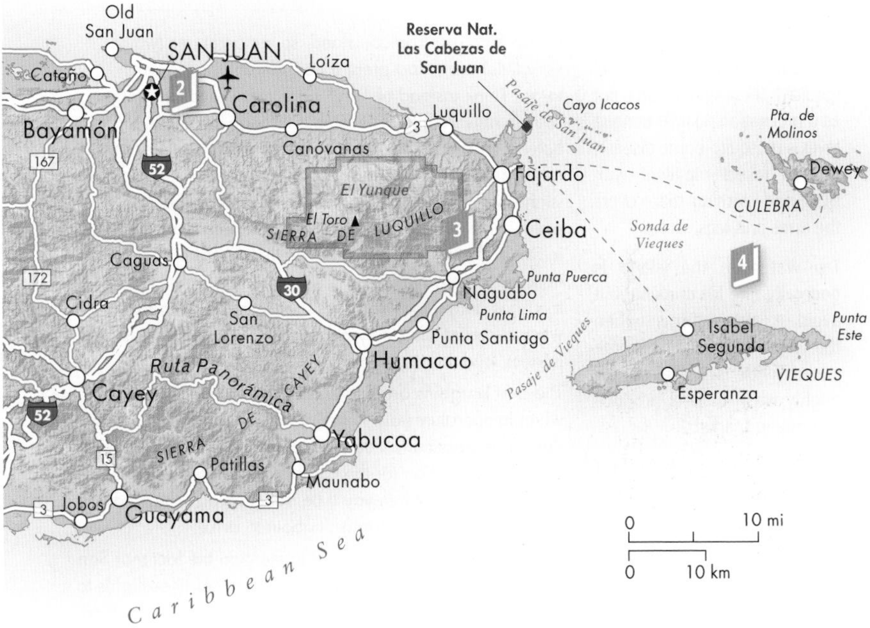

5 Ponce and the Southern Coast. Puerto Rico's southern coast is studded with tropical dry forests, such as Bosque Estatal de Guánica, a destination for hikers and birders. Be sure to explore the colonial center of Ponce, which has one of the finest art museums in the Caribbean. Offshore, "The Wall" gives scuba divers raptures of the deep.

6 Rincón and the Porta del Sol. The jagged coastline of the southwest is renowned for world-class surfing centered on Rincón, where dozens of beaches beckon those who like to hang 10. The Cabo Rojo offers great birding. Architecture buffs appreciate the grandeur of downtown Mayagüez and the charms of San Germán, a colonial hilltop.

7 The Ruta Panorámica. The rugged mountain spine that runs the width of the isle is festooned with forest. The roads of the scenic Panoramic Route wend through this tangled, lush terrain, linking yesteryear towns and indigenous sites. Several nature reserves along this rewarding drive provide delightful hiking jaunts.

PUERTO RICO PLANNER

Health

Few visitors experience health problems, and inoculations aren't required. There's no malaria, but as a precaution against dengue fever, a mosquito-borne disease, use an insect repellent with DEET and clothing that covers the arms and legs.

Tap water on the island is generally fine for drinking, but avoid it after storms (when the water supply can become mixed with sewage). Thoroughly wash or peel produce you buy in markets.

Health care is among the best in the Caribbean. All medical centers have English-speaking medical staff, and many large hotels have an English-speaking doctor on call.

Safety

San Juan, Mayagüez, and Ponce, like most other big cities, have their share of crime, so guard your wallet or purse in crowded areas; handbags should be worn bandolier style (across one shoulder and your chest). Avoid walking anywhere alone at night. Always lock your car, and do not leave any valuables in sight.

When to Go

Puerto Rico is a tropical island, so temperatures (which vary little) aren't too great a consideration as to when to go: Think instead of "dry" and "rainy" seasons. High season runs from mid-December through mid-April. Winter hotel rates are as much as 25% higher than off-season rates, and hotels tend to be packed. This doesn't mean the island won't have rooms in winter—rarely is space completely unavailable—but if you plan to beat that winter sleet in Duluth, make arrangements for flights and accommodations as far in advance as possible. A less expensive time to visit is during the "shoulder" seasons of fall and spring, when discount rates may be available, the weather is still perfect, and the tourist crush is less intense.

The best bargains are in the less busy summer season, when temperatures are hotter, it's rainier, and hurricanes are a slim possibility. Puerto Rico can be an excellent hurricane-season option for the Caribbean for last-minute flight and hotel deals, when you'll be able to watch the weather report and know a storm isn't about to strike.

However, business travel—not to mention the fact that San Juan serves as a major hub for American Airlines flights to the rest of the Caribbean—keeps the flights to Puerto Rico fairly full on weekdays all year long, while the El Yunque region can be deluged at any time of year, feeding the lush rain forest.

Climate

Puerto Rico's weather is moderate and tropical year-round, with an average temperature of about 82°F (26°C). Essentially, there are no big seasonal changes, although winter sees cooling (not cold) breezes from the north, and temperatures in higher elevations drop by as much as 20 degrees. The rainier summer months are hurricane season in the Caribbean, which runs July through November. The southwest is relatively dry year-round.

Festivals and Events

January. The annual season of the **Puerto Rico Symphony Orchestra,** in San Juan, begins with classical and pop performances by the island's finest orchestra.

The annual **Fiestas de la Calle San Sebastián** *(San Sebastián Street Festival)* features several nights of live music as well as food festivals and *cabezudos* parades, where folk legends are caricatured in oversize masks.

Each year the Puerto Rico film industry honors talent in the **Puerto Rico International Film Festival,** which showcases island-made films and works from around the world.

February–early March. In the weeks preceding Lent, Puerto Ricans celebrate **Carnival**, held island-wide, with flamboyant float parades, music, Carnival Queen pageants.

March. Held in Guayama, the two-day **Dulce Sueño Paso Fino Fair,** showcases the island's famous Paso Fino horses, which are bred and trained to walk with a distinctive, smooth gait.

Late August–early September. Anglers try their hand at snagging blue marlin and other game fish in the **International Light Tackle Blue Marlin Tournament**.

June. Old San Juan's Fortaleza Street is closed to traffic for the annual "South of Fortaleza" **SoFo Culinary Week,** when more than two-dozen restaurants set up outside.

The annual **Heineken JazzFest** attracts some 15,000 aficionados to San Juan for four days of outdoor concerts by the likes of Spyro Gyra and George Benson.

San Juan's annual **Casals Festival** honors native son Pablo Casals, the late, great cellist. The 10 days of classical-music performances feature the Puerto Rico Symphony Orchestra, as well as soloists from the island and around the world.

November. The **Festival of Puerto Rican Music,** held in San Juan and other locations, celebrates the vibrancy of the island's folk music, highlighted by a contest featuring the *cuatro,* a traditional guitar with five double strings.

December. The Puerto Rico National Folkloric Ballet performs its **Annual Criollísimo Show**, blending modern ballet with Puerto Rican and Caribbean music and themes. The Teatro Tapia in Old San Juan and the Centro de Bellas Artes Luis A. Ferré in Santurce post schedules.

The annual **Festival de los Máscaras** honors the mask-making traditions of Hatillo, where colorful masks used in religious processions have been crafted for centuries.

What to Pack

Although "casual" is the operative word for vacation clothes, Puerto Ricans dress up to go out, particularly in the cities. Pack some dressy-casual slacks and shirts, summer skirts for women, casual clothes for the resort, at least two bathing suits, and sturdy shoes for walking. A light sweater or jacket is also a good idea. And if planning on visiting nature reserves, pack long-sleeve shirts to guard against mosquitoes.

Visitor Information

In addition to the Puerto Rico Tourism Company's *Qué Pasa!*, pick up the Puerto Rico Hotel and Tourism Association's *Bienvenidos* and *Places to Go.* Among them you can find a wealth of information about the island and its activities. All are free and available at tourism offices and hotel desks. The Puerto Rico Tourism Company has information centers at the airport, Old San Juan, Ponce, Aguadilla, and Cabo Rojo. Most island towns also have a tourism office, usually in the city hall.

Contacts Puerto Rico Tourism Company (*La Princesa Bldg., Paseo de la Princesa, San Juan 00902* ☎ *800/866–7827* ✉ *135 W. 50th St.22nd fl., New York, NY 10020* ☎ *800/223–6530* ✉ *3575 W. Cahuenga Blvd., Suite 560, Los Angeles, CA 90068* ☎ *800/874–1230* ⊕ *www.gotopuertorico.com*).

PUERTO RICO TOP ATTRACTIONS

B

C

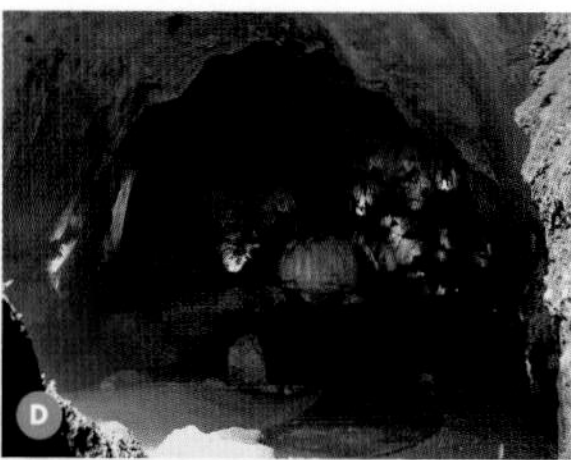
D

A

San Juan National Historic Site

(A) The U.S. National Parks Service maintains this huge colonial military complex, comprising Castillo El Morro and Castillo San Cristóbal. A visit to Old San Juan is not complete without exploring these twin fortresses. Park rangers offer fascinating tours of the tunnels, cannon batteries, and barracks, which today feature museum pieces recalling a once-glorious past.

El Yunque National Forest

(B) Pack your raingear and hike the crown jewel of Puerto Rico's national parks—carpeting the slopes of the rugged Luquillo Mountain Range. From the El Portal Visitor Center, the Sendero El Yunque climbs 1,365 feet through an eerie cloud forest. This 2.6-mile trail puts you atop the summit at 3,496 feet. When it's clear the 360-degree views are spectacular. Add a twist to your return hike by diverting along Forest Road 10 to the Mt. Britton observation tower, resembling a castle turret. A spiral staircase leads to a viewing platform.

Playa Flamenco

(C) Puerto Rico's best beach? Ask the thousands of *sanjuaneros* who fly or ferry out to the isle of Culebra on weekends and holidays. Long and broad enough to absorb the masses, this visual stunner tempts disbelief with its bright white sands and waters of Maxfield Parrish blues and greens. Snorkeling is tops thanks to an offshore reef, and when the wind is up, surfers are thrilled by the action.

Parque de las Cavernas del Rio Camuy

(D) Puerto Rico has some of the deepest and longest caves in the world, and it's a special thrill to rappel down a cliff-face to enter Cueva Camuy. Donned with life jacket and lamped helmet, you'll ever remember the 250-foot rope descent, Spider-Man-style into the gaping mouth of the Angeles cavern. Dripstone

formations take on surreal forms in the cool, moist depths, where you slide down mud chutes and body raft in the care of experienced guides. Aventuras Tierra Adento offers trips.

Bioluminescent Bay, Vieques

(E) A remarkable natural wonder, Vieques's world-famous Puerto Mosquito bay will make you giggle with childlike glee. Microscopic organisms that live in the lagoon light up around your kayak, enveloping you in a neon-like spectral glow. Choose a moonless pitch-black night for best effect. The experience is well worth the journey to Vieques, even if you do nothing else here. Several operators on the island offer trips.

Arecibo Observatory

(F) If this space-age facility deep in the mountains of northwest Puerto Rico looks like something from a sci-fi movie, it is. *Contact*, with Jodie Foster was filmed here. The view over the 1,000-ft.-wide dish (the largest such telescope ever built) is a jaw-dropper. The visitor center doubles as a superb museum on astronomy, the atmosphere, and Earth.

The Ruta Panorámica

(G) Puerto Rico's interior is a beautiful mountainous region with cooler climes and splendid climbs. The Ruta Panorámica, is network of roads that snakes through the entire region. Some are nicely maintained, others are little more than gravel. But the "Panoramic Route" lives up to its name, providing eye-catching vistas around every bend of the road. It's an exciting journey that reveals an enthralling vision of Puerto Rico undisclosed to those who don't venture beyond the city and shores.

HISTORY YOU CAN SEE

Precolonial Puerto Rico

The Taínos were the indigenous group that populated the island prior to its "discovery" by Christopher Columbus during his second trip to the New World in 1493. The Taínos' name for the island was Boriquen, and even today Puerto Ricans honor their Taíno heritage by referring to themselves as "boricuas."

What to See: The island's two main ceremonial centers—**Tibes** and **Caguana**—have preserved the limited artifacts of Taíno culture that have been discovered over the years. At Tibes, just north of Ponce, visitors can see reproductions of the *bohios* in which Taínos lived, as well as fields believed to be the sites of ceremonial events.

Closer to San Juan, those curious to get a window into the Taíno world can visit **La Cueva de Maria de la Cruz**, a cave in Loíza where archaeologists discovered Taíno artifacts in the mid-20th century. As of this writing, entry to the cave was free; there are no officials on-site.

Colonial Puerto Rico

Columbus arrived in 1493, and the Spanish crown controlled the island—though with a determinedly laissez-faire approach—until the Spanish American War of 1898 ended with the concession of Puerto Rico to the United States. The first Spanish governor of the island was Juan Ponce de Léon, the explorer famous for his tireless pursuit for the elusive fountain of youth. Spain's Queen Isabella charged de Léon with the task of "compel[ling] and forc[ing] the Indians to work for the Christian inhabitants." According to historian and archaeologist Ricardo Alegria, the Taínos were decimated, refusing to resist the Spanish conquistadores because they believed that Spaniards were immortal; thus, taking up arms against them was futile.

By the 1530s, Africans had been brought to the island for slave labor; they built San Juan's two biggest fortresses, Castillo San Felipe del Morro and Castillo San Cristóbal, massive construction projects that took more than 250 years of intense, arduous labor. Slavery in Puerto Rico was finally abolished in 1873.

What to See: Built in 1521, **Casa Blanca** was the intended home of Juan Ponce de Léon, who never actually lived here. His descendants, however, called the Old San Juan property home for 250 years. Today, it's a museum open to the public; a highlight is the quiet, intimate garden located on the property.

Castillo San Felipe del Morro and **Castillo San Cristóbal** aren't San Juan's only forts—there's also Fortin San Geronimo del Boqueron, located just behind the Caribe Hilton, and the Fuerte El Canuelo on Goat Island, visible across the San Juan Bay—but they're certainly the largest and most impressive. Both offer commanding views of the Atlantic from their upper levels.

Built between 1533 and 1540, **La Fortaleza** was intended to serve as a perch from which the Bay of San Juan could be monitored and protected. Its strategic limitations were soon discovered, though, and the UNESCO-recognized structure is home to Puerto Rico's governor, as it has been since the late 16th century. Guided tours allow the public to glimpse how the governor lives.

A predominantly Afro–Puerto Rican town, **Loíza** was founded in 1719 and was populated by escaped slaves. Separated from the mainland by the Rio Grande, the town remained geographically and

socially isolated until the mid 1970s, allowing many Afro–Puerto Rican traditions to be preserved. Called the capital of tradition, Loíza is home to popular *bomba* and *plena* (music and dance) and is famous for coconut masks, or *vejigantes*, used during annual festivals (*see also "The Masks of Puerto Rico" feature in Chapter 5*). Though it's most lively during early July, when the Santiago Apostol festival is under way, a visit at any other time of year should include a stop at **San Patricio**, one of the island's oldest churches and home to what may be the only black St. Patrick statue in the world.

The Transition to the Commonwealth

Though Puerto Rico was transferred from the Spanish to the Americans in 1898, the U.S. government maintained a similar posture toward the island that had characterized the colonial period. Puerto Rican historians Kal Wagenheim and Olga Jimenez de Wagenheim remarked that "[t]he invasion of Puerto Rico [by the U.S.] ended four centuries of oppressive Spanish colonial rule, only to replace it with a more subtle brand of colonialism."

The ways in which this colonialism was manifest are fascinating. Puerto Ricans were without formal citizenship for more than a decade. The educational system underwent frequent upheavals, as did the structure of the government, as the U.S. imposed policies reflecting evolving defense and economic interests. Even when U.S. citizenship was conferred in the 1916 passage of the Jones Bill, the development did little to resolve the ambiguous relationship between Puerto Rico and the United States. Citizenship for Puerto Ricans was not, after all, conferred with all the rights and privileges enjoyed by mainland citizens.

It would be almost 40 more years before the U.S. and Puerto Rico negotiated the island's current status—that of a commonwealth (or "free associated state"). But the commonwealth—a compromise status between statehood and independence—has its fair share of critics, and both statehood and independence movements are competing to shape Puerto Rico's future.

What to See: Built between 1919 and 1929, Puerto Rico's beaux arts–style **Capitol** building is an often-overlooked site that shouldn't be missed. Its rotunda is inlaid with colorful mosaic tiles depicting the major periods of Puerto Rican history, and the Puerto Rican Constitution is displayed in glass cases. Busts of important Puerto Rican politicians are also on display. Visitors will often encounter protesters on the Capitol steps; citizens gather here frequently to peacefully protest government policies.

The **Las Mercedes Cemetery,** located in Ponce, is the final resting place of some of Puerto Rico's most important and celebrated politicians, among them Don Luis A. Ferré, former governor and founder of the Museo de Arte in Ponce. The grand tombstones and mausoleums in this cemetery are photo worthy, as are the bones resting within your reach in open crypts at the back of the cemetery. ■ **TIP→ Every town has its own culture trolley, offering a historic guided tour of that area's highlights. The trolleys are often free. Stops can generally be found in the town's plaza, in front of its city hall.**

CRUISING TO PUERTO RICO

San Juan is a home base for many cruise ships and a staple of itineraries for cruise ships sailing from Florida. It's an excellent way for first-time visitors to sample Puerto Rico, as most cruise companies offer excursions beyond Old San Juan. At most, you'll get one or two days in San Juan, but some itineraries begin or end here—a chance for more extensive exploration.

Arriving in San Juan

Most cruise ships dock within a couple of blocks of Old San Juan; however, there is a second cruise pier across the bay at Isla Grande, and if your ship docks there you'll need to take a taxi to get anywhere on the island. The Paseo de la Princesa, a tree-lined promenade beneath the city wall, is a nice place for a quick stroll—you can admire the local crafts and stop at the refreshment kiosks. Fortunately, major sights in the Old San Juan area are mere steps from the piers. Two major tourist information booths are within one block of the cruise-terminal area.

Carnival Cruises. They call themselves "fun ships" for good reason, with lots of entertainment and youthful things to do aboard. Singles, couples, children, and even older folks will enjoy these cruises. In fact, the kids' programs earn rave reviews. ☎ *888/227–6482* 🌐 *www.carnival.com*

Celebrity Cruises. Celebrity's focus is on service, and it shows. From their waitstaff to their activity directors, every aspect of your trip has been well thought out. They cater to adults more than children, so this may not be the best line for families. ☎ *800/647–2251* 🌐 *www.celebrity.com.*

Costa Cruise. European flair distinguishes Costa, with its Italian staff and festive mood. ☎ *877/882–6782* 🌐 *www.costacruise.com.*

Holland America. The grande dame of cruise lines, Holland America has a reputation for service and elegance. This company includes Mayagüez, on Puerto Rico's west coast, on its itineraries departing from Fort Lauderdale and Tampa. ☎ *877/724–5425* 🌐 *www.hollandamerica.com.*

Norwegian Cruise Line. Billing its relatively relaxed, family-friendly cruises as "freestyle," NCL was one of the earliest companies to specialize in the Caribbean. It boasts the youngest fleet on the planet. ☎ *800/327–7030* 🌐 *www.ncl.com.*

Princess Cruises. Princess strives to offer affordable luxury. Its prices start out a little higher, but you get more bells and whistles (more affordable balcony rooms, nice décor, more restaurants to choose from, personalized service). It has a wide range of itineraries departing from Fort Lauderdale, but it also includes San Juan on cruises from New York. It aims to offer affordable luxury and draws a slightly older crowd. ☎ *800/774–6237* 🌐 *www.princess.com.*

Regent Seven Seas. Aiming for the high-end market with deluxe staterooms, noteworthy speakers, and performance troupes, this company's ships are among the most sophisticated afloat. ☎ *800/505–5370* 🌐 *www.rssc.com.*

Royal Caribbean. Royal Caribbean is known for its spacious and stylish mega-liners. In keeping with its reputation for being all things for all people, Royal Caribbean offers a huge variety of activities and services on board and more excursions on land than any other cruise line. ☎ *800/521–8611* 🌐 *www.royalcaribbean.com.*

Seabourn. With the most luxurious vessels afloat, Seabourn specializes in intimate service and a tranquil cruise experience

for the moneyed crowd, using small ships. ☎ *800/929–9391* 🌐 *www.seabourn.com.*

Silversea. Silversea serves deluxe cruisers with small vessels renowned for exquisite decor and attentive service. Expect classical performers among the entertainers. ☎ *800/722–9955* 🌐 *www.silversea.com.*

Windstar. Windstar is unique for its use of masted ships catering to an upscale niche. These are laid-back, albeit stylish, cruises without too much regimentation or arranged activities on board. ☎ *877/827–7245* 🌐 *www.windstarcruises.com.*

Although Puerto Rico is U.S. territory and no passport is required for U.S. citizens, you'll still need yours for ports of call in other Caribbean islands.

Almost all the ship's shore excursions can be arranged more cheaply with local tour operators. Taxis are also available near the dock. Within the city, metered cabs charge an initial $1; after that, it's about 10¢ for each additional 1/13 mi. You can negotiate with taxi drivers for specific trips, and you can hire a taxi for as little as $30 per hour for sightseeing tours. You can also prearrange a rental car if you'd prefer to drive yourself, but be sure you leave plenty of time to return it before your ship sails.

Most mainland cell phones will work in Puerto Rico, but that is not usually the case while at sea. Check with the cruise company before setting out.

SAN JUAN BEST BETS

Castillo San Felipe del Morro. Explore the giant labyrinthine fort.

El Yunque National Forest. This rain forest east of San Juan is a great half-day excursion.

Casa Bacardí. Rum lovers can jump on the public ferry and then taxi over to the factory.

Old San Juan. Walk the cobblestone streets of Old San Juan.

Shopping. Within a few blocks of the port there are plenty of factory outlets and boutiques.

WEDDINGS AND HONEYMOONS

Many other Caribbean destinations make a big pitch as wedding destinations, and Puerto Rico often gets overlooked. But it has all the ingredients of a spectacular place to wed and/or honeymoon. Gorgeous beaches dissolving into warm turquoise waters and a sensual tropical climate induce romance, and many an enamored couple has tied the knot here on the spur of the moment.

Choosing the Perfect Place

You can be as stylish or as informal as you wish. Although Puerto Rico has fewer ritzy beach resorts than many others islands, there's no shortage of exquisite boutique hotels with just the right ambience to inspire "I do." In San Juan, Casa Herencia and the El Convento have just the right romantic style. In Rincón, the Horned Dorest Primavera exudes honeymoon chic, and the Hix House Hotel, on Vieques, will suit honeymooners seeking a reclusive escape. Also on Vieques, the new W Beach Resort & Spa promises all the hip sophistication perfectly suited to young newlyweds, including sexy rooms and a holistic spa for Him and Her treatments. Puerto Rico has no couples-only "all-inclusives," such as the well-known Caribbean Sandals and SuperClubs chains, but the "W" promises to deliver all the right stuff. Also consider Copamarina Beach Resort & Spa, which has a "romance package" that includes a bottle of champagne plus massage. Many larger hotels have their own wedding planners to take care of all arrangements—a distinct advantage over smaller hotels if you're seeking to wed on the island.

Getting Your Licenses

You must get an application from the Demographic Registry Office. There are no special residency requirements, but U.S. citizens must produce a driver's license, and non-U.S. citizens must produce a valid passport for identification purposes. Medical certificates, which can be done by your own doctor and approved by a Puerto Rican one, are required. If either the bride or groom was previously married, certified copies of a divorce decree or death certificate must be produced. The filing cost is $20. Blood tests are required and must be done within 10 days of the marriage ceremony. The results must be certified and signed by a doctor or hotel physician in Puerto Rico. The cost for the laboratory test in Puerto Rico is about $15 to $25. Both parties must appear at the City Court office to purchase a marriage license. Marriages may then be performed by a judge or any clergyman. The marriage fee is usually between $150 and $350. Most large hotels on the island have marriage coordinators who can explain the necessary paperwork and help you complete it on time for your marriage ceremony.

Information **Demographic Registry Office** (✉ *Box 11854, Fernandez Juncos Station, San Juan 00910* ☎ *787/728–7980.*

GAY PUERTO RICO

In sophisticated San Juan, gays and lesbians will find it easy to mingle. Many gay-friendly hotels, restaurants, and clubs are scattered throughout the city, and the beaches at Condado and Ocean Park tend to attract a gay crowd. Many guesthouses here are gay-owned and oriented. The bohemian Old San Juan crowd is particularly friendly and—just as in Ocean Park and Condado—many businesses there are owned by gays or lesbians. However, in recent years the gay energy has moved south to relatively nontouristy but artsy and increasingly lively Santurce district; take a taxi to get there.

San Juan's gay hotspots include Angelu's, the Male Depot, and the erotically themed Krash Klub, which has cutting-edge music and occasional live music and even drag shows; go on Wednesday for Krash's happening Latin night. Lesbians should head to Cups, a tropical bar for women; it has live music. Both Cups and Krash are in Santurce. The Café Bohemia, in the gay-friendly Hotel El Convento, is another gathering spot, handily situated for enjoying the night scene along calles San Sebastián and Fortaleza.

Some clubs and bars also host a weekly "gay night." On the first Sunday in June a gay pride parade takes place in Condado and is preceded by a week of events, and the annual SanJuanBrothas gay parade, held each Memorial Day, is an annual highlight.

Other welcoming areas include Ponce in the south, Rincón in the west; and the island of Vieques in the east, although the local population here is more conservative and it's the large and bohemian expat crowd that is tolerant. Remember that Puerto Rico is a strongly Catholic nation, and state laws are not as tolerant of homosexuality as in the mainland USA. In rural areas and small towns, overt displays of affection between same-sex couples can cause problems.

The local newspapers *Connexion G* serves the gay and lesbian community. Frank Fournier of Connections Travel, which is a member of the **International Gay & Lesbian Travel Association** (✉ *915 Middle River Dr., Suite 306, Fort Lauderdale, FL 33304* ☎ *954/630–1637* 🌐 *www.iglts.org*) is a reliable local travel agent for gay and lesbian travelers. The association is a great resource for planning your trip.

STATE OF THE ARTS IN PUERTO RICO

Puerto Rico's visual arts have long been shaped by the influences of its African, Spanish, and indigenous roots. Though the history of Puerto Rican art can be categorized into several predominant thematic preoccupations, a close examination of seminal Puerto Rican works reveals the persistence of these diverse cultural influences.

The indigenous Taíno were living on the island at the time of Columbus's arrival in the late 15th century; their art consisted primarily of petroglyphs and daily-use or ceremonial objects made of ceramic or wood. Little survived Spanish colonization, but we know about its existence thanks to written accounts of Spanish priests like Fray Ramón Pané, who described Taíno *cemies*—ceremonial figures—in extensive detail. The few remaining Taíno objects are largely preserved in private collections, although small collections of representative pieces and some examples of petroglyphs can be seen at the **Parque Ceremonial Indigena de Tibes** (Tibes Indigenous Ceremonial Center) in Ponce and the **Parque Ceremonial Indigena de Caguana** (Caguana Indigenous Ceremonial Center) in Utuado.

The arrival of the Spanish also resulted in the introduction of new art forms. According to art historian Osiris Delgado, much of the art from the early colonial period was religious in nature and function, the most representative example being the *santos*—saint figurines carved of wood, an art form that endures on the island to this day *(see also "Santos" feature in chapter 5)*. It wasn't until the mid- to late-18th century that the "fine" arts began in earnest, with the works of Jose Campeche (1752–1809) being the most representative.

Campeche became known for his exceptional oil portraits of religious figures and the social elite; his renown was particularly noteworthy considering he was a self-taught artist with little formal education. Campeche's seminal works, including *Dama a caballo* (*Lady on Horseback*), can be seen at the **Museo de Arte in Ponce (MAP)** and at the **Museo de Arte de Puerto Rico** in San Juan.

Campeche was followed by Francisco Oller (1833–1917), a painter who remains a central figure in the narrative of Puerto Rican art. Also working primarily in oils, Oller turned his brush toward a realistic treatment of Puerto Rican life as he observed it. His paintings can be grouped into one of two broad categories: landscapes (*paisajes*) and folkloric images of daily life. *La ceiba de Ponce* (*The Ponce Ceiba Tree*) and *Hacienda Aurora* (*Aurora Hacienda*) are cornerstones in the permanent collection at the MAP and help viewers understand why Oller has been called "a realist of impressionism." *El Velorio* (*The Wake*), his most powerful and enduring work, is on display in the museum at the main campus of the **University of Puerto Rico.**

Oller not only established the subjects and styles that would dominate Puerto Rican art throughout most of the 20th century, but he also played a significant role in creating a community of artists and an artistic culture on the island. He opened Puerto Rico's first gallery in Old San Juan around 1870, exhibiting work of local artists. His influence is visible in the works of many 20th-century artists who are shown alongside Campeche and Oller in the permanent collections at the MAP and the Museo de Arte de Puerto Rico. An appreciation for rural landscapes and lifestyles, as well as its signature figure,

the *jíbaro*—a poor, humble, hard-working mountain man—became the stamp of Puerto Rican identity.

By the 1940s, the government started supporting the arts, and art institutions began to flourish, with the **Museo de la Universidad de Puerto Rico** opening in 1946.

During the 1950s artists turned their interests toward social justice and the urban proletariat, focusing on slums and poverty. The evolution of these motifs is evident in the work of Ramón Frade and Rafael Tufino, whose works are on display in San Juan's **Galeria Nacional**.

The Instituto de Cultura Puertorriquena (Institute of Puerto Rican Culture) was established in 1955 to promote Puerto Rican artists; today, the agency oversees many of the island's museums and art programs. In 1959, the MAP was founded by former governor, philanthropist, and passionate art collector, Luis A. Ferré. MAP houses a private collection of more than 2,400 works from the 14th through 19th centuries, including paintings by El Greco, Goya, Rubens, Cranach, Murillo, and Delacroix. The collection is particularly strong in Italian baroque and Pre-Raphaelite works, with good representation by Latin American and Puerto Rican artists from the 18th century to the present including Myrna Baez, Julio Rosado del Valle, and Antonio Martorell.

In the 1960s, as the art world moved away from socially committed art, Puerto Rican artists still struggled with nationalism and identity issues. Locally, this struggle resulted in a battle between abstraction—with artists such as Julio Rosado Del Valle, Olga Albizu, and Luis Hernández Cruz—and avant-garde expression that favored figurative and socially minded art considered "genuinely" Puerto Rican.

In the 1980s, abstract expressionists and other stylistic experimenters were granted a place at the table of Puerto Rican identity. These years opened art to the irreverent humor of Carmelo Sobrino, to the environmental activism of Carlos Marcial, and to aspects of the fantastic, as in the works of Marta Pérez, Jorge Zeno, and Rafi Trelles

By 1988, a group of artists, professors, critics, collectors, and other art lovers came together to establish the **Museo de Arte Contemporáneo de Puerto Rico** (Museum of Contemporary Art of Puerto Rico). The collection is composed mostly of works donated by the artists. Private collectors continued to expand their sphere of influence in the art world throughout the late 1980s and into the 1990s. Most notable among them are Diana and Moisés Berezdivin, whose collection became so extensive the museum acquired a space for part of the work and opened it to the public in 2005. Their **Espacio 1414** is dedicated to cultivating the visual arts in Puerto Rico and is one of the most interesting places on the island to see art.

The future is exciting as Puerto Rican art both brings art aficionados from abroad and travels beyond the island. The launch of the first annual **CIRCA Art Fair** in 2006 signaled Puerto Rico's readiness to take its place on the international art stage, bringing both exhibitors and collectors from near and far to see just how much Puerto Rican art has changed. Increasingly, Puerto Rican artists are showing their work abroad, engaging audiences in a more nuanced dialogue about what, exactly, Puerto Rican art is and what it's becoming.

FLAVORS OF PUERTO RICO

Puerto Rican cuisine has been experiencing a boom of sorts, with innovative, gourmet restaurants opening around the island. Today, more chefs and restaurateurs are developing menus in the line of a Nuevo Latino cuisine. Joyfully departing from traditional continental and Puerto Rican recipes, these chefs nevertheless include traditional ingredients and update old favorites. Standard meats like chicken, fish, and lamb are given an added zest by sauces made from such tropical fruits as tamarind, mango, or guava. Take your palate out for a few adventures. Puerto Rican cuisine may surprise and delight you with both new and old tastes.

Cocina Criolla

The origins of contemporary Puerto Rican cuisine can be traced to the Taíno people, who inhabited the island in the 15th century. Taíno staples still used today include yucca, peppers, and corn. The Taíno also are believed to have grown guava, pineapple, and soursop.

Cocina criolla—literally, the creole kitchen—is an aggregate of Caribbean cuisines, sharing basic ingredients common to Cuban, Dominican, and to some extent even Brazilian culinary traditions. Still, it has its own distinct flavorings.

When the Spaniards arrived on the island, they brought olives, eggplant, onion, garlic, rice, and cilantro. Wheat would not grow on the island, so yucca remained a staple, as did rice. Regional culinary specialties from Spain, such as *paellas*, came out of the Spanish-influenced kitchen. These specialties played an important role in the development of Puerto Rican recipes, recognizable today in such dishes as *arroz con pollo*. Lacking olive oil, early Puerto Ricans often used lard as a fat. African slaves brought by the Spanish from Guinea and the Gold Coast of Africa during the 16th century to toil in the sugar fields also left their marks on the Puerto Rican table. The slaves brought plantains, bananas, pigeon peas, okra, and yams. The Taíno used corn husks to wrap foods, but the Africans replaced them with plantain leaves. The African population developed a variety of coconut-based dishes and preferred frying foods to stewing them.

Local Seafood

Puerto Rico is home to an abundance of freshwater and saltwater fish, both native and introduced, and the island is readily associated with big-game fishing. Off the coast of Culebra, fishermen catch bonefish, tuna, blue and white marlin and dolphin fish, otherwise known as mahimahi. The island's more than twenty man-made lakes are stocked regularly with freshwater fish, and local restaurants take advantage of these fresh catches, offering inventive daily specials. Lunch and dinner generally start with appetizers, such as *bacalaitos*, (crunchy cod fritters) or *sopón de pescado*, a classic fish soup made with garlic and spices plus onions and tomatoes. Fried fish is also popular, served with *mojo isleño*, a sauce made with olives and olive oil, onions, pimientos, capers, tomato sauce, and vinegar. The seafood shacks of Joyuda are so well known for fresh fish that people come here from as far away as Ponce and San Juan. In Boquerón people line up at pushcarts where vendors sell oysters on the half shell. (Hot sauce is optional.) If you're in Rincón, the Horned Dorset Primavera has one of the most elegant eateries in the Caribbean.

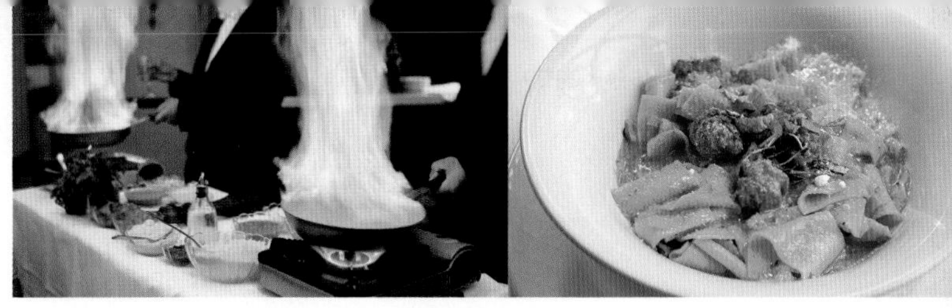

Indigenous Fruits and Vegetables

Tropical fruits often wind up at the table in the form of delicious juices. A local favorite is pineapple juice from crops grown in the north of the island. Coconut, mango, papaya, lime, and tamarind are other local favorites. Puerto Rico is home to lesser-known fruits that are worth trying if you find them; these include the *caimito* (which is also called a star apple and has a mild, grapelike flavor), *quenepa* (also called a Spanish lime, which has yellow sweet-tart pulp surrounded by a tight, thin skin), and *zapote* (a plum-size fruit that tastes like a combination of peach, avocado, and vanilla). The Plaza del Mercado in the Santurce sector of San Juan is a good place to look for the unusual.

Spices

Puerto Rican dishes often feature pepper, lime rind, cinnamon, cloves, fresh ginger, garlic, and the juice of the sour orange. Two popular herb seasonings are cilantro (coriander) and oregano. These ingredients, along with small sweet peppers, are commonly used to flavor soups and meats. The conventional wisdom says that the real secret of the *cocina criolla* depends on the use of *sofrito* (a sauce that may include tomatoes, onion, garlic, peppers, and coriander), *achiote* (the inedible fruit of a small Caribbean shrub whose seeds are sometimes ground as a spice), lard, and the *caldero* (cooking pot).

Plantains and Mofongo

Plátanos, or plantains, are related to bananas but are larger and starchier. They are served mostly as side dishes and may be eaten green (as *tostones,* which are salty) or ripe (as *amarillos,* which are sweet). They can be fried, baked, boiled, or roasted and served either whole or in slices. Sometimes whole amarillos are served with cinnamon as a dessert. *Pasteles,* boiled plantain leaves wrapped around fillings, tamale-style, are a Christmas specialty but can be eaten anytime.

Of all the delicious plantain preparations, one of the tastiest is also the simplest – *mofongo*. Green plantains are mashed with a wooden *pilón*, mixed with garlic and other flavorings and fried in a pan. Served plain, it's often a side dish. But when it's stuffed with chicken, beef, or some other meat, *mofongo* becomes one of Puerto Rico's signature entrées.

In the center of the island it's often made with pork. On the coast, however, *mofongo* is almost always stuffed with fresh fish or shellfish. Some restaurants are even known for what they put in their plantains. A neon sign outside Tino's, one of a long line of seafood restaurants in Joyuda, touts its signature dish: an earthenware goblet overflowing with plantains and seafood.

Rice

Rice is omnipresent on the Puerto Rican plate. It can be served "white" with kidney beans, or prepared with *gandules* (pigeon peas) or garbanzos (chickpeas); most often rice is simply served with *habichuelas* (red beans). Whatever the case, the accompaniment for rice is almost always some kind of bean, always richly seasoned. Rice stuck to the pot, known as *pegao,* is the most highly prized, full of all the ingredients that have sunk to the bottom.

Rum

As you enjoy your piña colada—a cocktail served in nearly every bar on the island—lift your glass to Christopher Columbus. Although the explorer didn't invent the fruity cocktail, he did bring sugarcane to the Caribbean on his second voyage in 1493. Sugarcane is native to Southeast

Asia, but it was cultivated in Spain at the time, and Columbus thought it would do well in the tropical "New World." Juan Ponce de Léon, the island's first governor, planted vast fields of the stuff. The first sugar mill was opened in 1524, leading to the distillation of what was then called *brebaje*. Although rum was first exported in 1897, it took a bit longer for it to become the massive industry it is today. The Bacardí family, after fleeing Cuba, set up shop near San Juan in 1959. Their company's product, lighter-bodied than those produced by most other distilleries, gained favor around the world. Today Puerto Rico produces more than 35 million gallons of rum a year. You might say it's the national drink.

ON THE MENU

Adobo: a seasoning made of salt, onion powder, garlic powder, and ground black pepper.

Aji-li-mojili: a dressing combining garlic and sweet, seeded chili peppers, flavored with vinegar, lime juice, salt, and olive oil.

Alcapurrias: banana croquettes stuffed with beef or pork.

Amarillos: fried ripe, yellow plantain slices.

Arepas: fried corn or bread cakes.

Batido: a tropical fruit-and-milk shake.

Bacalaítos: deep-fried codfish fritters.

Chimichurri: an herb sauce of finely chopped cilantro or parsley with garlic, lemon, and oil.

Empanadillas: turnovers, bigger than *pastelillos,* filled with beef, crabmeat, conch, or lobster.

Mofongo: a mix of plantains mashed with garlic, olive oil, and salt in a *pilón,* the traditional Puerto Rican mortar and pestle.

Mojo or Mojito Isleño: a sauce made of olives and olive oil, onions, pimientos, capers, tomato sauce, vinegar, garlic, and bay leaves.

Pasteles: corn or yucca stuffed with various fillings and wrapped in a plantain leaf.

Pastelillos: deep-fried cheese and meat turnovers; a popular fast-food snack.

Picadillo: spicy ground meat, which is used for stuffing or eaten with rice.

Pique: a condiment consisting of hot peppers soaked in vinegar, sometimes with garlic or other spices added.

Tembleque: a coconut custard, usually sprinkled with cinnamon or nutmeg.

Tostones: crushed fried green plantains.

DID YOU KNOW?

Much of El Yunque's forest canopy is dominated by the Puerto Rico Royal Palm, a relatively short tree (40 to 85 ft [12 to 18 m]) that thrives because it can withstand high, hurricane-force winds.

GREAT ITINERARIES

LIFE'S A BEACH

This itinerary takes you to the best beaches of the Porta del Sol, along the island's west coast, and it will get you home in a week. You can easily combine this with one of the other itineraries if you want to see more of the island.

Day 1: Dorado

From San Juan, head west to Dorado, one of the north coast's most stunning stretches of sand. This is a favorite weekend destination for *sanjuaneros*, so you won't have a problem finding a place to stay. One good choice is the Embassy Suites Dorado del Mar Beach & Golf Resort. There's a string of restaurants along the town's main drag, including El Ladrillo, a longtime favorite serving *zarzuela* (seafood stew) and other traditional Spanish dishes.

Logistics: After arriving at San Juan's Aeropuerto Internacional Luis Muñoz Marín, pick up the rental car that you have arranged in advance. Take Route 165 west of San Juan; then head west on Route 693.

Day 2: Isabela and Rincón

Your destination is Rincón, on the western coast. There's no need to hurry, however. If it's a weekend, take a detour to Lago Dos Bocas, where you can have lunch at one of the waterfront restaurants. You'll have to take a boat across the lake, but we think that adds to the appeal. If it isn't a weekend, stop for a bite in Isabela, a small town that overlooks the rocky shoreline. Ocean Front Restaurant , a seaside eatery that overlooks a stretch of shoreline called Playa Jobos, has a varied menu of great seafood and steak. You'll probably arrive in Rincón in early afternoon, giving you plenty of time to hit the beach. If you've just received a large inheritance, you'll want to stay at the Horned Dorset Primavera. Otherwise, there are any number of inexpensive lodgings on or near the beach.

Logistics: From Dorado, drive south on 165, then west on Route 2. If you're in a hurry, save a bit of time by taking Route 22, a toll road that runs parallel to Route 2 until they meet near Arecibo. From Route 2, Route 115 takes you to Rincón.

Day 3: Cabo Rojo

The term Cabo Rojo is confusing, as "Red Cape" refers to a region, a town, and the tiny peninsula that juts off the southwestern tip of the island. The last is where you are headed on your third day. Stop en route at Joyuda, known as the "Golden Mile" because of its string of seafood shacks. Make sure to stop at one for lunch. We like the food best at Tino's, even though it is one of the few places that doesn't have a view. Joyuda has no beachfront, so if you want to walk on the sand you'll have to head south to Boquerón. An even better idea is to continue on to El Combate. Here you'll find a less crowded beach near the neoclassical Cabo Rojo Lighthouse. (Be aware, though, that the rough road to the lighthouse is rocky.) Stay overnight in El Còmbate, perhaps at the recently expanded Bahía Salinas Beach Hotel.

Logistics: From Rincón, Route 115 takes you back to Route 2. Head south on Route 2 until you reach the turnoff for Route 100, which leads to all the coastal communities in Cabo Rojo.

Day 4: Bosque Estatal de Guánica

From Cabo Rojo it's an easy drive to the coastal town of Guánica. Drop your stuff off at your hotel—we recommend the expansive Copamarina Beach Resort—and head to the Bosque Estatal de Guánica. There are several entrances to the state park, but take Route 334, because it takes you past the park's ranger station, where you can pick up trail maps and park your car more securely. This is a dry forest, so the scenery is unlike that of any other part of the island. You'll see more than 700 species of plants, ranging from the prickly-pear cactus to the gumbo limbo tree. In the afternoon, head back to the hotel for some much-needed rest and relaxation. The beaches along the coast are beautiful, but you can also take a ferry to Gilligan's Island. The name may be a bit hokey, but the scenery is gorgeous. There's no better choice for dinner than Copamarina's elegant dining room, Alexandra.

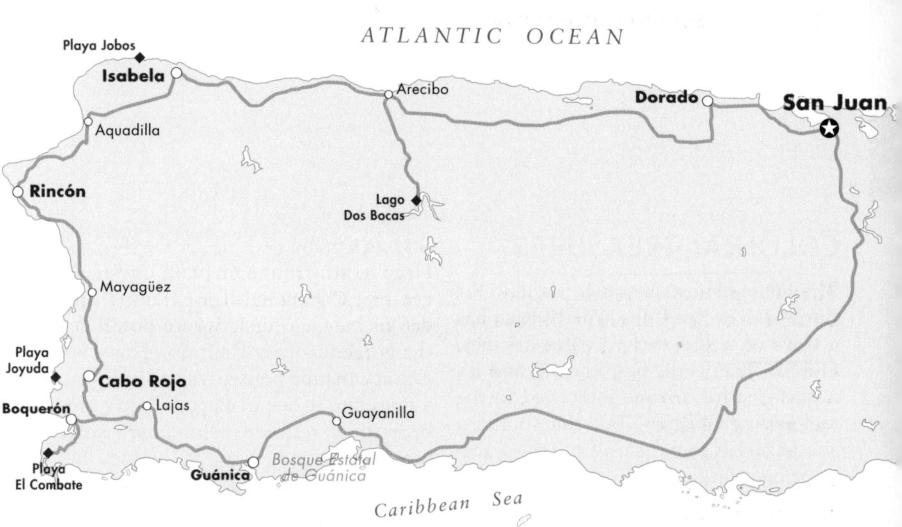

Logistics: From El Combate, head north on Route 100 until you reach the turn-off for Route 2. Follow it east until you reach Route 116, which leads south to Guánica. You can take a more direct route to Guánica, but the narrow roads won't save you any time.

Day 5: San Juan

If you have a flight home today, don't despair. The drive back to San Juan should take you less than two hours (except on a weekend or holidays), so you can probably spend the entire morning by the beach or beside the pool.

Logistics: Route 2 takes you to Ponce, and then Route 52 whisks you directly back to San Juan, or take Route 1 for a more leisurely journey.

TIPS

Book your hotels in advance. There are long stretches along the island's northern and western coasts that don't have any lodgings.

This drive is especially nice with a convertible. Ask your rental company about rates—you may be surprised to find they cost only $20 or $30 more a day than a compact.

The only traffic you're likely to encounter is in San Juan. If you're going to be driving through the city on a weekday morning or afternoon, add a half hour or more to your estimated time of arrival.

COLONIAL TREASURES

More than almost any other island in the Caribbean except Cuba, Puerto Rico has a trove of well-preserved colonial cities. Old San Juan is the best known, and it's a must-see for anyone interested in the region's rich history. But the southern coast also has some gems, from the graceful square in Coamo to the churches of San Germán to the heady mix of neoclassical and art deco masterpieces in Ponce.

Day 1: Old San Juan

If you truly want to experience Old San Juan, make sure you stay within the city walls. El Convento, once a Carmelite convent, is Old San Juan's most luxurious lodging. Gallery Inn, whose mascot is a cockatoo named Campeche, has the most personality; while Da House is cheap and funky. After you drop off your suitcases, hit the cobblestone streets. Make sure to stroll along the city walls and visit one of the forts—most people pick Castillo San Felipe del Morro, but the nearby Castillo San Cristóbal is equally impressive. Old San Juan isn't just for historical sightseeing, though. When the sun goes down, the streets of the historic district light up, becoming one of the city's nightlife centers. For dinner, head to Calle Fortaleza, where you'll find some of the city's best restaurants. Then you can while the night away at one of the happening bars or clubs.

Logistics: Believe us when we tell you that you don't want the headache of parking in Old San Juan. At San Juan's Aeropuerto Internacional Luis Muñoz Marín, take a *taxi turístico* (tourist taxi) to your hotel. The streets here were made for walking, and that's just what you'll do. Wait and pick up your car when you're ready to leave town for the countryside.

Day 2: Coamo

Head south from San Juan, and if you get an early enough start, take a short detour to Guayama, where you'll find the gorgeous Casa Cautiño. This 19th-century manor house, transformed into a museum, is one of Puerto Rico's most beautifully restored colonial-era structures. Continue west to Coamo, best known for its thermal springs. The best place to stay is the Parador Baños de Coamo, a rustic retreat with hot and cold pools. On Coamo's lovely main square is the gleaming white Iglesia Católica San Blás, one of the island's oldest churches. In terms of distance, Coamo isn't so far from San Juan—only about 60 mi km (96 km)—so you don't have to leave at the crack of dawn to have most of a day to explore the town.

Logistics: Ponce is reached by Route 52, a modern highway that heads south of San Juan. This is a toll road, so keep your change handy. Exit Route 52 and follow Route 15 to Guayama. Then take Route 3 west to Santa Isable; turn north on Route 53 for Coamo.

Day 3: Ponce

Your destination on your third day is Ponce, the "Pearl of the South." You'll know you've arrived when you drive through the massive letters spelling the name of the city. The main square, the Plaza de las Delicias, is a delight. Here you'll find the Catedral de Nuestra Señora de Guadalupe, a church dating from 1835, and the Parque de Bombas, a firehouse from 1882 that is painted in bold red and black stripes. There are several museums around the city, but the most interesting is the small Casa Wiechers-Villaronga, a house built in 1911. In a city filled with neoclassical confections, this is one of the most elaborate. Strolling the downtown streets, you'll also marvel at neoclassical and art deco architecture. Don't miss the Museo de Arte de Ponce, one of the Caribbean's best art museums.

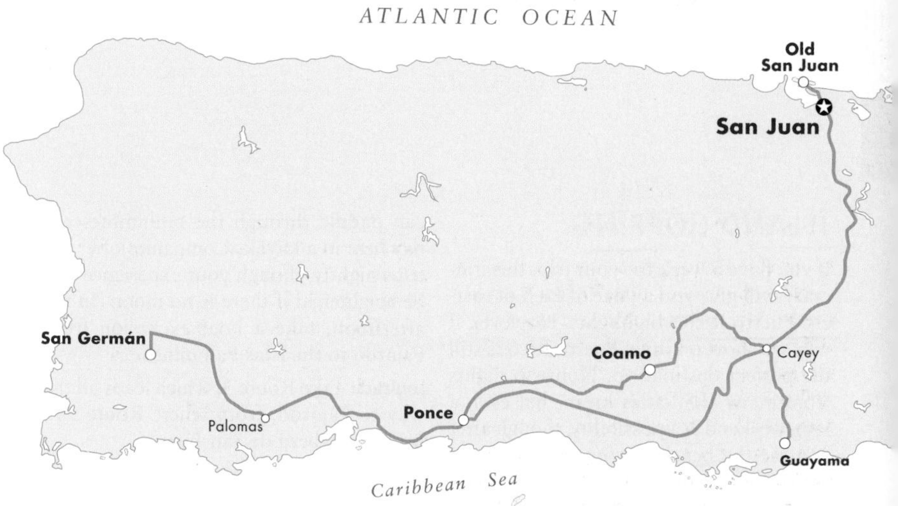

Logistics: Ponce is reached by Route 14 from Coamo. To get downtown, take Route 1.

Day 4: San Germán

Less than an hour west of Ponce is San Germán, a must-see for anyone interested in the colonial era. The best place to start a tour of San Germán is Plazuela Santo Domingo, the small park in the center of the historic district. At the eastern edge of the park is the Capilla de Porta Coeli. This chapel, at the top of some steep stone steps, is now a museum of religious art. Stroll west past the delightful assemblage of buildings of every architectural style from mission to Victorian. Make sure to see the other gorgeous church, the Iglesia de San Germán de Auxerre, a few blocks north. The best lodging in the area is the simple Villa del Rey, a few miles outside of town.

Logistics: San Germán is easy to reach—simply take Route 2 west of Ponce. When you reach Route 122, head south.

TIPS

If you're staying in Old San Juan, pick up your rental car at one of the hotel desks. You'll avoid an expensive taxi ride to the airport.

Bring comfortable shoes for exploring these colonial-era cities. You'll be glad you brought sneakers after a few hours traipsing around on the cobblestone streets.

Old San Juan is hillier than it first appears, and in Ponce avoid walking to Castillo Serallé—a stiff hike through an unsavory area. Take advantage of the free public transportation to the most popular tourist sites in both cities.

Day 5: San Juan

If you have time on your way back to San Juan, stop for lunch at one of the open-air eateries near Guavate, off Route 52. You can try *lechón,* whole suckling pig roasted on a spit.

Logistics: From San Germán, take Route 2 until you reach Ponce. Exit onto Route 52; a toll road takes you all the way to San Juan.

ISLAND HOPPING

If you have a week for your trip, this itinerary will give you a taste of each of eastern Puerto Rico's highlights. However, if you are short on time, Puerto Rico is still the perfect destination. Nonstop flights from many U.S. cities mean that even a long weekend is a possibility, though after you see the beaches, you may not want to limit yourself to just a night or two on Vieques or Culebra.

Day 1: El Yunque

East of San Juan is El Yunque, the undulating rain forest that covers much of the eastern edge of the island. It's a highlight of any trip to Puerto Rico, and you can still have a memorable time if you have only one day to spend there. Several of the trails can be done in an hour or less, including one leading to the spectacular waterfalls called the Cascada La Mina. Spend the night in Río Grande; our favorite hotel along this stretch of shoreline is Wyndham's upscale Rio Mar Beach Resort & Spa, known for its seaside golf courses, lovely beach, and first-class restaurants.

Logistics: Take Route 3 east of San Juan; then head south on Route 191, which leads through El Yunque.

Day 2: Reserva Natural Las Cabezas de San Juan

Head to Fajardo, on the northeastern tip of the island. Drop your stuff off at your hotel—we prefer the smaller ones like the Fajardo Inn—and then head out for a prearranged tour of the mangrove forests of the Reserva Natural Las Cabezas de San Juan. However, exploring this area isn't just a daytime experience. You may also want to head out at night to get a very different view of Las Cabezas; you can paddle through the bioluminescent bay here in a kayak. Companies offer the trips nightly, though your experience will be heightened if there is no moon. In the afternoon, take a boat excursion from Fajardo to the Islas Palominos.

Logistics: Take Route 3, which leads all the way to Fajardo, from where Route 987 leads to Cabeza de San Juan.

Days 3 and 4: Culebra

Culebra has some of the most beautiful, powdery soft beaches that you'll find in all of Puerto Rico. It's a small, quiet island, so you won't find much to do except relax. But then, that's the draw. There are no big hotels or fancy restaurants, only small guesthouses and some villas. If this sounds like too much of a get-away-from-it-all experience for your tastes, then skip Culebra and spend more time on Vieques, which has more resorts and better restaurants, and plenty of eco-focused activities. If you visit both islands, you can fly between Culebra and Vieques, but note that there's no ferry link.

Logistics: Drop off your rental car in Fajardo—you'll want to rent a sturdier four-wheel-drive vehicle once you get to Culebra. Take a 90-minute ferry trip or 10-minute puddle-jumper flight to the island. We recommend taking the plane, as the views are spectacular.

Days 5 and 6: Vieques

Close—both in terms of atmosphere and geography—to the U.S. Virgin Islands, Vieques has an entirely different feel from the rest of Puerto Rico. If you've never been to Vieques, we strongly recommend you spend at least one night there. The beaches are endless, the snorkeling is remarkable, and the bioluminescent bay is one of nature's best shows. A great way

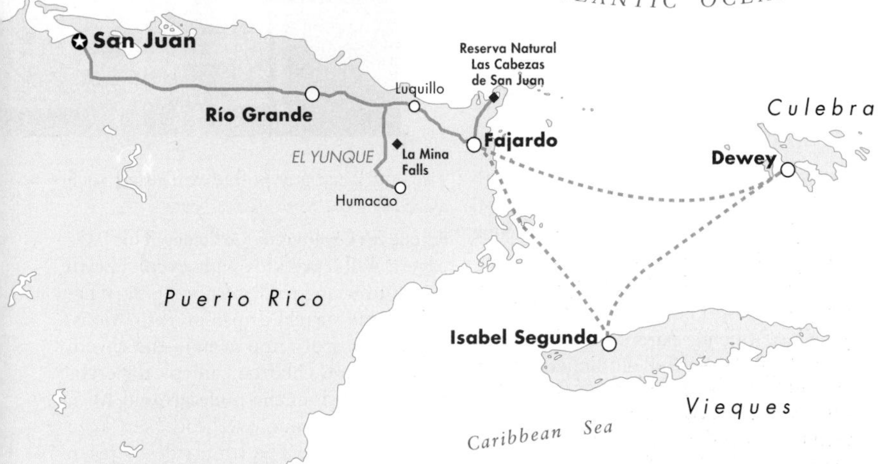

to explore the island is on a bicycle tour arranged by a local operator.

Logistics: You'll want to fly between Culebra and Vieques—there are scheduled direct flights between the islands. Otherwise you'll need to return to Fajardo, then take the ferry or fly to Vieques.

Day 7: San Juan

From Vieques, take a puddle-jumper flight back to San Juan (or to Fajardo's Ceiba airport to pick up your rental car). If you want to spend a day in Old San Juan, take a flight into Aeropuerto Fernando L. Rivas Dominici, which is a short taxi ride from San Juan's colonial heart. If you are connecting to a flight back home, then all you have to do is switch planes and you'll be on your way.

Logistics: If you are connecting to a flight back home, make sure your flight to San Juan is headed to Aeropuerto Internacional Luis Muñoz Marín. If it is going to San Juan's regional airport, Aeropuerto Fernando L. Rivas Dominici, you'll have to shuttle between the airports.

TIPS

Don't even think about taking your rental car to Vieques or Culebra—it's not allowed!

Check to see if you have to reserve in advance for certain tours, such as the daily trip to Fajardo's Reserva Natural Las Cabezas de San Juan.

Vieques and Culebra are both popular weekend destinations for Puerto Ricans, so the ferries become very crowded, and it's sometimes difficult to get on. If possible, plan your travel for a weekday.

KIDS AND FAMILY

Puerto Rico is a family-friendly isle, with no end of fun things for kids to see and do, including cave exploration, snorkeling with marine turtles, and going on nighttime excursions to bioluminescent lagoons. And many resort hotels arrange children's activities, freeing parents for romantic beach strolls and candlelit dinners.

Choosing a Place to Stay

Resort hotels make a point of catering to family needs. Most offer free rooms to children under 12 and can provide cribs. Here are a few questions to ask to gauge the level of family friendliness.

Are there discounted meals and activities? Do the restaurants have kids' menus? Are there children's programs, and is there an age range? A children's pool?

El Conquistador Resort, near Fajardo, has a long list of facilities for children, including the sensational Coqui Water Park. On the south coast, the Copamarina Beach Resort & Spa has two children's pools plus kayaks, pedal boats, tennis, and heaps of other activities.

Condos and vacation rentals offer an inexpensive option, especially for larger families. They typically have multiple bedrooms and you can cook for yourselves. ESJ Towers Condo Hotel, in Condado, is right on the beach in San Juan.

Things to Do

Vacationing in the Caribbean is all about the outdoors. Kids may even forget video games when they see the options: snorkeling, whale watching, Boogie boarding, and cave exploring. And the list of great beaches is endless. The wave-action around Rincón can be too rough for youngsters, but Vieques and Culebra have the most fantastic, reef-protected sands good for snorkeling, and kids can go kayaking and fishing. Many beaches have rip tides; always play safe, and heed any posted warnings, such as red flags.

Parque Las Cavernas de Río Camuy. This huge cavern will leave kids wide-eyed. They'll have fun trying to discern imaginary figures in the surreal dripstone formations. Tiny *coquí* frogs hop around the cavern entrance, and children can spy for crabs and blind fish in the underground river. Bats flitting about overhead help keep kids enthralled. The tram ride to reach the caverns is icing on the cake.

Arecibo Lighthouse & Historical Park. Local families love this small theme park built around the Faro de Los Morrillos lighthouse. It has a museum on seafaring, including pirates. In winter, kids can spy for whales from the lighthouse observation platform. The playground has a pirate's cave and replica galleon as well as a Taíno village.

Dr. Juan A. Rivera Zoo. Kids love animals—reason enough to visit this splendid zoo in Mayagüez, on the west coast. The highlight is an African wildlife park with elephants, giraffes, lions, and rhinos. There are also tigers, big apes, and camel rides.

Museo del Niño. While exploring San Juan, head to this small two-level museum in a colonial mansion opposite the cathedral. It's a great learning experience for younger children, with exhibits spanning hurricanes to interactive human biology, plus interactive displays including those in the NASA Space Place.

San Juan

WORD OF MOUTH

"Saturday we explored Old San Juan. There is rich history here. The narrow cobblestone streets are inviting and lend themselves to wonderful walking tours. There are many parks with fountains and benches where one can relax. And there is definitely no shortage of shops and restaurants."

—sunbabe

WELCOME TO SAN JUAN

TOP REASONS TO GO

★ **Take a Stroll:** Wander the cobblestone streets of Old San Juan, a UNESCO World Heritage Site.

★ **Climb a Battlement:** Explore Castillo San Felipe del Morro, the 16th-century fortress that dominates the waterfront; rangers provide a fascinating insight.

★ **Shop:** Head to Condado's Avenida Ashford, where you'll find most of the city's designer boutiques, including that of Nono Maldonado, one of the island's home-grown design talents.

★ **Catch Some Rays:** Balneario de Carolina, at the eastern tip of Isla Verde, is San Juan's best beach. Take time to parasail.

★ **Dine on the Strip:** Dine at Marmalade, just one of many stellar restaurants along the eastern end of Calle Fortaleza, a strip so trendy that locals call it "SoFo."

1 Old San Juan. Still enclosed by its original fortified city walls, this enclave of blue-cobbled streets is superbly preserved with more than 800 structures of historic importance. Many date back to the 16th century. Many of the city's best restaurants and bars are here, as well as boutiques spanning fare from cigars to designer clothing. Laid out in an easy-to-navigate grid, Old San Juan has enough sites and shops to enthrall for days.

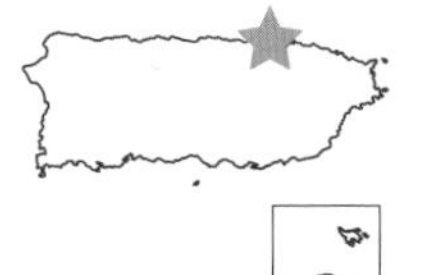

GETTING ORIENTED

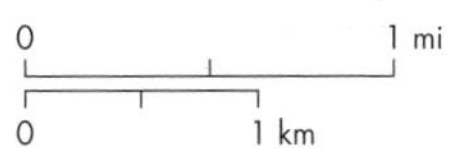

2 Greater San Juan. The sprawling modern metropolis opens out like a fan to three sides of Old San Juan. Condado and Isla Verde are superb venues for lazing on the beach by day and living it up by night at casinos and ritzy nightclubs—many associated with the upscale hotels that line the shorefront. Even teetotalers will enjoy an educational tour of the Bacardí rum factory, while culture vultures will delight in the Museo de Arte de Puerto Rico.

3 San Juan Environs. White- and golden-sand beaches unspool along the Atlantic shoreline to either side of the city. Several are developed as *balnearios* (public beaches), such as Playa Piñones; others, such as Dorado and Luquillo, boast several world-class hotels. They're popular with *sanjuaneros* on weekends, as is El Yunque National Forest. El Yunque offers fantastic hiking and birding, only a one-hour drive, yet a world away from San Juan.

San Juan wraps around the Bahía de San Juan (San Juan Bay) on the island's northern, Atlantic coast. Old San Juan, the original colonial city, occupies a long, slender isthmus on the northeast side of the bay and is connected by a bridge to Condado and, farther east, the districts of Ocean Park and Isla Verde (home of the international airport), which together make up San Juan's hip, touristy, 5-mi-long (8-km-long) coastal strip lined with gorgeous beaches. These districts have the lion's share of hotels, restaurants, entertainment, and sites to see. South of Condado and Ocean Park, the Santurce district—setting for the city's main art museums—melds into Hato Rey, the city's business district. The greater city fans out from here into suburbs with little touristic appeal.

SAN JUAN PLANNER

When to Go

During the high season, mid-December through mid-April, hotels tend to be packed, though rarely full, and rates are a bit higher than in the off-season. Fall and spring are less expensive. The weather's still fantastic, and the tourist crush is less intense. However, a winter visit may allow you to participate in many of San Juan's annual events. The January San Sebastián Street Festival, held in Old San Juan, consists of several nights of live music, food festivals, and *cabezudos* (parades). The Heineken JazzFest, each June, is the Caribbean's showcase for local and international talent. And the mid-November Festival of Puerto Rican Music takes place in both San Juan venues and elsewhere on the island. The festival celebrates Puerto Rico's traditional *plena* and *bomba* folk music with competitions and concerts.

San Juan's weather is moderate and tropical year-round, with an average temperature of about 82°F (26°C). And although it's true that hurricane season accounts for much of the summer and fall, San Juan's still an attractive destination during those months—hotels charge their lowest rates, restaurant reservations are easier to come by, and the streets are tourist free.

Getting Here

Air Travel. San Juan's busy **Aeropuerto Internacional Luis Muñoz Marín** (SJU ☎ *787/791–4670*) is the Caribbean hub of American Airlines, Continental Airlines, Delta, JetBlue, Spirit Air, United, and US Airways. International carriers include Air Canada from Toronto, Air France from Paris, Iberia from Madrid, and Condor from Germany. Air Flamenco, Isla Nena Air Service, and Vieques Air Link offer daily flights from SJU and Isla Grande Airport (SIG) in San Juan to Vieques and Culebra. Cape Air flies between SJU and Vieques.

Aeropuerto Fernando L. Rivas Dominici (☎ *787/729–8790*) is in Isla Verde, 11 mi (18 km) east of Old San Juan. It serves flights to and from Puerto Rico and Caribbean destinations.

⇨ *For airline contact information, see Air Travel in "Travel Smart."*

Before you leave for Puerto Rico, check with your hotel about transfers; many larger hotels provide transport from the airport, free or for a fee, to their guests. Otherwise, your best bets are *taxis turísticos* (tourist taxis). Uniformed officials at the airport can help you make arrangements. They will give you a slip with your exact fare written on it to hand to the driver. Rates are based on your destination. A *taxi turístico* to Isla Verde costs $10. It's $15 to Condado and $20 to Old San Juan. There's a $1 charge for each bag handled by the driver.

The Baldorioty de Castro Expressway (Route 26) runs from the airport into the city. Exits are clearly marked along the way, though you should check with your hotel to determine which one is best for you to take. Plan on 40 minutes for the drive from the airport all the way west to Old San Juan.

Ferry Travel. The **Puerto Rico Ports Authority** (☎ *787/723–2260* 🌐 *www.prpa.gobierno.pr*) runs passenger ferries from Fajardo to Culebra and Vieques. Service is from the ferry terminal in Fajardo, about a 90-minute drive from San Juan. There are a limited number of seats on the ferries, so get to the terminal in plenty of time. ⇨ *For schedule information, see Ferry Travel in "Travel Smart."*

Getting Around

Bus and Trolley Travel. The **AMA** (Autoridad Metropolitana de Autobuses ☎ *787/294–0500*) thread through San Juan, running in exclusive lanes on major thoroughfares and stopping at signs marked PARADA. Destinations are indicated above the windshield. Bus B-21 runs through Condado all the way to Plaza Las Américas in Hato Rey. Bus A-5 runs from San Juan through Santurce and the beach area of Isla Verde. Fares are 75¢ and are paid in exact change upon entering the bus. Most buses are air-conditioned and have wheelchair lifts and lock-downs.

The Municipio de San Juan operates free trolleys throughout Old San Juan. Trolleys run along three routes beginning at Pier 4, on Calle Gilberto Concepción de Gracia and running to the two castles plus Plaza de Armas.

Car Travel. Although car rentals are inexpensive (about $45 a day), we don't recommend that you rent a car if you're staying only in San Juan (at most, you might want to rent a car for a day to explore more of the island). Parking is difficult—particularly in Old San Juan—and many hotels charge hefty daily rates; also, traffic can be very heavy. With relatively reasonable taxi rates, it simply doesn't pay to rent a car unless you are leaving the city.

The main highways into San Juan are Route 26 from the east (it becomes the Baldorioty de Castro Expressway after passing the airport), Route 22 (José de Diego Expressway) from the west, and Route 52 (Luis A. Ferré Expressway) from the south.

International Agencies **Avis** (☎ *787/721–4499*). **Hertz** (☎ *787/791–0840*). **National** (☎ *787/791–1805*). **Thrifty** (☎ *787253–2525*).

Local Agencies **Charlie Car Rental** (☎ *787/728–2418* 🌐 *www.charliecars.com*). **Vias** (☎ *787/791–4120*).

Taxi Travel. *Taxis turísticos*, which are painted white and have the *garita* (sentry box) logo, charge set rates based on zones; they run from the airport and the cruise-ship piers to Isla Verde, Condado, Ocean Park, and Old San Juan, with rates ranging $10 to $20. Make sure to agree on a price before you get inside. City tours start at $30 per hour.

Although you can hail cabs on the street, virtually every San Juan hotel has taxis waiting outside to transport guests; if none are available, have one called. **Major Taxi** (☎ *787/723–2460*) is reliable. **Metro Taxi** (☎ *787/725–2870*) is recommended. Radioed taxis might charge an extra $1 for the pickup.

Visitor Information

You'll find Puerto Rico Tourism Company information officers (identified by their caps and shirts with the tourism company patch) near the baggage-claim areas at Luis Muñoz Marín International Airport.

In San Juan the tourism company's headquarters is at the Old City jail, La Princesa, in Old San Juan. Its main information bureau is opposite Pier 1, on Calle Gilberto Concepción de Gracia. Be sure to pick up a free copy of *Qué Pasa!*, the official visitor guide. Information officers are posted around Old San Juan (near the cruise-ship piers and at the Catedral de San Juan Bautista) during the day.

La Oficina de Turismo del Municipio de San Juan, run by the city, has information bureaus in Old San Juan and in Condado.

Information **Oficina de Turismo del Municipio de San Juan** (✉ *Calle Tetuán, corner Calle San Justo, Old San Juan* ☎ *787/721–6363* ✉ *Alcaldía, 153 Calle San Francisco, Old San Juan* ☎ *787/724–7171 ext. 2000* ✉ *999 Av. Ashford, Condado* ☎ *787/740–9270*). **Puerto Rico Tourism Company** (✉ *Edificio Ochoa, near Pier 1, Old San Juan* ☎ *787/721–2400* ✉ *Luis Muñoz Marín International Airport* ☎ *787/791–1014 or 787/791–2551* 🌐 *www.gotopuertorico.com*).

2

'HES OF SAN JUAN

Isla Verde beach is a beautiful strand that offers multiple water-sport and dining options or plenty of room to just stretch out and relax.

Just because you're staying in the city doesn't mean you'll have to forgo time on the *playa*. These beaches are among the island's best, and Condado, Isla Verde, and Ocean Park—to name a few—are always abuzz.

With 365 different beaches in Puerto Rico, choosing where to spread out your towel might seem like a daunting task. The decision is easier now that four have been designated with a Blue Flag. Chosen by the Foundation for Environmental Education, a nonprofit agency, Blue Flag beaches have to meet 27 criteria, focusing on water quality, the presence of a trained staff, and the availability of facilities such as water fountains and restrooms.

Playa Flamenco, on the island of Culebra, made the cut. After all, it's rated one of the world's best beaches. More surprisingly, two of the beaches are in San Juan: Balneario Escambrón, in Puerta de Tierra, and Balneario Carolina, in Isla Verde. The fourth is Luquillo's Balneario Monserrate. This means that three of Puerto Rico's finest beaches are within an hour's drive of the capital.

PUBLIC BEACHES

The government maintains 13 *balnearios* (public beaches), including two in the San Juan metro area. They're gated and equipped with dressing rooms, lifeguards, parking, and, in some cases, picnic tables, playgrounds, and camping facilities. Admission is free; hours are generally daily 9–5 in summer and Tuesday–Sunday 9–5 during the rest of the year.

The city's beaches can get crowded, especially on weekends. There's free access to all of them, but parking can be an issue in the peak sun hours—arriving early or in the late afternoon is a safer bet.

Balneario de Carolina. When people talk of a "beautiful Isla Verde beach," this is the one they're talking about. A government-maintained beach, this *balneario* east of Isla Verde is so close to the airport that the leaves rustle when planes take off. The long stretch of sand, which runs parallel to Avenida Los Gobernadores, is shaded by palms and almond trees. There's plenty of room to spread out and lots of amenities: lifeguards, restrooms, changing facilities, picnic tables, and barbecue grills. ✉ *Carolina* 🎫 *Parking $3* ⏲ *Daily 8–5.*

Balneario de Escambrón. In Puerta de Tierra, this government-run beach is just off Avenida Muñoz Rivera. The patch of honey-colored sand is shaded by coconut palms and has surf that's generally gentle. Favored by families, it has lifeguards, bathhouses, bathrooms, and restaurants. ✉ *Puerta de Tierra* 🎫 *Parking $4.28* ⏲ *Daily 6–7.*

Playa de Ocean Park. The residential neighborhood east of Condado and west of Isla Verde is home to this 1-mi-long (1½-km-long) stretch of golden sand. The waters are often choppy but still swimmable—take care, however,

as there are no lifeguards on duty. Windsurfers say the conditions here are nearly perfect. The tranquil beach is popular with young people, particularly on weekends, as well as gay men. Parking is a bit difficult, as many of the streets are gated and restricted to residents. ✉ *Ocean Park* ⏲ *Daily dawn–dusk.*

Playa del Condado. East of Old San Juan and west of Ocean Park, this long, wide beach is overshadowed by an unbroken string of hotels and apartment buildings. Beach bars, water-sports outfitters, and chair-rental places abound. You can access the beach from several roads off Avenida Ashford, including Calle Cervantes and Calle Candina. The protected water at the small stretch of beach west of the Conrad San Juan Condado Plaza hotel is particularly calm and popular with families; surf elsewhere in Condado can be a bit strong. The stretch of sand near Calle Vendig (behind the Atlantic Beach Hotel) is especially popular with the gay community. If you're driving, on-street parking is your only option. ✉ *Condado* ⏲ *Daily dawn–dusk.*

Revised and Updated by Christopher Baker and Heather Rodino

If you associate Puerto Rico's capital with the colonial streets of Old San Juan, then you know only part of the picture. San Juan is a major metropolis, radiating out from the bay on the Atlantic Ocean that was discovered by Juan Ponce de León. More than a third of the island's 4 million citizens proudly call themselves *sanjuaneros*. The city may be rooted in the past, but it has its eye on the future. Locals go about their business surrounded by colonial architecture and towering modern structures.

By 1508 the explorer Juan Ponce de León had established a colony in an area now known as Caparra, southeast of present-day San Juan. He later moved the settlement north to a more hospitable peninsular location. In 1521, after he became the first colonial governor, Ponce de León switched the name of the island—which was then called San Juan Bautista in honor of St. John the Baptist—with that of the settlement of Puerto Rico ("rich port").

Defended by the imposing Castillo San Felipe del Morro (El Morro) and Castillo San Cristóbal, Puerto Rico's administrative and population center remained firmly in Spain's hands until 1898, when it came under U.S. control after the Spanish-American War. Centuries of Spanish rule left an indelible imprint on the city, particularly in the walled area now known as Old San Juan. The area, with its cobblestone streets lined with brightly painted, colonial-era structures, has been designated a UNESCO World Heritage Site.

Old San Juan is a monument to the past, but most of the rest of the city is planted firmly in the 20th and 21st centuries and draws migrants from island-wide and farther afield to jobs in its businesses and industries. The city captivates residents and visitors alike with its vibrant lifestyle as well as its balmy beaches, pulsing nightclubs, globe-spanning restaurants, and world-class museums. Once you set foot in this city, you may never want to leave.

IF YOU LIKE

ARCHITECTURE

San Juan has been under construction for nearly 500 years, which shows in the city's wide range of architectural styles. The Old City's colonial Spanish row houses—brick with plaster fronts painted in pastel blues, oranges, and yellows—line narrow streets and alleys paved with *adoquines* (blue-gray stones originally used as ballast in Spanish ships). Several churches, including the Catedral de San Juan Bautista, were built in the ornate Spanish Gothic style of the 16th century. The massive, white marble El Capitolio, home of Puerto Rico's legislature, was completed in 1929. And firmly rooted in the 20th century are the gleaming high-rise resorts along the beaches in Condado and Isla Verde and the glistening steel-and-glass towers in the business and financial district of Hato Rey.

MUSIC

Music is a source of Puerto Rican pride, and it seems that increasingly everyone wants to live that *vida loca* (crazy life) espoused by Puerto Rico's own Ricky Martin. The brash Latin sound is best characterized by the music-dance form salsa, which shares not only its name with the word "sauce" but also its zesty, hot flavor. A fusion of West African percussion, jazz (especially swing and big band), and other Latin beats (mambo, merengue, flamenco, cha-cha, rumba), salsa music is sexy and primal. Dancers are expected to let go of all inhibitions.

NIGHTLIFE

As befits a metropolitan capital city, San Juan has a wide variety of restaurants and bars for people with all sorts of palates and party habits. Old San Juan and Condado, in particular, are big nighttime destinations. Many of the newer establishments have set their tables on terraces, the beach, indoor patios, or streetside to take advantage of the late-night atmosphere. Many clubs and discos stay open into the wee hours of morning.

EXPLORING SAN JUAN

San Juan's metro area stretches for 12 mi (19 km) along Puerto Rico's north coast, and defining the city is rather like assembling a puzzle. Neighborhoods are irregular and sometimes overlap—locals disagree, for example, about where Condado ends and Ocean Park begins. The areas most visited by tourists run along the coast.

Farthest west is Old San Juan, the showplace of the island's rich history. On this peninsula you will find some of the city's finest museums and shops, as well as excellent dining and lodging options. To the east is Puerta de Tierra, a narrow strip of land sandwiched between the ocean and the bay. The area is home to a couple of famous hotels and two noteworthy parks, the Parque de Tercer Milenio and the Parque Muñoz Rivera. Beyond Puerta de Tierra is Condado, an upscale older neighborhood that is a mix of beautiful Spanish-style homes, larger apartment buildings, and resort hotels. Here you'll find designer fashions in the boutiques and on the people strolling down the main drag of Avenida

Ashford. Ocean Park, to the east of Condado, is mostly residential, but the handful of inns and restaurants here are among the city's best. Beyond Ocean Park is Isla Verde, a more commercial zone and also where you'll find the biggest resorts on the best city beach.

You may want to explore a few other neighborhoods. South of Condado and Ocean Park lies Santurce, a business district with a growing artistic community, thanks to the Museo de Arte de Puerto Rico and the Museo de Arte Contemporáneo. Hato Rey is a busy financial district, where you'll find the large Plaza las Américas Mall. The mostly residential Río Piedras area is home of the Universidad de Puerto Rico.

OLD SAN JUAN

Old San Juan's 16th-century cobblestone streets, ornate Spanish town houses with wrought-iron balconies, ancient plazas, and eclectic museums are all repositories of the island's colorful history. Founded in 1521 by the Spanish explorer Juan Ponce de León, Old San Juan sits on a peninsula separated from the "new" parts of the city by a couple of miles and a couple of centuries. Ironically, its culture is youthful and vibrant, reflecting the sensibilities of stylish professionals, a bohemian art crowd, and skateboarding teenagers who populate the streets. You'll find more streetfront cafés and fine restaurants, more contemporary art galleries, more musicians playing in plazas, than anywhere else in San Juan.

Old San Juan slopes north, uphill, to Calle Norzagaray, which runs along the Atlantic shoreline and connects Castillo San Cristóbal to El Morro, the Old City's twin defensive bastions. On the north side of Calle Norzagaray you'll find a small neighborhood tucked beneath the city walls tight up against the ocean—this is La Perla, a rough area that you would be wise to avoid. The west end of the Old City overlooks San Juan Bay, and it's here that the rugged, towering walls of the original city are most evident. On Old San Juan's south side, along Calle Gilberto Concepción de Gracia, you'll find the commercial and cruise-ship piers that jut into San Juan Harbor.

GETTING AROUND

Don't consider driving in Old San Juan unless you enjoy sitting in traffic jams for much of the day, especially on Sunday. Old San Juan is a walking city, with narrow, one-way streets, narrower alleys, little parking, and sights and shops packed together in an area hardly larger than one square mile. Some of the streets are steep and many are paved with cobblestones, so wear comfortable shoes as well as a hat and sunscreen—and drink plenty of water.

FERRY The ferry between Old San Juan and Cataño is operated by the Autoridad de los Puertos. It costs a mere 50¢ one-way and runs daily every 15 or 30 minutes from 6 AM until 10 PM. The ferry, which departs from Pier 2, is the one to take if you wish to visit the Bacardí Rum Factory.

Information The **Autoridad de los Puertos** (☎ *787/788–0940*).

PARKING If you can't avoid taking a car into Old San Juan, park at La Puntilla, at the head of Paseo de la Princesa. It's an outdoor lot with the Old

Festive street musicians are frequently seen and heard throughout Old San Juan.

City's cheapest rates (they start at 50¢ an hour). You could also try the Felisa Rincón de Gautier lot on Calle Gilberto Concepción de Gracia or the Frank Santaella lot between Paseo de Covadonga and Calle Gilberto Concepción de Gracia. Parking starts at $1.25 for the first hour. The lots open at 7 AM and close at 10 PM weekdays and as late as 2 AM on weekends.

TROLLEYS Free trolleys swing through Old San Juan all day, every day—departing from the main bus terminal area across from Pier 4 and taking three routes through the Old City. One route heads north to Calle Norzagaray then west to El Morro, dropping you off at the long footpath leading to the fort. Then it retraces its route past Castillo San Cristóbal, west to Plaza de Armas, east on Fortaleza, west on Recinto Sur, and then back along Calle Gilberto Concepción de Gracia (also called Calle la Marina) to the piers. A second route takes you east to the Punta de Tierra district, then via Castillo San Cristóbal to El Morro, then via Calle Norzagaray and Plaza Colón and back to the piers. The third route follows a figure-8 route from Pier 4 north on Tanca, then west along San Francisco and east on Fortaleza, returning via Plaza Colón. The trolleys make regular stops (at 24 signs marked PARADA) on their routes. When you're finished touring, taxis can be found in several spots: in front of Pier 2, on the Plaza de Armas, or on Calle O'Donnell near the Plaza de Colón. A map of trolley routes is available from the Puerto Rico Tourism Company information offices.

SAFETY

Old San Juan is generally safe, but keep in mind that pickpockets visit the same places as tourists. Keep money and credit cards out of back pockets, and avoid carrying open handbags. Avoid the La Perla district and, if walking, stick to well-policed areas and well-lit streets by night. Women should take licensed taxis at night.

TIMING

Old San Juan is a small neighborhood, approximately seven city blocks north to south and eight east to west. In strictly geographical terms, it's easily traversed in a day. But to truly appreciate the numerous plazas, museums, boutiques, galleries, and cafés requires two or three days. *For a great half-day itinerary, see "A Stroll Through Old San Juan."*

TOUR OPTIONS

In Old San Juan free trolleys can take you around, and the tourist board can provide you with a copy of *Qué Pasa* and an Old San Juan map, which contains a self-guided walking tour.

Legends of Puerto Rico (☎ *787/605–9060* 🌐 *www.legendsofpr.com*) has tours of Old San Juan as well as the modern neighborhoods that few travelers ever visit.**Segway Tours of Puerto Rico** (☎ *787/598–9455* 🌐 *www.segwaytourspr.com)*offers group tours of the city's historic district using Segways for fun and easy transport. **Wheelchair Getaway** (☎ *787/883–0131 or 800/868–8028*) offers city sightseeing trips as well as wheelchair transport from airports and cruise-ship docks to San Juan hotels.

Numbers in the margin correspond to the "Exploring Old San Juan" map.

WHAT TO SEE

TOP ATTRACTIONS

19 **Casa Blanca.** The original structure on this site was a wooden house built in 1521 as a home for Ponce de León; he died in Cuba without ever having lived here. His descendants occupied the house's sturdier replacement, a lovely colonial mansion with tile floors and beamed ceilings, for the next 250 years. It was the home of the U.S. Army commander in Puerto Rico from the end of the Spanish-American War in 1898 to 1966. Several rooms decorated with colonial-era furnishings are open to the public. A guide will show you around, and then you can explore on your own. Don't miss the stairway descending from one of the bedrooms—which, despite local lore, leads to a small room and not to a tunnel to nearby El Morro. The lush garden, complete with watchtower, is a quiet place to unwind. As of this writing, Casa Blanca was closed for a lengthy restoration to last into 2010. ✉ *1 Calle San Sebastián, Old San Juan* ☎ *787/725–1454* 🌐 *www.icp.gobierno.pr* 🎟 *$3* ⏲ *Wed.–Sun. 9–noon and 1–4.*

5 **Catedral de San Juan Bautista.** The Catholic shrine of Puerto Rico had humble beginnings in the early 1520s as a thatch-roof, wooden structure. After a hurricane destroyed the church, it was rebuilt in 1540, when it was given a graceful circular staircase and vaulted Gothic ceilings. Most of the work on the present cathedral, however, was done in the 19th century. The remains of Ponce de León are behind a marble tomb in the wall near the transept, on the north side. The trompe l'oeil

Hear your footsteps echo throughout Castillo San Felipe's vast network of tunnels, designed to amplify the sounds of approaching enemies.

work on the inside of the dome is breathtaking. Unfortunately, many of the other frescoes suffer from water damage. ✉ *151 Calle Cristo, Old San Juan* ☎ *787/722–0861* 🌐 *www.catedralsanjuan.com* 💵 *$1 donation suggested* ⏲ *Mon.–Sat. 8–5, Sun. 8–4:30.*

22 **Castillo San Cristóbal.** This huge stone fortress, built between 1634 and 1785, guarded the city from land attacks from the east. Even larger than El Morro, San Cristóbal was known in the 17th and 18th centuries as the Gibraltar of the West Indies. Five freestanding structures divided by dry moats are connected by tunnels. You're free to explore the gun turrets (with cannon in situ), officers' quarters, re-created 18th-century barracks, and gloomy passageways. Along with El Morro, San Cristóbal is a National Historic Site administered by the U.S. Park Service; it's a World Heritage Site as well. Rangers conduct tours in Spanish and English. ✉ *Calle Norzagaray at Calle Muñoz Rivera, Old San Juan* ☎ *787/729–6777* 🌐 *www.nps.gov/saju* 💵 *$3; $5 includes admission to El Morro* ⏲ *Daily 9–6.*

Fodor's Choice ★

21 **Castillo San Felipe del Morro** *(El Morro).* At the northwestern tip of the Old City is El Morro ("the promontory"), a fortress built by the Spaniards between 1540 and 1783. Rising 140 feet above the sea, the massive six-level fortress was built to protect the harbor entrance. It is a labyrinth of cannon batteries, ramps, barracks, turrets, towers, and tunnels. Built to protect the port, El Morro has a commanding view of the harbor. You're free to wander throughout. The cannon emplacement walls and the dank secret passageways are a wonder of engineering. The fort's small but enlightening museum displays ancient Spanish guns and other armaments, military uniforms, and blueprints for Spanish forts

Fodor's Choice ★

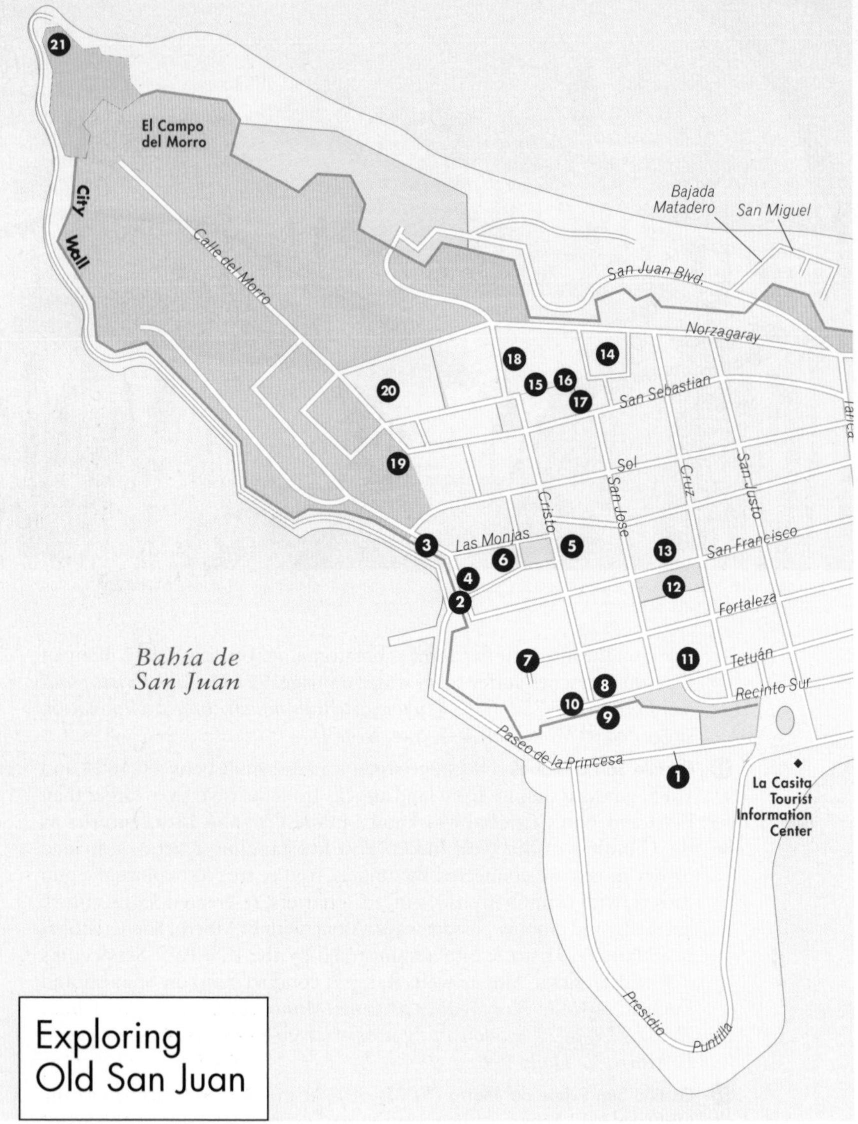

Exploring Old San Juan

Alcaldía **13**
Capilla del Cristo **9**
Case Blanca **19**
Casa de Ramón Power y Giralt **11**
Castillo San Cristóbal **22**
Castillo San Felipe del Morro (El Morro) **21**
Catedral de San Juan Bautista **5**
Convento de los Dominicos **18**
Iglesia de San José **15**
La Fortaleza **7**
Museo de las Américas ... **20**
Museo de la Casa del Libro **8**
Museo del Niño **6**
Museo de Nuestra Raíz Africana **17**
Museo de San Juan **14**
Museo Felisa Rincón de Gautier **4**
Museo Pablo Casals **16**
Parque de las Palomas ... **10**
Paseo de la Princesa **1**

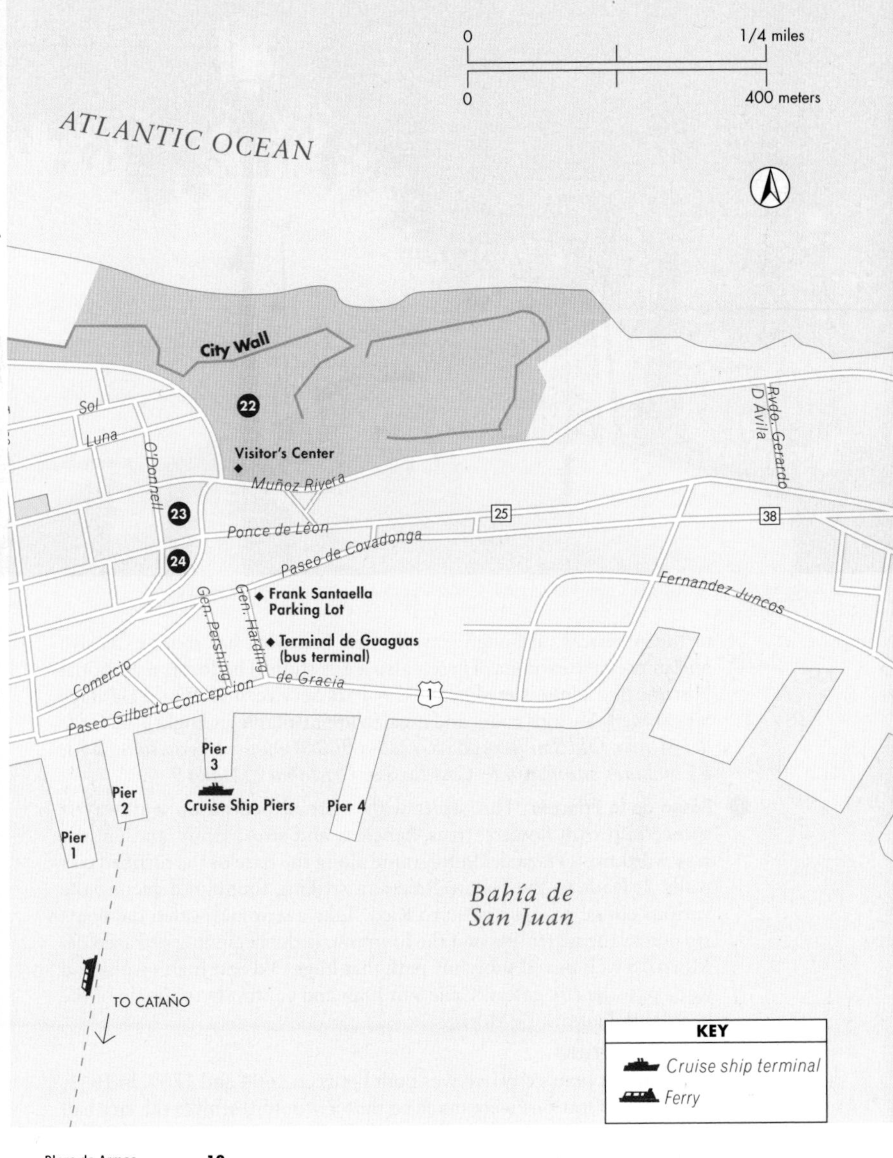
0
1/4 miles
0
400 meters
ATLANTIC OCEAN
City Wall
22
Sol
Luna
O'Donnell
Visitor's Center
Muñoz Rivera
23
Ponce de Léon
25
38
Rvdo. Gerardo D Avila
24
Paseo de Covadonga
Fernandez Juncos
Gen. Pershing
Gen. Harding
Frank Santaella Parking Lot
Terminal de Guaguas (bus terminal)
Comercio
de Gracia
1
Paseo Gilberto Concepcion
Pier 3
Pier 2
Pier 1
Cruise Ship Piers
Pier 4
Bahía de San Juan
TO CATAÑO
KEY
Cruise ship terminal
Ferry

La Muralla, the city wall, towers over the harbor-side walkway that winds around the Old City.

in the Americas, although Castillo San Cristóbal has more extensive and impressive exhibits. There's also a gift shop. The fort is a National Historic Site administered by the U.S. Park Service; it's a World Heritage Site as well. Various tours and a video are available in English. ✉ *Calle del Morro, Old San Juan* ☎ *787/729–6960* 🌐 *www.nps.gov/saju* 🎟 *$3; $5 includes admission to Castillo San Cristóbal* 🕒 *Daily 9–6.*

1 **Paseo de la Princesa.** This street with a broad pedestrian walkway is spruced up with flowers, trees, benches, and street lamps and unfurls westward from Plaza del Immigrante along the base of the fortified city walls. It leads to the Fuente Raices, a striking fountain depicting the various ethnic groups of Puerto Rico. Take a seat and watch the boats zip across the water. Beyond the fountain, is the beginning of Paseo del Morro, a well-paved shoreline path that hugs Old San Juan's walls and leads past the city gate at Calle San Juan and continues to the tip of the headland, beneath El Morro.

WORTH NOTING

13 **Alcaldía.** San Juan's city hall was built between 1604 and 1789. In 1841, extensive alterations were made so that it would resemble the city hall in Madrid, with arcades, towers, balconies, and an inner courtyard. Renovations have refreshed the facade of the building and some interior rooms, but the architecture remains true to its colonial style. Only the patios are open to public viewings. A municipal tourist information center and an art gallery with rotating exhibits are in the lobby. ✉ *153 Calle San Francisco, Plaza de Armas, Old San Juan* ☎ *787/724–7171* 🎟 *Free* 🕒 *Weekdays 8–4.*

9 **Capilla del Cristo.** According to legend, in 1753 a young horseman named Baltazar Montañez got carried away during festivities in honor of San Juan Bautista (St. John the Baptist), raced down Calle Cristo, and plunged over its steep precipice. A witness to the tragedy promised to build a chapel if the young man's life could be saved. Historical records maintain the man died, but legend contends that he lived. (Another version of the story has it that the horse miraculously stopped before plunging over the cliff.) Regardless, this chapel was built, and inside is a small silver altar dedicated to the Christ of Miracles. You can peer in through the wrought-iron gates, which are usually closed. ✉ *End of Calle Cristo, Old San Juan* ☎ *No phone* 🎟 *Free.*

8 **Museo la Casa del Libro.** This 18th-century house contains a museum dedicated to the artistry of the printed word. The 6,000-piece collection includes some 200 rare volumes dating back more than 500 years, as well as what appears to be legal writing on a fragment of clay from 2,000 years ago. Also on hand are several antique printing presses, one constructed in 1812 in France and later brought to Puerto Rico. There are interesting temporary exhibits as well. At this writing, repairs to the building had temporarily relocated the museum to the ground-floor courtyard of the Museo de las Américas. Construction was expected to continue into 2010, so call ahead. ✉ *255 Calle Cristo, Old San Juan* ☎ *787/723–0354* 🌐 *www.icp.gobierno.pr* 🎟 *$2 donation suggested* ⏱ *Tues.–Sat. 11–4:30.*

11 **Casa de Ramón Power y Giralt.** The restored home of 18th-century naval hero Don Ramón Power y Giralt is now the headquarters of the Conservation Trust of Puerto Rico. On-site are several displays highlighting the physical, cultural, and historical importance of land and properties on the island under the trust's aegis. You'll find a display of musical instruments that you can play, a bird diorama with recorded bird songs, an active beehive, and a seven-minute movie discussing the trust's efforts. Displays are in Spanish; the movie is in English or Spanish. A gift shop sells toys and Puerto Rican candies. ✉ *155 Calle Tetuán, Old San Juan* ☎ *787/722–5834* 🎟 *Free* ⏱ *Tues.–Fri. 9–5.*

18 **Convento de los Dominicos.** Built by Dominican friars in 1523, this convent often served as a shelter during Carib Indian attacks and, more recently, as headquarters for the Antilles command of the U.S. Army. Now home to some offices of the Institute of Puerto Rican Culture, the beautifully restored building contains the Galería Nacional, displaying religious manuscripts, artifacts, and art. The institute also maintains a book and music shop on the premises. Classical concerts are held here occasionally. However, it was closed at last visit until further notice pending repairs. ✉ *98 Calle Norzagaray, Old San Juan* ☎ *787/721–6866* 🎟 *Free* ⏱ *Mon.–Sat. 9–5.*

7 **La Fortaleza.** Sitting atop the fortified city walls overlooking the harbor, the Fortaleza was built in 1533 as a fortress—and not a very good one. It was attacked numerous times and was occupied twice, by the British in 1598 and the Dutch in 1625. When El Morro and the city's other fortifications were finished, the Fortaleza was transformed into the governor's palace. Numerous changes have been made to the original

primitive structure over the past four centuries, resulting in the current eclectic yet eye-pleasing collection of marble and mahogany, medieval towers, and stained-glass galleries. It is still the official residence of the island's governor and is the Western Hemisphere's oldest executive mansion in continual use. Guided tours are conducted several times a day in English and Spanish; both include a short video presentation. Call ahead, as tours are often canceled because of official functions. The tours begin near the main gate in a yellow building called the Real Audiencia, housing the Oficina Estatal de Preservación Histórica. ✉ *Western end of Calle Fortaleza, Old San Juan* ☎ *787/721–7000* 🌐 *www.fortaleza.gobierno.pr* 🎫 *Free* ⏲ *Weekdays 8–4.*

NEED A BREAK?

On your hike up hilly Calle Cristo, stop at Ben & Jerry's (✉ *61 Calle Cristo, Old San Juan* ☎ *787/977-6882*) at the corner of Calle Sol. Savor Vermont ice cream under a palm tree or enjoy fresh fruit smoothies next to a Green Mountain cow.

15 **Iglesia de San José.** With its vaulted ceilings, this little church is a splendid example of 16th-century Spanish Gothic architecture. It was built under the supervision of Dominican friars in 1532, making it one of the oldest churches in the Western Hemisphere. The body of Ponce de León, the Spanish explorer who came to the New World seeking the Fountain of Youth, was buried here for almost three centuries before being moved to the Catedral de San Juan Bautista in 1913. At this writing, much-needed renovations were still under way, but progress has been slow and the anticipated reopening date is now 2010. ✉ *Calle San Sebastián, Plaza de San José, Old San Juan* ☎ *787/725–7501.*

14 **Museo de San Juan.** A bustling marketplace in 1855, this handsome building now houses the small San Juan Museum (formerly the San Juan Museum of Art and History). You'll find exhibits of Puerto Rican art, plus tableaux and audiovisual shows that present the island's history. Concerts and other cultural events take place in the huge interior courtyard. ✉ *150 Calle Norzagaray, at Calle MacArthur, Old San Juan* ☎ *787/724–1875* 🎫 *Free* ⏲ *Tues.–Sun. 9–4.*

20 **Museo de las Américas.** On the second floor of the imposing former military barracks, Cuartel de Ballajá, the museum's permanent exhibit, "Las Artes Populares en las Américas," focuses on the popular art and folk art of Latin America, including religious figures, musical instruments, basketwork, costumes, and farming and other implements. It's a small exhibit, worth a look if you're visiting other nearby attractions. ✉ *Calle Norzagaray and Calle del Morro, Old San Juan* ☎ *787/724–5052* 🌐 *www.museolasamericas.org* 🎫 *$3* ⏲ *Tues.–Wed. and weekends 10–4, Thurs.–Fri. 9–4.*

4 **Museo Felisa Rincón de Gautier.** This tiny museum honors Felisa Rincón de Gautier, who served as San Juan's mayor from 1946 to 1968. Throughout her life, "Doña Felisa" worked tirelessly on various public causes, from women's voting rights to health care for the poor. She was a fascinating figure who rose to power at a time when women and politics were not mentioned in the same breath. Even if you have no interest in her story, you can peek inside one of the historic homes

of Old San Juan. ✉ *51 Caleta de San Juan, Old San Juan* ☎ *787/723–1897* 🌐 *www.museofelisarincon.com* 🎫 *Free* 🕒 *Weekdays 9–4.*

6 **Museo del Niño.** This three-floor, hands-on "museum" is pure fun for kids. There are games to play, clothes for dress-up, a mock plaza with market, and even a barbershop where children can play (no real scissors here). One of the newer exhibits is an immense food-groups pyramid, where children can climb to place magnets representing different foods. Older children will appreciate the top-floor garden where bugs and plants are on display, and the little ones can pretend to go shopping or to work at a construction site. For toddlers, there's a playground. Note that when it reaches capacity, the museum stops selling tickets. ✉ *150 Calle Cristo Old San Juan* ☎ *787/722–3791* 🌐 *www.museodelninopr.org* 🎫 *$5, $7 children* 🕒 *Tues.–Thurs. 9–3:30, Fri. 9–5, weekends noon–5:30.*

17 **Museo de Nuestra Raíz Africana.** The Institute of Puerto Rican Culture created this museum to help Puerto Ricans understand African influences in island culture. On display over two floors are African musical instruments, documents relating to the slave trade, and a list of African words that have made it into popular Puerto Rican culture. ✉ *101 Calle San Sebastián, Plaza de San José, Old San Juan* ☎ *787/724–4294* 🌐 *www.icp.gobierno.pr* 🎫 *$2* 🕒 *Tues.–Sat. 8:30–4:30.*

16 **Museo Pablo Casals.** The small, two-story museum contains memorabilia of the famed cellist, who made his home in Puerto Rico from 1956 until his death in 1973. Manuscripts, photographs, and his favorite cellos are on display, in addition to recordings and videotapes (shown on request) of Casals Festival concerts, which he instituted in 1957. The festival is held annually in June. ✉ *101 Calle San Sebastián, Plaza de San José, Old San Juan* ☎ *787/723–9185* 🎫 *$1* 🕒 *Tues.–Sat. 9:30–4:30.*

10 **Parque de las Palomas.** Never have birds had it so good. The small, shaded park bordering Old San Juan's Capilla del Cristo has a large stone wall with pigeonholes cut into it. Hundreds of *palomas* (pigeons) roost here, and the park is full of cooing local children chasing the well-fed birds. There's a small kiosk where you can buy refreshments and bags of seed to feed the birds. Stop to enjoy the wide views over Paseo de la Princesa and the bay.

12 **Plaza de Armas.** The Old City's original main square was once used as military drilling grounds. Bordered by Calles San Francisco, Rafael Codero, San José, and Cruz, it has a fountain with 19th-century statues representing the four seasons as well as a bandstand and a small café. The Alcaldía commands the north side. This is one of the most popular meeting places in Old San Juan, so you're likely to encounter everyone from artists sketching caricatures to street preachers imploring the wicked to repent.

NEED A BREAK?

At Café 4 Estaciones, on the Plaza de Armas in Old San Juan, tables and chairs sit under a canvas canopy surrounded by potted plants. This tiny kiosk-café is the perfect spot to put down your shopping bags and rest your tired feet. Grab a *café con leche* (coffee with hot milk), an espresso, or cold drink, and watch the children chase the pigeons. It's open 24 hours.

23 **Plaza de Colón.** A statue of Christopher Columbus stands atop a soaring column and fountain in this bustling Old San Juan square catercorner to Castillo San Cristóbal. Originally called St. James Square, it was renamed in honor of Columbus on the 400th anniversary of his arrival in Puerto Rico. Bronze plaques on the statue's base relate various episodes in the life of the great explorer. On the north side of the plaza is a terminal for buses to and from San Juan.

3 **Plazuela de la Rogativa.** According to legend, the British, while laying siege to the city in 1797, mistook the flaming torches of a *rogativa*—religious procession—for Spanish reinforcements and beat a hasty retreat. In this little plaza a monument of a bishop and three women commemorates the legend. The striking contemporary statue was created in 1971 by the artist Lindsay Daen to mark the Old City's 450th anniversary. The fine view of La Fortaleza and the harbor is a bonus. ✉ *Caleta de las Monjas, Old San Juan.*

2 **Puerta de San Juan.** Dating back to 1520, this was one of the five original entrances to the city and is the only one still in its original state. The massive gate, painted a brilliant shade of red, gave access from the port. It resembles a tunnel because it passes through La Muralla, the 20-foot-thick city walls. ✉ *Paseo de la Princesa, Old San Juan.*

24 **Teatro Tapia.** Named after the Puerto Rican playwright Alejandro Tapia y Rivera, this municipal theater was built in 1832 and remodeled in 1949 and again in 1987. It showcases ballets, plays, and operettas. Stop by the box office to find out what's showing. ✉ *Calle Fortaleza, Plaza de Colón, Old San Juan* ☎ *787/723–7800.*

GREATER SAN JUAN

Old San Juan may be Puerto Rico's jewel, but each of the other neighborhoods of San Juan has a distinctive character with its own special attractions. Just east of the Old City is **Puerta de Tierra**, home to a few notable hotels, a nice public beach, and several parks.

For multiple shopping and dining options all within walking distance, look to **Condado**. Once home to the city's moneyed elite, it's the most vibrant pedestrian neighborhood outside of Old San Juan. Here you'll find old Spanish-style homes next to sleek, modern apartment buildings and designer shops. The main street, Avenida Ashford, is fun to walk along, but the quieter residential areas are also very attractive. Many hotels are beachfront, though the beach is not as big or alluring as those in Isla Verde.

Ocean Park is a partially gated residential community with a laid-back feel. If you've dreamed of staying in a quiet guesthouse on a more secluded beach—away from the crowds—this might be the spot for you.

If you came to work on your tan—and you came to do it on a big, beautiful Caribbean beach—consider staying in **Isla Verde**, home to the nicest beach in the metropolitan area. The main commercial strip is not especially attractive: It's filled with fast-food restaurants and other businesses. You'll also need a car or taxi to get anywhere. That said, the resort-style hotels (many of them beachfront) offer so many amenities and so many restaurants on-site, you may not want—or need—to leave very often.

Continued on page 58

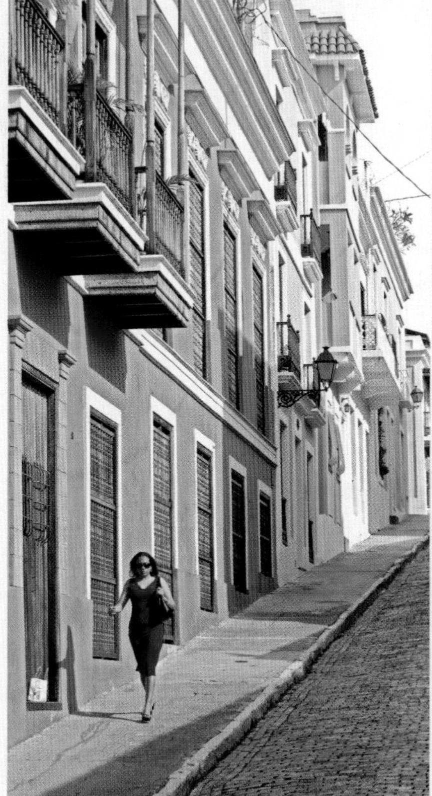

WALKING OLD SAN JUAN

Old San Juan is Puerto Rico's quintessential colonial neighborhood. Narrow streets and plazas are still enclosed by thick fortress walls, and bougainvillea bowers spill over exquisite facades. A walk along streets paved with slate-blue cobblestones leads past colonial mansions, ancient churches, and intriguing museums and galleries. Vivacious restaurants and bars that teem with life young and old are always nearby, making it easy to refuel and reinvigorate anytime during your stroll.

by Christopher P. Baker

left, strolling down Calle del Cristo; top right, a view from El Morro; bottom right, dancers in front of Castillo San Cristóbal

A STROLL THROUGH OLD SAN JUAN

La Fortaleza

This walk is best done in the morning to avoid the afternoon heat and cruise-ship crowds. The route is 2 mi (3 km); it will take half a day at a leisurely pace, with plenty of stops along the way.

❶ **Start at Plaza del Inmigrante.** This cobbled square facing the cruise port has impressive neoclassical and art deco buildings. From here, the **Paseo de la Princesa** promenade unfurls west beneath the ancient city wall, **La Muralla**. Artisans set up stalls under the palms on weekends. Midway along the brick-paved walkway, stop to admire the **Fuente Raices** monument and fountain: dolphins cavort at the feet of figures representing Puerto Rico's indigenous, Spanish, and African peoples.

❷ **Pass through the Puerta de San Juan.** This fortified entrance in La Muralla was built in 1520 and still retains its massive wooden gates, creaky on their ancient hinges. Immediately beyond, turn left and ascend to **Plazuela de la Rogativa**, a tiny plaza where a contemporary statue recalls the torch-lit procession that thwarted an English invasion in 1797. The harbor views are fantastic. Then, walk east one block to reach the **Catedral de San Juan Bautista**, the neoclassical 19th-century cathedral containing the mausoleum of Ponce de León.

❸ **Head south on Calle del Cristo.** Sloping gradually, this lovely cobbled street is lined with beautifully restored colonial mansions housing cafés, galleries, and boutiques. Pass-

Puerta de San Juan

Castillo San Cristóbal

Calle del Cristo

Catedral de San Juan Bautista

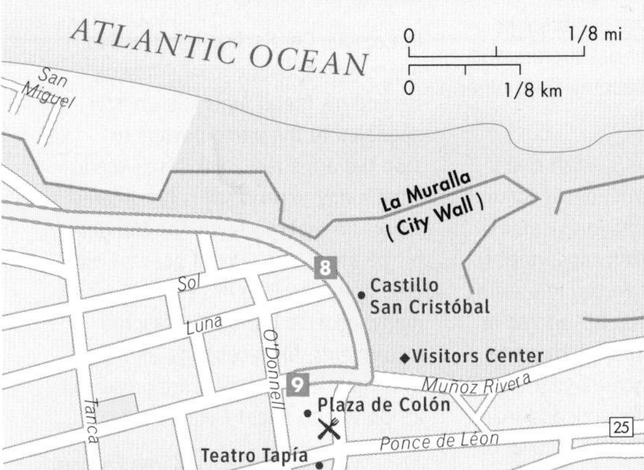

Castillo San Felipe del Morro

ing Calle Fortaleza, note **La Fortaleza,** the official residence of the Puerto Rican Governor at the end of the street. Calle del Cristo ends at **Capilla del Cristo**, a chapel adorned within by silver *milagros* (token requests).

❹ Return via Calle del Cristo and continue to Plaza de San José. Catercorner to the cathedral you'll find **El Gran Convento**, a former convent turned hotel, with an excellent restaurant, tapas bar, and café. At **Plaza de San José** visit the **Museo de Pablo Casals**, dedicated to the Spanish cellist, and the **Iglesia de San José**, a simple church dating from 1532.

❺ Walk west on Calle San Sebastián. This narrow street with colonial mansions painted in vibrant pastels ends at the gleaming white **Casa Blanca**. The oldest continually occupied residence in the Americas was originally the home of Ponce de León. Today it's a delightful museum furnished with period pieces. The garden is a tranquil spot for contemplation.

❻ Follow Calle del Morro north. One block from Casa Blanca you'll emerge upon a broad grassy headland—the Campo del Morro—popular with kite-flying families. It's skewered by an arrow-straight gravel path that aims at the imposing **Castillo San Felipe del Morro (El Morro)**, guarding the harbor entrance. Allow one-hour to roam the small museum, turrets, labyrinthine tunnels, and six levels of ramparts soaring 140 feet above the ocean.

❼ Retrace your steps and turn left on Calle Norzagaray. This street runs atop the Atlantic shoreline, offering sweeping ocean vistas. On your right you'll pass the **Plaza del Quinto Centenario**, pinned by an impressive statue: the *Tótem Telúrico*. Beyond, stroll past the Convento de los Dominicos to reach the **Museo de San Juan**. Housed in a former market, it traces the city's history and displays works by Puerto Rico's master painters.

❽ Continue east to Castillo San Cristóbal. Spanning 27 acres, this multitiered fortress was completed in 1771 with mighty bulwarks that protected the city from eastern attack by land. It features superb historical exhibits and reenactments by soldiers in period costumes.

❾ Exit the castle, turn south and walk one block to Plaza de Colón, This leafy square is lined with excellent cafés and restaurants where you can rest your feet and enjoy a great meal.

CLOSE UP

Peaceful Music

Cellist Pablo Casals was one of the 20th century's most influential musicians. Born in Catalonia in 1876, he studied in Spain and Belgium, settled for a time in Paris, then returned to Barcelona. Tours in Europe, the United States, and South America brought him artistic and financial success and opportunities to collaborate with other prominent musicians.

By the advent of the Spanish civil war, he was an internationally famous musician, teacher, and conductor. He was also an outspoken supporter of a democratic Spain. Forced into exile by Franco's regime, Casals arrived in Puerto Rico, his mother's birthplace, in 1956. Here the then-81-year-old maestro continued to work and teach. He established the Casals Festival of Classical Music, making the island a home for sublime orchestral and chamber works. During two weeks each June, the Puerto Rico Symphony Orchestra is joined by musicians from all over the world.

In Catalan, Casals' first name is Pau, which appropriately means "peace." He and his friend Albert Schweitzer appealed to the world powers to stop the arms race, and Casals made what many experts say is his greatest work—an oratorio titled *The Manger*—his personal message of peace. Casals died in Puerto Rico in 1973, but his many legacies live on. His favorite instruments, his recordings, and some of his numerous awards are preserved at the Museo Pablo Casals.

—Karen English

South of Condado is **Miramar**, home to a few hotels and some of the city's top restaurants. Seedy in spots, thriving in others, it's worth a visit if only to see what the innovative chefs are doing. From there you can venture into **Santurce,** a mostly commercial district with a growing artistic community, thanks to the Museo de Arte de Puerto Rico and the Museo de Arte Contemporáneo. You'll also find a thriving nightlife scene there on weekends. **Hato Rey** is a busy financial district, where you'll find the large Plaza las Américas Mall. The mostly residential **Río Piedras** area is home of the Universidad de Puerto Rico.

GETTING AROUND

Locals traveling in San Juan often complain about *el tapón* (traffic jam or, more literally, "cork"). A fifteen-minute drive can easily turn into forty-five minutes depending on the road conditions. In addition, drivers can be unpredictable, using the shoulder as a through-lane or drifting unpredictably from lane to lane, so be alert. If you choose to rent a car, get a good map. San Juan's roads are well marked, but one-way streets pop up out of nowhere.

Just east of Old San Juan, Avenidas Muñoz Rivera, Ponce de León, and Fernández Juncos are the main thoroughfares that cross Puerta de Tierra, leading to the neighborhoods of Condado, Ocean Park, and Isla Verde. Puente Dos Hermanos, the "Bridge of the Two Brothers," connects Puerta de Tierra with Condado. Avenida Ashford, which splits off into Avenida Magdalena for a few blocks, travels through Condado to Ocean Park. Calle Loíza connects Ocean Park with Isla Verde. These

The statues of Plaza de Armas's 19th-century fountain represent the four seasons.

streets can be choked with traffic, so if you are traveling more than a few blocks, consider taking the speedier Route 26.

TIMING

Depending on what mode of transportation you choose, you can see the Greater San Juan area sights in a day; if you linger in the museums, exploring might require two days. Buses are the least expensive but most time-consuming way to travel. Unfortunately, the beautiful new rapid-transit system, Tren Urbano, does not yet service the main tourist areas; however, if you're traveling to Bayamón, Guaynabo, Río Piedras, or another, more residential suburb, it's an option. Taxis are more convenient and you won't get lost—consider hiring a taxi by the hour and covering your selected sights in a couple of hours. Taxis charge $30 per hour for city tours, but the rate can be negotiable for long stretches of time.

Numbers in the margin correspond to the "Exploring Greater San Juan map."

WHAT TO SEE

TOP ATTRACTIONS

28 **Museo de Arte de Puerto Rico.** One of the biggest museums in the Caribbean, this 130,000-square-foot building was once known as San Juan Municipal Hospital. The beautiful neoclassical building, dating from the 1920s, proved to be too small to house the museum's permanent collection of Puerto Rican art dating from the 17th century to the present. The solution was to build a new east wing, which is dominated by a five-story-tall stained-glass window, the work of local artist Eric Tabales.

Fodor's Choice ★

Plucky pontiff: the bronze bishop of Plazuela de la Rogativa is a monument to the religious procession that, according to legend, repelled British invasion.

The collection starts with works from the colonial era, most of them commissioned for churches. Here you'll find works by José Campeche, the island's first great painter. His *Immaculate Conception,* finished in 1794, is a masterpiece. Also well represented is Francisco Oller y Cestero, who was the first to move beyond religious subjects to paint local scenes. His influence is still felt today. A gallery on the third floor is filled with works by artists inspired by Oller.

There's much more to the museum, including a beautiful garden filled with a variety of native flora and a 400-seat theater that's worth seeing for its remarkable hand-crocheted lace curtain. ✉ *299 Av. José De Diego, Santurce* ☎ *787/977–6277* 🌐 *www.mapr.org* 🎫 *$6* 🕐 *Tues.–Sat. 10–4, Sun. noon–4.*

26 ★ **Museo de Arte Contemporáneo de Puerto Rico.** This Georgian-style structure, once a public school, displays a dynamic range of works by both established and up-and-coming Latin American artists. Many of the works on display have strong political messages, including pointed commentaries on Puerto Rico's status as a commonwealth. Only a small part of the more than 900 works in the permanent collection is on display at any time, but it might be anything from an exhibit of ceramics to a screening of videos. ✉ *1220 Av. Ponce de León, at Av. R.H. Todd, Santurce* ☎ *787/977–4030* 🌐 *www.museocontemporaneopr.org* 🎫 *Free* 🕐 *Tues.–Sat. 10–4, Sun. noon–4.*

WORTH NOTING

25 **El Capitolio.** The white-marble Capitol, a fine example of Italian Renaissance style, dates from 1929. The grand rotunda, which can be seen from all over San Juan, was completed in the late 1990s. Fronted by

GREAT ITINERARIES

IF YOU HAVE 1 DAY

Many people find themselves with a single day—or even less—to explore San Juan. There should be no question about your destination—head to Old San Juan. Spend the entire day rambling around the cobblestone streets and ducking into the many shops, being sure to save plenty of time for exploring the turrets, towers, and dungeons of **Castillo San Felipe del Morro**, the original fortress on a rocky promontory at the Old City's northwestern tip (*see also "Great Walks: Old San Juan" feature*).

IF YOU HAVE 3 DAYS

It's only fitting that you spend the first day enjoying a walking tour of Old San Juan. What to see? **Castillo San Felipe del Morro** is at the top of the list. You might want to explore the equally enthralling **Castillo San Cristóbal,** which has underground tunnels and hidden passages, plus cannons and a more impressive museum than San Felipe del Morro. The city's original fortress, the **Fortaleza,** wasn't much protection from marauding pirates, but it does a great job at sheltering the governor and can be toured. And **Casa Blanca,** a home built for Juan Ponce de León, is a wonderful place to explore how the Spanish lived in the colonial days. Day two should be for lazing on a *playa* (beach). Choose from the city's finest at Condado, Ocean Park, or Isla Verde, and park yourself in a rented chair with a good book, a cold drink, and plenty of sunscreen. In the evening, make sure you enjoy the warm weather by dining alfresco. On your third day, hop the ferry across the bay to Cataño for a tour of the **Casa Bacardí Visitor Center.** Return in time for some shopping in the high-end shops and delightful art and crafts galleries along Calle Cristo, then dinner in one of the trendy eateries on Calle Fortaleza.

IF YOU HAVE 5 DAYS

Follow the itinerary above for your first three days in San Juan. On Day 4 head for the Santurce district. You can immerse yourself in island art at the **Museo de Arte Contemporáneo de Puerto Rico** and, nearby, the **Museo de Arte de Puerto Rico.** Afterward, wander through the produce stalls at the Plaza del Mercado in Santurce, with a fresh papaya or soursop shake in hand, and have your palm read. Be sure to note the giant bronze sculptures of avocados by artist Annex Burgos. On the morning of Day 5, hit the beach once more; then head to Avenida Ashford in Condado for an afternoon of shopping in its ritzy boutiques.

eight Corinthian columns, it's a very dignified home for the commonwealth's constitution. Although the Senate and the House of Representatives have offices in the more modern buildings on either side, the Capitol is where the legislators meet. You can also watch the legislature in action—note that the action is in Spanish—when it is in session, most often Monday and Thursday. Guided tours, which range between 30 minutes and two hours and include visits to the rotunda and other parts of the building, are by appointment only. ✉ *Av. Constitución, Puerta de Tierra* ☎ *787/721–5200, ext. 4609 or 4611* 🌐 *www.olspr.org* 🎟 *Free* ⏲ *Daily 8:30–5.*

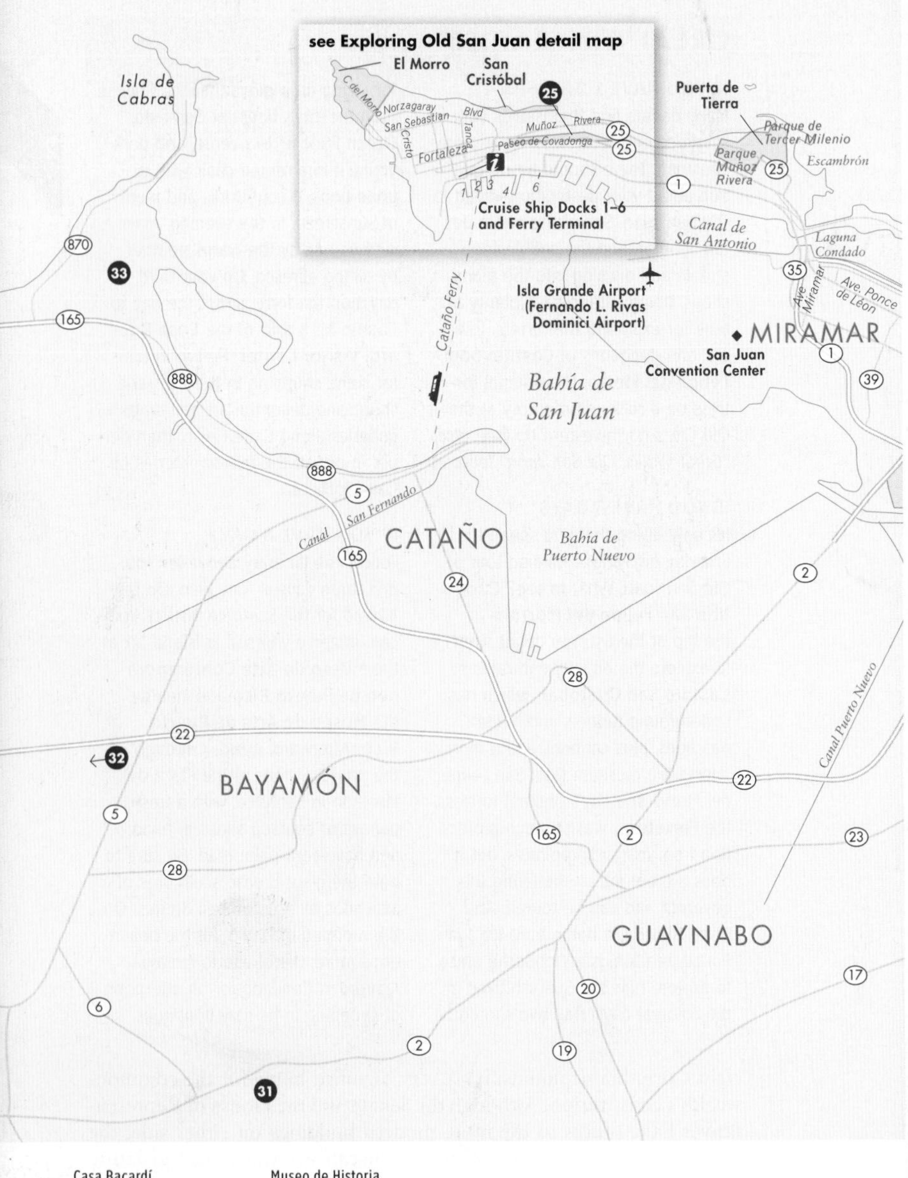
see Exploring Old San Juan detail map
El Morro
San Cristóbal
Isla de Cabras
C. del Morro
Norzagaray
San Sebastian
Blvd
Cristo
Tanca
Fortaleza
Muñoz
Rivera
Paseo de Covadonga
Cruise Ship Docks 1–6 and Ferry Terminal
Puerta de Tierra
Parque de Tercer Milenio
Parque Muñoz Rivera
Escambrón
Canal de San Antonio
Laguna Condado
Ave Miramar
Ave. Ponce de Léon
Isla Grande Airport (Fernando L. Rivas Dominici Airport)
MIRAMAR
San Juan Convention Center
Bahía de San Juan
Cataño Ferry
Canal San Fernando
CATAÑO
Bahía de Puerto Nuevo
Canal Puerto Nuevo
BAYAMÓN
GUAYNABO

Exploring
Greater San Juan
ATLANTIC OCEAN
0
1 mi
0
1 km
Condado
Joffre
Magdalena
Ashford
Santa Ana
C Italia
Punta las Marías
Wilson
Luchetti
C Mc Leary
C Cacique
Park Blvd
Guerrero
Noble
Loíza
Parque Barbosa
Taft
Mipillas
Túnel
Isla Verde
Ave Isla Verde
Gardenia
Amapola
Rosa
Violeta
SANTURCE
C5 Oeste
Laguna Los Corozos
C1 Este
Emma
Tapia
Avenida Eduardo Conde
C Sagrado Corazón de Jesus
Calle
Ave Hermanos Rodriguez
CAROLINA
Luis Muñoz Marín International Airport
Canal Martín Peña
RÍO PIEDRAS
Avenida Rexach
Constitución
Teodoro Moscoso Bridge
KEY
Ferry
Tourist Information

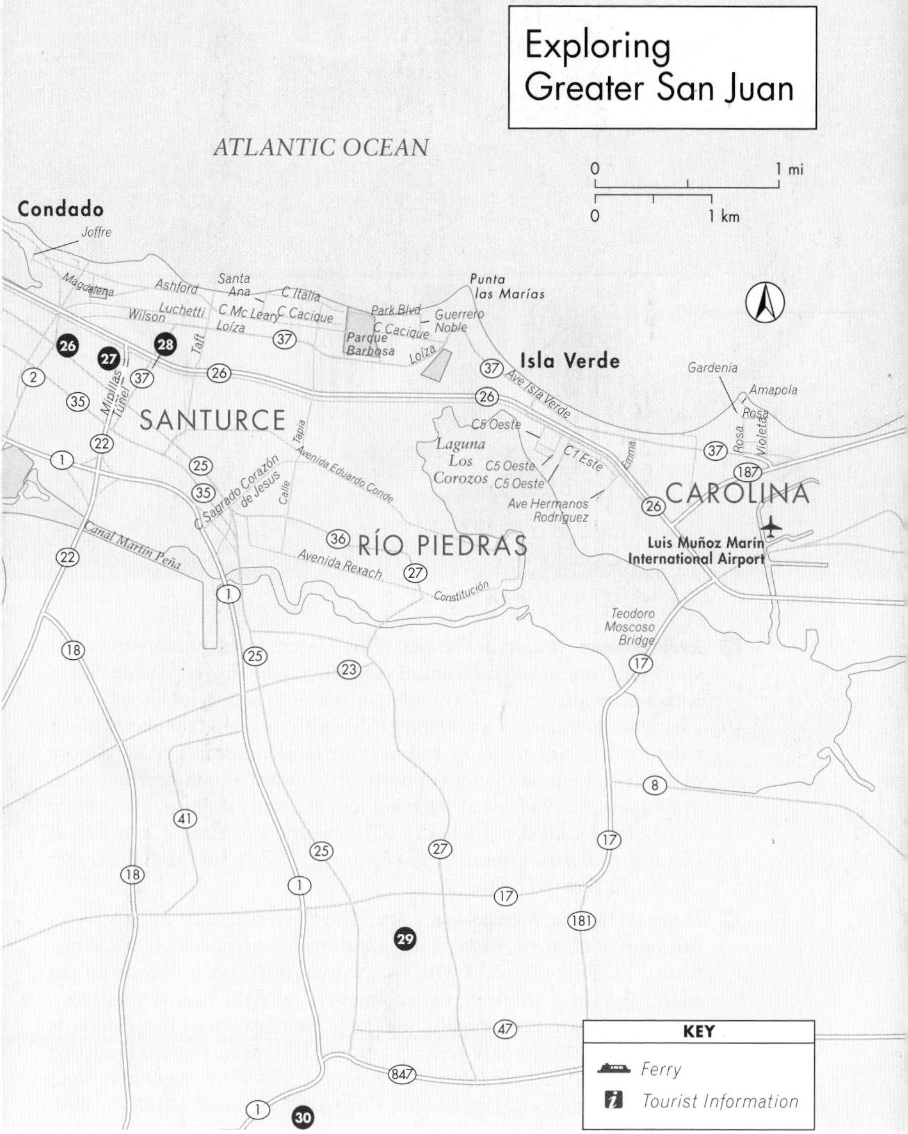

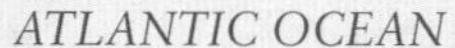

The stately lobby of the Museo de Arte de Puerto Rico

30 **Jardín Botánico** *(Botanical Garden)*. This 75-acre forest of more than 200 species of tropical and subtropical vegetation is the Universidad de Puerto Rico's main attraction. Gravel footpaths lead to a graceful lotus lagoon, a bamboo promenade, an orchid garden with some 30,000 plants, and a palm garden. Not all plants and trees are labeled, so the garden is more of a tranquil retreat than an opportunity to learn about the vegetation. Trail maps are available at the entrance gate, and groups of 10 or more can arrange guided tours ($25). ✉ *Intersection of Rtes. 1 and 847 at entrance to Barrio Venezuela, Río Piedras* ☎ *787/767–1710* 🌐 *www.upr.clu.edu* 🎫 *Free* 🕒 *Daily 6–6.*

29 **Museo de Historia, Antropología y Arte.** The Universidad de Puerto Rico's *Museum of History, Anthropology and Art* has archaeological and historical exhibits that deal with the Native American influence on the island and the Caribbean, the colonial era, and the history of slavery. Art displays are occasionally mounted; the museum's prize exhibit is the painting *El Velorio* (*The Wake*), by the 19th-century artist Francisco Oller. ✉ *Av. Ponce de León, Río Piedras* ☎ *787/764–0000 ext. 5852* 🌐 *www.uprrp.edu* 🎫 *Free* 🕒 *Mon.–Tues. and Thurs.–Fri. 9–4:30, Wed. 9–8:30, Sun. 11–5.*

27 **Plaza del Mercado.** Completely overlooked by tourists, the Plaza del Mercado is one of the most charming corners of San Juan. At its center is a market hall dating from 1910. Inside you'll find bushels of fruits and vegetables, many of which you probably haven't seen before. Many chefs from the top city restaurants come here to find their produce. If all this food makes you hungry, dozens of storefront restaurants face the central square. These places, mostly serving seafood, are quiet during

2

A GOOD TOUR

East of Old San Juan on Avenida Ponce de León you'll find **El Capitolio,** Puerto Rico's magnificent capitol building. Take Avenida Ashford east, branching off onto Avenida Magdalena and then Calle Loíza. At the corner of Avenida Ponce de León is the **Museo de Arte Contemporáneo de Puerto Rico,** with a fine collection of contemporary Latin American art. If you're hungry, stop for lunch at the nearby **Plaza del Mercado.** Afterward, head east on Avenida Ponce de León, then north on Avenida José de Diego to reach the **Museo de Arte de Puerto Rico,** a former hospital that has been transformed into the island's most ambitious art museum.

From the museum, it's a straight ride south on Avenida Ponce de León (Route 25) to the Río Piedras district, where you'll find the Universidad de Puerto Rico and its **Museo de Historia, Antropología y Arte.** Less than 1 mi (1½ km) to the west, at the junction of Routes 1 and 847, is the 75-acre **Jardín Botánico.**

the week but bustling on the weekends, especially in the evening. The area also has many *botánicas,* small shops that sell herbs, candles, and religious items. There may even be an in-house card or palm reader ready to show you your future. The square is between the Museo de Arte de Puerto Rico and the Museo de Arte Contemporáneo de Puerto Rico, making it a good place to stop for lunch if you are museum hopping. ✉ *Calle Dos Hermanos at Calle Capital, Santurce.*

SAN JUAN ENVIRONS

The suburbs of Cataño, Bayamón, and Guaynabo, west and south of San Juan, are separate municipalities but in many ways are indistinguishable from the city itself. Cataño, bordered by the Bahía de San Juan in the north, is an industrial suburb, perhaps most noted for its distillery belonging to Bacardí. Bayamón can be reached within 15 to 30 minutes from central San Juan; if you come by car, stop by the attractive central park, bordered by historic buildings. Guaynabo is a mix of residential and industrial areas and is worth visiting for its historical importance—Juan Ponce de León established the island's first settlement here in Caparra, and you can visit the ruins of the original fortification.

GETTING HERE AND AROUND

Avenida Kennedy runs mostly north–south and leads to the suburbs of Bayamón and Guaynabo. The Casa Bacardí Visitor Center is an easy trip from Old San Juan—you simply take a ferry across the harbor. The other sites are a challenge to reach, as you must navigate some of the region's most traffic-clogged streets. Do yourself a favor and take a taxi or book a tour.

WHAT TO SEE

33 **Casa Bacardí Visitor Center.** Exiled from Cuba, the Bacardí family built a small rum distillery here in the 1950s. Today it's the world's largest, with the capacity to produce 100,000 gallons of spirits a day and 21 million cases a year. You can hop on a little tram to take an approximately

CLOSE UP

Art Invasion

Public art is transforming the Puerto Rican capital: here a monolithic metal dove, there avocados so big you can stretch out on them. The stained-glass blades of a windmill spin above an oceanfront drive. A bright red jack towers over children at play in a park. These are only some of the 25 works that the city commissioned from 1996 to 2000, when Governor Sila María Calderón was its mayor.

Often the works seem perfectly at home in their environments. *Platanal,* by Imel Sierra Cabreras, has translucent panels that run across the ceiling of the restored Plaza del Mercado in Santurce. The avocados in *My Favorite Fruit* by Annex Burgos seem to spill from the entrance of this marketplace and across its front plaza. Although the large jack by María Elena Perales is a bit surreal, it's an appropriate addition to a playground in Parque Central Municipio de San Juan.

Some pieces attempt to soften or enliven their surroundings. Carmen Inés Blondet, whose *Fire Dance* is a collection of 28- to 35-foot spirals, created what seems an abstract forest in the midst of the concrete jungle. Crabs were once a common sight in Santurce (hence the name of the baseball team, the Santurce Crabbers), so Adelino González's benches for the area are bronze crabs. *Windmills of San Juan,* by Eric Tabales, is a whimsical tribute to the coast and its ocean breezes. The steel tower, with its rotating wheel of color, is on a restored ocean-side drive in Ocean Park.

The works haven't been without controversy. Many residents found *Paloma,* the metallic dove that towers over a busy Condado intersection, ugly; others went so far as to assert that it was the cause of traffic jams. Mayor Jorge Santini even threatened to remove it during his campaign. But it appears to be here to stay. To soften the piece, a fountain was added to its base, and it's now especially beautiful at night when the water is illuminated.

As a whole, however, the statues have made San Juan more interesting. And public art has spread around the island. In January 2002 Governor Calderón unveiled the Puerto Rico Public Art Project. Its budget of $15 million has funded about 100 new works. In San Juan these include stations of the urban train, the Luis Muñoz Marín International Airport, and several government buildings and city parks. The committee also envisions installing works at nature reserves, along highways, and in school playgrounds across the island. Soon, perhaps, that new bus stop, lifeguard station, or street-vendor stand you see will truly be a work of art.

—John Marino

45-minute tour of the visitor center, though you can no longer visit the distillery itself. Yes, you'll be offered a sample. If you don't want to drive, you can reach the factory by taking the ferry from Pier 2 for 50¢ each way and then a *público* (public van service) from the ferry pier to the factory for about $2 or $3 per person. ✉ *Road 165, Rte. 888, Km 2.6, Cataño* ☎ *787/788–1500 or 787/788–8400* 🌐 *www.casabacardi.org* 🎟 *Free* ⏲ *Mon.–Sat. 9–6, last tour at 4:30; Sun. 10–5, last tour at 3:45.*

31 **Ruinas de Caparra.** In 1508, Ponce de León established the island's first settlement here. The Caparra Ruins—a few crumbling walls—are what remains of an ancient fort. The small **Museo de la Conquista y Colonización de Puerto Rico** (Museum of the Conquest and Colonization of Puerto Rico) contains historical documents, exhibits, and excavated artifacts, though you can see the museum's contents in less time than it takes to say the name. Both the ruins and the museum are maintained by the Puerto Rican Institute of Culture. ✉ *Rte. 2, Km 6.6, Guaynabo* ☎ *787/781–4795* 🌐 *www.icp.gobierno.pr* 🎫 *Free* ⏲ *Weekdays 8:00–4:30.*

SAINTS ON PARADE

Each of Puerto Rico's 78 municipalities has a patron saint, and each one celebrates an annual festival near the saint's birthday, sometimes lasting a week or more. These festivals are a great opportunity to hear live music and buy local arts and crafts. San Juan celebrates its patron-saint feast in the *noche de San Juan* on June 23, when locals take to the beach. The event culminates at midnight, when crowds plunge into the Atlantic to flip over backward three times, a cleansing ritual expected to bring good fortune.

32 **Parque de las Ciencias Luis A. Ferré.** The 42-acre Luis A. Ferré Science Park contains a collection of intriguing activities and displays. The Transportation Museum has antique cars and the island's oldest bicycle. In the Rocket Plaza, children can experience a flight simulator, and in the planetarium the solar system is projected on the ceiling. Also on-site are a small zoo and a natural-science exhibit. It's a long drive from central San Juan, though. ✉ *Rte. 167, Bayamón* ☎ *787/740–6878* 🎫 *$5, $3 children* ⏲ *Wed.–Fri. 9–4, weekends 10–6.*

WHERE TO EAT

In cosmopolitan San Juan, European, Asian, Middle Eastern, and chic fusion eateries vie for your attention with family-owned restaurants specializing in seafood or *comida criolla* (creole cooking, or local Puerto Rican food). U.S. chains such as McDonald's and Subway compete with chains like Pollo Tropical and El Mesón, which specialize in local cuisine. Many of the most innovative chefs here have restaurants in the city's large hotels, but don't be shy about venturing into stand-alone establishments—concentrated in Condado and along Calles Fortaleza and San Sebastián, in Old San Juan.

WHAT IT COSTS IN U.S. DOLLARS

	¢	$	$$	$$$	$$$$
At Dinner	under $8	$8–$12	$12–$20	$20–$30	over $30

Prices are per person for a main course at dinner.

Dress codes vary greatly, though a restaurant's price category is a good indicator of its formality. For less expensive places, anything but beachwear is fine. Ritzier spots will expect collared shirts and long pants for

BEST BETS FOR SAN JUAN DINING

Fodor's Choice★

Il Mulino New York $$$$, p. 85
La Fonda del Jibarito $$, p. 74
Marmalade $$$, p. 75
Pamela's $$$, p. 84
Pikayo $$$, p. 82
St. Germain Bistro & Café, p. 76

By Price

$$

Bebo's Cafe, p. 80
Cafetería Mallorca, p. 69
El Patio de Sam, p. 72
La Bombonera, p. 73
La Fonda del Jibarito, p. 74
Lupi's, p. 74
Raices, p. 76

$$$

Ajili-Mójili, p. 77
Aureola, p. 69
Barú, p. 69
Café Berlin, p. 69
Chayote, p. 80
Delirio, p. 81
Dragonfly, p. 72
El Picoteo, p. 72
El Toro Salao, p. 73
Kasalta, p. 84
La Cucina de Ivo, p. 74
La Mallorquina, p. 74
La Ostra Cosa, p. 74
Parrot Club, p. 76
Pikayo, p. 82
Sofia, p. 76
Varita, p. 83

$$$$

Aguaviva, p. 68
Budatai, p. 80
Carli's Fine Dining & Piano, p. 72
Il Mulino New York, p. 85
Marmalade, p. 75
Panza, p. 75

By Experience

MOST ROMANTIC

Delirio, p. 81
La Ostra Cosa, p. 74
Pamela's, p. 84

BEST LOCAL FOOD

Ajili-Mójili, p. 77
Casa Dante, p. 85
La Fonda del Jibarito, p. 74

men (jacket and tie requirements are rare) and chic attire for women. When in doubt, do as the Puerto Ricans often do and dress up.

For breakfast outside of your hotel, cafés are your best bet. It's rare for such establishments to close between breakfast and lunch; it's slightly more common for restaurants to close between lunch and dinner. Although some places don't accept reservations, it's always a good idea to make them for dinner whenever possible. This is especially true during the busy season from November through April and on weekends at any time of the year.

OLD SAN JUAN

Use the coordinate (⊕ 1:A2) at the end of each listing to locate a site on the corresponding "Map 1: Where to Eat and Stay in Old San Juan."

$$$–$$$$ SEAFOOD ✕ **Aguaviva.** The name means "jellyfish," which explains why this ultracool, ultramodern place has dim blue lighting like a tranquil ocean, and lamps shaped like jellyfish floating overhead. Elegantly groomed oysters and clams float on cracked ice along the raw bar. Eating here is like submerging oneself into the ocean. The extensive menu is alive with inventive ceviches, some with tomato or roasted red peppers and olives, and fresh takes on such classics as paella. For something more filling,

try dorado served with a shrimp salsa or tuna accompanied by seafood enchiladas. You could also empty out your wallet for one of the *torres del mar,* or "towers of the sea." This gravity-defying dish comes hot or cold and includes oysters, mussels, shrimp—you name it. Oh, and don't pass up the lobster mashed potatoes. Those alone are worth the trip—and the wait. ✉ *364 Calle Fortaleza, Old San Juan* ☎ *787/722–0665* 🌐 *www.ooffestaurants.com* ✍ *Reservations not accepted* ▭ *AE, D, MC, V.* ⏲ *Closed Sun.* ✥ *1:F4*

2

$$–$$$ CARIBBEAN ✕ **Aureola.** Facing Plaza San José, this bright and airy restaurant (formerly Amadeus) often throws open its doors and lets its tables spill into the square. If you want a little more privacy, there's also a small, sunlit interior courtyard (for smokers) and an intimate dining room with whitewashed walls, linen tablecloths, and lazily turning ceiling fans. New owners have livened up the decor with fruity colors, and the new menu now includes such appetizer treats as *tostones* (fried plantains) with caviar, and mussels in meunière sauce and entrées such as mahimahi breaded with plantains. ✉ *106 Calle San Sebastián, Old San Juan* ☎ *787/977–0100* ▭ *AE, MC, V* ⏲ *Closed Mon.* ✥ *1:D3*

$$–$$$ ECLECTIC ✕ **Barú.** A global menu has earned Barú a solid reputation among *sanjuaneros,* so this stylishly contemporary restaurant in a colonial townhome with original tile floor is often crowded. The dishes, some served in medium-size portions so you can order several and share, range from Middle Eastern to Asian to Caribbean. Favorites include almond-crusted goat cheese with mango sauce and yucca chips, and carpaccio made from beef, tuna, or salmon. More substantial fare includes risotto with porcini mushrooms and goat cheese, filet mignon with horseradish mashed potatoes, and pork ribs with a ginger-tamarind glaze. The dining room, in a beautifully renovated colonial house, is dark and mysterious. You can dine on high stools at the bar. Wine servings here are generous. ✉ *150 Calle San Sebastián, Old San Juan* ☎ *787/977–7107* 🌐 *www.barupr.com* ▭ *AE, MC, V* ⏲ *Closed Mon. No lunch.* ✥ *1:D3*

$$–$$$ CAFE ✕ **Café Berlin.** A handful of tables spill onto a fairy-lit, sidewalk deck at this unpretentious place overlooking Plaza Colón. There's something on the menu for everyone, from turkey breast in a mustard-curry sauce and penne tequila shrimp to dorado in coconut sauce with garlic on a bed of mashed potatoes. The house signature dish is berenjera guisado—eggplant and chicken stew. There are even several good vegetarian dishes, including tofu in a mushroom sauce. Patrons get a free manjito cocktail with an entrée order. Inside is a small bar, one of the few places in Puerto Rico that serve draft beer. ✉ *407 Calle San Francisco, Old San Juan* ☎ *787/722–5205* ▭ *AE, MC, V.* ✥ *1:F3*

$–$$ CAFE ✕ **Cafetería Mallorca.** The specialty at this old-fashioned, yanqui-style 1950s diner is the *mallorca,* a sweet pastry that's buttered, grilled, and then sprinkled with powdered sugar. Wash one down with a terrific cup of café con leche. For something more substantial, try the breakfast mallorca, which has ham and cheese; the menu includes pancakes, egg dishes, and sandwiches, as well. The waitstaff—all dressed in crisp black uniforms and caps—are friendly and efficient. It gets packed on weekends with locals, for whom it's an institution. ✉ *300 Calle San Francisco, Old San Juan* ☎ *787/724–4607* ▭ *MC, V.* ✥ *1:E3*

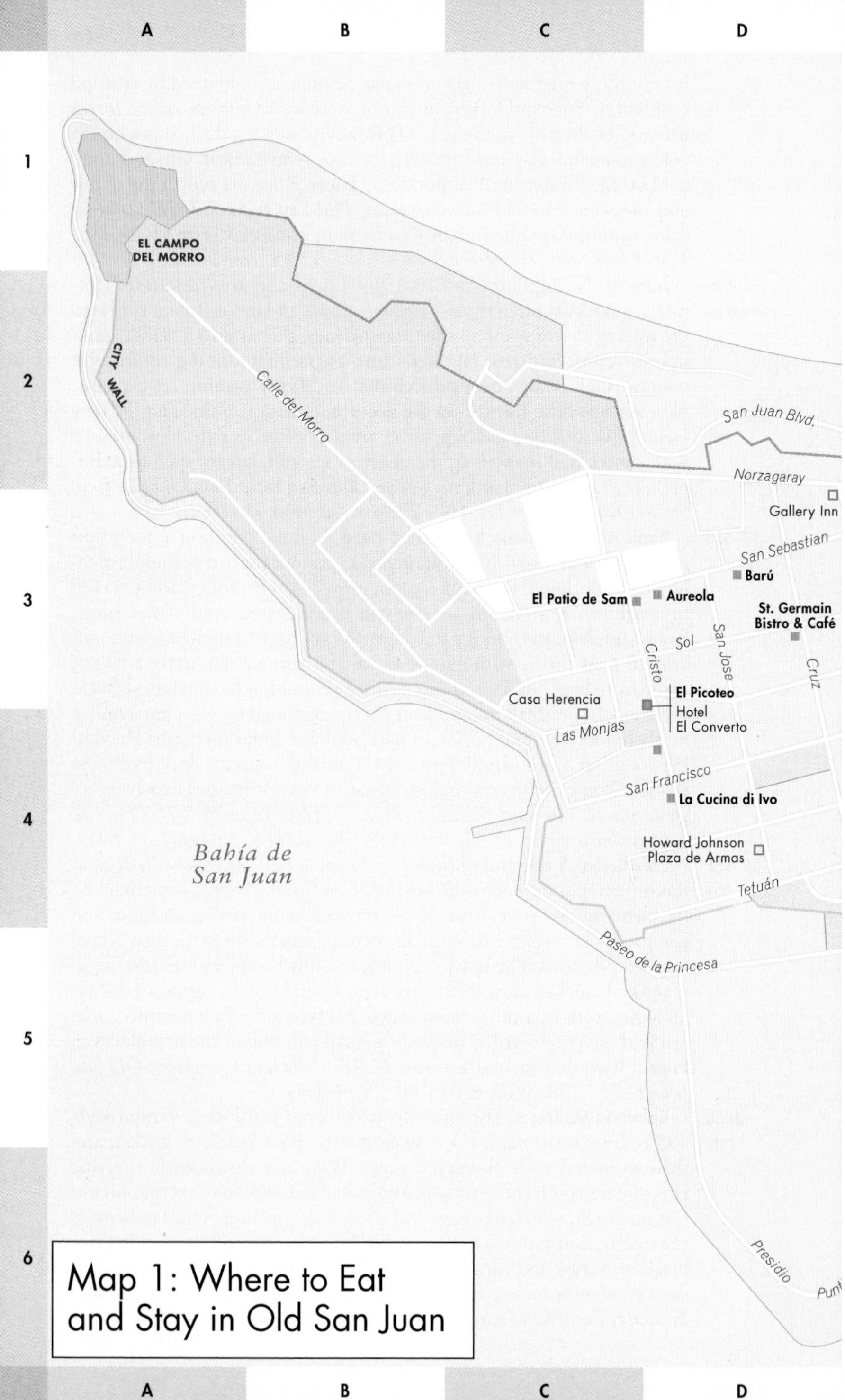

A
B
C
D
1
2
3
4
5
6
EL CAMPO DEL MORRO
CITY WALL
Calle del Morro
San Juan Blvd.
Norzagaray
Gallery Inn
San Sebastian
Barú
El Patio de Sam
Aureola
St. Germain Bistro & Café
Sol
San Jose
Cristo
Cruz
El Picoteo
Hotel El Converto
Casa Herencia
Las Monjas
San Francisco
La Cucina di Ivo
Howard Johnson Plaza de Armas
Tetuán
Bahía de San Juan
Paseo de la Princesa
Presidio
Map 1: Where to Eat and Stay in Old San Juan
A
B
C
D

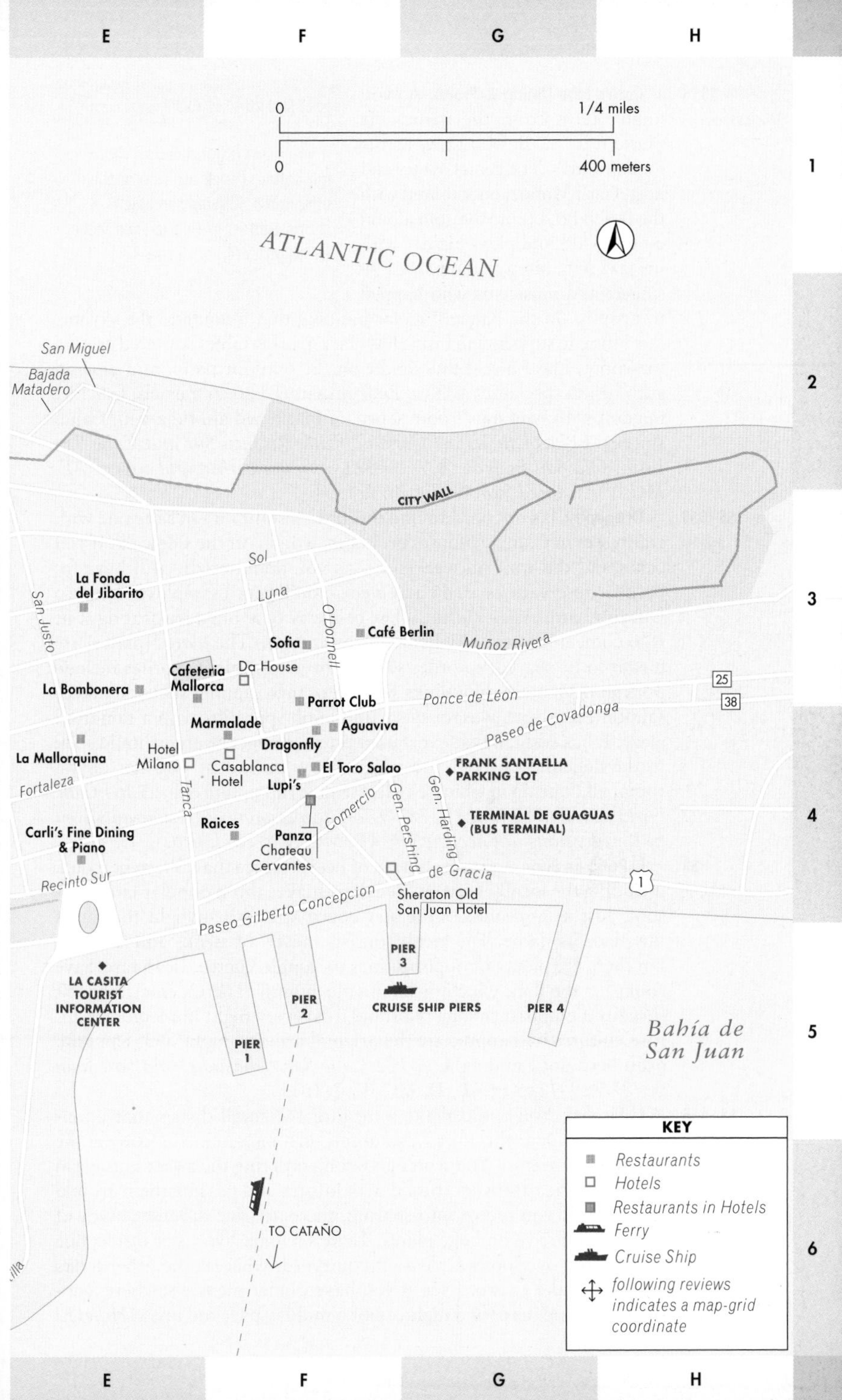

E
F
G
H
1
2
3
4
5
6
0
1/4 miles
0
400 meters
ATLANTIC OCEAN
San Miguel
Bajada Matadero
CITY WALL
Sol
Luna
San Justo
O'Donnell
Muñoz Rivera
Ponce de Léon
Paseo de Covadonga
25
38
La Fonda del Jibarito
Sofia
Café Berlin
Cafeteria Mallorca
Da House
La Bombonera
Parrot Club
Marmalade
Aguaviva
Dragonfly
La Mallorquina
Hotel Milano
Casablanca Hotel
El Toro Salao
Lupi's
FRANK SANTAELLA PARKING LOT
Fortaleza
Tanca
Comercio
Gen. Pershing
Gen. Harding
TERMINAL DE GUAGUAS (BUS TERMINAL)
Raices
Carli's Fine Dining & Piano
Panza
Chateau Cervantes
de Gracia
1
Recinto Sur
Paseo Gilberto Concepcion
Sheraton Old San Juan Hotel
PIER 3
LA CASITA TOURIST INFORMATION CENTER
PIER 2
CRUISE SHIP PIERS
PIER 4
PIER 1
Bahía de San Juan
TO CATAÑO
KEY
Restaurants
Hotels
Restaurants in Hotels
Ferry
Cruise Ship
following reviews indicates a map-grid coordinate

> **MORNING COFFEE**
>
> If you want a good cup of morning coffee, check out one of the ubiquitous Subway sandwich shops; outlets in Puerto Rico make excellent *café con leche.*

$$$$ MEDITERRANEAN ✕ **Carli's Fine Dining & Piano.** As you might guess from the name, the music is as much of a draw as the food at Carl's. The genial owner and host, Carli Muñoz, once toured with the Beach Boys (note the gold album on the wall) and plays nightly with his jazz trio, often accompanied by singers and musicians who happen to drop in. In the Banco Popular building that dominates the skyline, this intimate supper-club bistro has black-marble tables scattered around the room. Have a seat indoors or on the outdoor patio, and dine on such fusion specialties as New Zealand sautéed green mussels, U.S. filet mignon with wild mushroom sauce, or blackened ahi tuna with Cajun spices. ✉ *Plazoleta Rafael Carrión, Calle Recinto Sur and Calle San Justo, Old San Juan* ☎ *787/725–4927* 🌐 *www.carlisworld.com* ▭ *AE, MC, V* ⊗ *Closed Sun.* No lunch. ✣ *1:E4*

$$–$$$ ASIAN ✕ **Dragonfly.** It's not hard to find this little restaurant—it's the one with waitresses in Chinese blouses beckoning you in off the sidewalk. If you can stand the wait on weekends—as you undoubtedly will have to, because reservations aren't accepted—you'll get to sample chef Severo Duran's Latin-Asian cuisine. (The best way to avoid a frustrating wait is to come midweek, or when it opens at 6 PM.) The *platos* (plates) are meant to be shared, so order several for your table. Favorites include pork-and-plantain dumplings with an orange dipping sauce, smoked-salmon pizza with wasabi salsa, and lamb spareribs with a tamarind glaze. It has sushi, but at exorbitant prices. Budget hounds should stick to the delicious chicken and veggie chow mein. The two-tier dining room, all done up in Chinese red, resembles an opium den. ✉ *364 Calle Fortaleza, Old San Juan* ☎ *787/977–3886* 🌐 *www.oofrestaurants.com* ⚠ *Reservations not accepted* ▭ *AE, MC, V* ⊗ *No lunch.* ✣ *1:F4*

$$ ECLECTIC ✕ **El Patio de Sam.** A great selection of beers—more than 30, to be exact, including the locally brewed Medalla—makes this a popular late-night spot. Just as appealing is the airy courtyard with skylight that gives the place its name. The menu consists mostly of steaks and seafood, but there are plenty of opportunities to sample Puerto Rican fare. Save room for the flan, which melts in your mouth. There's entertainment (usually a guitarist singing old standards) every night but Sunday. Culture vultures will appreciate the original art, and night owls can grab grub here until midnight. ✉ *102 Calle San Sebastián, Old San Juan* ☎ *787/723–1149* ▭ *AE, D, MC, V.* ✣ *1:C3*

$$–$$$ SPANISH ✕ **El Picoteo.** You could make a meal of the small dishes that dominate the menu at this tapas restaurant, on a mezzanine balcony at the Hotel El Convento. You won't go wrong ordering the sweet sausage in brandy or the turnovers stuffed with lobster and passing them around the table. If you're not into sharing, there are five different kinds of paella that arrive on huge plates. There's a long, lively bar inside; one dining area overlooks a pleasant courtyard, whereas the other looks out onto Calle Cristo. Even if you have dinner plans elsewhere, consider stopping here for a nightcap or a midday pick-me-up. ✉ *Hotel El*

Hotel El Convento's El Picateo restaurant serves tasty tapas and generous paella

Convento, 100 Calle Cristo, Old San Juan ☎ *787/723–9202* 🌐 *www.elconvento.com* ▭ *AE, DC, MC, V.* ✥ *1:C3*

$$–$$$ SPANISH ✕ **El Toro Salao.** The name means "The Salty Bull," and there's something about this place that makes its moniker entirely appropriate. (And it's not just the bullfighting posters that decorate one of the two-story-high walls.) This popular tapas restaurant was opened by Emilio Figueroa, who helped turn the southern end of Calle Fortaleza into the city's top dining destination: He owns half a dozen restaurants at the east end of Calle Fortaleza and around the corner on Plaza Somohano. There are plenty of small dishes to share, as well as heartier fare such as blackened tuna in sweet paprika sauce and grilled octopus with a sundried-tomato vinaigrette. The dining room, with a bar illuminated in lusty red, is pleasant enough, but the tables that spill onto the adjacent cobblestone square are even better. ✉ *367 Calle Tetuán, Old San Juan* ☎ *787/722–3330* 🌐 *www.oofrestaurants.com* ▭ *AE, MC, V.* ✥ *1:F4*

$–$$ CAFE ✕ **La Bombonera.** You can't miss the stained glass and gorgeous Moorish-style tilework on the facade of this local landmark, which was established in 1903. In the window you'll see piles of freshly baked pastries. Inside there's a long counter with salmon-colored stools and a wall lined with booths of the same interesting shade. It's extremely popular in the morning—particularly on Sunday—but it's open until 8:30 for lunch and dinner. The menu spans simple sandwiches to hearty local dishes, including *asopao* (a stew with rice and seafood) and delicious flans among the desserts—all this even though the food is only average and the seemingly overworked waiters give the appearance of having worked here since the day it opened. ✉ *259 Calle San Francisco, Old San Juan* ☎ *787/722–0658* ▭ *AE, MC, V.* ✥ *1:E3*

$$–$$$ ITALIAN **La Cucina di Ivo.** A pretty courtyard just steps from the cathedral has been transformed into this traditional trattoria. The staff enters and leaves through leaded-glass doors on either side of the central courtyard that lead to the bar, the wine cellar, and intimate dining rooms. You'll want to dine alfresco, as ceiling fans keep everything cool. A fountain bubbles on one side of the courtyard, and rows of potted fig trees surround the wrought-iron café tables. The place is named for chef Ivo Bignami, and the kitchen turns out specialties of his native Milan. For a lighter meal, or a first course big enough to share with your date, order the light, fluffy gnocchi. Entrées include a wide range of pasta and gnocchi dishes, plus such mouthwatering temptations as filet mignon in truffle sauce. For dessert, try the classic and tasty tiramisu. ⊠ *202 Calle Cristo, Old San Juan* ☎ *787/729–7070* ⊕ *www.lacucinadiivo.com* ▭ *AE, MC, V.* ⊗ *Closed Sun.* ✣ *1:D4*

$$ CARIBBEAN Fodor's Choice ★ **La Fonda del Jibarito.** The menus are handwritten and the tables wobble, but *sanjuaneros* have favored this casual, no-frills, family-run restaurant—tucked away on a quiet cobbled street—for years. The conch ceviche, goat fricassee, and shredded beef stew are among the specialties on the menu of typical Puerto Rican comida criollo dishes. The tiny back porch is filled with plants, and the dining room is filled with fanciful depictions of life on the street outside. The ever-present owner, Pedro J. Ruíz, is filled with the desire to ensure that everyone is happy. Troubadors serenade patrons, among them plenty of cruise-ship passengers when ships are in dock. ⊠ *280 Calle Sol, Old San Juan* ☎ *787/725–8375* ⊕ *www.eljibaritopr.com* ✍ *Reservations not accepted* ▭ *AE, MC, V.* ✣ *1:E3*

$$–$$$ LATIN AMERICAN **La Mallorquina.** Dating from 1848, La Mallorquina is thought to be the island's oldest restaurant. The menu is heavy on such basic Puerto Rican and Spanish fare as *asopao* and paella, but the old-fashioned atmosphere is what really recommends the place. Nattily attired staffers zip between tables set against peach-colored walls and beneath the whir of ceiling fans. They can be a bit short with tourists, however. ⊠ *207 Calle San Justo, Old San Juan* ☎ *787/722–3261* ⊕ *www.lamallorquinapr.com* ▭ *AE, MC, V* ⊗ *Closed Sun.* ✣ *1:E4*

$$–$$$ ECLECTIC **La Ostra Cosa.** This restaurant's succulent prawns, grilled and served with garlic butter, are supposed to be aphrodisiacs. In fact, everything on the menu is rated for its love-inducing qualities. (Look out for those labeled "Ay, ay, ay!") There are some seats indoors, but opt for a seat beneath the shade of a mango tree in the walled courtyard. With moonlight streaming through the trees, it's one of the city's prettiest alfresco dining spots. The gregarious owner, Alberto Nazario, brother of pop star Ednita Nazario, genuinely enjoys seeing his guests satisfied. He'll sometimes take out a guitar and sing old folk songs. Don't be surprised if the locals sing along. ⊠ *154 Calle Cristo, Old San Juan* ☎ *787/722–2672* ▭ *AE, D, MC, V.* ✣ *1:D4*

$–$$ MEXICAN **Lupi's.** Dining in Old San Juan doesn't have to mean fighting for a table. With its colorful and earthy ambience, this Mexican restaurant is among the best of the string of quality eateries along Calle Recinto Sur. Plates of steaming hot tacos, burritos, and other reasonably authentic fare arrive at your table within minutes of ordering. And if you want to watch the big game—whatever it might be—it will doubtless be playing

Pineapples, plantains, and coconuts are among the bounty of locally grown produce found in markets and stands throughout the island.

on the television over the bar. Lupi's stays open late, so it is a good place to try when other kitchens are closing. ✉ *313 Calle Recinto Sur, Old San Juan* ☎ *787/722–1874* ▭ *AE, MC, V.* ✣ *1:F4*

$$$–$$$$ FUSION Fodor's Choice ★ ✕ **Marmalade.** "Wow!" could well be your first reaction to entering Old San Juan's hippest and finest restaurant. U.S.-born owner-chef Peter Schintler has created a chic class act, famous for its über-hip lounge bar. The restaurant's sensual and minimalist orange-and-white decor features high-back chairs and corner cushion banquets beneath recessed halogens. The menu features local ingredients prepared California-French fashion, resulting in complex flavors full of explosive fragrance. Begin with the scallop mojito with rum, mint, and fresh coconut and lime; then move to the honey and lime shrimp with baked jalapeño with sweet corn sauce and shellfish emulsion, or perhaps the braised Colorado lamb shank with Lebanese tabouleh pomegranate and minted yogurt. Leave room for the chocolate mousse—a divine work of art. Schintler, who apprenticed with Raymond Blanc and Gordon Ramsay, offers a monthly 5-course tasting menu and an 11-course dinner with wine pairings. A $25 wine sampler lets you taste from 40 labels. ✉ *317 Calle Fortaleza, Old San Juan* ☎ *787/724–3969* 🌐 *www.marmaladepr.com* ✍ *Reservations essential* ▭ *AE, D, MC, V* ⏲ *No lunch.* ✣ *1:F4*

$$$–$$$$ ECLECTIC ✕ **Panza.** Tucked discreetly within the lobby of Chateau Cervantes, this restaurant recently reopened after a total remake, with a new chef and menu and a trendy and sophisticated new livery. The menu is a wonderful mix of different-size dishes, so you can have your own or share a few with friends. Our favorites include cream of potato and truffle soup with crispy pancetta and tomato confit, and sautéed sea bass with Lyonnaisse potato, capers, and olives. The half-moon banquettes in the front window are the

perfect place to sample any of the 550 wines from the eatery's extensive cellars, or opt for a high stool at the bar with an oval recessed ceiling lit by hidden orange lamps. Nice! ✉ *Chateau Cervantes, 329 Calle Recinto Sur, Old San Juan* ☎ *787/724–7722 www.cervantespr.com* ✍ *Reservations essential* ▭ *AE, D, DC, MC, V* ⏲ *Closed Sun.* ✣ *1:F4*

$$–$$$ CARIBBEAN ✕ **Parrot Club.** Loud and lively, this place is intent on making sure everyone is having a good time. You're likely to strike up a conversation with the bartender as you enjoy a passion-fruit cocktail or with the couple at the next table in the covered courtyard. Something about the atmosphere—laid-back Caribbean decor, including murals of swaying palm trees—makes connecting easy. The menu has contemporary variations of Caribbean classics. You might start with mouthwatering crab cakes or crispy Latin calamari, followed by seared tuna in a spicy Caribbean rub with black bean reduction or grilled churrasco steak with yellow tomato chimichurri and sautéed potatoes. ✉ *363 Calle Fortaleza, Old San Juan* ☎ *787/725–7370* 🌐 *www.oofrestaraunts.com* ✍ *Reservations not accepted* ▭ *AE, DC, MC, V.* ✣ *1:F3*

$–$$ PUERTO RICAN ✕ **Raices.** You can't miss this lively restaurant thanks to the waitresses in all-white *campesina* (peasant) dresses beckoning you in off the sidewalk. Themed as a country venue, with artsy recreations of rustic life, Raices packs in the locals for tasty criolla fare, such as ceviche, and mofongo in various combinations. We recommend the garlic shrimp mofongo, served country-style in a faux wooden pestle. Drinks come in tin mugs, including delicious fruity frappes. On Thursday nights there's live music. ✉ *315 Calle Recinto Sur, Old San Juan* ☎ *787/729–2121* 🌐 *www.restauranteraices.com* ▭ *AE, MC, V* ⏲ *Closed Sun.* ✣ *1:F4*

$$–$$$ ITALIAN ✕ **Sofia.** Ignore the tongue-in-cheek recordings of "That's Amore." Everything else in this red-walled and warmly atmospheric trattoria is the real deal, from the gleaming vegetables on the antipasto table to the vintages on the small but well-chosen wine list. Start with the squid stuffed with sweet sausage; then move on to the linguine with clams and pancetta or the roasted pumpkin risotto. The plates of pasta are huge, so you might want to consider a half-order (which is more the size of a three-quarter order). It also has pizzas, and the braised osso buco with creamy polenta and baked tomatoes is a house specialty. Save room for—what else?—a tasty tiramisu or chocolate mousse. ✉ *355 Calle San Francisco, Old San Juan* ☎ *787/721–0396* ▭ *AE, MC, V.* ✣ *1:F3*

$–$$ VEGETARIAN ✕ **St. Germain Bistro & Cafe.** One of the city's hidden treasures, this charming little French-inspired café-restaurant is tucked away on a quiet cobbled street corner. The contemporary decor is clinically clean, with lots of whites, and colorful art festoons the walls. It's a great place to linger over cappuccino, but the menu delivers delicious gourmet sandwiches and salads (with creative dressings), quiches, plus pita pizzas, and a Sunday brunch menu spans omelets to baked eggs with salmon. Feeling adventurous? Try the buffalo mozzarella tower with tomatoes and pesto sauce. All the ingredients here are fresh as can be, and owners Pedro and Paola execute their culinary skills to perfection, and their young waitstaff are eager to please. ✉ *156 Calle Sol, Old San Juan* ☎ *787/725–5830* 🌐 *www.stgermainpr.com* ▭ *MC, V* ⏲ *Closed Mon.* ✣ *1:D3*

PUERTA DE TIERRA

Use the coordinate (⊕ 2:A1) at the end of each listing to locate a site on the corresponding "Map 2: Where to Eat and Stay in Greater San Juan."

$$$ SEAFOOD **Escambrón Beach Club.** You can see two of the forts of Old San Juan—Fuerte San Filipe del Morro and Fuerte San Cristóbal—from the covered terrace of this seafood restaurant. The beach itself is only a few feet away. The food here is more creative than you'd expect, with dishes ranging from shrimp with cilantro and roasted-garlic butter to lobster grilled with a rum-and-butter sauce. Not in the mood for seafood? There are plenty of meat dishes, including skirt steak and pork chops. The restaurant is walking distance from the Caribe Hilton. ✉ *Parque de Tercer Milenio, Playa Escambrón, Puerta de Tierra* ☎ *787/724–3344* 🌐 *www.escambron.com* 💳 *AE, MC, V.* ⊕ *2:A1*

$$$ ASIAN **Lemongrass.** Whether you sit inside the pagoda-style building or on the large outdoor terrace of this chic restaurant, you'll feel as if you've truly escaped to another world. The dishes are as memorable as the setting. Try the inventive sushi, such as the smoked salmon, brie, and lingonberry roll. If you're not in the mood for fish, the five-spice baby ribs with guava glaze are delicious, served with a side of pancetta fried rice. For dessert, there's an orange, ginger, and cardamom ice cream. ✉ *Caribe Hilton, 1 San Gerónimo Grounds, Puerta de Tierra* ☎ *787/724–5888* 🌐 *www.lemongrasspr.com* 💳 *AE, MC, V* ⏲ *No lunch.* ⊕ *2:B2*

$$$ SEAFOOD **Marisquería Atlántica.** This popular restaurant is across from its namesake, so it's no surprise that the seafood is the freshest around. Start with a plate of fried calamari, served lightly breaded and accompanied by a spicy sauce, and then move on to the broiled lobster tail or grilled red snapper in a garlic sauce. Locals swear by the paella, which is loaded with scallops, clams, shrimp, and squid. The restaurant is just west of Playa Escambrón. There's another branch in Isla Verde. ✉ *7 Calle Lugo Viñas, Puerta de Tierra* ☎ *787/722–0890* 🌐 *www.marisqueriaatlantica.com* 💳 *AE, MC, V* ⏲ *Closed Mon.* ⊕ *2:A1*

CONDADO

Use the coordinate (⊕ 2:A1) at the end of each listing to locate a site on the corresponding "Map 2: Where to Eat and Stay in Greater San Juan."

$$$ CARIBBEAN **Ajili-Mójili.** A Puerto Rico landmark with a noble objective: Cook as Grandma used to, largely with locally sourced ingredients. Gone are the white tablecloths, and the high prices that discouraged many. The food, however, is still executed with a flourish. The menu is a catalog of local favorites, including terrific *piononos* (meat or fish rolled in a sweet plantain with cheese), shrimp smothered in coconut, and mofongo with chorizo. Wash it all down with a delicious *mangó bajito* (rum with fresh mango juice). During the summer or fall the restaurant offers a taste of various Puerto Rican towns (El Sabor de los Pueblos), on a rotating two-week schedule. (By local demand, they repeat Loíza, known for its fritters.) ✉ *1006 Av. Ashford, Condado* ☎ *787/725–9195* 🌐 *www.ajilimojilipr.com* 💳 *AE, D, MC, V.* ⊕ *2:C2*

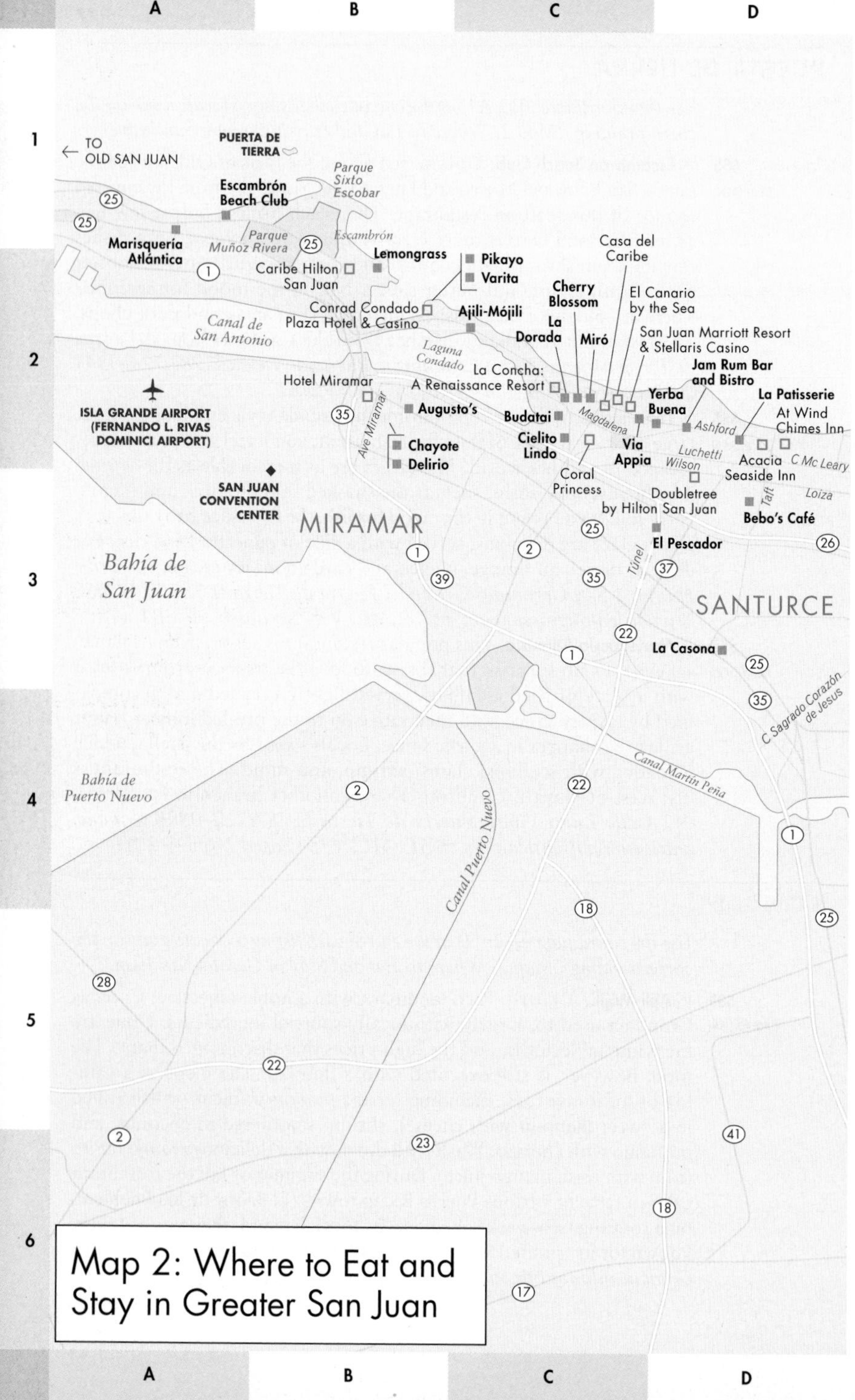

A
B
C
D
1
2
3
4
5
6
TO
OLD SAN JUAN
PUERTA DE
TIERRA
Parque
Sixto
Escobar
Escambrón
Beach Club
Marisquería
Atlántica
Parque
Muñoz Rivera
Escambrón
Lemongrass
Caribe Hilton
San Juan
Pikayo
Varita
Conrad Condado
Plaza Hotel & Casino
Ajili-Mójili
Canal de
San Antonio
Laguna
Condado
Casa del
Caribe
Cherry
Blossom
El Canario
by the Sea
La
Dorada
Miró
San Juan Marriott Resort
& Stellaris Casino
La Concha:
A Renaissance Resort
Hotel Miramar
Jam Rum Bar
and Bistro
Yerba
Buena
La Patisserie
At Wind
Chimes Inn
ISLA GRANDE AIRPORT
(FERNANDO L. RIVAS
DOMINICI AIRPORT)
Augusto's
Budatai
Magdalena
Ashford
Ave Miramar
Chayote
Delirio
Cielito
Lindo
Via
Appia
Luchetti
Wilson
Acacia
Seaside Inn
C Mc Leary
Coral
Princess
Doubletree
by Hilton San Juan
Loiza
Taft
SAN JUAN
CONVENTION
CENTER
MIRAMAR
Bebo's Café
El Pescador
Bahía de
San Juan
Túnel
SANTURCE
La Casona
C Sagrado Corazón
de Jesus
Canal Martín Peña
Bahía de
Puerto Nuevo
Canal Puerto Nuevo
Map 2: Where to Eat and
Stay in Greater San Juan

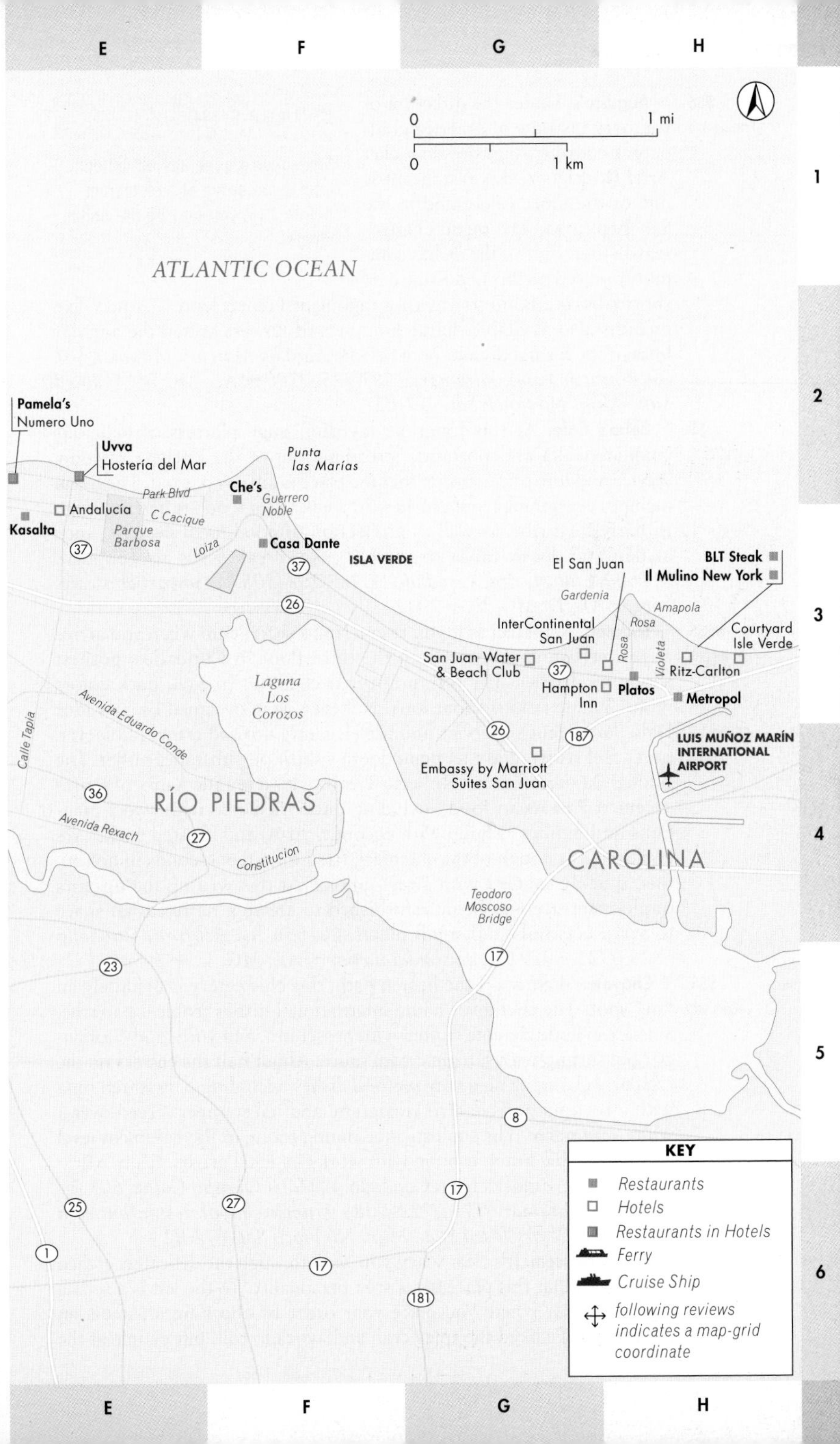

E
F
G
H
1
2
3
4
5
6
0
1 mi
0
1 km
ATLANTIC OCEAN
Pamela's
Numero Uno
Uvva
Hostería del Mar
Punta
las Marías
Park Blvd
Che's
Guerrero
Noble
Andalucía
C Cacique
Kasalta
Parque
Barbosa
Loiza
Casa Dante
ISLA VERDE
BLT Steak
El San Juan
Il Mulino New York
Gardenia
Amapola
InterContinental
San Juan
Rosa
Courtyard
Isle Verde
San Juan Water
& Beach Club
Rosa
Violeta
Ritz-Carlton
Laguna
Los
Corozos
Hampton
Inn
Platos
Metropol
Avenida Eduardo Conde
Calle Tapia
LUIS MUÑOZ MARÍN
INTERNATIONAL
AIRPORT
Embassy by Marriott
Suites San Juan
RÍO PIEDRAS
Avenida Rexach
Constitucion
CAROLINA
Teodoro
Moscoso
Bridge
KEY
Restaurants
Hotels
Restaurants in Hotels
Ferry
Cruise Ship
following reviews
indicates a map-grid
coordinate

$$$ CONTINENTAL **Augusto's.** Under the direction of Culinary Institute of America graduate and former Augusto's sous chef Ariel Rodríguez, this restaurant is one of the more celebrated in the San Juan area. The menu changes seasonally; some of the dishes commonly served are braised Kobe beef short ribs and lamb loin with a ragout of French lentils. A prix fixe menu is also available. Large bouquets of flowers soften the angular lines of the formal dining room ✉ *Courtyard by Marriott Miramar, 801 Av. Ponce de León, Miramar* ☎ *787/725–7700* ▭ *AE, MC, V* ⊗ *Closed Sun.–Mon. No lunch Sat.* ✣ *2:B2*

DINNER TIME

Sanjuaneros generally eat dinner late; if you arrive at a restaurant before 7 PM, you may be the only diners.

$$ LATIN AMERICAN **Bebo's Café.** At this longtime favorite, huge platters of delicious comida criolla are constantly streaming out of the kitchen. Friendly service and low prices ensure that the place is always packed. The menu includes everything from grilled skirt steak to seafood-stuffed mofongo to barbecued ribs, as well as a selection of good local desserts, such as flan and dense, moist *tres leches* cake. Breakfast is also popular. ✉ *1600 Calle Loíza, Condado* ☎ *787/268–5087* ⊕ *www.beboscafe.com* ▭ *AE, D, MC, V.* ✣ *2:D3*

$$$$ ASIAN **Budatai.** You'll feel as if you're entering a secret club when you arrive at this stylish spot located on the third floor in Condado's poshest shopping district. The restaurant is decked out in rich, dark colors with Chinese lanterns that look as if they were designed by Salvador Dalí. The attentive service and the elegantly dressed crowd, however, never feel stuffy, and the menu doesn't shirk on substance either. The brainchild of noted chef Roberto Treviño, it's a seamless mix of Latin-accented Pan-Asian food, including duck fried rice with sweet plantains and halibut sashimi with coconut, yuzu, and toasted garlic. We couldn't get enough of the calamari, fried for a few seconds in hot oil, then quickly sautéed with sweet onions. At this writing the upstairs outdoor terrace was being refurbished to create a more casual space to serve cocktails and small plates. ✉ *1056 Av. Ashford, Condado* ☎ *787/725–6919* ⊕ *www.budatai.com* ▭ *AE, MC, V.* ✣ *2:C2*

$$$ ECLECTIC **Chayote.** Slightly off the beaten path, this chic eatery is definitely an "in" spot. The chef gives haute international dishes tropical panache. Starters include chayote stuffed with prosciutto, and yuca- and chorizo-crusted shrimp with saffron cream sauce. About half the entrées on the regularly changing menu are seafood dishes, including pan-seared tuna with a coconut and cilantro vinaigrette and red snapper served over a white yam puree. The sophisticated dining room, in the basement level of a newly chic hotel, is hung with works by local artists. It's in Miramar, just a few blocks from Condado. ✉ *Hotel Olimpo Court, 603 Av. Miramar, Miramar* ☎ *787/722–9385* ⊕ *www.chayoterestaurant.com* ▭ *AE, MC, V* ⊗ *Closed Sun.–Mon. No lunch Sat.* ✣ *2:B2*

$$$ ASIAN **Cherry Blossom.** It's clear when you walk through the delicately etched glass doors that this place has a split personality. To the left is a sedate little sushi bar where you place your order by checking off items on the menu. (We liked the spicy crab and avocado roll, but people at the

next table seemed happy with their salmon skin roll.) To the right is a more boisterous dining room where the tables are arranged around teppanyaki tables. Chefs wearing tall red hats add drama to your meal, tossing knives and dodging flames as they prepare such dishes as sautéed scallops in garlic-sake sauce, beef stir-fried with scallions, and roast duck in savory spices. Wash everything down with a Sapporo beer or a fruity specialty cocktail. ✉ *1309 Av. AshfordCondado* ☎ *787/723-7300* ▭ *AE, D, MC, V* ⊙ *No lunch Sat.* ✣ *2:C2*

$$ MEXICAN ✕ **Cielito Lindo.** The moment you walk in the door you know that this is the real deal. The first clue is the smell of grilled meat coming from the kitchen. The juicy flank steaks are indeed standouts, but so are the burritos and fajitas that cater to the Tex-Mex crowd. There's also a wide selection of margaritas, each one iced to perfection and served with a lime wedge. The decor—paper streamers hanging from the ceiling—will remind you of eateries in small towns all over Mexico. ✉ *1106 Av. Magdalena, Condado* ☎ *787/723-5597* ▭ *AE, MC, V.* ⊙ *No lunch weekends.* ✣ *2:C2*

$$$ ECLECTIC ✕ **Delirio.** Set in a century-old family home, this sexy dining room has the look of a boudoir, decorated almost entirely in deep reds with paintings by local artists hanging on the walls. Chef and owner Alfredo Ayala's talent is widely admired—many younger chefs cite him as a source of inspiration. His menu, which changes frequently, takes the concept of Puerto Rican food to a new level, and his international training (with Joël Robuchon and others) shines through in entrées such as perfectly seared cod served over a puree of fresh corn and panko-crusted veal chop with small white beans and rice. ✉ *762 Av. Ponce de León, Miramar* ☎ *787/722-0444* 🌐 *www.deliriorestaurant.com* ▭ *MC, V* ⊙ *Closed Sun.–Mon. No lunch Sat.* ✣ *2:B2*

$$$ MEDITERRANEAN ✕ **Jam Rum Bar and Bistro Moderne.** This tucked-away spot may not look like a restaurant from the outside, but inside it's a study in modern design, in whites, oranges, greens, and other bright colors. Though it's only a block from touristy Avenida Ashford, the crowd is mostly locals in on the delicious secret. Appetizers include grilled peaches with lemon mascarpone and prosciutto, and red snapper ceviche with avocado, mango, and tomato. The menu uses local ingredients, most notably in the veal osso buco over porcini risotto. A rum bar showcases more than 50 rums from around the world and some creative cocktails. Surprisingly enough for a restaurant of this caliber, the place is extremely kid-friendly: there's a playroom if parents want to eat in peace, and kids eat free on Sunday. ✉ *Casabella Building, 1400 Av. Magdalena, Condado* ☎ *787/721-5991* ▭ *AE, MC, V.* ✣ *2:D2*

$$$ SEAFOOD ✕ **La Dorada.** This seafood establishment in the middle of Condado's restaurant row is surprisingly affordable. The dining room isn't much to look at—it's more along the lines of a diner. The focus here is the food. The grilled seafood platter is the specialty, but there are plenty of other excellent dishes, including mahimahi in caper sauce and codfish in green sauce. The friendly staff is genuinely welcoming. ✉ *1105 Av. Magdalena, Condado* ☎ *787/722-9583* ▭ *AE, MC, V* ⊙ *No lunch Mon.–Thurs.* ✣ *2:C2*

Dining alfresco is a favorite pastime in Puerto Rico.

$ CAFE ✕ **La Patisserie.** Everything—from pastries to pastas—is delicious at this café, which sits on a quiet block in Condado. For breakfast, wonderful omelets are stuffed with fresh vegetables and imported cheeses. Sandwiches—from pastrami to king crab—are served during lunch on croissants, baguettes, and other types of bread. Look also for various bargain lunch specials. For an early-bird dinner (they close at 6 PM), try grilled salmon, chicken in white wine, or pasta carbonara. Free valet parking is available. ⊠ *1504 Av. Ashford, Condado* ☎ *787/728–5508* ▭ *AE, MC, V.* ⊕ *2:D2*

$$$ SPANISH ✕ **Miró.** Like its namesake, the painter Joan Miró, this small restaurant draws its inspiration from the Catalan region of Spain, where the cuisine is heavy on seafood and hearty tapas. Start with steamed clams with garlic or braised chorizo and peppers. Main courses include sizzling lamb chops, as well as grilled tuna with anchovy and caper butter or codfish in a red-pepper and eggplant sauce. Prints by the artist hang on the walls, adding an authentic touch to the maze of tiny dining rooms. Its location, on busy Avenida Ashford across from the San Juan Marriott Resort, means that the place is always packed. ⊠ *1214 Av. Ashford, Condado* ☎ *787/723–9593* ▭ *AE, MC, V.* ⊕ *2:C2*

$$$ ECLECTIC Fodor's Choice ★ ✕ **Pikayo.** Celebrity chef and Puerto Rico native Wilo Benet's flagship restaurant has moved from its Santurce location in the Museo de Arte de Puerto Rico to this more accessible spot (for tourists and locals alike) at the Conrad San Juan Condado Plaza hotel. At 10,000 square feet, it's twice as large, and the impressive new digs are already drawing a big crowd. Works from local artists line the walls, and the atmosphere is elegant and formal, but never hushed. The menu offers a twist on traditional Puerto Rican classics as well as more international flavors.

Start with a glass of Benet's own wine, either a simple *tempranillo* (red) or an *albariño* (white). Then try some of the starters; particularly good are the pork belly sliders and the spicy tuna on crispy rice (known here as *pegao*). For main courses, Benet offers an addictive seafood risotto flecked with saffron, or tender Australian lamb chops with a rosemary demiglace. Don't be surprised if Benet himself stops by your table to make sure everything is just to your liking. ✉ *Conrad San Juan Condado Plaza, 999 Av. Ashford, Condado* ☎ *787/721–6194* 🌐 *www.wilobenet.com* ▭ *AE, D, DC, MC, V* ⏲ *No lunch.* ✣ *2:C2*

$$$ LATIN ✕ **Varita.** Chef Wilo Benet expands his empire with this twist on traditional Puerto Rican food. His version of *lechón* (roast pork) roasts Berkshire pigs a *la varita* (on the spit) with charcoal and applewood chips. The result is a tender and moist version you'd be hard-pressed to top elsewhere. Other options include mofongo, churrasco, and garlic shrimp. You'll want to save room for a decadent cheese flan or candied papaya with local cheese. This is a good place to start exploring the local cuisine, as cheerful servers are eager to assist. But it's no tourist trap. When we visited, the place was packed with local families. ✉ *Conrad San Juan Condado Plaza, 999 Av. Ashford, Condado* ☎ *787/723–8274* 🌐 *www.varitabbq.com* ▭ *AE, MC, V.* ✣ *2:C2*

$$ ITALIAN ✕ **Via Appia.** The food at this bustling no-frills café is just as authentic and tasty—from the pizza to the veal and peppers to the house red wine—as its higher-priced *paisanos*. During lunch, they even dish up some delicious comida criolla, with specials changing every day; try the *pollo guisado* (chicken stew)on Mondays. The outdoor-seating area looks out on Condado's busy Ashford Avenue, which is usually filled with people coming from and going to the beach. The wine bar next door has a bit more ambience. ✉ *1350 Av. Ashford, Condado* ☎ *787/725–8711* ▭ *AE, MC, V.* ✣ *2:C2*

$$$ CARIBBEAN ✕ **Yerba Buena.** Tables on the terrace are hard to come by at this restaurant, one of the most popular in Condado. That's fine, because the glassed-in dining room is even more comfortable and has exactly the same view. Cuban classics such as *ropa vieja* (meat cooked so slowly that it becomes tender shreds) seamlessly blend local dishes with imaginative presentation. The shrimp has a coconut-and-ginger sauce; the halibut fillet, one of mango and orange liqueur. The restaurant claims to use the "original" recipe for its *mojito*, Cuba's tasty rum, lime, and mint drink. Live Latin jazz is played many nights. ✉ *1350 Av. Ashford, Condado* ☎ *787/721–5700* 🌐 *www.yerbabuenapr.com* ▭ *AE, MC, V* ⏲ *No lunch.* ✣ *2:D2*

SANTURCE

Use the coordinate (✣ 2:A1) at the end of each listing to locate a site on the corresponding "Map 2: Where to Eat and Stay in Greater San Juan."

$$ SEAFOOD ✕ **El Pescador.** If you want food that's unmistakably Puerto Rican, head to Plaza del Mercado. Surrounding a fruit and vegetable market dating from 1910 are a few dozen restaurants that are the real deal. Our favorite is El Pescador, a narrow storefront selling the freshest of seafood. If you come in the evening it might be cool enough to eat at one of the

handful of tables on the square. If not, settle for the bright green dining room. The *chillo entero frito* (fried whole red snapper) and *camarones al ajillo* (shrimp with garlic) are tasty, but the standout is the *arroz con calamari* (rice with squid). This dramatic inky-black dish draws oohs and aahs from surrounding customers when it arrives at your table. Parking is tough here on weekends, so take a taxi. ✉ *178 Calle Dos Hermanos, Santurce* ☎ *787/721–0995* ✍ *Reservations not accepted.* ▭ *MC, V* ⊙ *Closed Mon.* ✥ *2:D3*

$$$ SPANISH ✕ **La Casona.** Business executives come here for power lunches, but La Casona is also a nice spot for a romantic dinner. The restored Spanish colonial residence in Santurce has well-appointed rooms and blooming gardens. The menu is based solidly in Spain but has many creative flourishes—start with the smoked salmon and move on to the duck breast in raspberry sauce or the rack of lamb, which is grilled a la plancha with herbs. ✉ *609 Calle San Jorge, Santurce* ☎ *787/727–2717* *www.lacasonapr.net* ▭ *AE, D, DC, MC, V* ⊙ *No lunch Sat. Closed Sun.* ✥ *2:D3*

OCEAN PARK

Use the coordinate (✥ 2:A1) at the end of each listing to locate a site on the corresponding "Map 2: Where to Eat and Stay in Greater San Juan."

$$$ ARGENTINE ✕ **Che's.** This Argentine-style steak house on the eastern edge of Ocean Park is worth the trip. If you haven't tried *churrasco*, the marinated skirt steak locals love, this is the place to do it. Another specialty is the grilled sweetbreads. The hamburgers are huge, and the french fries are fresh. The wine list, which tends toward Spanish and Argentine vintages, is also a winner. It's in Ocean Park, before you get to Isla Verde. ✉ *35 Calle Caoba, Punta Las Marías* ☎ *787/726–7202* 🌐 *www.chesrestaurant.com* ▭ *AE, D, DC, MC, V.* ✥ *2:F2*

$$–$$$ CAFE ✕ **Kasalta.** Those who think coffee can never be too strong should make a beeline to Kasalta, which has an amazing pitch-black brew that will knock your socks off. Make your selection from the display cases full of luscious pastries, particularly the famous *quesito* (cream-cheese-filled puff pastry) and other tempting treats. Walk up to the counter and order a sandwich, such as the savory Cubano, or other items such as octopus salad. For dinner there are fish dishes and other, more substantial fare. Occasionally quality can be uneven, though, and some staff members are curt with tourists. ✉ *1966 Calle McLeary, Ocean Park* ☎ *787/727–7340* 🌐 *www.kasalta.com* ▭ *AE, D, MC, V.* ✥ *2:E3*

$$$ CARIBBEAN Fodor's Choice ★ ✕ **Pamela's.** If you've always dreamed of a table for two on the beach, only steps from where crashing waves meet the shore, head to this local favorite in Ocean Park. If you prefer air conditioning, an elegant glassed-in solarium awaits, complete with black cobblestone floors and slow-turning ceiling fans. The menu is a contemporary, creative mix of Caribbean spices and other tropical ingredients. The restaurant prides itself on its fresh seafood; we liked the artfully plated crabmeat Napoleon, served with avocado, chayote, and black bean as an appetizer. But the real show-stopper was the entrée: codfish with a spicy shrimp sofrito. ✉ *Numero Uno Guesthouse, 1 Calle Santa*

Ana, Ocean Park ☎ *787/726–5010* 🌐 *www.numero1guesthouse.com* 💳 *AE, MC, V.* ✥ *2:E2*

$$$ MEDITERRANEAN ✕ **Uvva.** Sit on the deck at this romantic beachfront restaurant, where coconut palms wave in the breeze and the ocean gently laps right in front of you. Start with one of the most well-balanced mojitos we've tried, and then sample the falling-off-the-bone pork rib appetizer, served with a sweet and tangy ginger-tamarind sauce. Other than a few local favorites, the cuisine tends toward European staples with an Asian and Caribbean twist. The restaurant uses local seafood in terrific dishes such as fresh conch salad and Caribbean spiny lobster risotto. Vegetarian options are available as well. ✉ *Hostería del Mar, 1 Calle Tapia, Ocean Park* ☎ *787/727–0631* 🌐 *www.hosteriadelmarpr.com* 💳 *AE, D, DC, MC, V.* ✥ *2:E2*

ISLA VERDE

Use the coordinate (✥ 2:A1) at the end of each listing to locate a site on the corresponding "Map 2: Where to Eat and Stay in Greater San Juan."

$$$$ CONTINENTAL ✕ **BLT Steak.** Chef Laurent Tourondel's sprawling dining room in the Ritz Carlton invites you to relax. It's stylish and comfortable, with long leather banquettes and round booths, warm lighting, and glossy dark wood tables. Instead of bread, oversized warm popovers arrive at the table, complete with a take-home recipe. Entrées include classic steakhouse cuts, served with a choice of sauces (everything from chimichurri to classic peppercorn); an American Kobe beef burger served with fries and coleslaw; and Japanese Kobe strip steak, priced per ounce. For dessert, try the carrot cake with ginger ice cream. ✉ *The Ritz-Carlton, San Juan, 6991 Av. de los Gobernadores, Isla Verde* ☎ *787/253–1700, ext. 4240* 🌐 *www.ritzcarlton.com/sanjuan* 💳 *AE, D, DC, MC, V* ⏲ *Dinner only.* ✥ *2:H3*

$$ CARIBBEAN ✕ **Casa Dante.** If you're curious about mofongo—green plantains mashed with garlic and pork fat and filled with just about anything imaginable—head here for a stomach- and soul-satisfying version. Casa Dante offers four different types of the Puerto Rican specialty, including a noteworthy pinto version, blending both green and sweet plantains. Customers can then choose from various cuts of chicken, beef, or any combination of seafood. The restaurant's claim to fame is its excellent churrasco with chimichurri, of which owner Dante Marini sells 25,000 pounds per year. Vegetarian options are available. ✉ *3022 Av. Isla Verde, Isla Verde* ☎ *787/726–7310* 💳 AE, *MC, V* ✥ *2:F3*

$$$$ ITALIAN Fodor's Choice ★ ✕ **Il Mulino New York.** You'll want for nothing at the San Juan outpost of the famed Manhattan restaurant, where a team of tuxedoed waiters effortlessly coordinates your entire meal experience. The dark-wood-paneled walls and heavy velvet drapes are an odd juxtaposition with the tropical climate, but everything about this place is elegant and tasteful. Garlic bread and antipasti arrive moments after you sit down, though you'll want to pace yourself and leave room for the mammoth entrées to come. Standouts include rigatoni Bolognese, stuffed whole branzino (deboned tableside), and fresh pappardelle with sausage. A side of fried zucchini is a must. There's no fusion or haute cuisine here, just solid

DID YOU KNOW?

The city wall (la muralla) once encircled all of the Old City. It was built between 1539 and 1641 with sandstone blocks, some of which are 20 feet thick, and is 3.4 miles (5.5 km) long.

Italian dishes, painstakingly executed to perfection. All this perfection comes at a price, though the shot of homemade grappa they offer at the end might help ease the shock. ✉ *The Ritz-Carlton, San Juan, 6991 Av. de los Gobernadores, Isla Verde* ☎ *787/791–8632* 🌐 *www.ilmulino.com* ✍ *Reservations essential* ▭ *AE, D, DC, MC, V* ⊗ *No lunch.* ✥ *2:H3*

$$ CARIBBEAN ✕ **Metropol.** Across the street from a string of major hotels, this casual restaurant won't necessarily charm you with its decor, but it will impress you with solid versions of Cuban and Puerto Rican favorites at reasonable prices. Tasty options include Cornish game hen stuffed with *congri*, a mixture of black beans and rice; perfectly seasoned and tender veal churrasco; and fried chickpeas with ham and chorizo. The crowd is a pleasant mix of tourists and locals, families and groups of friends enjoying a relaxed evening out. The restaurant has several branches around the island, most in the metro area. ✉ *Av. Isla Verde, Isla Verde* ☎ *787/791–5585* 🌐 *www.metropolpr.com* ▭ *AE, D, DC, MC, V* ✥ *2:H3*

$$$ CARIBBEAN ✕ **Platos.** In the heart of Isla Verde, this restaurant attracts a young, hip crowd. The menu is a combination of something old, something new. Puerto Rican favorites are jazzed up, serving skirt steak with pumpkin risotto and covering grilled pork with a guava glaze. The bar is a great place for a beer in the early evening or for cocktails before heading to the clubs. There's live music on Fridays. ✉ *2 Calle Rosa, Isla Verde* ☎ *787/791–7474* 🌐 *www.platosrestaurant.com* ▭ *AE, MC, V* ⊗ *No lunch Mon.–Sat.* ✥ *2:H3*

WHERE TO STAY

San Juan prides itself on its plentiful clean, comfortable accommodations, and hoteliers, by and large, aim to please. All rooms are now no-smoking rooms. Big hotels and resorts, several with casinos, and a few smaller establishments line the sandy strands along Condado and Isla Verde. Between these two neighborhoods, the Ocean Park area has homey inns, as do the districts of Miramar and Santurce, although the latter two areas aren't directly on the beach. Old San Juan has a smaller selection, one of which has a casino, but most of the city's best boutique hotels are here.

Staying in a self-catering apartment or condo has advantages over a resort, especially for families. You can cook when and what you want, and you can enjoy considerable autonomy. Several companies represent such properties in San Juan. When booking, be sure to ask about maid service, swimming pools, and any other amenities that are important to you.

PRICES

The city's rooms aren't inexpensive: for a high-end beach-resort room, expect to pay at least $200 to $300 for a double in high season—roughly mid-November through mid-April. For smaller inns and hotels, doubles start at $100 to $150. As a rule, if your room is less than $50 in high season, then the quality of the hotel might be questionable. Although most hotels operate on the European plan (EP, no meals included), some establishments do include breakfast or offer other meal plans and/or all-inclusive packages; there's only one true all-inclusive hotel in Puerto Rico, and it's not in San Juan.

	WHAT IT COSTS IN U.S. DOLLARS				
	¢	$	$$	$$$	$$$$
FOR TWO PEOPLE	under $80	$80–$150	$150–$250	$250–$350	over $350

Prices are for a double room in high season, excluding 9% tax (11% for hotels with casinos, 7% for paradores) and typical 5%–12% service charge.

2

APARTMENT RENTALS

Caleta 64 Apartments (✉ *64 Calle de San Juan Old San Juan,* ☎ *787/667–4926* 🌐 *www.caleta64.com*) has four delightfully furnished boutique apartments just steps from the cathedral and Calle Cristo.

Puerto Rico Vacation Apartments (✉ *Calle Marbella del Caribe Oeste S-5, Isla Verde,* ☎ *787/727–1591 or 800/266–3639* 🌐 *www.sanjuanvacations.com*) represents some 200 properties in Condado and Isla Verde.

OLD SAN JUAN

Use the coordinate (⊕ 1:A2) at the end of each listing to locate a site on the corresponding "Map 1: Where to Eat and Stay in Old San Juan."

$–$$ HOTEL **Casablanca Hotel.** Mere steps away from some of the best dining in town, this boutique hotel in the heart of SoFo opened in February 2009, adding Moroccan-theme panache to Old San Juan. The lobby makes a big splash with its silk pillows, Oriental antiques, and blood-red sofas as counterpoints to dramatic, contemporary photo-realist pop-art by noted painter Carlos Mercado. The individually themed guest rooms blend the same mix of modern art with antique and ethnic pieces—gilt mirrors, Moroccan tea sets, mirrored cushions, and spreads—including queen beds framed with gauzy drapes. Quirky and fun, the overall effect is smile-inducingly stylish. At this writing, an elevator was planned for 2010, as was a bar. Until then, you'll need to climb five flights of stairs to soak in one of the rooftop's five stone hot tubs. **Pros:** Exotic decor; close to restaurants and nightclubs. **Cons:** Some rooms dark; noise from street and bars; no restaurant. ✉ *316 Calle Fortaleza, Old San Juan* ☎ *787/725–3436* 🌐 *www.hotelcasablancapr.com* *34 rooms, 1 suite* *In-room: safe (some), DVD. In-hotel: laundry service, Internet terminal, Wi-Fi, some pets allowed, no-smoking rooms.* 💳 *AE, MC, V.* ⊕ *1:F4*

$$ HOTEL **Casa Herencia.** From the same owners as Casablanca Hotel and DaHouse, this intimate property transports guests metaphorically back to the 19th century. The setting is an exquisitely restored former mansion that retains time-worn bare walls and original floral tile floors and beamed ceilings. Individually styled guest rooms are on two levels: Those below are in the original house and open to a narrow patio with fountain; those above are in a modern rooftop extension. All are graced by a mix of original antiques such as armoires, and retro-themed contemporary furniture straight from the pages of *Vogue*. Many have canopied beds. Plasma TVs are a nod to modernity. **Pros:** delightful furnishings; romantic to the max; close to shops and cafés of Calle Cristo. **Cons:** No on-site services. ✉ *23 Calle de las Monjas, Old San*

BEST BETS FOR SAN JUAN LODGING

Fodor's Choice ★

El San Juan Hotel & Casino $$$, p. 99

Hotel El Convento $$$$, p. 91

The Ritz-Carlton, San Juan $$$$, p. 100

By Price

$

Acacia Seaside Inn, p. 94

Andalucía, p. 97

Da House, p. 90

$$

Casablanca, p. 89

Casa Herencia, p. 89

Coral Princess, p. 95

Doubletree by Hilton San Juan, p. 95

Hotel Milano, p. 92

Howard Johnson Plaza de Armas, p. 92

Numero Uno, p. 98

San Juan Water & Beach Club, p. 100

$$$

Chateau Cervantes, p. 90

Conrad San Juan Condado Plaza, p. 95

El San Juan Hotel & Casino, p. 99

Gallery Inn, p. 91

$$$$

Hotel El Convento, p. 91

The Ritz-Carlton, San Juan, p. 100

Sheraton Old San Juan, p. 93

By Experience

BEST FOR ROMANCE

Hotel El Convento, p. 91

Numero Uno, p. 98

The Ritz-Carlton, San Juan, p. 100

San Juan Water & Beach Club, p. 100

BEST BEACHFRONT

El San Juan Hotel & Casino, p. 99

The Ritz-Carlton, San Juan, p. 100

BEST POOL

Caribe Hilton San Juan, p. 93

Gallery Inn, p. 91

The Ritz-Carlton, San Juan, p. 100

Juan ☎ 787/977–1180 🌐 www.casaherencia.com ⇆ 7 rooms, 1 suite ♨ In-room: DVD (some), Internet, Wi-Fi (some). In-hotel: room service, laundry service, no-smoking rooms. ▭ MC, V. ⊕ 1:C4

$$$ HOTEL **Chateau Cervantes.** The brainchild of local fashion icon Nono Maldonado, this luxury lodging has a look that's completely au courant. Bursts of color from red pillows or gold upholstery on the banquettes add considerable warmth to the sexily sophisticated modern decor. And the amenities, which include plasma TVs and Wi-Fi, are above and beyond other hotels. Splurge for one of the larger suites and you'll get a butler who will mix cocktails; the two-level presidential suite comes with a car and driver. A rooftop lounge bar was due to open at this writing. **Pros:** Gorgeous rooms; luxurious bathrooms; great restaurant. **Cons:** No views; very pricey; some rooms get street noise. ✉ *329 Calle Recinto Sur, Old San Juan ☎ 787/724–7722 🌐 www.cervantespr.com ⇆ 6 rooms, 6 suites ♨ In-room: safe, Wi-Fi. In-hotel: restaurant, bar, concierge, laundry service ▭ AE, D, DC, MC, V 🍽 EP. ⊕ 1:F4*

$ HOTEL **Da House.** This hotel occupies the same building as the fabled Nuyorican Café, a concert hall that many patrons simply refer to as Da House. But if you're expecting this hangout for musicians, artists, and writers to be dark and smoky, think again. Sunlight pours in through the front windows of the bright and airy hotel centered on a skylit

PARADORES

The small, government-sponsored inns called *paradores* are primarily *en la isla* (out on the island) rather than in San Juan.

atrium. Most rooms are bigger than you'd expect in a former convent, especially those with small sitting areas at the front of the building. The original tile floors have been preserved, and many of the furnishings are antiques, contrasting with pop-art chairs and lively contemporary art. During the 1970s the building housed an artist collective, the Centro Nacional de las Artes, and continues in this vein by naming each of the 27 rooms for a different local artist. The paintings hanging in your room are all for sale. If you're an early-to-bed person, you'll probably want a room on the top floor. (We found 402 and 403 to be the quietest.) If you plan on staying downstairs until the last encore, it won't matter which room you take. **Pros:** Hip vibe, artsy types to mingle with; great rooftop bar. **Cons:** Noise from nearby bars; on a steep alley; simple accommodations. ✉ *312 Calle San Francisco (entrance on Callejón de la Capellia), Old San Juan* ☎ *787/977–1180* 🌐 *www.dahousehotelpr.com* *27 rooms* *In-room: no TV, Internet. In-hotel: bar, no elevator, public Wi-Fi* 💳 *AE, MC, V* *EP.* ⊕ *1:F3*

$$–$$$ HOTEL **Gallery Inn.** Nothing like this hotel exists anywhere else in San Juan—or Puerto Rico, for that matter. You can shop from your bed at this 200-year-old mansion, as owner Jan D'Esopo has filled the rooms with her own artworks. But it's not only the rooms; the hallways, the staircases, and the roof are lined with her fascinating bronze sculptures, ceramic busts and plaques, and eclectic paintings. D'Esopo and her equally gregarious husband, Hernán "Manuco" Gandía, are terrific hosts, not least at the daily happy hour with wine on the new poolside patio, with its dozens of potted plants. No two rooms are alike here, but all have four-poster beds, hand-woven tapestries, and quirky antiques in every nook and cranny. You can view the coastline from several rooms and from the rooftop terrace. **Pros:** One-of-a-kind lodging; ocean views; wonderful classical music concerts. **Cons:** No restaurant; an uphill walk from rest of Old San Juan; sometimes raucous pet macaws and cockatoos. ✉ *204–206 Calle Norzagaray, Old San Juan* ☎ *787/722–1808* 🌐 *www.thegalleryinn.com* *13 rooms, 10 suites* *In-room: no a/c (some), refrigerator (some), no TV. In-hotel: restaurant, no elevator, no-smoking rooms* 💳 *AE, DC, MC, V* *CP.* ⊕ *1:D3*

$$$$ HOTEL Fodor's Choice ★ **Hotel El Convento.** Carmelite nuns once inhabited this 350-year-old convent, but they never had high-tech gadgets such as in-room broadband connections or plasma TVs. The accommodations here beautifully combine the old and the new. All the guest rooms are lavish and inviting and have a mix of wrought-iron and hand-hewn wood furniture, shuttered windows, and mahogany-beamed ceilings, but some have extra appeal—hence the hotel was featured in the May 2002 issue of *Architectural Digest.* Room 508 has two views of the bay, while Rooms 216, 217, and 218 have private walled patios. Guests gather on the second floor for the complimentary wine and hors d'oeuvres that are served before dinner, with a lovely view over the nearby cathedral. The second-floor El Picoteo and the courtyard Café del Níspero are good

The narrow streets and sloping hills of Old San Juan are fantastic for walking. Driving? Not so much.

dining choices. **Pros:** Lovely building; atmosphere to spare; plenty of nearby dining options. **Cons:** Near some noisy bars. ✉ *100 Calle Cristo, Old San Juan* 📭 *Box 1048, 00902* ☎ *787/723–9020 or 800/468–2779* 🌐 *www.elconvento.com* *63 rooms, 5 suites* *In-room: safe, DVD, Ethernet, Wi-Fi. In-hotel: 3 restaurants, bars, pool, gym, concierge, laundry service, public Internet, public Wi-Fi, parking (fee), no-smoking rooms* ▭ *AE, D, DC, MC, V* *EP.* ✢ *1:D3*

$–$$ HOTEL **Hotel Milano.** This affordable and conservative hotel is near the best and worst of Old San Juan. On the plus side, it's on a lively street lined with interesting shops. On the other hand, the street can be noisy. For less clamor, opt for a room at the back of the five-story building. Rooms here won't win any prizes, but they are clean and comfortable. The open-air restaurant on the top floor has expansive views of the barrel-tile rooftops and beyond. The friendly staff goes above and beyond the call of duty, arranging for your laundry to be washed or confirming that your flight is departing on time. **Pros:** Budget-friendly rates; walk to shops and restaurants. **Cons:** A bit staid; on a busy street; noise from nearby bars. ✉ *307 Calle Fortaleza, Old San Juan* ☎ *877/729–9050* 🌐 *www.hotelmilanopr.com* *30 rooms* *In-hotel: restaurant, bar, Wi-Fi, laundry service, no-smoking rooms* ▭ *AE, MC, V* *CP.* ✢ *1:E4*

$–$$ HOTEL **Howard Johnson Plaza de Armas.** Located on Old San Juan's main square, this hotel couldn't be more convenient. All the most popular sites are within easy walking distance. Some of the building's best architectural details, such as the tile floors, have been preserved. The best rooms are in the front, where shuttered doorways lead to balconies overlooking the Plaza de Armas. Some of the inner rooms are a bit cramped, as is the lobby, which has a streetfront café with Internet. Decor is a tad frumpy, but all the essentials are in place and the hotel is kept spic and span. The interior courtyard has a hip little bar area. **Pros:** Great location; quiet courtyard; good value. **Cons:** Some rooms have very small windows; some street noise. ✉ *202 Calle San José, Old San Juan* ☎ *787/722–9191* 🌐 *www.hojo.com* *51 rooms* *In-room: refrigerator (some). In-hotel: bar* 💳 *AE, D, DC, MC, V* *CP.* ✥ *1:D4*

WORD OF MOUTH

"I have stayed at the Caribe Hilton twice and found it to be a well-run resort with good service, decent food and extensive facilities. I thought it was a particularly good value for a Caribbean vacation in high season. It's a short cab ride to Old San Juan and other areas of the city.... And the pool is large, too."

—eileen

$$$$ HOTEL **Sheraton Old San Juan Hotel.** This hotel's triangular shape subtly echoes the cruise ships docked nearby. Rooms facing the water have dazzling views of these behemoths as they sail in and out of the harbor. (Interior rooms, however, face black concrete walls.) The plushly furnished rooms have nice touches like custom-designed beds, but they feel institutional. On the top floor you'll find a sunny patio with a pool and whirlpool bath, as well as a spacious gym with the latest equipment. Facilities here include two restaurants—a steak house and a burger joint—and a casino, which dominates the lobby. **Pros:** Harbor views; near many dining options; good array of room types. **Cons:** Motel feel to guest rooms; noise from casino overwhelms lobby and restaurants; extra charges for everything from bottled water to Internet access. ✉ *100 Calle Brumbaugh, Old San Juan* ☎ *787/721–5100 or 866/376–7577* 🌐 *www.sheratonoldsanjuan.com* *200 rooms, 40 suites* *In-room: safe, refrigerator, Ethernet. In-hotel: restaurant, room service, bar, pool, gym, laundry service, executive floor, public Internet, parking (fee), no-smoking rooms* 💳 *AE, D, DC, MC, V* *EP.* ✥ *1:F4*

PUERTA DE TIERRA

Use the coordinate (✥ 2:A1) at the end of each listing to locate a site on the corresponding "Map 2: Where to Eat and Stay in Greater San Juan."

$$$ RESORT **Caribe Hilton San Juan.** Not many hotels can lay claim to their own fort, but Fortín San Gerónimo del Boquerón, which once guarded the entrance to San Juan Bay, is on the grounds of this sprawling resort, the second largest in Puerto Rico. It has a private beach, a multilevel pool with swim-up bar, a luxurious spa, and one of the best-developed kids' programs on the island. The property is also being certified as a green hotel, with receptacles for recycling (a rarity in Puerto Rico) as well as the beginnings of a green roof. The airy Oasis lobby bar makes one of the more legitimate claims to inventing the piña colada; it holds an official government certification. **Pros:** Family-friendly atmosphere; private beach; lovely pool area. **Cons:** Ongoing construction of villas; parts of hotel still unrenovated; noisy lobby area. ✉ *1 San Gerónimo Grounds, Puerta de Tierra* ☎ *787/721–0303 or 800/468–8585* 🌐 *www.hiltoncaribbean.com/sanjuan* *872 rooms, 38 suites* *In-room: safe,*

kitchen (some), refrigerator, Internet. In-hotel: 6 restaurants, room service, bars, tennis courts, pools, gym, spa, beachfront, water sports, bicycles, concierge, children's programs (ages 4–12), laundry service, public Wi-Fi, parking (fee) ▭ AE, D, DC, MC, V 🍴 EP. ✥ 2:B2

CONDADO

$ HOTEL **Acacia Seaside Inn.** This chic spot, a sister property to At Wind Chimes Inn, falls somewhere between a boutique hotel and a casual guesthouse. Low-slung leather couches line the lobby entrance, and a giant Buddha statue with running water greets you in the hallway. A wave effect is echoed in everything from the curved staircases and balconies to the undulating granite wall of the impressive pool-size hot tub. The rooms are comfortable, but not all the decor seems to match the sleeker feel of the larger hotel. Niche, a matchbox-size restaurant serving creative Puerto Rican food, is tucked away on the first floor. While the hotel is not beachfront, you can walk there in less than two minutes. **Pros:** Enormous hot tub with ocean views; good value for the neighborhood; can use facilities at At Wind Chimes Inn. **Cons:** Several minutes' walk to most shops and restaurants; some outdated decorations in the rooms. ✉ *8 Calle Taft, Condado* ☎ *787/725–0068 or 877/725–0668* 🌐 *www.acaciaseasideinn.com* 🛏 *15 rooms, 6 suites* 👍 *In-room: safe (some), refrigerator (some). In-hotel: restaurant, room service, bar, laundry service, Wi-Fi, parking (paid)* ▭ *AE, D, MC, V* 🍴 *EP.* ✥ *2:D2*

$ HOTEL **At Wind Chimes Inn.** Hidden behind a whitewashed wall covered with bougainvillea, this Spanish-style villa gives the impression of an exclusive retreat. Much about the place invites you to relax: the patios shaded by royal palms, the terra-cotta-tiled terraces, two sun decks, and the small pool. And the soft, ever-present jingling of wind chimes reminds you that the beach is a block away. The inn has spacious, tropical guest rooms, and the Boat Bar, open only to guests, serves a light menu from 7 AM to 11 PM. The inn's sister property, Acacia Seaside Inn, is only a block away. **Pros:** Charming architecture; on the edge of Condado; can use facilities at Acacia Seaside Inn. **Cons:** On a busy street; old-fashioned rooms; only a few rooms have closets. ✉ *1750 Av. McLeary, Condado* ☎ *787/727–4153 or 800/946–3244* 🌐 *www.atwindchimesinn.com* 🛏 *17 rooms, 5 suites* 👍 *In-room: safe (some), kitchen (some). In-hotel: room service, bar, pool, laundry service, public Wi-Fi, parking (paid), some pets allowed* ▭ *AE, D, MC, V* 🍴 *EP.* ✥ *2:D2*

$ HOTEL **Casa del Caribe.** Tucked discreetly off Ashford Avenue, this guesthouse is one of the most affordable hotels in Condado. It's surrounded by a wall, which blocks most of the traffic noise from nearby Avenida Ashford. Rooms decorated with works by local artists are simple but comfortable. The wraparound veranda, surrounded by an overgrown garden, is the perfect place for a siesta, and the beach is only a few minutes away. Monthly rates are available. **Pros:** Near plenty of restaurants; on quiet side street. **Cons:** Staff sometimes surly; common areas are unkempt. ✉ *57 Calle Caribe, Condado* ☎ *787/722–7139* 🌐 *www.casadelcaribe.net* 🛏 *12 rooms, 1 suite* 👍 *In-room: safe, kitchen (some). In-hotel: laundry service, Wi-Fi, parking (fee), some pets allowed* ▭ *AE, D, MC, V* 🍴 *CP.* ✥ *2:C2*

2

$$$ HOTEL **Conrad San Juan Condado Plaza.** Fresh off a $78 million top-to-bottom renovation, this gorgeous hotel feels like a thriving hotspot. More like a boutique hotel in design, it has common areas that are crisp and clean and feature the wave pattern from the hotel's logo on everything from the ultramodern lighting fixtures to the art on the walls. Rooms are eye-popping—the ocean wing is cherry red, the bay wing glimmers in gold—with sleek furnishings such as the low-slung sofas near the massive windows. An ample pool area, including a saltwater pool, makes up for a small beachfront. The latest jewel in its crown is the acquisition of Wilo Benet's Pikayo, perhaps Puerto Rico's most notable restaurant by its most renowned chef. Noise can be a problem. At night we could hear doors opening and closing, as well as conversations in the hallways. The casino is a box-like room with gaming tables and slot machines. **Pros:** Lovely interiors; friendly staff; great ocean views from some rooms; several excellent dining options. **Cons:** Noisy rooms; on a disappointingly small public beach; a bit of a walk to center of Condado. ✉ *999 Av. Ashford, Condado* ☎ *787/721–1000* 🌐 *www.condadoplaza.com* *570 rooms, 62 suites* *In-room: safe, refrigerator, Internet, Wi-Fi. In-hotel: 5 restaurants, room service, 5 bars, tennis courts, pools, gym, beachfront, concierge, water sports, laundry facilities, laundry service, Internet terminal, Wi-Fi, parking (fee)* *AE, D, DC, MC, V* *EP.* ✢ *2:B2*

$$ HOTEL **Coral Princess.** This Art Deco building—one of the few left in Condado—has personality to spare. The guest rooms subtly reflect the boutique hotel's heritage with crisp lines, modern furnishings, and marble floors. We loved the attention to detail: fruit and cheese plates, jetted bathtubs, pillow-top beds, blackout shades, and even—shockingly—an affordable minibar. A good choice for a quiet, romantic getaway, the hotel is only a block from the neighborhood's main drag, and the beach is five minutes away. You can also take advantage of the small swimming pool on the palm-shaded terrace or the hot tub on the rooftop. **Pros:** Excellent value; friendly staff; comfortable common areas. **Cons:** Short walk to the beach. ✉ *1159 Av. Magdalena, Condado* ☎ *787/977–7700* 🌐 *www.coralpr.com* *25 rooms* *In-room: kitchen (some), Internet, Wi-Fi. In-hotel: bar, pool, public Wi-Fi* *AE, D, DC, MC, V* *CP.* ✢ *2:C2*

$$ HOTEL **Doubletree by Hilton San Juan.** Formerly the Best Western Pierre, this hotel has been taken over by the Hilton group and given a remarkable top-to-bottom renovation. The immaculate rooms are modern, yet warm, decorated in rich reds and browns. Some also have a Murphy bed (of the same mattress quality as the main bed) that can be folded up for more space. With Neutrogena products in the bathroom, Wolfgang Puck coffee and a coffeemaker in each room, ergonomic desk chairs, and warm cookies at check-in, there's clearly an emphasis on comfortable details that make a hotel stay more pleasant. And for the price, it can't be beat. It's geared slightly more to business travelers but offers an excellent value for anyone who doesn't need to be in central Condado or on the beach. Location-wise, it's across the street from a 24-hour supermarket, near the on-ramp to a major highway, and within walking distance of the main attractions and restaurants. **Pros:** Excellent value for the neighborhood; attractive rooms; good on-site dining options **Cons:** A bit of a walk to the beach and the main drag

in Condado. ✉ *105 Av. de Diego, Condado* ☎ *787/721–1200* 🌐 *www.hilton.com* *184 rooms* *In-room: safe, refrigerator, Internet. In-hotel: 4 restaurants, room service, 3 bars, pool, gym, laundry facilities, laundry service, Internet terminal, Wi-Fi, parking (paid)* 💳 *AE, D, MC, V.* 🍽 *EP.* ✥ *2:D3*

$ HOTEL **El Canario by the Sea.** You can't see the ocean from the rooms of this modest three-story hotel wedged between blocky condo complexes. Walk out the front door, however, and you can be on the beach in less than a minute. Rooms are comfortable, but relatively dated and humble, which may be fine for travelers who just need a place to crash. Some rooms have two twin beds instead of a full or queen, so keep this in mind when booking a reservation. Continental breakfast is served on a pretty brick patio. If this location is booked, the company has two more properties in Condado. **Pros:** Near beach, shops, and restaurants; good value for the budget traveler. **Cons:** Limited facilities; drab rooms need updating. ✉ *4 Av. Condado, Condado* ☎ *787/722–8640 or 800/533–2649* 🌐 *www.canariohotels.com* *25 rooms* *In-room: safe.* 💳 *AE, DC, MC, V* 🍽 *CP.* ✥ *2:C2*

$ HOTEL **Hotel Miramar.** This high-rise sits in the middle of Miramar, an up-and-coming neighborhood located halfway between Condado and Old San Juan. It's a good area if you want to be close to the historic district but don't want the hassle of driving through the narrow streets. There's no beach, but some of the city's best are nearby, and there's a bus stop right outside that will take you to Old San Juan in just a few minutes. The generously sized rooms have microwaves and refrigerators, and many of those on the upper floors have nice views of Condado Bay. **Pros:** Short drive to Old San Juan and Condado; walk to excellent restaurants. **Cons:** Drab decor; not the most interesting neighborhood. ✉ *606 Av. Ponce de León, Miramar* ☎ *787/977–1000* 🌐 *www.miramarhotelpr.com* *50 rooms* *In-room: safe, refrigerator, Wi-Fi. In-hotel: restaurant, bar, gym, laundry facilities, laundry service, public Wi-Fi, parking (free)* 💳 *AE, MC, V* 🍽 *CP.* ✥ *2:B2*

$$$ RESORT **La Concha—A Renaissance Resort.** After a multiyear, $220 million renovation, La Concha—an icon of Tropical Modernist architecture—reopened in late 2007. It has since become the envy of the hospitality industry and the center of social life in San Juan for travelers and locals (including politicians and celebrities) alike. The sprawling open-air lobby is a hive of dancing, drinking, and socializing most nights of the week, though if you're looking for a respite from DJ beats or live music, head poolside for comfortable chaises, umbrellas, and a surprising amount of privacy. Though La Concha hums with activity, the rooms offer a good night's sleep, not to mention exceptional amenities and extraordinary views. With four restaurants and a casino in-house, you'll be tempted not to step outside, but a carefully groomed beach awaits. **Pros:** Stunning Tropical Modernist architecture; most rooms have ocean views; numerous on-site social activities. **Cons:** Noise from bar/lobby, particularly when there's live music, can be heard from some of the rooms ✉ *1077 Av. Ashford, Condado* ☎ *787/721–7500* 🌐 *www.laconcharesort.com* *248 rooms, 16 suites* *In-room: safe, refrigerator, Internet, Wi-Fi. In-hotel: 4 restaurants, room service, bars, pool, beachfront, laundry*

service, fitness center, public Wi-Fi, no smoking rooms ☰ *AE, D, DC, MC, V* 🍽 *EP.* ✣ *2:C2*

$$$ RESORT **San Juan Marriott Resort & Stellaris Casino.** The shape and color of a cardboard box, this hotel doesn't add much to the skyline of Condado. Nothing about the hotel hints that it's in the Caribbean. The nondistinctive hanger-like lobby reverberates with the exceptionally loud music of the lounge and the ringing of slot machines in the adjoining casino. It's only in the rooms that there's a bit of flair—tropical fabrics and bright colors lighten the mood considerably—and there's a view of the ocean from most of the balconies. The high points are undoubtedly the pair of pools, which add a bit of whimsy with their gushing fountains and swirling mural. **Pros:** Many available amenities; on one of the area's best beaches; near dozens of dining options. **Cons:** Uninspired architecture; lots of conventions; overworked staff. ✉ *1309 Av. Ashford, Condado* ☎ *787/722–7000 or 800/465–5005* 🌐 *www.marriottsanjuan.com* *513 rooms, 12 suites* *In-room: safe, refrigerator, DVD, Internet, Wi-Fi. In-hotel: 4 restaurants, room service, 4 bars, tennis courts, pool, gym, spa, beachfront, bicycles, children's programs (ages 4–12), laundry facilities, laundry service, Internet terminal, public Wi-Fi, parking (fee)* ☰ *AE, D, DC, MC, V* 🍽 *EP.* ✣ *2:C2*

WORD OF MOUTH

"Both the best and worst part of staying in Ocean Park was the location. It's absolutely fantastic if you never intend to leave the beach. However, if you want to be around constant nightlife and want to have it all at your front door, then you might be better off staying in Old Town or near the casino area."

—Magellan

OCEAN PARK

$ INN **Andalucía.** In a Spanish-style house, this friendly little inn lives up to its name with such details as hand-painted tiles and ceramic pots filled with greenery. A kidney-shaped hot tub in the central courtyard is big enough for you and four or five of your closest friends. The individually decorated rooms are bright and clean. Owners Esteban Haigler and Emeo Cheung give you the warmest welcome imaginable, making you feel that their home is yours. Feel free to borrow their beach chairs, umbrellas, and Boogie boards. And if you forget your sunscreen, grab a bottle from a table near the door. One of the prettiest beaches in the city is a five-minute walk away. **Pros:** Terrific value; helpful hosts; gorgeous courtyard. **Cons:** Not right on the beach; some rooms are smaller than others; small sign can be easy to miss when you are driving by. ✉ *2011 Calle McLeary, Ocean Park* ☎ *787/309–3373* 🌐 *www.andalucia-puertorico.com* *11 rooms* *In-room: no phone, kitchen (some), refrigerator, Wi-Fi. In-hotel: public Internet, public Wi-Fi, parking (some free), no smoking* ☰ *MC, V* 🍽 *EP.* ✣ *2:E3*

$ INN **Hostería del Mar.** This breezy inn tucked away in residential Ocean Park is the place to go if you want to be right on a quiet beach and far from the big-name Isla Verde and Condado hotels. You'll probably pause, as most people do, to admire the pond filled with iridescent goldfish before continuing into the lobby, with whitewashed walls and dark wood paneling. Though the rooms are relatively simple and could use updating, the beachy vibe can't be beat. You'll definitely want an ocean-view room, preferably on the second floor, since first-floor rooms open right onto the deck of the terrific on-site restaurant, Uvva—a possible downside for those who plan to use their patio. For larger groups, apartments are available in a separate back building. **Pros:** Right on the beach; lovely building; great on-site dining. **Cons:** Rooms could use some updating; a long walk to other restaurants. ✉ *1 Calle Tapia, Ocean Park* ☎ *787/727–3302* 🌐 *www.hosteriadelmarpr.com* *20 rooms, 4 suites* *In-room: safe, kitchen (some), refrigerator (some). In-hotel: restaurant, bar, beachfront* ▭ *AE, D, DC, MC, V* *CP.* ✥ *2:E2*

WORD OF MOUTH

"I stayed for a week at the Numero Uno Guest House... right on the beach! Thanks to the wonderful staff, this was by far the most relaxing beach vacation I've ever had. The staff members and the owners were very professional, but also friendly and fun—full of good tips and information.

—sunbabe

$$ HOTEL **Numero Uno.** Although the name refers to the hotel's address, Numero Uno is how guests rate this small hotel. It's common to hear people trading stories about how often they've returned to this relaxing retreat. Behind a whitewashed wall is a patio where you can catch some rays beside the small pool, enjoy a cocktail at the bar, or dine in the restaurant. (It's so good that it draws locals.) A few steps away, a sandy beach beckons, where you can relax on beach chairs and under umbrellas. Instead of having the usual tropical colors, the rooms are decorated in shades of cream and gray, with custom-made furnishings, including sleek writing desks. **Pros:** Friendly atmosphere; great restaurant; good value. **Cons:** A long walk to other restaurants; small pool. ✉ *1 Calle Santa Ana, Ocean Park* ☎ *787/726–5010 or 866/726–5010* 🌐 *www.numero1guesthouse.com* *12 rooms, 4 apartments* *In-room: safe, kitchen (some), refrigerator, Internet, Wi-Fi. In-hotel: restaurant, room service, bar, pool, beachfront, Wi-Fi, some pets allowed* ▭ *AE, MC, V* *CP.* ✥ *2:E2*

ISLA VERDE

$$$ HOTEL **Courtyard by Marriott Isla Verde Beach Resort.** This 12-story hotel tries to be all things to all people—and succeeds to a great degree. Harried business executives appreciate its location near the airport and high-tech offerings such as high-speed Internet connections. Families prefer the many dining options and the fact that the city's best beach is just outside. The place is buzzing during the day, especially around the three swimming pools. At night the action centers on the lobby bar, where people often dance to the live salsa music. (If you don't know how, you can take lessons on Thursday nights.) **Pros:** On a great beach; family-friendly environment. **Cons:** Noise from lobby. ✉ *7012 Av. Boca de Cangrejos, Isla Verde* ☎ *787/791–0404 or 800/791–2553* 🌐 *www.sjcourtyard.com* *260 rooms, 33 suites* *In-room: safe, refrigerator, DVD, Internet, Wi-Fi. In-hotel: 5 restaurants, room service, bars, pools, gym, beachfront,*

laundry facilities, laundry service, Internet terminal, public Wi-Fi, parking (fee) ☐ *AE, D, DC, MC, V* 🍴 *EP.* ✥ *2:H3*

$$$ RESORT Fodor's Choice ★ **El San Juan Hotel & Casino, The Waldorf Astoria Collection.** For decades this iconic hotel was the don't-miss destination in Isla Verde, and now it's on everyone's list again after a complete renovation in 2007. First, what hasn't changed: the intricately hand-carved mahogany walls and ceiling in the lobby. There are three new bars beneath the coffered ceiling. The Blue Bar is in the center, down a few steps from the lobby, and set below a massive oval-shaped chandelier. You'll find the burnished warmth of Gold Bar on the right and the shimmering Silver Bar on the left. Just outside is the pool area, furnished with a trio of poolside cabanas with such unbelievable amenities as television and four-poster beds hung with gauzy curtains—all of which can be reserved in advance. (Some people even opt for breakfast in these beds.) Brava, a two-level nightclub, draws a hip crowd. Rooms are larger than most on the island and have modern white furnishings with a few colorful accents. All have high-tech conveniences such as CD players and iPod docks. **Pros:** Beautiful pool; great dining options in and near hotel; on a fantastic beach. **Cons:** Noise in the lobby from bars and casino; self-parking lot is a long walk from the hotel entrance. ✉ *6063 Av. Isla Verde, Isla Verde* ☎ *787/791–1000* 🌐 *www.elsanjuanhotel.com* *386 rooms, 57 suites* *In-room: safe, kitchen (some), refrigerator, Internet, Wi-Fi. In-hotel: 9 restaurants, room service, 15 bars, tennis courts, pools, gym, spa, beachfront, concierge, water sports, children's programs (ages 5–17), laundry service, Internet terminal, public Wi-Fi, parking (fee), some pets allowed* ☐ *AE, DC, MC, V* 🍴 *EP.* ✥ *2:G3*

$$$ HOTEL **Embassy Suites San Juan Hotel & Casino.** Overshadowing neighbors with more prestigious names, the coral-colored Embassy Suites is one of the prettiest hotels in Isla Verde. The glass elevators that whisk you up to your room overlook the plant-filled atrium, which includes a pond and waterfall. Outside is a lagoon-style pool and an adjacent bar. The suites are not luxurious, but they are spacious enough for a family. The location—1 mi (1½ km) from the airport—makes the hotel popular with business travelers. The one drawback is that while the beach is nearby, you have to cross some busy streets to get to it. **Pros:** Family-friendly environment; pretty pool; full cooked-to-order breakfast and cocktail reception included. **Cons:** Not on beach; chain-hotel feel; highway noise in pool area. ✉ *8000 Calle Tartak, Isla Verde* ☎ *787/791–0505 or 888/791–0505* 🌐 *www.embassysuitessanjuan.com* *299 suites* *In-room: safe, refrigerator, Internet, Wi-Fi. In-hotel: 2 restaurants, room service, bars, pool, gym, laundry facilities, laundry service, Internet terminal, public Wi-Fi, parking (fee)* ☐ *AE, D, DC, MC, V* 🍴 *BP.* ✥ *2:G4*

$$ HOTEL **Hampton Inn & Suites San Juan.** If you can live without being directly on the beach, you can get a room here for much less than at many of the resort's competitors across the road. The palm-shaded pool is so pleasant that you might not even make it to the beach. The guest rooms are standard issue, decorated in tropical colors, and count coffeemakers and irons among their amenities. Free coffee and tea are available around the clock in the lobby. The Guacamayo Pool Bar & Grill has a basic menu of hamburgers, fries, and the like. **Pros:** Good value; helpful

staff. **Cons:** Long walk to beach; chain-hotel feel. ✉ *6530 Av. Isla Verde, Isla Verde* ☎ *787/791–8777 or 800/426–7866* 🌐 *www.hamptoninn.com* *147 rooms, 54 suites* *In-room: safe, refrigerator (some), Internet, Wi-Fi. In-hotel: restaurant, bar, pool, gym, laundry facilities, laundry service, Wi-Fi, parking (fee)* *AE, MC, V* *BP.* *2:H3*

$$$ HOTEL **InterContinental San Juan Resort & Casino.** Despite its name, this 16-story hotel in the heart of Isla Verde is downright dowdy. The curvy balconies on the facade are old-fashioned, and the low-ceilinged lobby does not invite you to linger. But the spacious rooms have pleasant views of the ocean or the city; suites overlook the palm-shaded pool area. The jangling casino is just off the lobby, and on-site restaurants include the poolside restaurant Ciao Mediterranean, Ruth's Chris Steak House, and the Japanese restaurant Momoyama. **Pros:** Lovely pool; on one of the city's best beaches. **Cons:** Chain-hotel feel; unattractive facade; cramped lobby. ✉ *5961 Av. Isla Verde, Isla Verde* ☎ *787/791–6100 or 800/443–2009* 🌐 *www.intercontinental.com/sanjuan* *380 rooms, 22 suites* *In-room: safe, refrigerator, Internet, Wi-Fi. In-hotel: 5 restaurants, room service, bars, pool, gym, spa, beachfront, children's programs (ages 4–13), concierge, laundry service, Internet terminal, Wi-Fi, parking (paid)* *AE, D, MC, V* *EP.* *2:G3*

$$$$ RESORT Fodor's Choice ★ **The Ritz-Carlton, San Juan.** Elegant marble floors and fountains won't undermine the feeling that this is a true beach getaway. The hotel's sandy stretch is lovely, as is the cruciform pool, which is lined by statues of the chain's signature lion. Works by Latin American artists adorn the lobby lounge and the hallways leading to the well-equipped business center. Rooms have a mix of traditional wooden furnishings and wicker pieces upholstered in soft fabrics. Though most room windows are sealed shut to muffle airport noise, many suites open onto terraces, and numerous rooms have balconies. You can pamper yourself at the full-service spa with spirulina algae body wraps and *stone* massages. The lavish casino—the largest on the island—has a separate entrance from the lobby. **Pros:** Top-notch service; excellent restaurant options; pretty pool area. **Cons:** Not much is within walking distance; very expensive for San Juan lodging. ✉ *6961 Av. de los Gobernadores, Isla Verde* ☎ *787/253–1700 or 800/241–3333* 🌐 *www.ritzcarlton.com/sanjuan* *416 rooms, 11 suites* *In-room: safe (some), refrigerator, DVD, Internet, Wi-Fi. In-hotel: 5 restaurants, room service, 5 bars, tennis courts, pool, gym, spa, beachfront, water sports, concierge, children's programs (ages 4–12), laundry service, public Wi-Fi, parking (paid)* *AE, D, DC, MC, V* *EP.* *2:H3*

$$ HOTEL **San Juan Water & Beach Club.** Stepping into the elevators decked out in black lights at this hotel is almost like entering a nightclub. Water is everywhere, from the droplets that decorate the reception desk to the deluge that runs down the glass walls of the elevators. The soft-blue neon glow in the guest rooms, all of which are decorated in a minimalist style, adds to your under-the-sea experience. All the suites are equipped with telescopes for stargazing or peoplewatching along the beach, and all rooms have iPod docks. No matter which room you choose, you'll have a view of the ocean. Wet, the rooftop bar, lets you recline on white leather sofas as you take in the view of the skyline. Tangerine, the street-level restaurant, serves international tapas. **Pros:** Fun atmosphere; interesting

Fodor's Choice ★

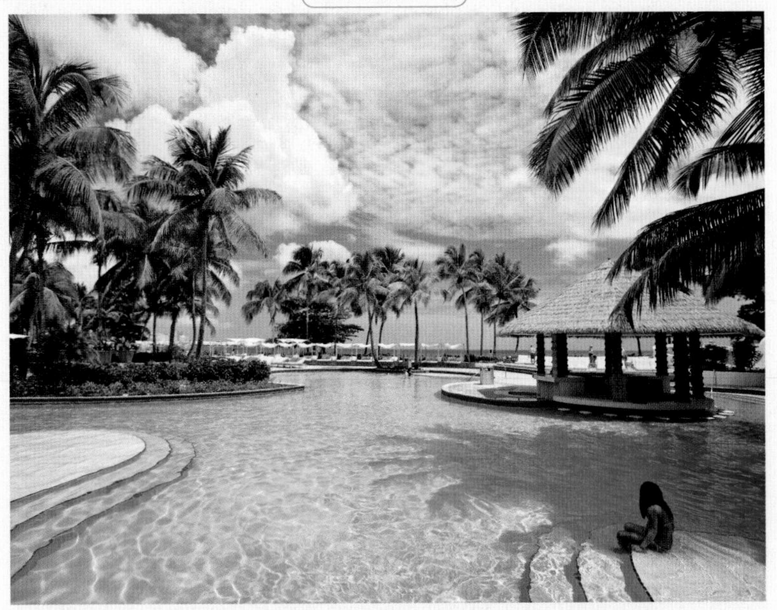

El San Juan Hotel & Casino

The Ritz-Carlton, San Juan

El Convento Hotel

design; great nightlife option. **Cons:** Lack of closet space in rooms. ✉ 2 *Calle Tartak, Isla Verde* ☎ *787/728–3666 or 888/265–6699* 🌐 *www.waterandbeachclubhotel.com* ⇨ *74 rooms, 4 suites* ♨ *In-room: safe, refrigerator, Internet, Wi-Fi. In-hotel: restaurant, room service, bars, pool, gym, beachfront, bicycles, concierge, laundry service, Internet terminal, public Wi-Fi, parking (fee)* ▭ *AE, MC, V* 🍽 *CP.* ⊕ *2:G3*

NIGHTLIFE AND THE ARTS

Several publications will tell you what's happening in San Juan. *Qué Pasa!,* the official visitors' guide, has current listings of events in the city and out on the island. For more up-to-the-minute information, pick up a copy of the *Puerto Rico Daily Sun,* the island's English-language daily. *Bienvenidos,* published by the Puerto Rico Hotel & Tourism Association, is also helpful. *Metro San Juan* (www.metrosanjuan.com) has restaurant reviews and cultural articles.

There are also publications for Spanish-speaking visitors, including the weekend section of the Spanish-language newspaper *El Nuevo Día*; the paper also gives a weekly rundown of events on its Web site, 🌐 *www.elnuevodia.com. Sal!* (🌐 *www.sal.pr*) includes brief restaurant reviews and articles about dining and nightlife. (It's available as an English-language guidebook in bookstores throughout the island.) *Noctámbulo* is a Spanish-language pocket-size music and nightlife guide aimed at island youth that has extensive listings and is distributed in area clubs, bars, and restaurants.

NIGHTLIFE

From Thursday through Sunday, it's as if there's a celebration going on nearly everywhere in San Juan. Be sure you dress to party, particularly on Friday and Saturday nights; Puerto Ricans have flair, and both men and women love getting dressed up to go out. Bars are usually casual, but if you have on jeans, sneakers, and a T-shirt, you may be refused entry at nightclubs and discos.

Well-dressed visitors and locals alike often mingle in the lobby bars of large hotels, many of which have bands in the evening. Some hotels also have clubs with shows and/or dancing; admission starts at $10. Casino rules have been relaxed, injecting life into what was once a conservative hotel gaming scene, but you still won't be allowed in if you're wearing a tank top or shorts. There are more games as well as such gambling perks as free drinks and live music.

In Old San Juan, Calle San Sebastián is lined with bars and restaurants, although the hottest clubs are along and just off Calle Fortaleza. Salsa music blaring from jukeboxes in cut-rate pool halls competes with mellow Latin jazz in top-flight nightspots. The young and the beautiful often socialize in Plaza San José. Late January sees the Fiestas de la Calle San Sebastián, one of the Caribbean's best street parties.

Young professionals as well as a slightly older bohemian crowd fill Santurce, San Juan's historical downtown area, until the wee hours. The revitalized Plaza del Mercado (Calle Dos Hermanos at Calle Capital) has structures—many painted in bright colors—dating from the 1930s or earlier. On weekend nights the area's streets are closed to vehicular traffic. You can wander from dive bars to trendy nightspots and sway to music that pours from countless open-air establishments and the marketplace's front plaza.

BARS

Barlovento. Packed on weekends, this "in" spot is a great place to sip tropical drinks oceanside. It's on a breezy plaza, across from some of the luxury retail shops in Condado. It also has a menu if hunger strikes. ✉ *Plaza Alberto Escudero, 1043 Av. Ashford, Condado* ☎ *787/724–7286.*

Coaches. This typical sports pub is well outfitted with televisions if your travel plans coincide with that game you just can't miss. Local Ivy League graduates often congregate here to watch big sporting events showcasing their alma maters. The annual Harvard–Yale football game can get ugly. The restaurant-bar also becomes a venue for live rock, Latin pop, and reggae bands at night, especially on weekends. Food offerings include U.S.-style burgers, chicken, steaks, and salads, as well as some Mexican food and local goodies. ✉ *137 Av. Roosevelt, Hato Rey* ☎ *787/758–3598.*

El Batey. This wildly popular hole-in-the-wall bar won't win any prizes for its decor. Grab a marker to add your own message to the graffiti-covered walls, or put your business card alongside the hundreds that cover the lighting fixtures. The ceiling may leak, but the jukebox has the best selection of oldies in town. Join locals in a game of pool. ✉ *101 Calle Cristo, Old San Juan* ☎ *787/725–1787.*

Eternal. Decorated in the same modern style of the Condado Plaza hotel, this sleek lounge hosts a range of acts on the weekends, including DJs and live bands, most often salsa, merengue, or Spanish pop. It's a comfortable spot for an evening cocktail during the week as well. ✉ *Conrad San Juan Condado Plaza, 999 Av. Ashford, Condado* ☎ *787/721–1000* 🌐 *www.condadoplaza.com.*

Jam Rum Bar + Bistro Moderne. You can come here earlier in the evening to eat a terrific meal, but this hidden spot in the heart of Condado is also a great place for a drink. The bar showcases more than 50 rums from around the world, including all the rums of Puerto Rico. You can try rum flights or one of many inventive rum-based cocktails—in addition to the regular bar. There's live music from Thursday to Saturday. ✉ *Casabella Building, 1400 Av. Magdalena, Condado* ☎ *787/721–5991.*

Old Harbor Brewery. Serious sudsters know to head to this authentic brewpub close to the harborfront. More clubby than pubby, it packs in locals as well as tourists who come to taste brewmaster Peter Boettcher's five delicious German-style beers. Order the five-beer sampler before making a selection for a pint-glass or liter stein. Jazz buffs should call in on Saturday night for live music. (✉ *202 Calle Tizol at Calle Recinto Sur, Plaza del Inmigrante, Old San Juan* ☎ *787/721–2100* 🌐 *www.oldharborbrewery.com.*

Wet. On the roof of the San Juan Water & Beach Club Hotel, this sexy spot offers some of the best ocean views anywhere in Isla Verde. On the weekends there's a DJ, and locals pack in to relax at the bar or on the leather beds reserved for bottle service. ✉ *San Juan Water & Beach Club, 2 Calle Tartak, Isla Verde* ☎ *787/725–4664.*

CASINOS

By law, all casinos are in hotels, and the government keeps a close eye on them. They're allowed to operate twenty-four hours a day, but individual casinos set their own hours. In addition to slot machines, typical games include blackjack, roulette, craps, Caribbean stud poker (a five-card stud game), and *pai gow* poker (a combination of American poker and the ancient Chinese game of *pai gow*, which employs cards and dice). That said, an easing of gaming regulations has set a more relaxed tone and made such perks as free drinks and live music more common. The range of available games has also greatly expanded. The minimum age is 18. Dress for the larger casinos in San Juan tends to be on the formal side, and the atmosphere is refined. Tank tops or shorts are usually not acceptable attire.

The Casino at The Ritz-Carlton, San Juan. With its golden columns, turquoise and bronze walls, and muted lighting, the Ritz casino is refined by day or night. There's lots of activity, yet everything is hushed. ✉ *6991 Av. de los Gobernadores, Isla Verde* ☎ *787/253–1700.*

Conrad San Juan Condado Plaza Hotel & Casino. Popular with locals, the casino at the Condado Plaza received a top-to-bottom makeover in 2007. But it's still one of the least interesting of the city's gaming rooms, worth a visit only if you're staying in the hotel or if you're looking for one open 24 hours a day. ✉ *999 Av. Ashford, Condado* ☎ *787/721–1000.*

InterContinental San Juan Resort & Casino. You may feel as if you're in Las Vegas here, perhaps because this property was once a Sands. Inside, a garish chandelier dripping with strands of orange lights runs the length of a mirrored ceiling. ✉ *5961 Av. Isla Verde, Isla Verde* ☎ *787/791–6100.*

El San Juan Hotel & Casino, The Waldorf Astoria Collection. Neither the clangs of the slots nor the sounds of the salsa band disrupt the semblance of Old World. The polish continues in the adjacent lobby, with its huge chandeliers and mahogany paneling. ✉ *6063 Av. Isla Verde, Isla Verde* ☎ *787/791–1000.*

San Juan Marriott Resort & Stellaris Casino. The crowd is casual, and the decor is tropical and bubbly at this spacious gaming room. A huge bar, where Latin musicians perform on weekends, and an adjacent café are right outside. ✉ *1309 Av. Ashford, Condado* ☎ *787/722–7000.*

Sheraton Old San Juan Hotel & Casino. It's impossible to ignore this ground-floor casino, the only place to gamble in Old San Juan. You can see the gaming room—expanded in 2007—from the hotel's main stairway, the balcony above, and the lobby. Light bounces off the Bahía de San Juan and pours through its many windows; passengers bound off their cruise ships and pour through its many glass doors. ✉ *101 Calle Brumbaugh, Old San Juan* ☎ *787/721–5100.*

Continued on page 109

Salsa

A Guide to Puerto Rico's Favorite Music and Dance

Salsa: its hip-shaking rhythms and sensual moves embody the spirit of the Caribbean and Latin America. The songs and the steps create a language all their own—one that's spoken by passionate dancers and musicians the world over. But it's the Puerto Ricans who are the most fluent. Welcome to the home of salsa! Are you ready to dance?

As the first notes of the song sound, dancers come alive, eager to take their place on the floor with a partner whose skill matches their own. These are the most daring salsa devotees who are found in every corner of the island, dancers who won't quit moving until the music stops. Even as a bystander, it's impossible to stand still.

Salsa isn't a passive rhythm: it's animated, hot, and sensual, a metaphor for the Caribbean itself. In general, the themes of the songs mirror the moves of the dance, with choruses alluding to love, both forbidden and open. In the music and the movement, there's occasional improvisation among those who know the genre. Hips shake to the clave, which marks the basic rhythm, and shoulders shake from one side to the other, fanning the air. It's a democratic form, where experimentation is encouraged . . . you just have to be willing to get out there.

by Julie Schwietert Collazo

SALSA HISTORY

Timbale master Tito Puente

Though salsa has its roots outside Puerto Rico, the island is directly responsible for the rhythm known by this name. As a musical form, the components of salsa can be traced back to Europe and Africa. During the colonial period, Spanish conquistadores arriving from the West Indies brought island rhythms along with them. They also brought the complex, multi-rhythmic riffs of Arabic music, an artifact of the Muslim conquest of the Iberian Peninsula that had become embedded in the music of Spain and Portugal. In Puerto Rico, all of these musical strands came together to create a new rhythm known as bomba.

The emergence of salsa was deeply influenced by musical forms from nearby Cuba and other parts of the Caribbean, as well as musical experimentation by diaspora Puerto Ricans living in New York. Among the most important of these mainland musicians was percussionist and band leader Tito Puente.

The history of salsa is the history of the new world. In salsa, there's evidence of rhythms from past ages, as well as the musical history of our own time. Salsa isn't a "pure" musical form, but represents—like Puerto Rico itself—a mixture of rhythmic elements, adapted by the inhabitants of the new world.

DID YOU KNOW?

- The first use of the word "salsa" related to music was in 1937 by Cuban composer Igancio Pineiro in his popular song, "Echale Salsita." It continues to be a frequently recorded song today by artists in and outside Cuba.
- The song "Oye Como Va" was originally composed by Tito Puente in 1963 and later recorded by Carlos Santana, who made it a number-one hit.
- The contribution of salsa to jazz music dates from 1940, when Dizzie Gillespie and Stan Kenton incorporated salsa in their tunes, giving birth to "Latin jazz."
- More than 30 countries celebrate salsa with annual festivals, among them, Poland, Israel, France, Serbia, and Japan.

SALSA SPEAK

ABRAZO: The *abrazo* is the positioning of the partners' hands and arms. The woman's left hand rests lightly on her partner's shoulder, while his right hand is placed on the small of her back to guide her. The abrazo establishes the space each partner maintains during turns.

Abrazo

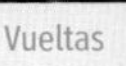

Vueltas

VUELTAS: *Vueltas*, turns, are an important component of salsa. There are numerous styles, and they can occur in both directions, but all are determined and initiated by the male partner. Turns are spontaneous; their complexity depends upon the skill and experience of the dancers.

Solos

SOLOS: Solos—a favorite move of experienced dancers—are moments when the partners separate to move independently though still in response to each other. These are often synchronized with the solos of percussion musicians. Solos are also used as a means of rest after a series of complex turns before the pair comes together again for even more intricate turns.

SALSA STYLE

Two elements define salsa fashion: comfort and sensuality. Men and women both draw from the best of their wardrobes, with men often dressed in guayabera shirts, linen pants, and two-toned dance shoes. Suede shoes permit optimal movement for men and add a touch of elegance. Women typically wear dresses—often knee length or shorter—and open-toed, medium-heeled dance shoes with ankle support. For both men and women, freedom of movement and maximum ventilation are important elements of a salsa wardrobe.

The dance is an opportunity to show off your elegance and your sensuality, but your clothing should also honor the significance of the event and venue. Many dance organizers impose dress policies, prohibiting running shoes, sleeveless shirts, and overly informal or provocative clothing. Dress to impress.

Salsa dance shoes

NEXT STEPS

If you're ready to take to the dance floor, here are some of the best places to learn—and then show off—your moves.

LESSONS

The Academia de Baile Julie Mayoral. On the Plaza de las Delicias in Ponce, Mayoral's second floor studio is steaming hot, and her young, enthusiastic instructors will have you doing proper vueltas in no time. For a bit more than $5 for an hour lesson, Mayoral probably offers the best deal in Puerto Rico. Mayoral also has studios in Coamo and Yauco. Call her Ponce studio (☎ 787/843–2830) for information about lessons at any of the three studios.

In San Juan, dancer Paulette Beauchamp offers salsa classes for adults on Tuesday and Thursday. Her studio, **DanzActiva** (☎ 787/775–9438 ⊕ www.danzactiva.com), is in the historic Cuartel de Ballaja building in Old San Juan.

HOTELS

Locals and tourists alike take to the dance floor at the **San Juan Marriott Resort** and **Stellaris Casino** on weekends, when homegrown musicians provide a soundtrack for the salsa experience. Entry is free, but you'll need to purchase drinks if you decide to rest at one of the tables circling the dance floor.

CLUBS

Old San Juan's **Nuyorican Café** looks like a dive—and it is—but it's the heart of Puerto Rico's salsa scene. Though the café also hosts jazz and rock groups as well as poetry readings and experimental theatre, its reputation for world-class salsa has expanded far beyond the island. Call ahead for the current schedule (☎ 787/977–1276).

FESTIVALS

As the home of salsa, Puerto Rico hosts an annual **International Salsa Congress.** It's held in San Juan each July, though the site changes each year. The congress attracts thousands of aficionados from the island and from surprisingly far-flung places, including Japan, Korea, and Norway.

(left) A couple prepares for competition at the International Salsa Congress held in San Juan. (right) Young dancers performing at the International Salsa Congress.

CLOSE UP

The Piña Colada Wars

This mixture of pineapple juice, coconut cream, and liberal amounts of rum, always garnished with a wedge of pineapple and a maraschino cherry, was invented by Ramón Marrero at the Caribe Hilton in 1954 or by Ramón Portas Mingot at the Barranchina Bar in 1963, depending on whom you believe. Was it Marrero, a young bartender who is said to have spent three months on a concoction that would appeal to patrons at the Beachcomber's Bar? (His secret? Using only fresh pineapple juice.) Or was it Mingot, an elderly bartender who was satisfying the whims of patrons at the bar in Old San Juan? (He said his were so frothy because he froze the pineapple juice and coconut cream mixture instead of simply adding crushed ice.)

The two venues have fought over bragging rights for decades. The Caribe Hilton issues press release after press release reminding people that the drink was born in its seaside bar. (If what its public relations department says is true, the drink celebrated its 50th anniversary in 2004.) The Barranchina Bar put up a plaque that tells passersby that it is the true birthplace of the beverage. The Caribe Hilton seems to have the edge. Coco López, the company that makes the coconut cream most often used in the drink, honored Marrero in 1978. In gratitude for his contributions to the "bartending arts," they presented him with a color television set. But the origins of the piña colada—which means "strained pineapple"—remains as unclear as the cocktail itself. You may have to sample several before you make up your own mind.

—Mark Sullivan

DANCE CLUBS

Blend. This hip SoFo nightspot draws fashionistas enamored of the black walls, neon-blue lighting, and eye-candy female waitstaff. You can settle in at the marble-topped bar, nestle cozily in a banquet sofa, or dance to salsa, techno, and world beat music in the dancehall to the rear. It serves late-night nouvelle native cuisine. ✉ *309 Calle Fortaleza, Old San Juan* ☎ *787/977–7777.*

Brava. A long line of young people can be spotted at the door of this chic club at the El San Juan Hotel & Casino. The two-level club, each with its own DJ and dance floor, is one of the best places for dancing. There's a different theme party Thursday through Saturday. ✉ *6063 Av. Isla Verde, Isla Verde* ☎ *787/641–3500* 🌐 *www.bravapr.com.*

Club Lazer. This multilevel club has spots for quiet conversation, spaces for dancing to loud music, and a landscaped roof deck overlooking San Juan. The crowd changes every night; Saturday is ladies' night, when male strippers sometimes perform. ✉ *251 Calle Cruz, Old San Juan* ☎ *787/725–7581.*

The Noise. A young crowd frequents this tunnel-like Old San Juan dance club to listen to hip-hop, reggae, and underground music. Long lines often spill out the door Thursday through Saturday nights. ✉ *203 Calle Tacna, Old San Juan* ☎ *787/724–3426.*

GAY AND LESBIAN BARS AND CLUBS

With its sophisticated nightlife, San Juan has become a popular destination for gay and lesbian tourists. The Condado, perhaps the heart of gay San Juan, is a favorite destination for happy hour. It hosts an annual gay-pride march each June, full of music and dancing, that rivals those in similar cities around the world. Santurce, just south of Condado, is packed with bars and clubs that cater to men and women of all ages. Most are located on or near Avenida Ponce de León.

REGGAETÓN

If you go out to San Juan's popular dance clubs, you're likely to hear this hip-hop–influenced mix of Jamaican reggae and dancehall styles along with some Latin rhythms. The music has a strong electronic drum-machine beat, and the lyrics are in Spanish. Many believe the music got its start in Puerto Rico, but its popularity has spread much farther.

Puerto Rico Breeze (🌐 *www.orgulloboricua.net*) is a monthly newspaper covering Puerto Rico's gay and lesbian community. It's chock-full of listings, articles, and advertisements on dining options, entertainment, and lodging alternatives.

Atlantic Beach. The oceanfront-deck bar of this hotel is famed in the gay community for its early-evening happy hours. But the pulsating tropical music, exotic drinks, and ever-pleasant ocean breeze make it a hit regardless of sexual orientation. Good food is also served on deck. ✉ *1 Calle Vendig, Condado* ☎ *787/721–6900.*

Cups. This women-oriented bar in the middle of Santurce has been a mainstay of San Juan's nightlife since 1980. Karaoke on Thursday night is especially popular. It's open Thursday through Sunday. ✉ *1708 Calle San Mateo, Santurce* ☎ *787/268–3570.*

Krash. A balcony bar overlooks all the drama on the dance floor at this popular club. Most of the time DJs spin music ranging from house and hip-hop to salsa and *reggaetón*, but occasionally disco nights send you back to the music of the 1970s and '80s. It's open Wednesday through Saturday. ✉ *1257 Av. Ponce de León, Santurce* ☎ *787/722–1131* 🌐 *www.krashklubpr.com.*

Junior's. Open every evening, this neighborhood bar attracts nearly equal numbers of men and women. The jukebox plays a constant stream of salsa, which often draws crowds to the dance floor. It has some of the cheapest drinks in town. ✉ *613 Av. Condado, Santurce* ☎ *787/723–9477.*

Starz. Dancing at this cavernous club starts at 10 PM on Friday and Saturday nights, but most people don't arrive until after midnight. There's also a popular after-the-beach party on Sunday evening. ✉ *365 Av. de Diego, at Av. Ponce de León, Santurce* ☎ *787/721–8645* 🌐 *www.starzclub.com.*

LATIN MUSIC

Hijos de Borinquen. Famed artist Rafael Tufiño, who stops in once in a while and has a stool with his name on it, immortalized this beloved bar in one of his paintings. The audience, which packs in like sardines, often sings along with the Puerto Rican ballads; some even play maracas, cowbells, or bongos. The pitch is fevered during Andrés Jiménez's revolutionary anthem, "Despierta Borinquen." It's closed Monday but on other nights often keeps going until sun-up. ✉ *151 Calle San José, at Calle San Sebastián, Old San Juan* ☎ *787/723–8126.*

★ **Nuyorican Café.** There's something interesting happening at this hipper-than-hip, no-frills, wood-paneled performance space nearly every night, be it an early evening play, poetry reading, or talent show or, later on, a band playing Latin jazz, Cuban son, Puerto Rican salsa, or even rock. During breaks between performances the youthful, creative set converses in an alley outside the front door. It's usually closed on Monday. ✉ *312 Calle San Fransico (entrance on Callejón de la Capellia), Old San Juan* ☎ *787/977–1276* 🌐 www.nuyoricancafepr.com.

Rumba. The air-conditioning blasts, the music thumps, and the under-30s crowd pretends not to notice how hip the place has become. With a large dance and stage area and smokin' Afro-Cuban bands, it's one of the best parties in town. Things cool down for jazz on Wednesday night. ✉ *152 Calle San Sebastián, Old San Juan* ☎ *787/725–4407.*

NIGHT BITES

San Juan is a cosmopolitan city by Caribbean standards, welcoming to all kinds of visitors, with plenty of late-night places. The establishments listed here are generally open until at least midnight during the week and 2 AM on weekends. But many are open much later. Old San Juan's Brickhaus, for example, proudly proclaims that its kitchen doesn't close until 3 AM.

Brickhaus Sports Bar & Grill. This friendly bar and sidewalk café on Old San Juan's bustling Plaza Somohano is adjacent to the Teatro Tapia. You can get tasty burgers until 3 AM as well as plenty of good conversation. If you eat elsewhere, you might run into your server here, after his or her shift ends. ✉ *359 Calle Tetuán, Old San Juan* ☎ *787/724–3359* 🌐 www.thebrickhaus.net.

Burén. Across the street from the Hotel El Convento, this funky, tropical-color bistro with a charming interior patio serves good pizza and pasta as well as Caribbean- and Mediterranean-inspired dishes until midnight. You can also get bargain-priced martinis and mojitos on weekdays. The house wines by the glass are all good, and there's often live jazz or flamenco music. ✉ *103 Calle Cristo, Old San Juan* ☎ *787/977–5023.*

Hard Rock Cafe. Are you really surprised to find that there's a Hard Rock in Old San Juan? This one attracts a surprising number of locals for its well-versed upscale ambience, musicians' memorabilia, and eclectic menu. ✉ *253 Recinto Sur, Old San Juan* ☎ *787/724–7625* 🌐 www.hardrock.com.

Makarios. Italy meets the Middle East, brick-oven pizza meets hummus, and crostinis meet falafel on a big outdoor-seating area that spills onto a plaza. The first indoor level is a sleek, modern bar with Western music and a small dining area that serves pizza and snacks. Upstairs is more serious Middle Eastern cuisine, hypnotic rhythms, and a skillful belly dancer on Friday and Saturday nights. ✉ *356 Calle Tetuán, Old San Juan* ☎ *787/723–8653.*

El Patio de Sam. The clientele swears that this Old San Juan institution serves the island's best burgers. Potted plants and strategically placed canopies make the outdoor patio overlooking Plaza San José a fine place to eat in any weather. ✉ *102 Calle San Sebastián, Old San Juan* ☎ *787/723–1149.*

Señor Frog's. Latin America's answer to the Hard Rock Cafe, Señor Frog's attracts the cruise-ship crowd—no surprise, as it recently relocated to a spot directly in front of the dock. The menu is a nod to Mexico, with south-of-the-border favorites like nachos and quesadillas. And there's now live music nightly. ✉ *Paseo Gilberto Concepción de Gracia, corner of Brumbaugh, Old San Juan* ☎ *787/977–4142.*

THE ARTS

San Juan is arguably one of the most important cultural centers of the Caribbean, both for its homegrown culture and the healthy influx of visiting artists that the local population supports. The city hosts the Puerto Rico Symphony Orchestra, the world-renowned Pablo Casals classical-music festival in winter, and an annual series of opera concerts. Many hit plays in New York and other large markets get produced locally, and there are often three or four other local theatrical productions taking place on any given weekend, many of them downright adventurous.

If you're in town on the first Tuesday of the month, take advantage of Old San Juan's **Noches de Galerias** (☎ *787/723–6286*). Galleries and select museums open their doors after hours for viewings that are accompanied by refreshments and music. Afterward, people head to bars and music clubs, and the area remains festive until well past midnight. The event is so popular that finding a parking space is difficult; it's best to take a cab.

ISLAND CULTURE

The year-round festival called **Le Lo Lai** *(☎ 787/721–2400 🌐 www.gotopuertorico.com)*celebrates Puerto Rico's Taíno Indian, Spanish, and African heritage. Performances showcasing island music and folklore take place Tuesday, Friday, and Saturday around San Juan. It's sponsored by the Puerto Rico Tourism Company.

PERFORMING ARTS

MAJOR EVENTS **The Casals Festival** (☎ *787/721–7727* 🌐 *www.festcasalspr.gobierno.pr*) has been bringing some of the most important figures in classical music to San Juan ever since Pablo Casals, the famous cellist, conductor, and composer, started the festival in 1957. Casals went on to direct it until his death in 1973. It has continued to serve as a vibrant stage for top-notch classical performers since then. Most of the shows are held at the Centro de Bellas Artes Luis A. Ferré, but performances are also at the University of Puerto Rico and other venues. The festival takes place from mid-February through mid-March. Tickets are available at the box office of the Centro de Bellas Artes Luis A Ferré.

San Juan is a great place to hear jazz, particularly Latin jazz, and the annual **Puerto Rico Heineken Jazzfest** (☎ *866/994–0001 or 787/294–0001* 🌐 *www.prheinekenjazz.com*), which takes place in late May at the Tito Puente Amphitheater, is one of the best opportunities for it. Each year's festival is dedicated to a particular musician. Honorees have included Chick Corea, Mongo Santamaria, and Tito Puente.

TICKETS Two major outlets sell tickets for events throughout Puerto Rico. **Ticket Center** (✉ *Plaza Las Américas, 525 Av. Franklin Delano Roosevelt, Hato Rey*

☎ 787/792–5000 🌐 *www.tcpr.com*) can get you seats to most large-scale events. **Ticketpop** (✉ *Banco Popular, 1500 Av. Ponce de León, Santurce* ☎ *866/994–0001 or 787/294–0001* 🌐 *www.ticketpop.com*) also sells tickets to popular events.

ART FOR ART'S SAKE

Many galleries stay open during Old San Juan's Noches de Galerías, held from 6 pm to 9 pm on the first Tuesday of the month, September to December and February to May.

PERFORMANCE VENUES

Anfiteatro Tito Puente *(Tito Puente Amphitheater)*. Surrounded by lagoons and trees, the open-air theater is a great spot to hear hot Latin jazz, reggae, and Spanish pop music. It's named after the late, great musician who is widely credited with bringing salsa to the rest of the world. Shows usually take place Thursday through Sunday nights. ✉ *Parque Luis Muñoz Marín,Hato Rey* ☎ *787/294–0001 or 866/994–0001.*

Centro de Bellas Artes Luis A. Ferré *(Luis A. Ferré Center for the Performing Arts)*. With three different theaters, the largest of which holds up to 1,800 people, this is the largest venue of its kind in the Caribbean. There's something going on nearly every night, from pop or jazz concerts to plays, operas, and ballets. It's also the home of the Puerto Rico Symphony Orchestra. ✉ *Av. Ponce de León, Parada 22½, Santurce* ☎ *787/725–7334.*

Coliseo Roberto Clemente. The arena has become an important island venue for concerts in addition to its status as a sports facility. Rap, reggae, salsa, jazz, and pop musicians all play this venue, which holds 10,000 people. ✉ *500 Av. Roosevelt across from Plaza las Américas, Hato Rey* ☎ *787/754–7422.*

Estadio Hiram Bithorn *(Hiram Bithorn Stadium)*. Particularly big acts often use this outdoor stadium adjacent to the Coliseo Roberto Clemente, which hosts baseball games and large concerts. There's seating capacity for at least 18,000, more when the infield is used for fans. ✉ *Av. Roosevelt at Plaza las Américas, Hato Rey* ☎ *787/725–2110.*

Teatro Tapia. Named for Puerto Rican playwright Alejandro Tapia y Rivera, the theater hosts traveling and locally produced theatrical and musical productions. Matinee performances with family entertainment are also held here, especially around the holidays. ✉ *Calle Fortaleza, Plaza Colón, Old San Juan* ☎ *787/723–7800.*

GROUPS

Orquesta Sinfónica de Puerto Rico *(Puerto Rico Symphony Orchestra)*. The island's orchestra is one of the most prominent in the Americas. Under the direction of conductor Maximiano Valdés, its 80 members perform a full 52-week season that includes classical-music concerts, operas, ballets, and popular-music performances. The orchestra plays most shows at Centro de Bellas Artes Luis A. Ferré, but it also gives outdoor concerts at museums and university campuses around the island, and it has an educational outreach program in island schools. Pablo Casals, the impetus for this group, helped create it in 1956. ☎ *787/721–7727* 🌐 *www.sinfonicapr.gobierno.pr.*

SHOPPING

In Old San Juan, Calle Fortaleza and Calle San Francisco have everything from T-shirt emporiums to jewelry stores to shops that specialize in made-to-order Panama hats. Running perpendicular to those streets is Calle Cristo, lined with factory-outlet stores, including Coach, Gant, Guess, and Ralph Lauren. On weekends, artisans sell their wares at stalls around Paseo de la Princesa.

With many stores selling luxury items and designer fashions, the shopping spirit in Condado is reminiscent of that in Miami. Avenida Ashford is considered the heart of San Juan's fashion district. High-end chain stores such as Chanel, Ferragamo, and Gucci are huddled together in what was formerly a derelict shopping strip. They are betting that the newly renovated, luxury hotel La Concha will attract people ready to plunk down their platinum credit cards. A little farther west along Avenida Ashford are the one-of-a-kind clothing retailers that make this a not-to-be-missed neighborhood.

Just as in most other American cities, however, the real shopping occurs in the mall, and the upscale mall here, Plaza Las Américas—the largest in the Caribbean—is not to be missed. Known to locals simply as "Plaza," it's often host to artisan crafts fairs, art exhibitions, antique shows, live Latin music, and pageants, depending on the time of year.

Thanks to Puerto Rico's vibrant art scene, numerous galleries and studios are opening, and many are doing so in Santurce and other neighborhoods outside the Old City walls. If you prefer shopping in air-conditioned comfort, there are plenty of malls in and just outside San Juan.

MARKETS AND MALLS

★ Look for vendors selling crafts from around the island at the **Artesanía Puertorriqueña** (✉ *Plaza de la Dársena, Old San Juan* ☎ *787/722–1709*). It's convenient for cruise-ship passengers, as it's across from Pier 1. Several vendors also sell handbags, hats, and other items along nearby Paseo de la Princesa.

About 10 minutes east of San Juan, you'll find **Plaza Carolina** (✉ *Av. Fragosa, Carolina* ☎ *787/768–0514*). Get there via Route 26. **Plaza del Sol** (✉ *725 West Main Ave., Bayamón* ☎ *787/778–8724*) includes Old Navy and Banana Republic. It's about 30 minutes west of San Juan. For a complete shopping experience, head to **Plaza Las Américas** (✉ *525 Av. Franklin Delano Roosevelt, Hato Rey* ☎ *787/767–5202*), which has more than 300 retailers, including the world's largest JCPenney store, Borders, Build-A-Bear Workshop, Gap, Sears, Macy's, Sephora, Coach, Forever 21, BCBG Maxazria, L'Occitane, Godiva, and Armani Exchange, as well as restaurants and movie theaters. Off Avenida John F. Kennedy, about 15 minutes south of San Juan, **Plaza San Patricio** (✉ *100 Av. San Patricio at Av. Franklin Delano Roosevelt, Guaynabo* ☎ *787/792–1255*) has a Boston Shoe and a Footaction USA, as well as restaurants and movie theaters.

FACTORY OUTLETS

With no sales tax, Old San Juan has turned into an open-air duty-free shop for people pouring off the cruise ships. Because they have only a few hours in port, they often pass by more interesting shops and head directly for the factory outlets on and around Calle Cristo. The prices aren't particularly good, but nobody seems to mind. Designer bags can be had at **Coach** (✉ *158 Calle Cristo* ☎ *787/722–6830*). Taking up several storefronts, **Ralph Lauren** (✉ *Calle Cristo and Calle Fortaleza* ☎ *787/722–2136*) has perhaps the best deals around. Stop here toward the end of your trip, as there are plenty of items such as pea coats and scarves that you won't be wearing until you get home.

There's clothing for men and women at **Tommy Hilfiger** (✉ *206 Calle Cristo* ☎ *787/729–2230*). The staff is eager to please.

★ It's not in Old San Juan, but **Belz Factory Outlet World** (✉ *18400 Rte. 3, Km 18.4,* ☎ *787/256–7040*) has more than 135 factory outlet stores, including BCBG, Children's Place, Nautica, Nike, Guess, Gap, and Polo Ralph Lauren. It's in Canóvanas, about 20 minutes east of San Juan.

SPECIALTY SHOPS

ART

★ The very influential **Galería Botello** (✉ *208 Calle Cristo, Old San Juan* ☎ *787/723–9987* 🌐 *www.botello.com*) displays the works of the late Angel Botelli, who was hailed as the "Caribbean Gauguin" as far back as 1943. His work, which often uses the bright colors of the tropics, usually depicts island scenes. His paintings hang in the Museo de Arte de Puerto Rico. There are works on display here by other prominent local artists as well.

★ Among those who have displayed their works at **Galería Petrus** (✉ *726 Calle Hoare, Miramar* ☎ *787/289–0505* 🌐 *www.petrusgallery.com*) are Dafne Elvira, whose surreal oils and acrylics tease and seduce (witness a woman emerging from a banana peel); Marta Pérez, another surrealist, whose bewitching paintings examine such themes as how life on a coffee plantation might have been; and Elizam Escobar, a former political prisoner whose oil paintings convey the horrors human beings must endure. Petrus also sells the architectonic designs of Imel Sierra (who created the sculpture *Paloma* in Condado), which combine wood and metal elements.

Galería San Juan (✉ *204–206 Calle Norzagaray, Old San Juan* ☎ *787/722–1808*) shows sensuous sculptures of faces and bodies by artist Jan D'Esopo. The gallery—a part of the guesthouse she runs—is a work of art in itself. It is a bit hard to find, so look for the busts over the front door.**Galería Viota** (✉ *793 Av. San Patricio, Las Lomas* ☎ *787/782–1752* 🌐 *www.violetagallery.com*) offers regularly changing works by contemporary Latin American artists.

CIGARS

The **Cigar House** (✉ *255 Calle Fortaleza, Old San Juan* ☎ *787/723–5223* 🌐 *www.thecigarhousepr.com*) has a small, eclectic selection of local and imported cigars. It has two other locations nearby.

CLOTHING

MEN'S CLOTHING

At **El Galpón** (✉ *154 Calle Cristo, Old San Juan* ☎ *787/725–3945* 🌐 *www.elgalpon.net*), knowledgeable owners Betsy and Gustavo will fit you with a Panama hat, from $45 to $900.

After many years of catering to a primarily local clientele, **Clubman** (✉ *1351 Av. Ashford, Condado* ☎ *787/722–1867*) is still the classic choice for gentlemen's clothing. **Monsieur** (✉ *1126 Av. Ashford, Condado* ☎ *787/722–0918*) has stylish casual clothing for men. In his shop called **Otto** (✉ *69 Av. Condado, Condado* ☎ *787/722–4609*), local designer Otto Bauzá stocks his own line of casual wear for younger men.Aficionados of the famous Panama hat, made from delicately hand-woven straw, should stop at **Olé** (✉ *105 Calle Fortaleza, Old San Juan* ☎ *787/724–2445*). The shop sells top-of-the-line hats for as much as $1,000.

MEN'S & WOMEN'S CLOTHING

With a hipper style than that of most other Condado boutiques, **Abitto** (✉ *1124 Av. Ashford, Condado* ☎ *787/724–0303*) is always filled with young people waving around their credit cards. ★ **Casa Galesa** (✉ *108 Calle Cruz, Old San Juan* ☎ *787/977–0400*) has gorgeous older pieces mixed in with some lovely reproductions. Prolific designer **David Antonio** (✉ *69 Av. Condado, Condado* ☎ *787/725–0600*) runs a shop that's small but full of surprises. His joyful creations range from updated versions of the men's classic *guayabera* shirt to fluid chiffon and silk tunics and dresses for women.

★ For nearly two decades, Robert and Sharon Bartos of **El Alcázar** (✉ *103 Calle San José, Old San Juan* ☎ *787/723–1229*) have been selling antiques and objets d'art from all over the world.

★ **Nono Maldonado** (✉ *1112 Av. Ashford, 2nd floor, Condado* ☎ *787/721–0456*) is well known for his high-end, elegant designs for men and women. He should know a thing or two about style—he worked for many years as the fashion editor of *Esquire* and presents a twice-yearly couture collection.

WOMEN'S CLOTHING

E'Leonor (✉ *1310 Av. Ashford, Condado* ☎ *787/725–3208*) is a well-established store for bridal apparel, evening gowns, and cocktail dresses as well as more casual attire. Look for designs by Vera Wang and St. John. **Harry Robles** (✉ *1752 Calle Loíza, Ocean Park* ☎ *787/727–3885*) sells his elegant gowns in this shop.**Lisa Cappalli** (✉ *151 Av. José de Diego, Condado* ☎ *787/724–6575*) sells her lacy, sensuous designs in this boutique. **Mademoiselle** (✉ *1504 Av. Ashford, Condado* ☎ *787/728–7440*) sells mostly European apparel, including NewMan, Bianca, and Cambio.

Mia (✉ *1104 Av. Ashford, Condado* ☎ *787/724–2147*) is the place for sophisticated outfits that look as if they belong in an art gallery—either on display or on one of the artists.

The window displays at **Nativa** (✉ *55 Calle Cervantes, Condado* ☎ *787/724–1396*) are almost as daring as the clothes it sells. **Pasarela** (✉ *1302 Av. Ashford, Condado* ☎ *787/724–5444*), which means "catwalk" in Spanish, seems a fitting name for a boutique offering designs by the likes of Nicole Miller, Luca Luca, La Perla, and Renato Nucci. **Verovero** (✉ *1302 Av. Ashford, Condado* ☎ *787/725–2332*) stocks women's shoes that look as if they were dreamed up by engineers. These gravity-defying styles are mostly from Italian designers.

San Juan shopping options include Plaza las Américas, the largest mall in the Caribbean.

FURNITURE AND ANTIQUES

★ For nearly two decades, Robert and Sharon Bartos of **El Alcázar** (✉ *103 Calle San José, Old San Juan* ☎ *787/723–1229*) have been selling antiques and objets d'art from all over the world.

Casa Galesa (✉ *108 Calle Cruz, Old San Juan* ☎ *787/977–0400*) has gorgeous older pieces mixed in with some lovely reproductions.

GIFTS

Exotic *mariposas* cover the walls of **Butterfly People** (✉ *257 Calle de la Cruz, Old San Juan* ☎ *787/732–2432* 🌐 *www.butterflypeople.com*). Clear plastic cases hold everything from a pair of common butterflies to dozens of rarer specimens in this lovely shop. Only the YOU BREAK IT, YOU BOUGHT IT signs detract from the colorful display. You can find many unique spices and sauces from around the Caribbean, kitchen items, and cookbooks at **Spicy Caribbee** (✉ *154 Calle Cristo, Old San Juan* ☎ *787/725–7259* 🌐 *www.spicycaribbee.com*).

HANDICRAFTS

★ **Arte & Máscaras** (✉ *222 Calle San José, Old San Juan* ☎ *787/724–9020*) has walls covered with festival masks made all over Puerto Rico. The **Haitian Gallery** (✉ *206 Calle Fortaleza, Old San Juan* ☎ *787/721–4362* 🌐 *www.haitiangallerypr.com*) carries Puerto Rican crafts as well as folksy, often inexpensive paintings from around the Caribbean. **Magia** (✉ *99 Calle Cristo, Old San Juan* ☎ *787/386–6164*) is the most clever shop in San Juan. At first the items on display look like traditional crafts, but look closer and you'll notice that everything is a bit offbeat. A little wooden shrine, for example, might be sheltering an image of Marilyn Monroe.

CLOSE UP

Design Lions

Puerto Rico's young fashion designers have opened many a boutique and atelier in metropolitan San Juan during the last few years. Their styles may differ, but these young lions all share an island heritage—complete with a tradition of true craftsmanship—and a level of sophistication acquired after studying and traveling abroad. The result is a fascinating assortment of original, exclusive, high-quality designs.

With all the warmth and sun, it goes without saying that Puerto Rico's designers are most inspired when it comes to creations for the spring and summer seasons. Lacy, flowing creations and lightweight, if not sheer, fabrics dominate designs for women. For men the trend is toward updated linen classics in tropical whites and creams. Whatever you find will be one of a kind, with stylish—if not playful or downright sexy—lines. Some of these designers have their own shops in San Juan.

Which designers should you check out? Lisa Cappalli, a graduate of New York City's Parsons School of Design, favors lace, as lace making is a tradition in her family. David Antonio uses upbeat colors—bold reds and vibrant oranges—in his updated classics. Harry Robles is a bit more established than his peers; he specializes in gowns for women, and his draping designs are often dramatic and always elegant. Each of these young designers has a shop in San Juan.

To see their collections, consider visiting during San Juan Fashion Week, which takes place each year in March and September. The events are full of shows and cocktail parties, all organized by the Puerto Rico Fashion Designers Group under the leadership of island-fashion icons Nono Maldonado and Mirtha Rubio.

—Isabel Abislaimán

★ Near Old San Juan's main square, **Mundo Taino** (✉ *151 San José, Old San Juan* ☎ *787/724–2005*) sells high-quality folk art from around the island. **Mi Pequeño San Juan** (✉ *107 Calle Cristo, Old San Juan* ☎ *787/977–1636* 🌐 *www.mipequenosanjuan.com*) specializes in tiny versions of San Juan doorways. These ceramics, all created by hand right in the shop, are a wonderful souvenir to remember your stay. You might even find the hotel where you stayed reproduced in plaster. For one-of-a-kind *santos*, art, and festival masks, head for **Puerto Rican Arts & Crafts** (✉ *204 Calle Fortaleza, Old San Juan* ☎ *787/725–5596* 🌐 *www.puertoricanart-crafts.com*).

JEWELRY

Aetna Gold (✉ *111 Calle Gilberto Concepción de Gracia, Old San Juan* ☎ *787/721–4756*), adjacent to the Sheraton Old San Juan Hotel, sells exquisite gold jewelry designed in Greece. For an array of watches and jewelry, visit the two floors of **Bared** (✉ *154 Calle Fortaleza, Old San Juan* ☎ *787/722–2172*), with a charmingly old-fashioned ambience. Look for the massive clock face on the corner.

Club Jibarito (✉ *202 Calle Cristo, Old San Juan* ☎ *787/724–7797* 🌐 *www.clubjirarito.com*) has a fantastic collection of high-end watches by Jaeger-LeCoultre and other designers.

Cristobal (✉ *Plaza Ventana al Mar, 1049 Av. Ashford, Condado* ☎ *787/721–8385*) sells glittery pieces in gold and silver that appeal to more modern tastes. With the huge panes of glass facing the street, it's a great place to window-shop.

2

Diamonds and gold galore are found at **Joseph Manchini** (✉ *101 Calle Fortaleza, Old San Juan* ☎ *787/722–7698*). **Joyería Cátala** (✉ *Plaza de Armas, Old San Juan* ☎ *787/722–3231*) is known for its large selection of pearls. **Joyería Riviera** (✉ *257 Fortaleza St., Old San Juan* ☎ *787/725–4000* 🌐 *www.joyeriariviera.com*) sells fine jewelry by David Yurman and Rolex watches.

N. Barquet Joyeros (✉ *201 Calle Fortaleza, Old San Juan* ☎ *787/721–3366* 🌐 *www.nbarquet.com*), one of the bigger stores in Old San Juan, carries Fabergé jewelry, pearls, and gold as well as crystal and watches. **Portofino** (✉ *250 Calle San Francisco, Old San Juan* ☎ *787/723–5113*) has an especially good selection of watches.

Rheinhold Jewelers (✉ *Plaza Las Américas, 525 Av. Franklin Delano Roosevelt, Hato Rey* ☎ *787/767–7837* ✉ *El San Juan Hotel & Casino, 6063 Av. Isla Verde, Isla Verde* ☎ *787/791–2521*) sells exclusive designs by Stephen Dweck and Tiffany's.

SPORTS AND THE OUTDOORS

Many of San Juan's most enjoyable outdoor activities take place in and around the water. With miles of beach stretching across Isla Verde, Ocean Park, and Condado, there's a full range of water sports, including sailing, kayaking, windsurfing, kiteboarding, jet skiing, deep-sea fishing, scuba diving, and snorkeling.

Land-based activities include tennis and walking or jogging at local parks. With a bit of effort—meaning a short drive out of the city—you'll discover a world of championship golf courses and rain-forest trails. Baseball is big in Puerto Rico, and the players are world-class; many are recruited from local teams to play in the U.S. major leagues. The season runs from October through February. Games are played in San Juan venues, as well as others around the island.

BASEBALL

Does the name Roberto Clemente ring a bell? The late, great star of the Pittsburgh Pirates, who died in a 1972 plane crash delivering supplies to Nicaraguan earthquake victims, was born near San Juan and got his start in the Puerto Rican pro leagues. Many other Puerto Rican stars have played in the U.S. major leagues, including the brothers Roberto Alomar and Sandy Alomar Jr.; their father, Sandy Alomar; and Hall of Fame inductees Tony Perez and Orlando Cepeda. Baseball games in the San Juan area are played at **Estadio Hiram Bithorn** (✉ *Hato Rey* ☎ *787/725–2110*), named for the first Puerto Rican to play in the major leagues. It's home to the Cangrejeros de Santurce, which means the Santurce Crabbers. (No, that last part was not a joke.)

BIKING

Most streets don't have bike lanes, and auto traffic makes bike travel somewhat risky; further, all the fumes can be hard to take. That said, recreational bikers are increasingly donning their safety gear and wheeling through the streets, albeit with great care.

Your best bet is to look into a bike tour offered by an outfitter. One popular 45-minute trip travels from Old San Juan's cobblestone streets to Condado. It passes El Capitolio and runs through either Parque del Tercer Milenio (ocean side) or Parque Luis Muñoz Rivera, taking you past the Caribe Hilton Hotel and over Puente Dos Hermanos (Dos Hermanos Bridge) onto Avenida Ashford. The truly ambitious can continue east to Ocean Park, Isla Verde, and right on out of town to the eastern community of Piñones and its beachside bike path.

At **Hot Dog Cycling** (✉ *Plazoleta Isla Verde, 6150 Av. Isla Verde, Isla Verde* ☎ *787/791–0776* 🌐 *www.hotdogcycling.com*), Raul del Río and his son Omar rent mountain bikes for $30 a day in addition to repair and sales.

DIVING AND SNORKELING

The waters off San Juan aren't the best places to scuba dive, but several outfitters conduct short excursions to where tropical fish, coral, and sea horses are visible at depths of 30 to 60 feet. Escorted half-day dives range from $45 to $95 for one or two tanks, including all equipment; in general, double those prices for night dives. Packages that include lunch and other extras start at $100; those that include accommodations are also available.

Snorkeling excursions, which include transportation, equipment rental, and sometimes lunch, start at $55–$60. Equipment rents at beaches for about $10. Avoid unsupervised areas, as rough waters and strong undertows make some places dangerous.

Eco Action Tours (✉ *1035 Av. Ashford, Condado* ☎ *787/791–7509* 🌐 *www.ecoactiontours.com*) offers diving trips for all skill levels. **Ocean Sports** (✉ *77 Av. Isla Verde, Isla Verde* ☎ *787/723–8513* 🌐 *www.osdivers.com*) offers certified scuba courses; specialty courses in nitrox diving; diving trips; airtank fill-ups; and equipment repairs, sales, and rentals. It also rents surfboards by the day.

FISHING

Puerto Rico's waters are home to large game fish such as snook, wahoo, dorado, tuna, and barracuda; as many as 30 world records for catches have been set off the island's shores. Prices for fishing expeditions vary, but they tend to include all your bait and tackle, as well as refreshments, and start at $600 (for a boat with as many as six people) for a half-day trip to around $1,000 for a full day. Other boats charge by the person, starting at around $200 for a full day.

Half-day and full-day excursions can be arranged through **Mike Benítez Sport Fishing** (✉ *Club Náutico de San Juan, 480 Av. Fernández Juncos, Miramar* ☎ *787/723–2292* 🌐 *www.mikebenitezsportfishing.com*). From the 45-foot *Sea Born* you can fish for sailfish, white marlin, and blue marlin.

GOLF

Puerto Rico is the birthplace of golf legend and raconteur Chi Chi Rodriguez—and he had to hone his craft somewhere. The island has more than a dozen courses, including some of championship caliber. Several make good day trips from San Juan. Be sure to call ahead for details on reserving tee times; hours vary, and several hotel courses allow only guests to play or give preference to them. Greens fees start at $25 and go as high as $190.

A GOLF GREAT

Juan "Chi Chi" Rodriguez, who was born in Río Piedras, was the first Puerto Rican golfer to be inducted into the World Golf Hall of Fame.

Three golf clubs are within fairly easy striking distance of San Juan. The four 18-hole golf courses at the **Hyatt Hacienda del Mar** are just west of San Juan. *For more information, see "Golf" under "Dorado" in Chapter 6, Rincón & the Porta del Sol.*

There are more options to the east of the city. **Palmas del Mar Country Club** has two good golf courses. *For more information see "Golf" under "Humacao" in Chapter 2, El Yunque & the Northeast.* The spectacular **Rio Mar Beach Resort & Spa** has a clubhouse with a pro shop and two restaurants set between two 18-hole courses. *For more information see "Golf" under "Río Grande" in Chapter 3, El Yunque & the Northeast.*

HIKING

El Yunque is the only tropical rain forest within the U.S. National Forest System. The park is officially known as the Bosque Nacional del Caribe (Caribbean National Forest) and is within easy striking distance of San Juan, about an hour's drive east. *(For more information, see Chapter 3.)*

Eco Action Tours (✉ *1035 Av. Ashford, Condado* ☎ *787/791–7509* 🌐 *www.ecoactiontours.com*) organizes a variety of hikes and excursions throughout the island, including in El Yunque.

HORSE RACING

Try your luck with the exactas and quinielas at **Hipodromo Camarero** (✉ *Rte. 3, Km 15.3, Canóvanas* ☎ *787/641–6060* 🌐 *www.hipodromo-camarero.com*), a large Thoroughbred racetrack about 20 minutes east of San Juan. On race days the dining rooms open at 12:30 PM. Post

San Juan's well-equipped balnearios (public beaches) are among the best on the island.

time is at 2:30 PM every day except Tuesday and Thursday. There's an air-conditioned clubhouse and restaurant, as well as a bar where people occasionally dance to live rumba music. Parking and admission to the grandstand and clubhouse are free.

KAYAKING

The Laguna del Condado is popular for kayaking, especially on weekends. You can simply paddle around it or head out under the Puente Dos Hermanos to the San Gerónimo fort right behind the Caribe Hilton and across from the Conrad San Juan Condado Plaza. Kayaks rent for $25–$35 an hour.

SPAS

Olas Spa at the Caribe Hilton. This full-service spa on the grounds of the Caribe Hilton offers a range of luxurious treatments, including the popular four-hand massage, hydrotherapy, facials, and other body treatments. An Aveda salon is also on site. ✉ *Los Rosales Street, Gerónimo Grounds, Puerta de Tierra* ☎ *787/977–5500 or 877/888–6527* 🌐 *www.olasspa.com.*

The Ritz-Carlton Spa, San Juan. Popular treatments at this posh spa include stone therapy, the balancing lomilomi massage, and the Ritz-Carlton signature facial. You can also take private yoga or salsa lessons. ✉ *6961 Av. de los Gobernadores, Isla Verde* ☎ *787/253–1700* 🌐 *www.ritzcarlton.com.*

Zen Spa. This family-run spa focuses on wellness, with staff trained in Chinese and Ayurvedic techniques, but all kinds of treatments are available. One facial uses silk fibers to firm and tone skin. You can also get a coffee-infused clay wrap or a lymphatic drainage massage. An attached shop sells Kiehl's and Eminence Organics products, as well the house line, Zendera. ✉ *1054 Av. Ashford, Condado* ☎ *787/722–8433 or 866/936–7720* 🌐 *www.zen-spa.com.*

SURFING

★ *See also "Surfing Puerto Rico" feature in Chapter 6.* Although the west-coast beaches around Isabela and Rincón are considered *the* places to surf in Puerto Rico, San Juan was actually the place where the sport got its start on the island. In 1958 legendary surfers Gary Hoyt and José Rodríguez Reyes began surfing at the beach in front of Bus Stop 2½, facing El Capitolio. Although this spot is known for its big waves, the conditions must be nearly perfect to surf here. Today many surfers head to Puerta de Tierra and a spot known as La Ocho (in front of Bus Stop 8 behind the Dumas Restaurant). Another, called the Pressure Point, is behind the Caribe Hilton Hotel.

In Condado you can surf La Punta, a reef break behind the Presbyterian Hospital, with either surfboards or Boogie boards. In Isla Verde, white water on the horizon means that the waves are good at Pine Grove, the beach break near the Ritz-Carlton. East of the city, in Piñones, the Caballo has deep-to-shallow-water shelf waves that require a big-wave board known as a "gun." The surf culture frowns upon aficionados who divulge the best spots to outsiders. If you're lucky, though, maybe you'll make a few friends who'll let you in on where to find the best waves.

At Ocean Park beach, famous surfer Carlos Cabrero, proprietor of **Tres Palmas Surf Shop** (✉ *1911 Av. McLeary, Ocean Park* ☎ *787/728–3377*), rents boards (daily rates are $25 for Boogie boards, $30 for short boards, $35 for foam boards, and $40 for long boards), repairs equipment, and sells all sorts of hip beach and surfing gear.

TENNIS

If you'd like to use the tennis courts at a property where you aren't a guest, call in advance for information about reservations and fees. The four lighted courts of the **Club Tennis de Isla Verde** (✉ *Calles Ema and Delta Rodriguez, Isla Verde* ☎ *787/727–6490*) are open for nonmember use at $4 per hour, daily from 8 AM to 10 PM. The **Parque Central Municipio de San Juan** (✉ *Calle Cerra, exit on Rte. 2, Santurce* ☎ *787/722–1646*) has 23 lighted courts. Fees are $3 per hour from 6 AM to 6 PM and $4 per hour from 6 PM to 10 PM.

WINDSURFING AND KITESURFING

★ The waves can be strong and the surf choppy, but the constant wind makes for good sailing, windsurfing, or kiteboarding (maneuvering a surfboard using a parachutelike kite), particularly in Ocean Park and Punta Las Marías (between Ocean Park and Isla Verde). In general, you can rent a Windsurfer for about $25 an hour (including a lesson).

You'll get the best windsurfing advice and equipment from Jaime Torres at **Velauno** (✉ *2430 Calle Loíza, Punta Las Marías* ☎ *787/728–8716* 🌐 *www.velauno.com*), the second-largest full-service windsurfing center in any U.S. territory. It sells surfboards, kites, and paddle boards and offers repair services and classes. The store also serves as a clearinghouse for information on windsurfing events throughout the island.

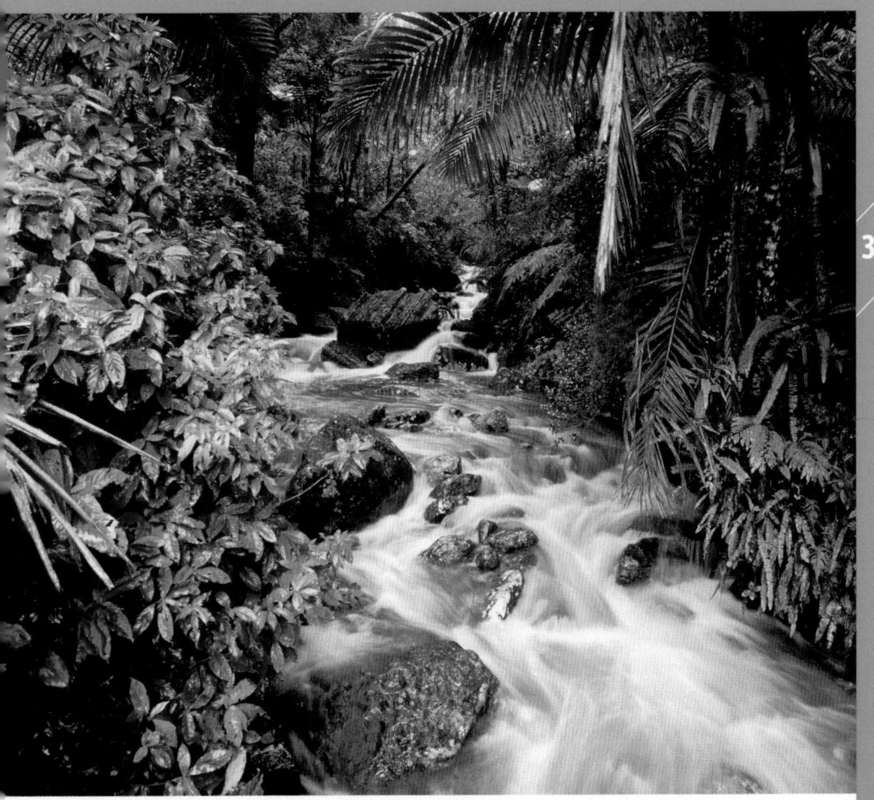

3

El Yunque and the Northeast

WORD OF MOUTH

"Please . . . make the hike [to the falls in El Yunque) in sneakers. The trail is very muddy, rocky, and slippery—after all, it's a rain forest! I was amazed at the people trying to make the hike in flip-flops or, yes, even heels!"

—Eileen

WELCOME TO EL YUNQUE AND THE NORTHEAST

TOP REASONS TO GO

★ **Take a hike:** Take in the spectacular waterfalls of El Yunque, the only rain forest within the U.S. National Forest system.

★ **Take a dip:** Relax at the Balneario de Luquillo, one of the prettiest beaches in Puerto Rico and a family favorite.

★ **Take a seat:** Hang with locals at one of the dozens of outdoor seafood shacks on the highway before you get to the Balneario de Luquillo. There are at least 50 to choose from.

★ **Hit the links:** Tee off at the tree-lined fairways of the two good golf courses at Palmas del Mar.

1 The Northeastern Coast. Head southeast and inland of San Juan to escape the city crowds and discover Río Grande's natural greenland and its long strips of pristine beach. Its closest neighbor is the region's magnificent natural wonder, El Yunque, a park you can explore in the air-conditioned comfort of a car in a few hours or hike for days and still not see all the greenery, waterfalls, and views. Nearby, Balneario de Luquillo (Luquillo Beach), Reserva Natural Las Cabezas de San Juan, and Fajardo are all worth exploring.

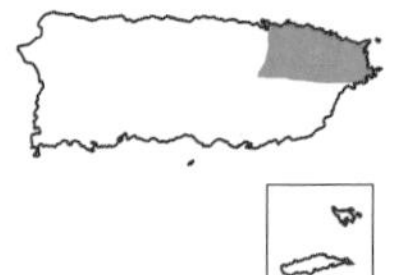

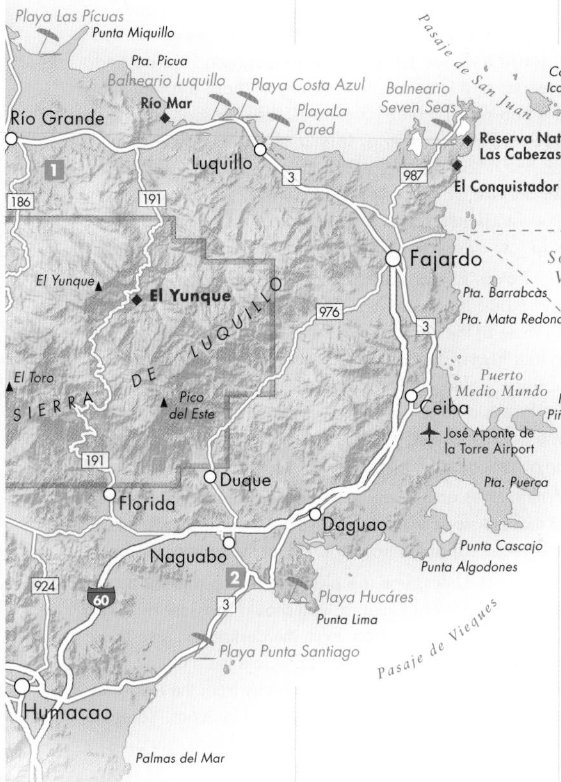

GETTING ORIENTED

If you seek an alternative to the hectic urban environs of San Juan, head to the pristine coastal towns and charming inland locales found along Puerto Rico's northeast corridor. Easily reached by car, El Yunque and northeast Puerto Rico are convenient enough for a quick day trip but beg exploration of at least two days. Kayak the lagoon in Piñones, take a surf lesson in Luquillo, sunbathe at Seven Seas Beach in Fajardo, horseback ride in the foothills of El Yunque—the list of exciting and/or relaxing activities in this region goes on and on.

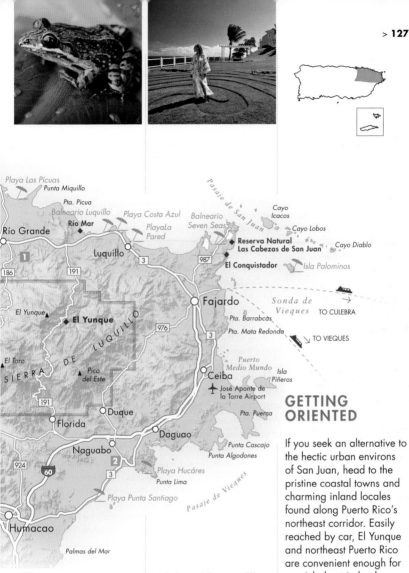

2 The Eastern Coast. Puerto Rico's eastern coast is home to some of the island's most popular attractions. Be sure to check out the beautiful beaches and crystal-clear snorkeling conditions of Fajardo before heading south to Naguabo. Naguabo is said to be the birthplace of the *pastelillo de chapín*, a popular dish that consists of trunkfish wrapped inside a deep-fried flour dough. Farther south and west, travelers will stumble upon Humacao, home of the island's largest resort, Palmas del Mar.

EL YUNQUE AND THE NORTHEAST PLANNER

When to Go

In general, the island's northeast coast—preferred by those seeking abandoned beaches and nature reserves rather than casinos and urban glitz—tends to be less in demand than San Juan. The exception is at Easter and Christmas, when Luquillo and Fajardo become crowded with local sun worshippers, merrymakers, and campers. Island festivals also draw crowds, but planning a trip around one of them will give you a true sense of the region's culture. Be sure to make reservations well in advance if you're visiting during high season, which runs from December 15 through April 15.

Safety

Although crime isn't as high in the island's eastern areas as it is in San Juan, use prudence. Avoid bringing valuables with you to the beach; if you must do so, be sure not to leave them in view in your car. It's best to keep your car locked while driving, and steer clear of out-of-the-way beaches after sunset.

Getting Here and Around

Air Travel. Air Flamenco, Isla Nena Air Service, and Vieques Air Link offer several daily flights between Fajardo and San Juan, as well as between Fajardo and Vieques and Culebra. Trips to any of these destinations are between 10 and 15 minutes; the cost ranges from $60 to $180 round-trip. **Information Air Flamenco** (☎ *787/724–1818* 🌐 *www.airflamenco.net*). **Isla Nena Air Service** (☎ *787/741–6362 or 877/812–5144* 🌐 *www.islanena.8m.com*). **Vieques Air Link** (☎ *787/741–8331 or 888/901–9247* 🌐 *www.vieques-island.com/val*).

Bus Travel. *Públicos*(a cross between a privately owned taxi and a bus) travel between San Juan and Fajardo, stopping en route at the ferry terminal. The full journey can take up to four hours, depending on where you board, frequency of stops, traffic, and where you are dropped off. However, the fare is a huge bargain at about $6 (pay the driver as you board). To get to Fajardo, simply flag down a público anywhere along Route 3.

Within cities and towns, local buses pick up and discharge at marked stops and cost 35¢–50¢. Enter and pay (exact fare required) at the front and exit at the front or the back.

Car Travel. Unless you are planning to hop directly onto a ferry to Vieques or Culebra, you should consider renting a car in eastern Puerto Rico. Even the destination resorts are fairly isolated, and you may appreciate the mobility if you want to get out and have a meal away from the resort, or explore El Yunque or some of the great beaches. Rates start at about $40 a day, but it may be possible to rent directly from your lodging, so ask about packages.

From San Juan the east coast is accessible via Route 3, or Route 187 if you want to visit Loíza. At Fajardo the road intersects with Route 53, which continues down the coast. Route 3 also continues along the coast, but provides a more scenic, if slower, trip.

Taxi Travel. You can flag cabs down on the street, but it's faster and safer to have your hotel call one for you. Cabs are usually metered, make sure it's clear whether a flat rate or a meter will determine the fare. Instead of renting a car, consider taking a taxi to Fajardo. The cost from the San Juan area should be about $80 for up to five people.

About the Restaurants

Some restaurants carry the tourist board's *meson gastronómico* designation. Such establishments specialize in typical island food. The eastern region has both formal restaurants, where reservations are very necessary, and casual beach-side eateries, where you can walk in unannounced in beach attire and have a fine meal of fresh fish. Bills generally don't include service charges, so a 15% tip is customary and expected. Most restaurants are open for dinner from late afternoon until at least 10 PM.

About the Hotels

The east coast has a wide variety of lodgings from small lodges in the mountains to large, lavish resorts along the coast. Also available are government-approved *paradores*. Often translated as "country inn," *paradores* offer affordable Puerto Rican hospitality and the cozy comforts of home outside of the San Juan metro area. These small, privately owned properties are usually quite picturesque and found throughout the island's interior and more remote coastal towns. If you wish to get away from it all with a neatly packaged trip, eastern Puerto Rico has some of the island's top resorts: the El Conquistador Resort and the Westin Río Mar. You'll also find the island's only all-inclusive resort, the Paradisus Puerto Rico. The extensive facilities and luxury services at these large, self-contained complexes make the list of regional offerings more than complete.

WHAT IT COSTS IN DOLLARS

	¢	$	$$	$$$	$$$$
Restaurants	under $8	$8–$12	$12–$20	$20–$30	over $30
Hotels	under $80	$80–$150	$150–$250	$250–$350	over $350

Restaurant prices are based on the median main course price at dinner. Hotel prices are for a double room in high season, excluding 9% tax (11% for hotels with casinos, 7% for *paradores*) and 5%–12% service charge.

El Yunque Packing

When you come to El Yunque, bring binoculars, a camera with a zoom lens, bottled water, and sunscreen; wear a hat or visor, good walking shoes, and comfortable clothes. Although daytime temperatures rise as high as 80°F (27°C), wear long pants, because some plants can cause skin irritations. There are no poisonous snakes in the forest (or on the island as a whole), but bugs can be ferocious, so a strong repellent is a must. And remember: This is a rain forest, so be prepared for frequent showers.

Visitor Information

The cities usually offer information through offices connected to city hall, and most are open only during business hours on weekdays.

Information **Fajardo Tourism Office** (✉ *6 Av. Muñoz Rivera, Fajardo* ☎ *787/863–1400*). **Luquillo Tourism Office** (✉ *154 Calle 14 de Julio, Luquillo* ☎ *787/889–2851*). **Río Grande Office of Tourism and Culture** (✉ *Calle San José, Plaza de Recreo, Río Grande* ☎ *787/887–2370*).

EL YUNQUE NATIONAL FOREST

El Toro Mountain rises more than 3,500 ft (1,070 m), and on a clear day the view from the peak extends to the Atlantic Ocean.

The more than 100 billion gallons of precipitation that El Yunque receives annually, spawns rushing streams and cascades, outsize impatiens and ferns, and 240 tree species. In the evening millions of inch-long *coquís* (tree frogs) begin their calls. El Yunque is also home to the *cotorra,* Puerto Rico's endangered green parrot, as well as 67 other types of birds

El Yunque is the only tropical rain forest in the U.S. National Forest System, spanning 28,000 acres, reaching an elevation of more than 3,500 ft. and receiving an estimated average of 200–240 inches of rain each year. The forest's 13 hiking trails are extremely well maintained; many of them are easy to navigate and less than 1 mi long. If you prefer to see the sights from a car, as many people do, simply follow Route 191 as it winds into the mountains and stop at several observation points along the way.

WHEN TO GO

It's about 73°F year-round, so weather isn't much of a factor for seasonal planning. For easy parking and fewer crowds, be sure to arrive early in the day, although the park rarely gets crowded by U.S. National Park standards. Expect rain nearly every day, but keep eyes peeled post-showers for the best bird-watching.

PARK HIGHLIGHTS

FLORA AND FAUNA

Each year, more than a million visitors from all over the world come to El Yunque to experience the rain forest's ecological treasures. Rivers and streams provide aquatic habitats for freshwater snails, shrimp and crabs, while approximately 35 species of migratory birds either winter or pass through El Yunque. Sonorous *coqui* frogs (endemic tree frogs found only in Puerto Rico), 14 different lizard species, and more than 1,200 insect species ranging from ants to beetles to flies all inhabit the forest.

Four major forest types, roughly stratified by elevation, are home to thousands of native plants including 150 fern species, 240 tree species (88 of these are endemic or rare and 23 are exclusively found in this forest). Two of the islands highest peaks rise out of the forest: El Toro and El Yunque, both more than 3,500 ft (1,070 m).

El Yunque doesn't have bigger wildlife species like monkeys, large cats, and poisonous snakes, but there are hundreds of small creatures that find ecological niches. Many of these species exist nowhere else on the planet, such as the endangered Puerto Rican parrot (only 30 parrots survive in the wild), Puerto Rican Boa, and Puerto Rican Sharp-Shinned Hawk. If you're interested in bird-watching, pack your binoculars because Puerto Rican Tody, Puerto Rican Lizard Cuckoo, hummingbirds, flycatchers and warblers are commonly spotted.

VISITOR CENTER

Carve out some time to stop at the cathedral-like **El Portal Visitor Center.** Enter via an elevated walkway that transports visitors across the forest canopy, 60 feet above the ground. Signs identify and explain the birds, animals, and other treasures seen among the treetops.

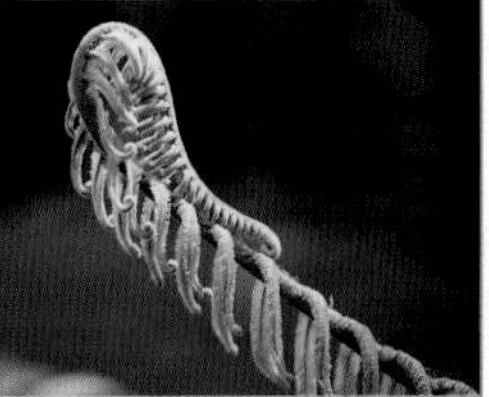

STAY THE NIGHT

If you're thinking about a second day at El Yunque, book a room near the rain forest instead of schlepping back to San Juan. (There is no lodging available within the reserve.) Rio Del Mar Beach Resort & Spa, a Wyndham Grand Resort and Gran Meliá Puerto Rico are both within a 10-minute drive in Rio Grande, but the two cottages at Sue's Place in Barrios Sabana, above the town of Luquillo cannot be beat. For a taste of local flavor, visitors leaving the El Yunque area may want to consider stopping off at the *friquitines* (seafood kiosks) that line Route 3 west of the beach turnoff. Frequented mostly by local families, truckers and business people, the kiosks are open all day and serve cold drinks, plates of fried fish (head and tail still attached), conch salad and fritter (usually codfish or corn).

3

BEST ONE-DAY ITINERARY

Start at the **El Portal Rain Forest Center.** Drive about 2 1/2 mi to **La Coca Falls**—one of the best photo ops in the park. View it from your car or climb up slippery rocks to the base of the falls. Back in the car for about half a mile to **Torre Yokahú** *(Yokahú Observation Tower)*, a lookout with vistas of 1,000-year-old trees, exotic flowers, and birds in flight. The parking lot has restrooms. Continue just beyond the halfway point to the **Area Pasadías Palma de Sierra.** Rangers here have information on closures, trail conditions, and daily activities. The Center and the next two parking lots, Caimitillo and Palo Colorado, have trailheads to both **El Yunque Summit** (about a half-day adventure) and **La Mina Falls.** Casual hikers should follow the moderate **Big Tree Trail** to reach the falls—about a half-hour hike. Bring a swimsuit for the falls and water shoes or sandals to navigate the slippery rocks. More advanced hikers can follow **La Mina Falls Trail.** It's only .7 mi long, but climbs to 2,132 ft. Plan 30–45 minutes each way. A little more than a mile up the road is one more trail, **Baño de Oro.**

Below the walkway, find a ground-level nature trail with stunning views of the lower forest and coastal plain. Inside the Center interactive exhibits explain the El Yunque National Forest's history, topography, flora and fauna. And watch "El Yunque: Journey into a Tropical Rain Forest." The 15-minute film provides a greater understanding of the ecology, environment, and history of the El Yunque National Forest. The facility also has a well-stocked bookstore and gift shop, filled with useful tools for exploring the park, like trail maps printed on recycled plastic paper. On a sticky day, the air conditioning, clean restrooms, and benches overlooking the forest make for a pleasant post-hike respite.

CASCADA LA COCA

The first spectacular sight you're likely to see in El Yunque is **Cascada La Coca** *(La Coca Falls)*, which plunges 85 feet down a flat sheet of solid rock. The waterfall is inches from the road, so it's visible from your car. The gate to the park, which opens at 7:30 AM and closes at 6 PM, is just before the falls. ✉ *Rte. 191, Km 8.1.*

BEST WAY TO EXPLORE

HITTING THE TRAILS

The 13 official trails throughout El Yunque are quite civilized—paved, well-marked and easy for both beginners and children. The trails on the north side of El Yunque, the park's main tourist hub, tend toward folks with minimal or no hiking experience. There are several short trails (about ½ mile) that are completely paved. On the south side, expect fewer people and moderate to challenging hikes. These trails are not as well-maintained as the marked trails found lower in the forest. Regardless of where you go, you'll be immersed in the sounds, smells and scenic landscape of the park. For

avid outdoor adventurers, it's possible to hike between the north and south sides of El Yunque.

DRIVING

A leisurely drive-thru may not be as immersive as a hike, but you'll still encounter beautiful waterfalls, hibiscus, banana and orchid plants, geckos, and the occasional vista over the forest and out to the Atlantic Ocean. The main and most direct route to El Yunque, Route 3, is a multilane highway dotted with places to stop for cold drinks and typical Puerto Rican snacks. Obey the speed limit, as rental cars are frequently pulled over. From the highway, hop onto Route 191, the only road through the preserve. When hurricanes and mud slides haven't caused portions of the road to be closed, you can drive straight from the entrance to Km 13, the base of Pico El Yunque. A stop at El Portal Visitor Center will teach you everything you need to know about your majestic surroundings. Make another quick stop to climb the winding stairs of Yokaho Tower for breathtaking views of the rain forest and the island. En route back, stop at El Bosque Encantado, a food *kiosko* with *empanadas*, cold coconut drinks and cliff's-edge views (located on Route 191, 7.2 km). Take note that drivers don't always recognize common road courtesies, such as slow cars to the right, stop signs and signals.

ZIPLINING

This adrenaline-fueled, half-day activity enables visitors to take a tree-to-tree canopy tour via a network of platforms, cables, and pulleys. Step off a platform more than 80 feet in the sky and fly through the air as you take in bird's-eye views of the northern limit of El Yunque National Forest and El Yunque & Este peaks. For more information contact **Yunke Zipline Adventure** (*http://yunkezipline.wordpress.com* ☎ *787/242–3368*).

FUN FACTS

The roots of the rain forest trees do not grow very deep. They find food and water in dead plant parts, fallen tree trunks and a very thin layer of surface soil.

El Yunque has had many names. President Theodore Roosevelt named it the Luquillo Forest Reserve in 1903, and President Franklin Roosevelt changed its name to the Caribbean National Forest. In 2007 the area officially became El Yunque National Forest.

ECO-STAYS

Casa Cubuy Ecolodge is a bit remote, located above Naguabo the south side of the rain forest, but it's worth the trek. Guests of the tranquil bed and breakfast are treated to the sound of nearby waterfalls and are within walking distance of the Cubuy and Icacaos Rivers and jungles of bamboo. Sunbathe on granite slabs and boulders or slip into a natural Jacuzzi. A short uphill trek from the house on a paved road takes you to the new El Yunque National Forest recreational facility, where interpretive guides offer forest hikes. At night, the serenading of the *coquis* lull weary travelers to sleep. The emphasis here is on unplugging—rooms are television and phone-free—and soaking up nature. Environmental friendly features of this property include: recycled water, solar panels to heat water, composted garbage to fertilize the fruit trees; eco-smart lightbulbs, erosion prevention techniques for trails.

3

BEACHES OF THE NORTHEAST

Playa Luquillo is one of four beaches in Puerto Rico to be awarded a Blue Flag, a distinction that recognizes superior water quality and accessible facilities.

The Atlantic east coast is edged with sandy, palm-lined shores that are occasionally cut by rugged stretches. Some of these beaches are quiet, isolated escapes. Others—such as Luquillo and Seven Seas near Fajardo—are jammed with water-loving families, especially on weekends and during the Easter holidays.

Known as "La Capital del Sol" (sun capital) and "La Riviera de Puerto Rico" (Puerto Rico's riviera), Luquillo is beloved for its towering palm trees and shimmering sand. Its public beaches are among the nicest in the San Juan area, making it a popular stop on the coastal highway.

Fajardo has a vibrant boating community with many hotels and inns. Its marina is a prime launching point for day trips to Culebra and Vieques, while snorkelers revel in Fajardo's crystal clear waters and at night, its bioluminescent lagoons. In Piñones you can find solitary coastline. The surf here is strong, and swimming—especially in winter—can be dangerous at some beaches.

DIVE IN

The waters off eastern Puerto Rico are probably the best for scuba diving and snorkeling and compare favorably to other Caribbean diving destinations. Operators will take you on dives to 65 feet. The east has a good mix of coral, as well as a large variety of marine life. Fine snorkeling and diving spots can be found offshore from Fajardo, and there are many uninhabited islets from which to dive just off the coast.

PIÑONES

You'll find **Playa de Piñones** right in front of the cluster of food kiosks built by the government for resident cooks. A large barrier reef blocks the strong currents and serves as the foundation for the large bathing pools in front of a sandy beach. ✉ *Route 187, Km 8.*

LUQUILLO

Fodor's Choice Just off Route 3, gentle **Playa Luquillo** (or Balneario La Monserrate) is a magnet for families. It's well equipped with restrooms, showers, lifeguards, guarded parking, food stands, picnic areas, and even cocktail kiosks. Lounge chairs and umbrellas are available to rent. Its most distinctive facility is the Mar Sin Barreras (Sea Without Barriers), a low-sloped ramp leading into the water that allows wheelchair users to take a dip. The beach is open daily. Admission is $2 per car, $3 for minivans. ✉ *Off Rte. 3.*

Waving palm trees and fishing boats add charm to the small **Playa Costa Azul,** although the ugly residential buildings along the water make an unattractive backdrop. The water here is good for swimming, and the crowds are thinner than elsewhere, but there are no facilities. ✉ *Off Rte. 193, near Rte. 3.*

Playa La Pared, literally "The Wall Beach," is a surfer haunt. Numerous local competitions are held here throughout the year, and several surfing shops are close by in case you need a wet suit or a wax for

your board. The waves here are medium-range. It's very close to Playa Luquillo but has a separate entrance. There are no facilities. ✉ *Off Rte. 3.*

FAJARDO

A long stretch of powdery sand near the Reserva Natural Las Cabezas de San Juan, **Balneario Seven Seas** may turn out to be the best surprise of your trip. Facilities include picnic tables, changing areas, restrooms, and showers. Many restaurants are just outside the gates. Its calm, clear waters are perfect for swimming. ✉ *Rte. 987, Las Croabas.*

NAGUABO

Playa Húcares is *the* place to be. Casual outdoor eateries and funky shops vie with the water for your attention. Two Victorian-style houses anchor one end of the waterfront promenade; a dock with excursion boats anchors the other. ✉ *Off Rte. 3, south of Naguabo.*

HUMACAO

Right beside the Refugio de Vida Silvestre de Humacao, **Playa Punta Santiago** is a long shore with closely planted palm trees that are perfect for stringing up hammocks. There's changing facilities with showers and restrooms, food kiosks, and lifeguard stations. Parking is $3. ✉ *Rte. 3, northeast of Humacao.*

Updated by Charyn Pfeuffer

Tree frogs, rare parrots, and wild horses only start the list of northeastern Puerto Rico's offerings. The backdrops for encounters with an array of flora and fauna include the 28,000-acre El Yunque tropical rain forest, the seven ecosystems in the Reserva Natural Las Cabezas de San Juan, and Laguna Grande, where tiny sea creatures appear to light up the waters.

As the ocean bends around the northeastern coast, it laps onto beaches of soft sand and palm trees, crashes against high bluffs, and almost magically creates an amazing roster of ecosystems. Beautiful beaches at Luquillo are complemented by more rugged southeastern shores. Inland, green hills roll down toward plains that once held expanses of coconut trees, such as those still surrounding the town of Piñones, or "sugarcane," as evidenced by the surviving plantations near Naguabo and Humacao.

The natural beauty and varied terrain continue in the area's other towns as well. Río Grande—which once attracted immigrants from Austria, Spain, and Italy—sits on the island's only navigable river. Naguabo overlooks what were once immense cane fields as well as Cayo Santiago, where the only residents are monkeys.

You can golf, ride horses, hike marked trails, and plunge into water sports throughout the region. In many places along the coast, green hills cascade down to the ocean. On the edge of the Atlantic, Fajardo serves as a jumping-off point for diving, fishing, and catamaran excursions. Luquillo is the site of a family beach so well equipped that there are even facilities enabling wheelchair users to enter the sea.

THE NORTHEASTERN COAST

Just east of San Juan, at the community of Piñones, urban chaos is replaced with the peace of winding, palm-lined roads that are interrupted at intervals by barefoot eateries and dramatic ocean views.

3

IF YOU LIKE

GREAT FOOD

Puerto Ricans love sybaritic pleasures, and that includes enjoying a well-prepared meal—whether it be Continental, Nueva Latina, or authentically native cuisine. In the east you'll find fine fare of all types. On the traditional side, look for the deep-fried snacks (often stuffed with meat or fish) known as *frituras*, as well as numerous dishes laced with coconut. Plantains are the star ingredient in the hearty *mofongo*, a seafood-stuffed dish, or as *tostones* (fried plantain chips). Fresh fish is commonly prepared with tomatoes, onions, and garlic, or some combination of the three.

GOLF

There's something to be said for facing a rolling, palm-tree-lined fairway with the distant ocean at your back. And then there are the ducks, iguanas, and pelicans that congregate in the mangroves near some holes. That's what golf in eastern Puerto Rico is all about. The Arthur Hills–designed course at El Conquistador is one of the island's best. The Flamboyán course, a Rees-Jones creation at Palmas del Mar Country Club, consistently gets raves, as do the courses at the Westin Río Mar. An old-time favorite is the Bahía Beach Plantation course, which was developed on a former coconut plantation.

Farther southeast and inland is Río Grande, a community that grew by virtue of its location beside the island's only navigable river. The river rises within El Yunque, the short name for El Yunque National Forest, a sprawling blanket of green covering a mountainous region south of Río Grande. Back on the coast, Balneario de Luquillo (Luquillo Beach) has snack kiosks, dressing rooms, showers, and facilities that enable wheelchair users to play in the ocean.

Southeast of Luquillo sits the Reserva Natural Las Cabezas de San Juan, with its restored lighthouse and variety of ecosystems. Anchoring the island's east coast is Fajardo, a lively port city with a large marina, ferry service to the outer islands, and a string of offshore cays. Catamarans based here sail to and from great snorkeling spots, yachts stop by to refuel or stock up on supplies, and local fishing craft chug in and out as part of a day's work. ■ **TIP→ Leave yourself plenty of time for driving to El Yunque or any of the resorts in the northeast. Route 3, the main route east, is notorious for its bumper-to-bumper traffic.**

PIÑONES

10 mi (16 km) east of San Juan.

Funky Piñones is little more than a collection of open-air seaside eateries. Sand floors, barefoot patrons, and tantalizing seafood—traditionally washed down with icy beer—have made it popular with locals, especially on weekend evenings. Chilled *agua de coco* is served right from the coconut. During the day you can rent a bike and follow the marked seaside trail that meanders for 7 mi (11 km) through the mangrove forest and along the northern coastline. It takes about two hours

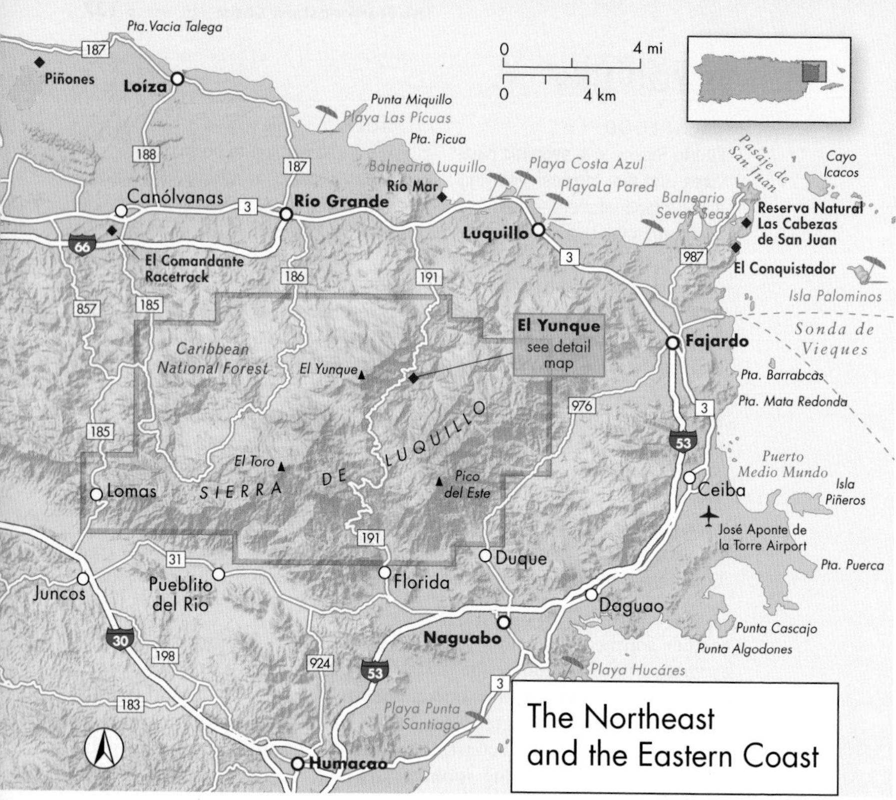

The Northeast and the Eastern Coast

to bike from one end and back, but allow some time to stop and take pictures, grab something to eat, and explore the scenic beach areas.

The area has grown as a nightlife designation, as fancier establishments, some with live music, have opened up. And there are raucous open-air dance halls playing mostly Dominican merengue or local rap, which is influenced by salsa and reggae. But the action begins to cook before sunset. As mid-afternoon turns into evening and people begin to leave the beach for refreshments, the air is thick with smoke from grilled fish, beef and chicken kabobs, and the kettles of oil used to fry codfish and crab fritters. When the giant orange Caribbean sun starts to fall behind the San Juan skyline, salsa and merengue—not to mention reggae and Latin pop—start to blare out from the jukeboxes and sound systems of the dozens of ramshackle establishments dotting Route 187, the sector's main road. Traffic on the two-lane road into and out of the area is daunting on Friday and Saturday nights, when many of these open-air bars host merengue combos, Brazilian-jazz trios, or reggae bands.

GETTING HERE AND AROUND

The approach to Piñones from San Juan is simple. Take Route 26 east or Route 37 east, follow signs for the Balneario de Carolina, then go straight on Route 187, and cross Punta Cangrejos. Door-to-door, the

GREAT ITINERARIES

IF YOU HAVE 1 DAY

If you have only a day, or even less than a day, to visit eastern Puerto Rico, you should make a beeline to **El Yunque.** Route 3 is the quickest way. This rain forest has hiking trails of various lengths leading to secluded waterfalls and mountaintop towers with spectacular views. It's wonderful to explore even if you never get out of your car. If you are staying overnight, your best bet is nearby **Río Grande.**

IF YOU HAVE 3 DAYS

If you have a bit more time, you can see much more of the region. To avoid the unrelenting string of strip malls along Route 3, take Route 187 as it winds along the coast. Stop for lunch at one of the seafood shacks that line the beach at **Piñones.** Spend the night in or near **Río Grande,** a town that makes a good base for exploring the region. On your second day, get up early to beat the crowds to **El Yunque.** Make sure to bring binoculars and watch for the rare Puerto Rican green parrot. On Day 3 you should head to **Luquillo,** which has one of the prettiest beaches on the island. Make sure to stop for lunch in one of the *kioskos* (food stands) on Route 3 just before you reach the town.

IF YOU HAVE 5 DAYS

If you have five days, follow the three-day itinerary above. On Day 4 head east along Route 3 to the coastal city of **Fajardo,** which has plenty of accommodations in every price range. Make sure you have called ahead to reserve a spot on a tour of Reserva Natural Las Cabezas de San Juan. If there's no moon, sign up for a late-night excursion to the reserve's bioluminescent bay. On Day 5 take a snorkeling trip to some of the nearby coral reefs. Many people who travel to Fajardo take advantage of the ferry service to the smaller islands of Vieques or Culebra.

3

trip should take about 15 minutes. You can also get a taxi out to Piñones or take the bus for about 75¢ (via C45 or B40) but it takes more than an hour. To avoid getting stranded, prearrange a pickup time for your taxi driver to return. Another option is to make Soleil Beach Club your destination. Yes, it's one of the priciest beachfront restaurants in Piñones, but it offers a complimentary shuttle for pickup and drop-off, which helps avoid the risks of drinking and driving.

Taxis **AA American Taxi, Inc.** ☎ *787/982–3466* **Astro Taxi** ☎ *787/727–8888*).

EXPLORING

One of the most pleasant ways to pass the time is walking along the **Paseo Piñones.** This 6½-mi (10½-km) boardwalk passes through sand dunes and crosses lagoons and mangrove forests. All the while, a line of coconut palms shades you from the sun. You'll share the path with bikers, joggers, and in-line skaters. Food kiosks abound.

WHERE TO EAT

$$–$$$ SEAFOOD ✕ **Bamboo Bei.** You can't miss this tiki-bar-esque beachfront hangout because of its eye-catching color scheme. But behind the brilliant blue building is a great deck that looks across a bike path to the beach. There's always live music on weekends—jazz on Saturday, something

else on Friday. Other times you can just enjoy the rhythms floating out from the speakers. The menu is reasonably priced and pretty much what you'd expect—heavy on the seafood—but lots of coconut and tropical fruit jazz things up. ✉ *Rte. 187, Km 5* ☎ *787/253–0948* ▭ *MC, V.*

$–$$ SEAFOOD ✕ **Pulpo Loco by the Sea.** Talk about truth in packaging—the Crazy Octopus has its palm-shaded tables planted firmly in the sand just a few yards from the ocean. As you might guess, octopus, oysters, mussels, and crab lead the lineup at this colorful seafood shack, though you can always munch on local favorites such as *bacalaito*, or fried codfish fritters. If your thirst is greater than your hunger, opt for Puerto Rican brew, Medalla Light, served in a plastic cup. The friendly staff seems to know all the customers on a first-name basis. ✉ *Rte. 187, Km 4.5* ☎ *787/791–8382* ▭ *AE, MC, V.*

CHIMICHURRI

When you get a steak in Puerto Rico, it usually is served with a little glass jar of a green herb-filled sauce with a small, plastic spoon. This is *chimichurri*, the traditional accompaniment to grilled steak. The sauce, made from finely chopped cilantro or parsley, garlic, lemon, and oil, can be sprinkled liberally or sparingly over the meat to give it a slight kick. You will rarely find steak sauce in Puerto Rico, except at an American chain, though you can frequently get ketchup if *chimichurri* isn't to your liking.

$ SEAFOOD ✕ **The Reef Bar & Grill.** This place has one of the most dazzling views of San Juan, especially in the evening, when the city lights are twinkling. Perched atop a coastal bluff, it's located at the first left once you cross the bridge into Piñones. Grab one of the tables on the deck and order an *ensaladas de mariscos*, a refreshing seafood salad with conch, shrimp, or octopus, or *mofongo relleno*, mofongo stuffed with chicken or your pick of seafood. ✉ *Off Rte. 187, Km 1* ☎ *787/791–1973* ▭ *MC, V.*

$$–$$$ SEAFOOD ✕ **Soleil Beach Club.** A bit more refined than some of its neighbors, this restaurant actually sits on a wooden platform positioned *above* the sand. Even nicer is the upstairs deck that lets you gaze at the ocean instead of the parking lot. The grilled USDA steak served with chimichurri is as good as it gets, and the fresh halibut fillet with beurre blanc and cassava mofongo is equally tasty. Save room for *postres* (dessert)—the coconut ice cream is worth every calorie. There are a couple of bars, and bands playing Latin music set the scene on weekend nights. Call ahead and you can arrange free transportation to and from your hotel—a very good deal. ✉ *Rte. 187, Km 4.6* ☎ *787/253–1033* 🌐 *www.soleilbeachclub.com* ▭ *AE, MC, V.*

$$–$$$ SEAFOOD ✕ **The Waterfront and Bar.** Farther down the beach than its rowdier rivals, this restaurant attracts a slightly older crowd of *sanjuaneros* whose primary objective is eating rather than drinking. The menu is also more mature, offering such entrées as red snapper in garlic sauce or lobster tails in lemon butter. If you can't decide, the sampler platter has everything from fried fritters to fresh oysters. You can choose a table in the dimly lighted dining room or outside on the covered patio. ✉ *Rte. 187, Km 5* ☎ *787/791–5859* ▭ *AE, MC, V.*

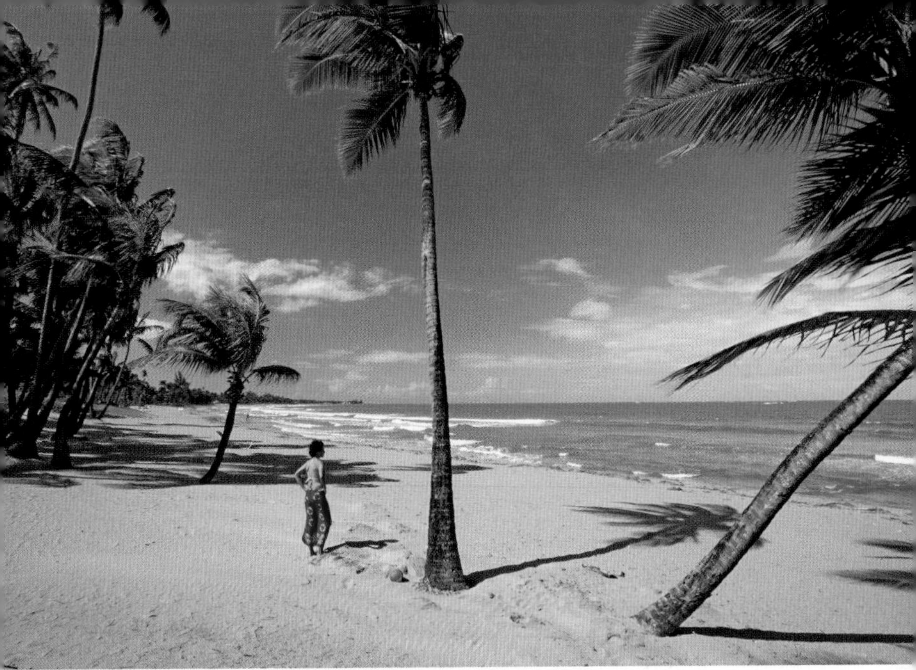

Soft sand and leaning palm trees are hallmarks of Luquillo beaches.

NIGHTLIFE

Nearly all the restaurants and cafés in Piñones have bands on weekends, mostly playing roof-shaking jazz and island rhythms, and locals go as much for the drinks and live entertainment as for the food. A largely Dominican clientele frequents many of these beachfront dance halls, and you're likely to see some smoking merengue dancing. Couples also twirl to salsa, bounce to *bomba*, or move to the grittier beats of local rap. You'll easily find several open-air establishments drawing weekend crowds for their steamy dance floors inside and smoking barbecue pits outside.

The Reef Bar & Grill (✉ *Off Rte. 187, Km 1* ☎ *787/791–1973*) has a jukebox for those rare evenings when there isn't live music. You can also shoot some eight ball at one of the pool tables. **Soleil Beach Club** (✉ *Rte. 187, Km 4.5* ☎ *787/253–1033*) has bars upstairs as well as down, so you never have to go far to order a drink. This place can get packed on weekends.

SHOPPING

Just west of Piñones is the town of Loíza, where you'll find **Artesanías Castor Ayala** (✉ *Rte. 187, Km 6.6, Loíza* ☎ *787/876–1130*). Among the offerings here are coconut-shell festival masks dubbed "Mona Lisas" because of their elongated smiles. Craftsman Raúl Ayala Carrasquillo has been making these pieces for more than 40 years, following in the footsteps of his late father. Collectors prize these wild masks, most with tentacle-like horns. ⚠ **Buyer beware: These masks have been much-copied by other artisans, so look for the signature on the back.** His one-room shop, in a shack that was painted yellow many years ago, is on the road between Loíza and Río Grande.

At **Estúdio de Arte Samuel Lind** (✉ *Rte. 187, Km 6.6, Loíza* ☎ *787/876–1494*), located on a short, dusty lane across the street from the Artesanías Castor Ayala, artist Samuel Lind sculpts, paints, and silk-screens images that are quintessentially Loízano. Lind's work is displayed in the two floors of his latticework studio. Of special note are his colorful folk-art posters.

SPORTS AND THE OUTDOORS

Piñones is bordered by a 10-mi (16-km) strip of beaches along the coast, which winds to a bluff called Vacia Talega, a once infamous lovers' lane with a wonderful view of an unspoiled coast lined with dense palm groves and towering sea grapes. The area has some fine surf, and several spots have become favorites of local and visiting surfers. You'll also find good fishing, snorkeling, and scuba opportunities. Away from the coast is Torrecilla Baja, one of the largest mangrove swamps on the island.

BICYCLING

The area's big outdoor attraction is a bike path that follows the swaying coconut palms on a quiet, breezy stretch, sometimes crossing over the main roadway but mostly running parallel to it. Along most of its 7 mi (12 km), it's a wooden boardwalk for bicycles. On weekends and holidays you can rent bikes from several places along Route 187 and explore the path on your own. The going rate is $5 per hour. Many are clustered at the start of the bike trail, at the first left once you cross the bridge into Piñones. If you want to rent a bike, head to **Pulpo Loco by the Sea** (✉ *Rte. 187, Km 5* ☎ *787/791–8382*).

DIVING AND FISHING TRIPS

Locals go fishing and crabbing right off the coast, and it's likely that the crab fritters you eat in any beachfront shack are local as well. Boating, deep-sea fishing, and scuba-diving trips are run out of the marina right below the bridge from Isla Verde. **Cangrejos Yacht Club** (✉ *Rte. 187, Km 1* ☎ *787/791–1015* 🌐 *www.cangrejosyachtclub.com*) is open Monday through Saturday from 8 to 5 and Sunday from 10 to 3. At **Puerto Rico Angling** (☎ *787/724–2079* 🌐 *www.puertoricofishing.com*), José Campos and his son run deep-sea fishing trips for up to six people. They also offer fishing trips through the area's lagoon system.

RÍO GRANDE

35 km (21 mi) southeast of San Juan.

This urban cluster of about 50,000 residents proudly calls itself "The City of El Yunque," as it's the closest community to the rain forest and most of the reserve falls within its district borders. Two images of the rare green parrot, which makes its home in El Yunque, are found on the city's coat of arms; another parrot peeks out at you from the town's flag. The city is also near the posh Rio Mar Beach Resort & Spa, a Wyndham Grand Resort, which is known for its seaside golf courses, lovely beach, and first-class restaurants.

Río Espíritu Santo, which runs through Río Grande, begins in El Yunque's highest elevations and is the island's only navigable river. It was once used to transport lumber, sugar, and coffee from plantations, and immigrants flocked to the region to take advantage of the employment opportunities. Many of today's residents can trace their families to Spain, Austria, and Italy.

GETTING HERE

Located only 30 minutes from San Juan, in the Northern Coastal Valley, Río Grande is easy to get to. From San Juan, take Road 26 toward Carolina until you reach Road 3. Then take Road 3 towards Fajardo for approximately 20 minutes until you see signs for Río Grande.

Car Rental Avis ✉ *Rio Mar Beach Resort & Spa, a Wyndham Grand Resort6000 Río Mar Blvd., Río Grande* ☎ *787/888–6638* 🌐 *www.avis.com*

IT'S THE BOMBA

The *bomba*—a dance for which the northeastern coast is famous—can be traced to the Kongo people of West Africa. Sometimes wearing a flouncy white dress, the woman of a dancing couple moves in a relatively fixed pattern of steps while her partner improvises to the drumbeat. A lead singer and a choir perform a call-and-response song—recounting a local story or event—while percussionists play maracas, *fuas* (wooden sticks that are smacked against a hard surface), *buleadores* (low-timbre, barrel-shape drums), and *subidores* (higher-pitch drums).

3

EXPLORING

The **Museo del Cartel José Hernández** is devoted to posters and the artists who design them. The collection dates from the 1950s and includes many eye-popping posters created for island festivals and art exhibits. ✉ *37 Calle Pimentel, El Centro* ☎ *787/887–2370* *Free* ⏲ *Tues.–Sun. 9–5.*

WHERE TO EAT

$–$$ CARIBBEAN ✕ **Antojitos Puertorriqueñes.** The menu here couldn't be simpler—dishes like fried pork with plantains or stewed crab with beans and rice are your best options. The premises are just as straightforward, a covered patio with plastic tables and chairs. But at these prices, who can complain? ✉ *160 Río Mar Blvd., Río Grande* ☎ *787/888–7378* ▭ *No credit cards.*

$$$–$$$$ ITALIAN ★ ✕ **Palio.** Northern Italian dishes, such as rack of lamb with olive tapenade and fillet of beef with a sweet Muscat grape reduction, are the star attractions at this top-notch restaurant. The amiable staff serves everything with a flourish, whipping up the salads and other dishes beside your table. Specialty coffees are served in mugs engulfed in blue flames, a showstopper that people at neighboring tables applaud. The dining room, with its black-and-white checkerboard floor and darkwood paneling, is among the island's most elegant. You can catch a glimpse of the sea through the floor-to-ceiling windows. ✉ *Rio Mar Beach Resort & Spa, a Wyndham Grand Resort, 6000 Río Mar Blvd., Río Grande* ☎ *787/888–6000* 🌐 *www.wyndhamriomar.com* *Reservations essential* ▭ *AE, D, DC, MC, V* ⏲ *No lunch.*

$–$$$ SEAFOOD ✕ **Richie's Café.** Perched on a mountaintop, this restaurant—a well-located option for Westin Río Mar guests who don't want to dine on-property but are willing to pay on par with hotel prices—has a pair of open-air dining rooms with views to Vieques on a clear day. It's no surprise that seafood is the specialty here—try the fried plantains

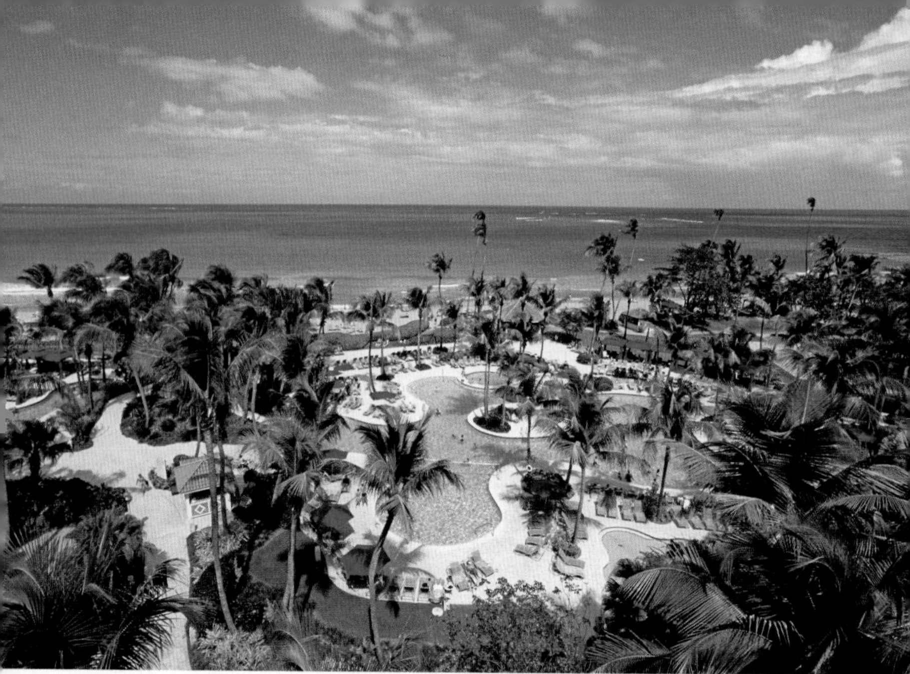

Water-recreation options abound in the enormous pools of The Rio Mar Beach Resort.

filled with shrimp, conch, octopus, or lobster for an appetizer, and then move on to grouper stuffed with crab and served in a spicy sauce. Bring some insect repellent at night, as some readers have mentioned problems with mosquitoes. ✉ *Río Mar Blvd., just past entrance to the Rio Mar Beach Resort & Spa, a Wyndham Grand Resort, Río Grande* ☎ *787/887–1435* or *787/547–1435* 🌐 *www.richiescafepr.com* 💳 *AE, MC, V.*

$ ITALIAN ✕ **Zary's Pizza.** If you simply want to grab a pizza, calzone, lasagna or plate of spaghetti, Zary's is a safe bet for tasty fare. ✉ *Route 3, Km 6 (east of the turnoff for Coco Beach), Río Grande* ☎ *787/645–3895* 💳 *MC, V.*

WHERE TO STAY

$$$$ RESORT **Gran Meliá Puerto Rico.** Located on an enviable stretch of pristine coastline is this massive resort, formerly an all-inclusive hotel called Paradisus Puerto Rico. The open-air lobby, with its elegant floral displays, resembles a Japanese garden, and the swimming pool's columns call to mind ancient Greece. Although the mishmash of styles doesn't quite come together in a coherent way, the resort does a decent job of being all things to all people. The 500 suites, many of which have hot tubs, are spread among two-story bungalows. Loads of them look onto the two 18-hole golf courses that, with patches of dead grass, are in need of some grooming. **Pros:** Beautiful setting; lovely pool area; short walk to the beach. **Cons:** Parking spots are scarce; facade is blank and uninviting; rooms are temperature controlled and tend to be on the chilly side. ✉ *Rte. 968, Km 5.8, Coco Beach* ☎ *787/657–1026 or 800/336–3542* 🌐 *www.meliahotels.com* *500 suites* *In-room: safe, refrigerator. In-hotel: 6*

restaurants, room service, bars, golf courses, tennis courts, pool, gym, spa, beachfront, diving, water sports, children's programs (ages 4–12), concierge, laundry service, public Internet ▭ *AE, D, MC, V* 🍽 *EP.*

$$$$ RESORT ★ **Rio Mar Beach Resort & Spa, a Wyndham Grand Resort.** On more than 500 acres, this sprawling resort is geared toward outdoor activities. Many people come to play the championship golf courses or hike in the nearby rain forest. But the biggest draw is the 2-mi-long (3-km-long) stretch of sand just steps from the door. There's a kiosk near the swimming pools that rents sailboats and other equipment; a dive shop organizes excursions to nearby places of interest. Even the extensive programs for children are mostly outdoors. The seven-story hotel, which wraps around lush gardens, never feels overwhelming. Some rooms are on the small side but are cleverly designed to make use of all the available space. Wyndham took over the property in 2007 and, among other improvements, added its comfy "Be Well" beds. More recently, the Wyndham Rio Mar added a new fire pit overlooking the beach. In addition to daily happy hour from 5 to 7 PM featuring Puerto Rican rum mixes, sangria, and a sizzling s'mores menu, guests can enjoy the theme nights, like Latin/Tropical Dance Lessons, Hawaiian Nights, and International Karaoke by the fire. There are also free Spanish lessons every Monday and Wednesday by the pool at 1 PM. The Mandara Spa transports you to the South Pacific with its hand-carved wood furnishings from Bali. **Pros:** On one of the island's best beaches; great restaurants in and near the hotel; plenty of outdoor activities. **Cons:** Dark and depressing parking garage; long lines at check-in desk. ✉ *6000 Río Mar Blvd., Río Grande* ☎ *787/888–6000 or 877/636–0636* 🌐 *www.wyndhamriomar.com* ⇨ *528 rooms, 72 suites, 59 villas* ♿ *In-room: safe, VCR, Internet. In-hotel: 7 restaurants, bars, golf courses, tennis courts, pools, gym, spa, beachfront, diving, water sports, bicycles, children's programs (ages 4–12), concierge, laundry service, public Internet, public Wi-Fi, airport shuttle* ▭ *AE, D, DC, MC, V* 🍽 *EP.*

NIGHTLIFE

Pick a game—Caribbean stud poker, blackjack, slot machines—and then head to the Las Vegas–style casino at the **Rio Mar Beach Resort & Spa, a Wyndham Grand Resort** (✉ *6000 Río Mar Blvd., Río Grande* ☎ *787/888–6000*). If all that betting makes you thirsty, step into the Players Bar, which is connected to the gaming room.

SPORTS AND THE OUTDOORS

Activities in the Río Grande region are mostly oriented around the two big resorts, the Rio Mar Beach Resort & Spa, a Wyndham Grand Resort and the Grand Meliá Puerto Rico.

DIVING AND SNORKELING The **Dive Center** (✉ *Rio Mar Beach Resort & Spa, a Wyndham Grand Resort, 6000 Río Mar Blvd., Río Grande* ☎ *787/888–6000* 🌐 *www.wyndhamriomar.com*) offers scuba and snorkeling rentals and lessons. Large catamaran snorkeling trips leave from the resort for the calm, crystal-blue seas; beautiful coral reefs; and deserted islands off the coast of northeastern Puerto Rico. The cost is $105 per person, including a buffet lunch, limited open bar, and snacks. If you don't want to invest in a full-day, half-day snorkeling excursions are also available ($75 per person).

GOLF The **Berwind Country Club and Golf Course** (✉ *Rte. 187, Km 4.7* ☎ *787/876–3056*) has an 18-hole course known for its tight fairways and demanding greens. It's open to nonmembers from Tuesday through Friday, with greens fees of $65, which includes a cart and bucket of balls. On Sunday afternoons nonmembers can play if they make arrangements in advance.

Trump International Golf Course (✉ *Grand Melía Puerto Rico, 100 Clubhouse Dr.* ☎ *787/657–2000* 🌐 *www.trumpgolfclubpuertorico.com*), the former Coco Beach Golf & Country Club, features two 18-hole courses designed by PGA Professional Tom Kite, bordered by 100 acres of coastline and outstanding views of El Yunque. Greens fees range from $120 for the Twilight Rate to $200 for the 18-hole Championship Course.

★ The spectacular **Río Mar Country Club** (✉ *Rio Mar Beach Resort & Spa, a Wyndham Grand Resort, 6000 Río Mar Blvd., Río Grande* ☎ *787/888–7060* 🌐 *www.wyndhamriomar.com*) has a clubhouse with a pro shop, two restaurants between two 18-hole courses, and a recently added fire pit that doubles as a place to grab a quick beverage and bite. The River Course, designed by Greg Norman, has challenging fairways that skirt the Mameyes River. The Ocean Course, designed by Tom and George Fazio, has slightly wider fairways than its sister; iguanas can usually be spotted sunning themselves near its fourth hole. If you're not a resort guest, be sure to reserve tee times at least 24 hours in advance. Greens fees for hotel guests range from $70 to $199, depending on tee time. Fees for walk-ins start at $150.

HORSEBACK RIDING ★ **Hacienda Carabalí** (✉ *Rte. 992, Km 4, north of entrance to El Yunque* ☎ *787/690–3781*), a family-run operation, is a good place to jump in the saddle and ride one of Puerto Rico's Paso Fino horses. Hour-long rides ($32) take you around the 600-acre ranch, while two-hour treks take you to a river where you and your horse can take a dip. If you prefer something more high tech, rent a four-wheeler for an excursion through the foothills of El Yunque. At this writing, plans were in the works for a late-2010 canopy tour and guided nature walks in the lowlands of El Yunque rain forest.

TENNIS The facilities at the **Peter Burwash International Tennis Center** (✉ *Rio Mar Beach Resort & Spa, a Wyndham Grand Resort, 6000 Río Mar Blvd., Río Grande* ☎ *787/888–6000* 🌐 *www.pbitennis.com*) are the best in the area. Besides the 13 courts with spectacular views, there are lessons for everyone from novices to old pros.

WATER SPORTS You can rent sea kayaks ($25 an hour for single-person kayaks, $35 and $45 for two- and three-person models, respectively) from **Iguana Water Sports** (✉ *Rio Mar Beach Resort & Spa, a Wyndham Grand Resort, 6000 Río Mar Blvd., Río Grande* ☎ *787/888–6000* 🌐 *www.wyndhamriomar.com*). The helpful staff also rents everything from rafts ($10 a day) to windsurfing equipment ($25 an hour) and offers complimentary beginner sailing clinics.

Look closely at the small tree branches at the side of El Yunque's nature trails and you may spot creatures such as the mountain garden lizard.

SHOPPING

The picturesque **Treehouse Studio** (✉ *unmarked road off Rte. 3* ☎ *787/888–8062*), not far from the rain forest, sells vibrant watercolors by Monica Linville Laird, who also gives workshops. Call for an appointment and directions.

EL YUNQUE

Fodor's Choice ★ 7 mi (11 km) southeast of Río Grande; 26 mi (43 km) southeast of San Juan.

For more information on El Yunque, see the special feature at the beginning of the chapter.

GETTING HERE AND AROUND

You can take a taxi from San Juan to El Yunque (metered rates outside San Juan run about $36 per hour), but to get the most out of the rain forest, it's best to rent a car, even if you have only a few hours to explore. From the greater San Juan area, take the Airport Expressway, Highway 26 (Baldorioty de Castro Avenue) and follow signs east to Carolina; once you are on the expressway, follow it to the end (approximately 14 mi [22½ km]). At the final exit (Carolina), stay in the left-hand lane until you merge with PR Road #3. Continue on PR #3 approximately 13 mi (21 km) until you see the signs for Palmer–El Yunque. Turn right at the traffic signal and follow the road through the village of Palmer until you see the sign for PR Road #191. Turn left on PR #191 and follow it approximately 2 mi (3 km) until you see the El Yunque National

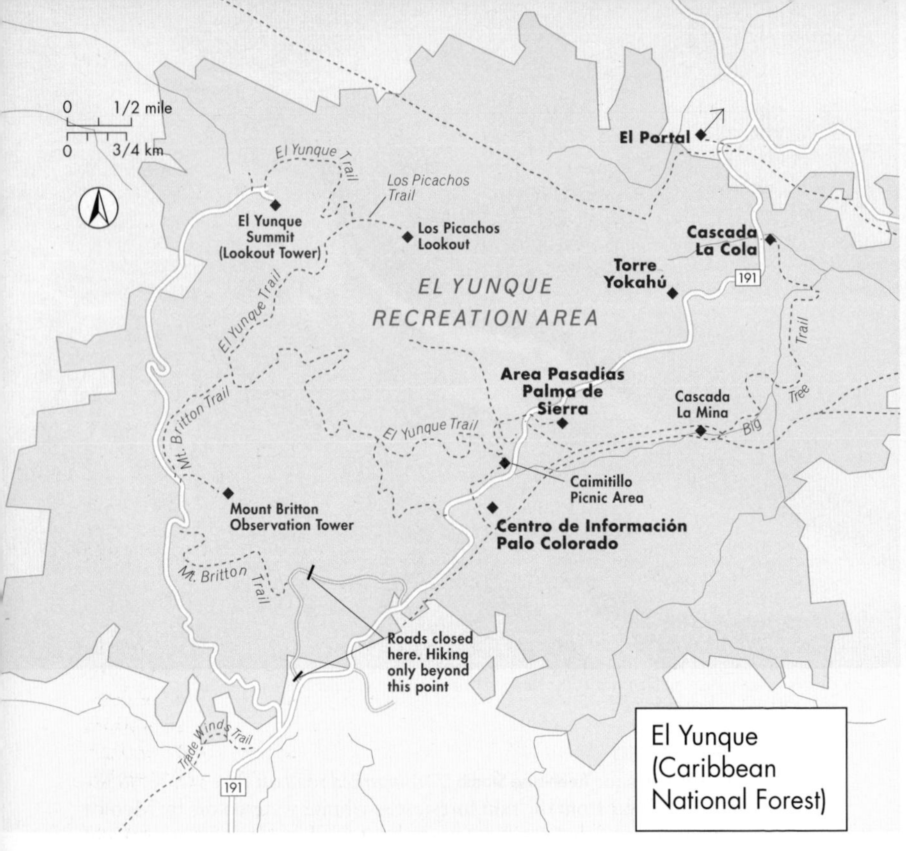

Forest sign. The entrance to the El Portal Rain Forest Center is on your right just after you enter the forest.

TOUR OPERATORS

Many companies in San Juan offer excursions to El Yunque. A National Forest Service ranger leads one-hour English and Spanish tours from the **Palo Colorado Information Center** along the Caimitillo and Baño de Oro trails (⏲ 10:30 AM–2:30 PM; 🎟 $3). Tours are first-come, first-served.

Eco Action Tours will pick you up at your hotel and take you to the rain forest, where small groups will hike, swim in the falls, and learn about the flora and fauna. Half-day rates are reasonable, starting at $58.

Book a half-day excursion with **Acampa Nature Adventure Tours** and choose from a moderate hike at lower elevations of the forest to more challenging treks to the El Yunque peak at 3,500 feet. Rates start at $85, with a six-person minimum.

ESSENTIALS

Admission Fees. There is no entrance fee for the El Yunque National Forest itself. There's an optional admission fee for the El Portal Rainforest Center ($3 adults, $1.50 children and senior citizens).

Admission Hours. The road into El Yunque opens (closes at 6 PM. Ranger stations are open 9–5.

Emergencies. If you witness an accident or the commi ful act or felony, or if you see something happening or suspicious, please contact the Law Enforcement Patrol, José Ayala, at 787/888--5675 (office), 787/ radio paging) or 787/549–0075 (cellular).

Restrooms. There are picnic areas with sheltered tables and bathrooms as well as several basic eateries along the road through the rain forest.

EXPLORING

Before you begin exploring El Yunque, check out the high-tech, interactive displays—explaining rain forests in general and El Yunque in particular—at **El Portal Rainforest Center,** the information center near the northern entrance. The beautifully designed facility is where you can pick up a map of the park and talk to rangers about which trails are open. You can stock up on water, snacks, film, and souvenirs at the small gift shop. ✉ *Rte. 191, Km 4.3, off Rte. 3* ☎ *787/888–1880* 🌐 *www.fs.fed.us/r8/caribbean* 🎟 *$3* ⏲ *Daily 9–5.*

WHERE TO EAT

$$–$$$ CARIBBEAN ✕ **Las Vegas.** The food is a slight cut above what you'd expect to find in such an out-of-the-way place. Be sure to try the rum punch, the corn fritters as an appetizer, then think about the roasted lamb in a wine-and-herb sauce as a hearty dinner. In a region where eating outdoors on plastic tables and chairs is the norm, the dining room's wooden furnishings are a blessing. ✉ *Rte. 191, Km 1.3* ☎ *787/887–2526* 💳 *AE, MC, V* ⏲ *Closed Mon.–Tues.*

¢ CARIBBEAN ✕ **Muralla.** The rangers at El Yunque swear by this place, a cement-block building just past Cascada La Cola. You won't find a cheaper meal anywhere in Puerto Rico, that's for sure. The *arroz habichuela con pollo* (fried chicken with rice and beans) is a steal at less than $5. The barking dog on the roof and the unusual artwork in the open-air dining room—a huge blob of papier-mâché that may or may not be a boulder—add to the atmosphere. Get here early, as the place closes at 5 PM. ✉ *Rte. 191, Km 7.4* ☎ *No phone* 💳 *No credit cards* ⏲ *Closed Thurs. No dinner.*

$ CARIBBEAN ✕ **Yuquiyú Delights.** If you've been hiking all morning in the rain forest, this open-air dining room will be a sight for sore eyes. The covered terrace is scattered with tables whose copper tops add a touch of elegance. The chalkboard out front usually lists a few specials, often local favorites such as *chuleta frita* (fried pork chop). Even if you're not looking for a full meal, there's a little shop where you can stock up on water for the trail or snacks for the ride home. ✉ *Rte. 191, Km 11.3* ☎ *787/396–0970* 🌐 *www.yuquiyudelightspr.com* 💳 *No credit cards* ⏲ *Closed Tues. No dinner.*

SHOPPING

While in El Yunque, buy a recording of the tree frog's song, a video about the endangered green parrot, or a coffee-table book about the rain forest at the large **El Yunque Gift Shop** (✉ *El Portal, Rte. 191, Km 4.3*

☎ *787/888–1880*). Tucked among the rain-forest gifts are other Puerto Rican items, including note cards, maps, soaps, jams, and coffee.

★ Not far from the entrance to El Yunque are half a dozen souvenir shops selling identical T-shirts. A cut above the rest is **Coquí International** (✉ *Rte. 955, near intersection of Rte. 191* ☎ *787/888–1880*). A trail of colorful *coquís* (tree frogs) painted on the floor takes you past artists selling original paintings, handwoven placemats, and one-of-a-kind items of clothing. And if you have to buy a T-shirt, the designs here can be found nowhere else.

LUQUILLO

8 mi (13 km) northeast of Río Grande; 28 mi (45 km) east of San Juan.

Known as the Sun Capital of Puerto Rico, Luquillo has one of the island's best-equipped family beaches. It's also a community where fishing traditions are respected. On the east end of Balneario de Luquillo, past the guarded swimming area, fishermen launch small boats and drop nets in open stretches between coral reefs.

Like many other Puerto Rican towns, Luquillo has its signature festival, in this case the Festival de Platos Típicos (Festival of Typical Dishes), a late-November culinary event that revolves around one ingredient: coconut. During the festivities, many of the community's 18,000 residents gather in the main square, Plaza de Recreo, to sample treats rich with coconut or coconut milk. There's also plenty of free entertainment, including folk shows, troubadour contests, and salsa bands.

GETTING HERE AND AROUND

Públicos run between San Juan to Fajardo and will let travelers off at Luquillo (about a 45-minute ride). Driving takes about the same amount of time. From San Juan, head out Highway 3, get off at Route 193, and follow signs for Luquillo. If you want to explore the town (it's small but well worth the time), a car is helpful. Take note not to park in places where the curb is painted yellow—it's a parking violation.

WHERE TO EAT AND STAY

$–$$ SOUTHWESTERN ✕ **Brass Cactus.** "Gringoland" is how one local described this Tex-Mex eatery. So many English-speaking tourists frequent the place that management doesn't bother printing the menu in Spanish. But the tender ribs and burgers melt in your mouth, and the helpings of crispy fries are generous. Nearly every dish—from the jalapeño burger to the mahimahi wrap—is made to be washed down with beer. Televisions broadcast the latest sporting events, and on the weekend bands often replace the jukebox. Free Wi-fi is available. ✉ *Off Rte. 3, near main entrance to Luquillo* ☎ *787/889–5735* ▭ *AE, MC, V.*

$$ CARIBBEAN ✕ **La Parrilla.** There are more than 50 *kioskos,* or food stands, along the highway on the way to Luquillo Beach. They range from full-service restaurants to standing-room-only stands, and all serve basically the same thing—fried seafood and empanadas. Unlike its weekends-only neighbors, this place is so popular with locals that it's open every day. True to its name, it also has a grill, so you can add some sizzle to your shrimp, salmon, or red snapper; deboned, stuffed with shrimp and

CLOSE UP

210 Parrots and Counting

The Taíno Indians called it the *iguaca,* Spanish speakers refer to it as the *cotorra,* and scientists know it as *Amazona vittata.* Whatever moniker it takes, the Puerto Rican green parrot—the only one native to the island—is one of the world's rarest birds. It nests primarily in the upper levels of El Yunque and in the nearby Sierra de Luquillo. The bird is almost entirely green, though there are touches of blue on its wings, white rings around its eyes, and a red band just above its beak. It's only about 12 inches long, and its raucous squawk doesn't match its delicate appearance. The parrots mate for life. In February (the rain forest's driest season), they build nests within tree hollows and lay three to four eggs. Both parents feed the young.

When the Spanish arrived, the parrot population was an estimated 1 million on the main island, Vieques, and Culebra. But deforestation, hurricanes, and parasites have reduced the population (parrot hunting was common before being outlawed in 1940). By 1967 there were only 19 birds; a 1975 count totaled only 13.

But things are looking up, especially with work beginning on a $2.5 million, state-of-the-art breeding facility in El Yunque. At this writing, an estimated 30 green parrots were living in the wild, and another 180 were in captivity. Officials are optimistic that the numbers will continue to grow. If you're very observant (and very lucky), you just might spot one.

grilled to perfection, it's grilled-fin heaven. There are even a couple of steaks on the menu that are guaranteed to satisfy the biggest carnivores. Like all of its neighbors, this place faces the street, but there's a comfortable patio in the rear where you can kick back with an icy-cold beer or sangria and escape the traffic noise. ✉ *Luquillo Beach, Kiosk #2* ☎ *787/889–0590* ▭ *No credit cards.*

¢–$ MEXICAN ✕ **Lolita's.** When it comes to Mexican food, this place is the real deal. Sure, you could order one of the dozen or so burritos, but why play it safe? Order *carne tampiqueña* (marinated skirt steak), *enchiladas suizas* (enchiladas in a mild green sauce), or *mole con pollo* (chicken in a spicy sauce laced with chocolate) and you'll know where you want to go for your next trip. There's a reason why devoted travelers have been returning for more than a decade. Generous portions are washed down with oversize margaritas, of course. Those who eschew tequila can try the house sangria or one of the many Mexican beers. There's also an unusually varied wine list. The pleasant dining room, decorated with slightly kitschy paintings of village life, is on the second floor of a building just east of Luquillo. Parking can be tricky. ✉ *Rte. 3, Km 41.3, Barrio Juan Martín* ☎ *787/889–5770 or 787/889–0250* ▭ *AE, MC, V.*

¢–$ **Yunque Mar.** A sign near the door says WELCOME TO PARADISE. That might be overstating its charm a bit, but this low-slung hotel is certainly pleasant. It has the barrel-tile roofs and white stucco walls that typify Spanish colonial style. The modest rooms line corridors on two floors; the ocean-view rooms upstairs cost more but are worth it. For another $10 you get a private balcony that's a stone's throw from the water.

DID YOU KNOW?

El Yunque Forest is divided into four forest types according to their elevations. At 2,500 ft. (762 m) above sea level, Cloud Forest is the highest and receives nearly constant rainfall.

The calm waters of Playa Luquillo are a draw for families and beachgoers looking for a relaxing ocean dip.

It's just west of the Balneario de Luquillo, but the beach here is nearly as nice and almost always deserted. The on-site seafood restaurant, La Yola, is a favorite with locals. **Pros:** On a lovely beach; great restaurant; friendly owners; rooms boast only basic amenities but are clean. **Cons:** Building is on a crowded street; bland decor; no in-room safe; no elevator. ✉ *6 Calle 1, Fortuna* ☎ *787/889–5555* *15 rooms, 2 suites* *In-hotel: restaurant, bar, pool* ▭ *AE, MC, V* *EP.*

SPORTS AND THE OUTDOORS

SURFING Not far from Playa La Pared, **La Selva Surf Shop** (✉ *250 Calle Fernández Garcia Luquillo* ☎ *787/889–6205* 🌐 *www.rainforestsafari.com/selva.html*) has anything a surfer could need, including news about current conditions. The family-run shop sells sunglasses, sandals, bathing suits, and other beach necessities.

FAJARDO

7 mi (11 km) southeast of Luquillo; 34 mi (55 km) southeast of San Juan.

Fajardo, founded in 1772, has historical notoriety as a port where pirates stocked up on supplies. It later developed into a fishing community and an area where sugarcane flourished. (There are still cane fields on the city's fringes.) Today it's a hub for the yachts that use its marinas, the divers who head to its good offshore sites, and the day-trippers who travel by catamaran, ferry, or plane to the islands of Culebra and Vieques. With the most significant docking facilities on the island's eastern side, Fajardo is a bustling city of 37,000—so bustling, in fact, that its unremarkable downtown is often congested and difficult to navigate.

GETTING HERE AND AROUND

Getting around Fajardo is tricky without a car, especially if you plan on visiting several of the sights. **Travel with Padin** (☎ *787/644–3091or 787/355–6746*) will take passengers from the San Juan Airport to the ferry for $60 (two people) with prior reservations. Públicos are also an option, albeit time-consuming—be sure to ask your driver to take you all the way to the port.

Fajardo is served by the one-room **Aeropuerto Diego Jiménez Torres,** (☎ *787/860–3110*) just southwest of the city on Route 976, with flight service to Vieques, San Juan, St. Thomas, and St. Croix via Air Flamenco, Isla Nena, and Vieques Air Link. The landing field at **Aeropuerto Regional de Humacao** (☎ *787/852–8188*) is used mostly by private planes.

Car Rental Avis (✉ *El Conquistador Resort & Golden Door Spa, 1000 Av. El Conquistador, Fajardo* ☎ *787/863–2735* 🌐 *www.avis.com.* **L&M Car Rental** (✉ *Hwy. 3, Km 43.7, in El Conquistador Hotel, Fajardo* ☎ *787/860–6868.* **Leaseway of Puerto Rico** (✉ *Rte. 3, Km 44.4, Fajardo* ☎ *787/860–5000).* **World Car Rental** (✉ *Calle Únion 466 [entrance on Calle Cometa], Fajardo* ☎ *787/863–8696 or 787/860–4808).*

EXPLORING

Las Croabas. A few miles north of Fajardo is this fishing area, where seafood is sold in open-air restaurants along the ocean. In the middle of town is a small park with a lovely waterfront walk. ✉ *Rte. 3, Km 51.2.*

Marina Puerto del Rey. Home to 1,100 boats, this is one of the Caribbean's largest marinas. This is the place to hook up with a scuba-diving group, arrange an excursion to Vieques's bioluminescent bay, or charter a fishing boat. The marina, located south of Fajardo, also has several restaurants and boating-supply stores. ✉ *Rte. 9987, off Rte. 987* ☎ *787/860–1000* 🌐 *www.puertodelrey.com.*

Reserva Natural Las Cabezas de San Juan. The 316-acre reserve on a headland north of Fajardo is owned by the nonprofit Conservation Trust of Puerto Rico. You ride in open-air trolleys and wander down boardwalks through seven ecosystems, including lagoons, mangrove swamps, and dry-forest areas. Green iguanas skitter across paths, and guides identify other endangered species. A half-hour hike down a wooden walkway brings you to the mangrove-lined **Laguna Grande,** where bioluminescent microorganisms glow at night. The restored **Fajardo Lighthouse** is the final stop on the tour; its Spanish-colonial tower has been in operation since 1882, making it Puerto Rico's second-oldest lighthouse. The first floor houses ecological displays; a winding staircase leads to an observation deck. The only way to see the reserve is on a mandatory guided tour; reservations are required. ✉ *Rte. 987, Km 6* ☎ *787/722–5882 weekdays or 787/860–2560 weekends* 🌐 *www.fideicomiso.org* 🎟 *$7* 🕓 *Tours Wed.–Sun. at 8:30, 9:30, 10, 10:30, and 2.*

Villa Marina. The second-largest marina in Fajardo, it's home to charter-fishing boats as well as several catamaran operators who give day tours for swimming and snorkeling to the deserted islands right off

Puerto Rico's northeast coast. ✉ *Rte. 987, Km 1.3* ☎ *787/863–5131* 🌐 *www.villamarinapr.com.*

WHERE TO EAT

$$–$$$ SEAFOOD ✕ **Anchor's Inn.** Seafood is the specialty at this shipshape restaurant. It's a great place to sample such local favorites as *chillo entero* (fried whole red snapper), among others. When the porthole windows are flung open, a nice breeze blows through the dining room. The convenient location, down the road from El Conquistador Resort, lures travelers who have had enough hotel food. ✉ *Rte. 987, Km 2.7* ☎ *787/863–7200* *Reservations not accepted* 💳 *AE, MC, V* ⏲ *Closed Tues.*

$$$–$$$$ ASIAN ✕ **Blossoms.** Hung with elaborate lanterns, this dining room is a fanciful version of the Far East. The first thing you'll notice is the sound of meats and vegetables sizzling on the large teppanyaki tables. The chefs here know they're on stage and perform with a flourish. Despite the abundance of fresh fish, sushi bars are a rarity in this part of Puerto Rico. But the excellent one here has a seemingly endless array of dishes. Want traditional Chinese fare? Try the fancifully named "Passion Love Boat" (lobster and shrimp) or "Full Steam Ahead" (steamed fish with scallions and black mushrooms). ✉ *El Conquistador Resort & Golden Door Spa, Rte. 987, Km 3.4* ☎ *787/863–1000* 🌐 *www.elconresort.com/resort_activities/blossoms.cfm* *Reservations essential* 💳 *AE, D, DC, MC, V* ⏲ *No lunch Mon.–Sat.*

$$$ SEAFOOD ✕ **Calizo.** There's a string of seafood shacks on the island's northeastern coast, all serving delicious fried fish. This open-air eatery, one of the best in the village of Las Croabas, takes things up a notch or two. Look for dishes like conch salad in a spicy vinaigrette, mahimahi in a honey-and-white-wine sauce, or chunks of lobster sautéed in garlic. Wash it all down with an icy-cold beer on tap. It's almost across from the Balneario Seven Seas, making it a great place to refuel after a day at the beach. The only drawback is that it's a bit on the pricey side. ✉ *Rte. 987, Las Croabas* ☎ *787/706–7337* 💳 *MC, V.*

$$$ CARIBBEAN ✕ **Pasión por el Fogón.** The name refers to the passion that chef Myrta Pérez Toledo possesses for taking traditional dishes and making them into something special. Pérez loves to present her dishes in unexpected ways—for example, the flank steak is rolled into a cylinder and stands on one end. But what makes this dish remarkable is the slightly sweet tamarind sauce that brings out the meat's earthy flavors. If you're a seafood lover, start with the lemony ceviche, and then move on to the lobster medallions broiled in butter. Owner Norma Guadaloupe, who will no doubt greet you at the door, often wears a brilliant shade of red that matches the main dining room's walls. It seems to be a case of a food lover wearing her heart on her sleeve. ✉ *Rte. 987, Km 2.3* ☎ *787/863–3502* 🌐 *www.pasioporelfogon.com* 💳 *MC, V.*

$–$$ SEA FOOD ✕ **Rosa's Sea Food.** Despite its name, this family-run restaurant just outside the gates of Marina Puerto Real is also a good spot for beef and chicken. But if you want to see what people from all around the island are raving about, stick with the seafood. The specialty here is pieces of lobster, simmered with onions, tomatoes, and red peppers. Grilled and sautéed selections of fresh fish, from tuna to red snapper, are also a success. You can't miss the restaurant, as it's inside a two-story house painted a

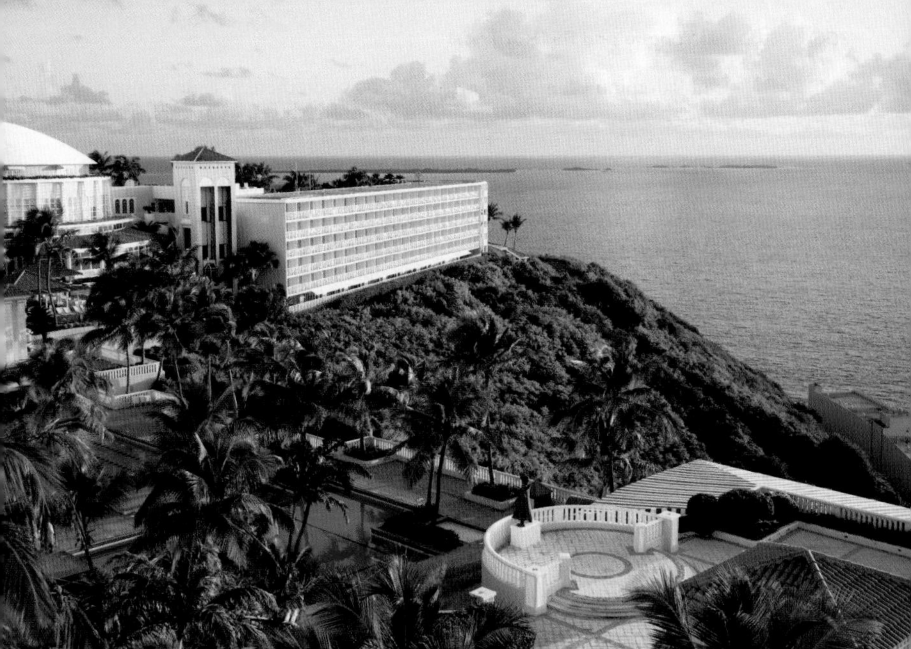
High on top of a bluff, the El Conquistador Resort has commanding views of the ocean.

vivid shade of pink. ✉ *536 Calle Tablazo, off Rte. 195* ☎ *787/863–0213* *Reservations not accepted* ▭ *AE, MC, V* ⊙ *Closed Wed.*

WHERE TO STAY

$ INN **Ceiba Country Inn.** Although it's close to the rain forest, Fajardo has few lodgings that take advantage of the area's gorgeous greenery. For that reason you might want to drive 5 mi (8 km) south to the town of Ceiba, where amid the rolling hills you'll find this unassuming little inn. Colorful birds—the same ones you'll see in nearby El Yunque—flutter through the tropical foliage. Don't worry—you won't miss the ocean. From the sunny patio you have a view of Culebra, one of the small islands to the east of Puerto Rico. The same seascape is available from several of the simply furnished rooms—just ask for Room 1, 2, 8, or 9. Owners Sue Newbauer and Dick Bray, along with several dogs, will make you feel right at home. **Pros:** Gorgeous setting; friendly owners; proximity to El Yunque. **Cons:** Very steep driveway; hard to find; far from tourist areas; not for those with pet allergies; no elevator. ✉ *Rte. 977, Km 1.2, Ceiba* ☎ *787/885–0471* 🌐 *www.geocities.com/countryinn* *9 rooms* *In-room: refrigerator. In-hotel: bar* ▭ *AE, MC, V* *CP.*

$$$–$$$$ RESORT Fodor's Choice ★ **El Conquistador Resort & Golden Door Spa.** The name means "The Conqueror," and this sprawling complex certainly has claimed the northeastern tip of the island. Perched on a bluff overlooking the ocean, it is one of Puerto Rico's loveliest destination resorts. Arranged in five "villages," the whitewashed buildings bring to mind the colonial era. Guest rooms were completely renovated—right down to the floors—in 2007. The ultramodern furnishings are all low to the ground, making sure nothing obscures the ocean views. The resort's beach is just offshore

on Palomino Island; a shuttle boat takes you there in eight minutes. At the resort there are several different pools, as well as a water park for kids (and kids at heart). For grown-ups, the Japanese-influenced Golden Door is widely considered among the Caribbean's best spas. The Strip House is the newest of the cluster of top-drawer restaurants. **Pros:** Some of the island's best rooms; unbeatable views of the nearby islands; good dining options in and near hotel. **Cons:** Must take a boat to the beach; long waits at the funicular taking guests between levels; self-parking lot is a long distance from the front door. ✉ *1000 Av. El Conquistador, Box 70001, Fajardo 00738* ☎ *787/863–1000 or 800/468–0389* 🌐 *www.elconresort.com* *750 rooms, 17 suites, 155 villas* *In-room: safe, refrigerator, VCR, Wi-Fi. In-hotel: 17 restaurants, bars, golf course, tennis courts, pools, gym, spa, beachfront, diving, water sports, children's programs (ages 4–12), laundry service, public Wi-Fi, airport shuttle, parking (fee)* *AE, D, DC, MC, V* *EP.*

$–$$ HOTEL **Fajardo Inn.** The butterscotch-colored buildings that make up this hilltop hotel offer lovely views of the islands poking out of the Atlantic Ocean. A bit closer is the pool lined with shimmering aquamarine tiles, surrounded by gardens filled with wild ginger and other colorful plants. All rooms have simple furnishings and white-tile floors; some have balconies that let you enjoy the sunrise. Two restaurants, Starfish and Blue Iguana, are so good that they attract locals. The closest beach is the public Balneario Seven Seas, about a five-minute drive away. **Pros:** Beautiful grounds; family-friendly environment; good value. **Cons:** Not on the beach; motel-like rooms. ✉ *Rte. 195, 52 Parcelas, Beltran Sector, Fajardo* ☎ *787/860–6000 or 888/860–6006* 🌐 *www.fajardoinn.com* *54 rooms* *In-room: kitchen (some), refrigerator (some). In-hotel: 2 restaurants, bar, pool, tennis court, public Internet, laundry service, parking (no fee), no-smoking rooms* *AE, MC, V* *EP.*

NIGHTLIFE

Most of the evening action takes place in the El Conquistador Resort's lounges, but there are a few neighborhood bars where locals drink beer. You can play slots, blackjack, roulette, and video poker at **El Conquistador Casino** (✉ *El Conquistador Resort & Golden Door Spa, 1000 Av. El Conquistador* ☎ *787/863–1000*), a typical hotel gambling facility within the resort's lavish grounds.

SHOPPING

Maria Elba Torres runs the **Galería Arrecife** (✉ *El Conquistador Resort & Golden Door Spa, 1000 Av. El Conquistador* ☎ *787/863–3972*), which shows only works by Caribbean artists. Look for ceramics by Rafael de Olmo and jewelry made from fish scales. Chocolate-loving Laurie Humphrey had trouble finding a supplier for her sweet tooth, so she opened the **Paradise Store** (✉ *Rte. 194, Km 0.4* ☎ *787/863–8182*). Lindt and other gourmet chocolates jam the shop, which also sells flowers and such gift items as Puerto Rican–made soaps.

SPORTS AND THE OUTDOORS

GOLF ★ The 18-hole, Arthur Hills–designed course at **El Conquistador Resort & Golden Door Spa** (✉ *1000 Av. El Conquistador* ☎ *787/863–6784*) is famous for its 200-foot changes in elevation. From the highest spot, on the 15th hole, you have great views of the surrounding mountains. The trade winds make every shot challenging. Greens fees for resort guests range from $100 to $165 and are even steeper for nonguests.

DAY SAILS Several reputable catamaran and yacht operators in Fajardo make excursions to the reefs and sparkling blue waters surrounding a handful of small islets just off the coast. Many of the trips include transportation from San Juan and transportation to and from San Juan–area hotels. Whether or not you're staying in Fajardo, if you take a day trip on the water, you'll see classic Caribbean scenes of coral reefs rife with sea life, breathtakingly clear water, and palm-fringed, deserted beaches. The day sails, with stops for snorkeling, include swimming breaks at deserted beaches and picnic lunches. Most of the craft are outfitted for comfort, with quality stereo systems and full-service bars. Many competent operators offer a nearly identical experience, so your selection will probably be based on price and which operators serve your San Juan hotel, or which operate out of the marina in Fajardo that you are visiting. Prices range from $55 to $95; price is affected by whether you join a trip in San Juan or in Fajardo and by what is included in the cost. Ask if extras, such as picnic lunches and a full-service bar, are included. They are quickly becoming standard features.

At **East Winds Excursions** (✉ *Marina Puerto del Rey, Rte. 3, Km 51.4* ☎ *787/860–3434 or 877/937–4386* 🌐 *www.eastwindcats.com*) catamarans ranging in size from 45 feet to 65 feet take you offshore for snorkeling. Two of the catamarans are powered, and this cuts down tremendously on the travel time to outlying islands. Trips include stops at isolated beaches and a lunch buffet, included in the price. All craft are outfitted with swimming decks, freshwater showers, and full-service bars. These vessels are some of the plushest for day sails in the area.

Erin Go Bragh (✉ *Marina Puerto del Rey, Rte. 3, Km 51.4* ☎ *787/860–4401 or 787/409–2511* 🌐 *www.egbc.net*) is a sailing yacht based in Fajardo that takes a tour of the glistening waters and nearby islands. It is known for its barbecue picnic lunches. Snorkel and fishing equipment are provided. Longer charters are available for groups.

At Villa Marina, **Fajardo Tours** (✉ *Villa Marina, Rte. 987, Km 1.3* ☎ *787/863–2821* 🌐 *www.travelerpr.com*) has a 54-foot catamaran called the *Traveler* that takes you to pristine coral reefs for an afternoon of snorkeling. Of course, there's the usual lunch buffet and plenty of rum punch.

The ***Spread Eagle II*** (✉ *Puerto del Rey Marina, Rte. 3, Km 51.4* ☎ *787/887–8821 or 888/523–4511* 🌐 *www.snorkelpr.com*) is a 51-foot catamaran that heads out to isolated beaches on the islands off Fajardo. The trip includes an all-you-can-eat buffet and unlimited piña coladas. To top it off, you get a free snorkel to bring home. Sunset and moonlight cruises are also available.

DIVING **La Casa del Mar Dive Center** (✉ *El Conquistador Resort & Golden Door Spa, 1000 Av. El Conquistador* ☎ *787/863–1000 ext. 7919 or 787/860–3483* ✉ *lacasadelmar@hotmail.com*) focuses its scuba and snorkeling activity on the islets of Palominos, Lobos, and Diablo. It also offers boating charters and trips to Vieques's bioluminescent bay. A two-tank morning dive costs $99–$124, depending on your equipment needs; single-tank afternoon dives are $69–$94. An afternoon of snorkeling costs $50 per person.

At **Sea Ventures Pro Dive Center** (✉ *Marina Puerto del Rey, Rte. 3, Km 51.4* ☎ *787/863–3483* 🌐 *www.divepuertorico.com*) you can get your diving certification, arrange dive trips to 20 offshore sites, or organize boating and sailing excursions. A two-tank dive for certified divers, including equipment, is $119.

KAYAKING Several tour operators, including some based in San Juan, offer nighttime kayaking tours in the bioluminescent bay at the Reserva Natural Las Cabezas de San Juan, just north of Fajardo.

Eco Action Tours (☎ *787/791–7509 or 787/640–7385* 🌐 *www.ecoactiontours.com*) provides transportation and gives kayak tours of the shimmering Fajardo bay every night, with pickup service in the Fajardo area and San Juan hotels. The outfit also offers sailing tours to Culebra, daylong snorkeling trips, and Jet Ski rentals.

THE EASTERN COAST

From Fajardo, a good way to explore the southeast is to travel along the old coastal road, Route 3, as it weaves on and off the shoreline and passes through small towns. The route takes a while to travel but offers terrific beach and mountain scenery.

NAGUABO

11 mi (18 km) southwest of Fajardo.

In this fast-growing municipality's downtown, pastel buildings give the main plaza the look of a child's nursery: A golden-yellow church on one side faces a butter-yellow city hall, and a pink-and-blue amphitheater anchors one corner. It's a good spot for people watching until the heat drives you to the beach.

Offshore, Cayo Santiago—also known as Monkey Island—is the site of some of the world's most important rhesus monkey research. A small colony of monkeys was introduced to the island in the late 1930s, and since then scientists have been studying their habits and health, especially as they pertain to the study of diabetes and arthritis. You can't land at Cayo Santiago, but Captain Frank Lopez sails a small tour boat—*La Paseadora Naguabeña*—around it.

GETTING HERE AND AROUND

To reach Naguabo, it takes about an hour driving from San Juan. It's just south of Fajardo off of Highway 53, along Route 31. From Route 31, turn down Calle Garzot , to reach the town square. Although públicos run to and from Naguabo, public transportation within Naguabo is extremely limited, so a rental car is your best transportation option.

WHERE TO EAT AND STAY

$ SEAFOOD ✕ **Chumar.** As at the other seafood shacks along Playa Húcares, you order at the counter and then grab a seat at one of the plastic tables lining the sidewalk. It's right on the ocean, so you are almost guaranteed fresh fish.

Paper plates and plastic cutlery accompany the down-home seafood. Afterward you can stroll along the waterfront walkway across the street. ✉ *Rte. 3, Km 66, Playa Húcares* ☎ *787/874–0107* ▭ *MC, V.*

$ **Casa Cubuy Ecolodge.** El Yunque's southern edge is the setting for this hotel. If you're up for a hike, set off on your own for a short one or hire a local guide for a daylong adventure that takes you through thick rain forest to hidden waterfalls. If you'd rather relax, hammocks await you on the tiled veranda. Guest rooms are simple—no phones or TVs—but comfortable, with tile floors, rattan furniture, and windows that show off one of the island's best views. You must climb many stairs to reach the upper rooms; if this is a problem, request one on the lower level. The proprietor, who believes that healthful eating translates into healthful living, serves tasty and wholesome breakfasts. Light picnic lunches can also be ordered in the morning to take with you on hikes, and dinner is available for groups of four or more. **Pros:** Spectacular setting; close to some of the island's best hiking trails; doting staff. **Cons:** Basic rooms; up a terrible road; lower-level rooms are small. ✉ *Rte. 191, Km 22, Barrio Río Blanco* ☎ *787/874–6221* 🌐 *www.casacubuy.com* *8 rooms* *In-room: no a/c, no TV. In-hotel: no elevator* ▭ *AE, MC, V* *BP.*

3

SPORTS AND THE OUTDOORS

Captain Frank Lopez will sail you around Cayo Santiago aboard ***La Paseadora*** (✉ *Playa Húcares dock, Rte. 3, Km 66.6* ☎ *787/850–7881*). Lopez, a charming, well-informed guide, gears the outings to the group. In an hour or 90 minutes, you can motor around the island and watch the monkeys. You can also make arrangements in advance for snorkeling stops or for the captain to drop you off at another islet and pick you up later.

HUMACAO

9 mi (15 km) southwest of Naguabo; 55 km (34 mi) southeast of San Juan.

Travelers flock to the Humacao area for one reason: the sprawling resort community called Palmas del Mar and its two world-class golf courses, the Flamboyán and the Palm. Although it's not thought of as a tourist destination, Humacao does have a handful of interesting neocolonial buildings along its traffic-clogged downtown streets. These are worth a peek if you're stuck here on a rainy day.

GETTING HERE AND AROUND

Huamaco is served by two highways and one toll expressway. Highway 30 serves as the main highway coming from points west (Caguas and Las Piedras), while Highway 53 serves destinations to the north (Fajardo and Naguabo). Highway 3, the main highway bordering the eastern coastline of the island from San Juan, passes through Humacao.

Car Rental Avis ✉ *170 Candelero Dr., Humacao* ☎ *787/285-1376* 🌐 *www.avis.com*

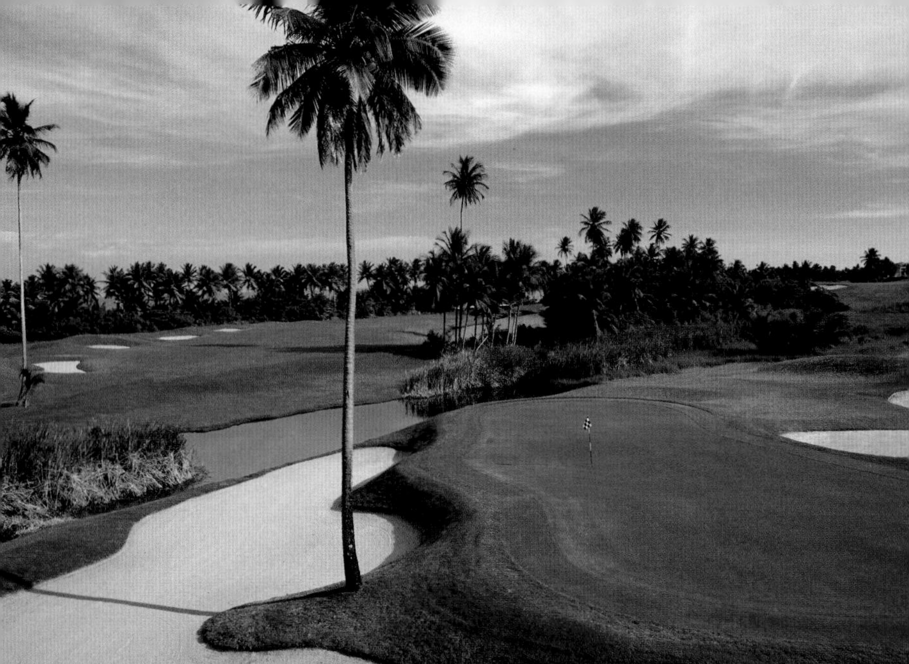
The Palmas del Mar Country Club features the Reese Jones-designed Flamboyán course.

EXPLORING

The former residence of sugar baron Antonio Roig Torruellas, **Museo Casa Roig** was built in 1919. Czech architect Antonio Nechodoma designed the facade, unusual for its wide eaves, mosaic work, and stained-glass windows with geometric patterns. This building, which bears more than a passing resemblance to those of Frank Lloyd Wright, was Puerto Rico's first 20th-century building to be included on the register of National Historic Places. The Roig family lived in the home until 1956; it was then abandoned before being turned over to the University of Puerto Rico in 1977. It's currently a museum and cultural center that houses historical photos, furniture, and rotating exhibits of works by contemporary island artists. ✉ *66 Calle Antonio López* ☎ *787/852–8380* 🌐 *www.uprh.edu/~museocr* 🎫 *Free* 🕑 *Wed.–Fri. and Sun. 10–4.*

Plaza de Humacao, downtown's broad square, is anchored by the pale pink Catedral Dulce Nombre de Jesús (Sweet Name of Jesus Cathedral), which dates from 1869. It has a castlelike facade, and even when its grille door is locked, you can peek through to see the sleek altar, polished floors, and stained-glass windows dominated by blues. Across the plaza, four fountains splash under the shade of old trees. People pass through feeding the pigeons, children race down the promenade, and retirees congregate on benches to chat. Look for the little monument with the globe on top; it's a tribute to city sons who died in wars. ✉ *Av. Font Martel at Calle Ulises Martinez.*

As you travel from Naguabo to Humacao, you'll pass stretches of beach and swaths of undeveloped land, including the swamps, lagoons, and forested areas of the **Refugio de Vida Silvestre de Humacao.** This nature reserve has an information office, restrooms, and campsites. ✉ *Rte. 3, Km 74.3* ☎ *787/852–4440* *Free* ⏲ *Weekdays 7:30–4:30.*

WHERE TO EAT AND STAY

$–$$ CAFE ✕ **Bistro Rico.** You can't eat at Chez Daniel every night, which is probably why Daniel Vasse opened this bistro a stone's throw away from his original restaurant. The menu here is mostly made up of sandwiches, but don't expect anything too ordinary. The sliced duck breast with caramelized red onions is simple but satisfying, as is the codfish with slices of hard-boiled eggs or the filet mignon with béarnaise sauce. The handful of entrées includes—of course—a smashing quiche Lorraine. The staff is friendly, and the simple decor is livened up with some slightly kitschy seaside murals. ✉ *Palmas del Mar, Anchor's Village Marina, Rte. 906, Km 86.4* ☎ *787/850–3838* 💳 *AE, MC, V* ⏲ *Closed Sun.*

3

$$$–$$$$ FRENCH Fodor's Choice ★ ✕ **Chez Daniel.** When the stars are out, it would be hard to find a more romantic setting than this waterfront eatery in the Anchor's Village Marina. Dozens of gleaming white boats are anchored so close that you could practically hit them with a baguette. The dining room has a chummy atmosphere, probably because many patrons seem to know each other. If you'd prefer alone time, ask for a table on one of the private terraces. Chef Daniel Vasse's French-country-style dishes are some of the best on the island. The exceptional Catalan-style bouillabaisse is full of fresh fish and bursts with the flavor of a white garlic sauce. Pair it with a bottle from the extensive wine cellar. Sunday brunch, with its seemingly endless seafood bar, draws people from all over the island. ✉ *Palmas del Mar, Anchor's Village Marina, Rte. 906, Km 86.4* ☎ *787/850–3838* 🌐 *www.chezdanielpalmasdelmar.com* *Reservations essential* 💳 *AE, MC, V* ⏲ *Closed Tues. No lunch Mon.–Thurs.*

$$ HOTEL **Four Points by Sheraton at Palmas del Mar Hotel & Casino.** The only hotel in Palmas del Mar, the Four Points by Sheraton, sits amid acres and acres of condo developments. It's surprisingly modest in scale, given its opulent surroundings. The rooms could be at any hotel, but those fitted with plantation-style furnishings are more luxurious. None of the rooms have a view of the ocean, but all of them have balconies overlooking the infinity pool or the lush grounds. Because you have access to the facilities at Palmas del Mar, you can stroll around the marina, play a few games of tennis, or hit the links at the two championship golf courses. **Pros:** Access to all the resort's amenities; near excellent restaurants; beautiful pool area; outgoing staff. **Cons:** Uninspired architecture; standard-issue albeit slightly rundown rooms; small casino. ✉ *170 Candelero Dr.* ☎ *787/850–6000* 🌐 *www.starwoodhotels.com* *107 rooms* *In-room: safe, Wi-Fi. In-hotel: restaurant, room service, bars, golf courses, tennis courts, pool, gym, beachfront, diving, water sports, public Wi-Fi, airport shuttle* 💳 *AE, D, DC, MC, V* *EP.*

$ HOTEL **Parador Palmas de Lucía.** Lights shaped like palm trees illuminate the pool area at this family-run hotel. The rooms are larger than you'd expect for the price and have spotless kitchenettes. Kids like chatting with Coquí, the M&M-munching macaw that resides in the lobby. The hotel is in Yabucoa, several miles south of Humacao. **Pros:** An off-the-beaten-path feel; friendly staff. **Cons:** A 15-minute drive to restaurants;

a bit difficult to find. ✉ *Rte. 901 at Rte. 9911, Yabucoa* ☎ *787/893–4423* 🌐 *www.palmasdelucia.com* ⇨ *34 rooms* ♿ *In-room: refrigerator. In-hotel: restaurant, laundry service* ▭ *AE, MC, V* 🍴 *EP.*

NIGHTLIFE

The small casino at the **Four Points by Sheraton Palmas del Mar Resort** (✉ *170 Candelero Dr.* ☎ *787/850–6000*) offers everything from blackjack to slot machines. The action is liveliest on weekends.

SPORTS AND THE OUTDOORS

FISHING

At **Karolette Sport Fishing** (✉ *Palmas del Mar, Anchor's Village Marina* ☎ *787/850–7442* 🌐 *www.puertoricodeepseafishing.com*), you're in the capable hands of Captain Bill Burleson, who has fished these waters since 1966. He'll take you out for excursions in his bright yellow Bertram powerboat. A half day of fishing along the continental shelf costs $680, while a full day (usually more than nine hours) of deep-water fishing costs $1,250. If nobody makes a catch, he'll cut the fee in half.

Maragata Charters (✉ *Palmas del Mar, Anchor's Village Marina* ☎ *787/850–7548 or 637–1802* 🌐 *www.maragatacharters.com*) takes anglers out to the continental shelf on a 38-foot power catamaran. For a four-hour tour, the cost starts at $105 per person, while an eight-hour tour starts at $200 per person.

GOLF

★ **Palmas del Mar Country Club** (✉ *Rte. 906* ☎ *787/285–2256* 🌐 *www.palmascountryclub.com*) has two good golf courses: The Rees Jones–designed Flamboyán course, named for the nearly six dozen flamboyant trees that pepper its fairway, has been rated one of the top five courses in the world. The older Gary Player–designed Palm course has a challenging par 5 that scoots around wetlands. Greens fees are $80–$100.

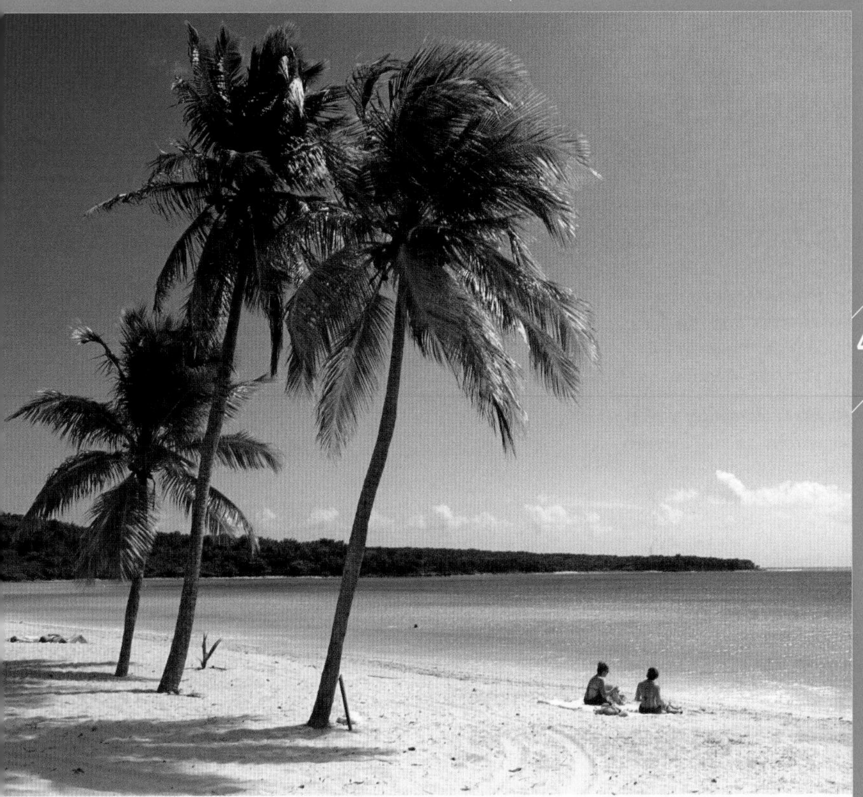

Vieques and Culebra

WORD OF MOUTH

"The open-air bars let in afternoon breezes and time quickly passed as we plied ourselves with pina coladas and mojitos. We floated through tunnels of mangroves, watching the herons fly, and the black crabs scuttle through the trees. At night, the stars in the sky mirrored the pixie lights in the bioluminescent bay. Vieques just feels good."

—akila

WELCOME TO VIEQUES AND CULEBRA

TOP REASONS TO GO

★ **Puerto Mosquito:** Kayak after dark on the astounding bioluminescent bay on Vieques.

★ **Playa Flamenco:** Catch some rays on this Culebra bay, consistently ranked as one of the world's best white-sand beaches.

★ **Bicycle Refugio Nacional de Vida Silvestre de Vieques:** Explore around the base of Monte Pirata on the western side of the island.

★ **El Resuelve:** Sample real Puerto Rican fare with the locals at this colorful roadside restaurant on Vieques.

★ **Playa Carlos Rosario:** Simply walk into the waters off this deserted Culebra beach to snorkel a fabulous coral reef.

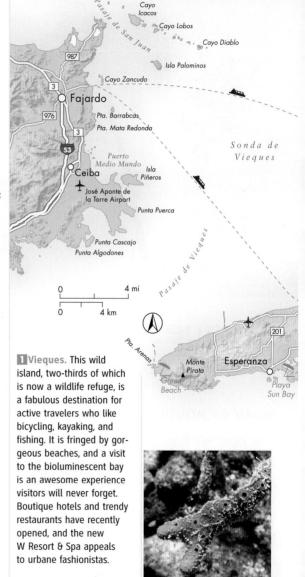

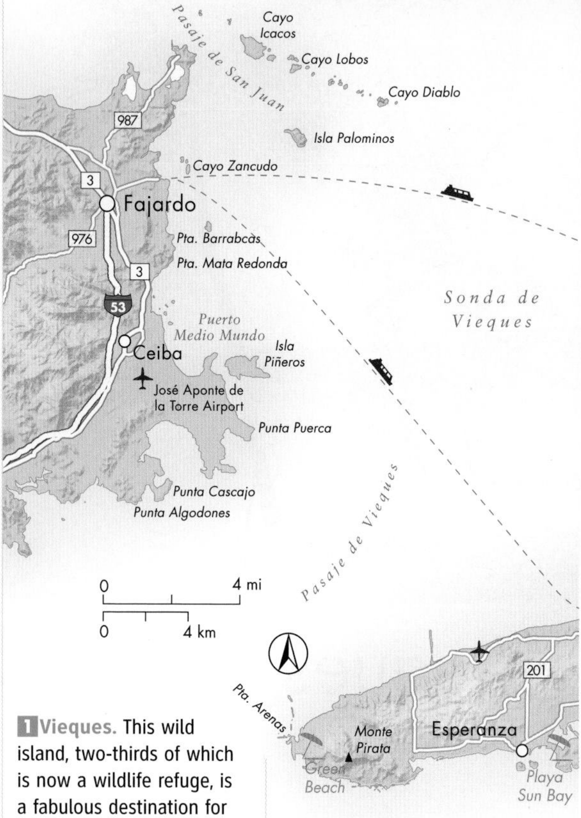

1 Vieques. This wild island, two-thirds of which is now a wildlife refuge, is a fabulous destination for active travelers who like bicycling, kayaking, and fishing. It is fringed by gorgeous beaches, and a visit to the bioluminescent bay is an awesome experience visitors will never forget. Boutique hotels and trendy restaurants have recently opened, and the new W Resort & Spa appeals to urbane fashionistas.

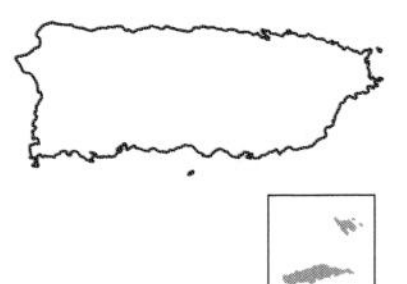

GETTING ORIENTED

Vieques is 21 mi (33½ km) long and 4 mi (6½ km) wide and has two small communities. Isabel Segunda, on the northern shore, is the main town, where the ferry docks. On the southern shore is the village of Esperanza, little more that a string of low-cost bars, restaurants, and hotels along a waterfront promenade. Nearby is the world-famous bioluminescent bay Puerto Mosquito. The bulk of the island is a national park, the Vieques National Wildlife Refuge. Within the park you'll find dozens of beaches with names such as Caracas, Plata, and Chiva, as well as many more that have no official name. At 7 mi (11 km) long and 4 mi (6½ km) wide, Culebra is much smaller and less developed than Vieques. There's only one community, the tiny town of Dewey.

2 Culebra. The island is mostly unspoiled, a quality that brings many people back year after year. People come to Culebra to laze on Playa Flamenco, consistently rated one of the top ten most beautiful beaches in the world, as well as many lesser-known but sensational beaches. Snorkeling and diving on the cays surrounding Culebra are rated world-class.

4

VIEQUES AND CULEBRA PLANNER

When to Go

Roughly speaking, high season runs from December 15 through April 15. Puerto Ricans flock at Christmas and Easter, when Vieques and Culebra are packed with families enjoying the sun and sand. Be sure to make reservations well in advance if you're visiting during the holidays. The shoulder season, when prices are a bit lower, is a good option. Remember, however, that some restaurants and hotels are only open during the high season. The only time you might want to avoid is late August through late October, when hurricanes can strike the area.

Safety

Vieques is relatively crime-free compared to San Juan, although it pays to be on your guard. Avoid bringing valuables to the beach, and don't leave any personal items in your car. Rental agencies advise that you leave your car unlocked when parked at a beach so thieves won't break the windows to get inside. There's very little crime on Culebra.

Getting Here and Around

Air Travel. **Air Flamenco** (☎ *787/724–1818* 🌐 *www.airflamenco.net*) flies daily from San Juan's Isla Grande Airport to Vieques and Culebra. **Vieques Air Link** (☎ *888/901–9247* 🌐 *www.vieques-island.com/val*) flies from Isla Grande and the international airport. **Cape Air** (☎ *800/352–0714* 🌐 *www.flycapeair.com*) flies between the international airport and Vieques. These companies also fly from Ceiba (Fajardo). Flights from San Juan are 20 to 30 minutes, and one-way fares are between $60 and $100; flights from Ceiba are about 10 minutes with one-way fares between $25 and $40. Small propeller planes that hold up to nine passengers are used.

Most international travelers fly from San Juan's Aeropuerto Internacional Luis Muñoz Marín (SJU) or Aeropuerto Fernando L. Rivas Dominici (SIG; more commonly known as Aeropuerto Isla Grande). Most of the companies that fly from San Juan also fly from Ceiba's Aeropuerto José Aponte de la Torre (RVR) about 7 mi (12 km) south of Fajardo.

Car Travel. It's nearly impossible to see either island without renting a car. Scooters are another option, especially on Culebra, but not if you're headed to the beach. Road conditions and local driving habits are spotty. Both islands have local agencies, including several that specialize in SUVs. Rates are between $40 and $80 a day. It's cheaper to book a hotel-rental car package.

Ferry Travel. The **Puerto Rico Ports Authority** (☎ *800/981–2005*) runs passenger ferries from Fajardo to Culebra and Vieques. Service is from the ferry terminal in Fajardo, about 90 minutes' drive from San Juan. Car ferries also link Fajardo to Vieques and Culebra, but rental agencies won't let you take their vehicles between the mainland and islands. A municipal parking lot next to the ferry costs $5 a day. No ferries link Vieques and Culebra.

There's limited seating, so arrive about an hour ahead of the departure time. The Ports Authority claims to take phone reservations daily from 8 to 11 and 1 to 3, but it's difficult to get anyone to answer this number. Ferry schedules change often. Call the **Fajardo Terminal** (☎ *787/863–4761*) to confirm before you plan your trip.

About the Restaurants

Most of the restaurants on Vieques and Culebra are extremely casual. Because even the most formal restaurants on the islands are on covered terraces or in open-air dining rooms, there's not a single establishment where you'll be frowned on for wearing shorts. Pack a couple of nice shirts and you'll be set.

You'll find seafood at almost every eatery on Vieques and Culebra. The fish is as fresh as you'll find anywhere, since that red snapper was probably splashing around in the Caribbean that very morning. Here you can order your fish in any number of ways. Chefs are experimenting with European and Asian cooking techniques, so you may find your fish smoked or in a sushi roll.

Even if a restaurant focuses on a different type of food, you can be sure that mangos, papayas, and other tropical fruits will make an appearance. Bills often include a service charge; if it isn't included, a 15% tip is customary. Most restaurants are open for dinner from about 6 PM until at least 10 PM.

About the Hotels

Vieques has a wide variety of lodgings, from surf shacks across from the beach to boutique hotels high up on secluded hillsides. There's something here for everyone. Looking for tropical splendor? Try Hacienda Tamarindo. Sexy sophistication? Head to the W Resort & Spa. Interesting architecture? There's Hix Island House. An intimate inn where you'll meet fellow travelers? Head to Hector's or Trade Winds.

Culebra has fewer options. Dewey, the island's only town, has a handful of small inns that are easy on the wallet. Scattered around the island are a couple of more luxurious lodgings plus villa rentals. Nothing remotely resembles a chain hotel, and that's how the locals like it.

WHAT IT COSTS IN U.S. DOLLARS

	¢	$	$$	$$$	$$$$
Restaurants	under $8	$8–$12	$12–$20	$20–$30	over $30
Hotels	under $80	$80–$150	$150–$250	$250–$350	over $350

Prices are for a double room in high season, excluding 9% tax (7% for paradores) and 5%–12% service charge.

What to Pack

Vieques has a pharmacy and a hospital, and Culebra's small hospital has a prescription-only pharmacy. Stock up on all supplies—such as allergy medications, contact-lens solution, or feminine supplies—before heading to the islands. Snorkel gear can be rented, but bring your own if you have it.

Visitor Information

The island's tourism offices are hit and miss when it comes to offering helpful material. The **Vieques Tourism Office** (✉ *449 Calle Carlos Lebrón, Isabel Segunda, Vieques* ☎ *787/741–0800*), across from the main square in Isabel Segunda, has a friendly staff that has very little to give you. If you need information, ask them to print out a complete list of local businesses. It's open Monday–Saturday 8–4:30.The **Culebra Tourism Office** (✉ *250 Calle Pedro Marquez, Dewey, Culebra* ☎ *787/742–3116*), near the ferry dock, has very little information on hand. The staffers will help you as best they can, even recommending restaurants that are off the beaten path. The office is open weekdays 8–4:30.

BEACHES OF VIEQUES AND CULEBRA

Head to the beautiful semi-circular shore of Playa Sun Bay on weekdays for less crowds and enjoy a stroll on more than a mile of soft, white sands.

Vieques and Culebra are where you'll find Puerto Rico's most serene shores. Ideal for romantic strolls or family swims, the calm waters and long unspoiled stretches here are what you probably had in mind when you envisioned a Caribbean beach paradise.

Many of the beaches around Vieques were once named by the U.S. Navy, which assigned them random colors: Red Beach, Blue Beach, and Green Beach. Most beaches have since been renamed in Spanish by locals. Islanders know Sun Bay as Sombé. Those within the Vieques National Wildlife Refuge are open 6 AM–sunset. Of Vieques's more than three-dozen beaches, Sun Bay east of Esperanza is easily the most popular. Although both islands' beaches are favored for their comparative isolation, crowds can gather on weekends at the most popular spots such as Culebra's spectacular Playa Flamenco. On weekdays, however, it's not uncommon for large swaths of shore on either island to be sparsely populated.

WORD OF MOUTH

"Flamenco beach is a must see. White, soft powdery sand, clear water. Water may or may not be calm depending on the time, but there is a shallow, calm area close to the rock pier that is good for kids to play. I recommend MamaCita's for lunch or dinner. [But] if you don't feel like going to town, you can get a decent barbecue chicken/pork-and-rice dish for about $5 at the picnic area at the end of the beach." —bluecow

VIEQUES

Green Beach. On the western edge of the island, this beach faces the Vieques Passage. Miles of coral reef just offshore attract snorkelers and divers, but caution is required due to strong currents. From the shore you can catch a glimpse of El Yunque on the mainland. ✉ *At the western end of Rte. 994, off Rte. 200.*

La Chiva. Once known as Blue Beach, this is the most beautiful beach on Vieques. It has a handful of covered cabañas and strong surf in some spots, making swimming difficult. ✉ *Off Rte. 997, 2½ mi (4 km) east of Esperanza.*

Playa Media Luna. Ideal for families because the water is calm and shallow, this is also a good spot to try your hand at snorkeling. There are no facilities. ✉ *Off Rte. 997, east of Playa Sun Bay.*

Playa Caracas. Located on former U.S. Navy land on the eastern end of Vieques, this tiny yet beautiful beach is reached via a well-maintained dirt road. The water is crystal clear, and its location in Bahía Corcho means that it is sheltered from waves. ✉ *Off Rte. 997, east of Playa Media Luna.*

Playa Sun Bay. The 1-mi-long (1½-km-long) white sands skirt a crescent-shaped bay. You'll find food kiosks, picnic tables, and changing facilities. It gets packed on holidays and weekends. On weekdays, when the crowds are thin, you might see wild horses grazing among the palm trees. Parking is $3, but often no one is at the gate to take your money. ✉ *Rte. 997, east of Esperanza.* ☎ *787/741–8198.*

CULEBRA

Fodor's Choice **Playa Flamenco.** Consistently ranked one of the most beautiful in the world. Snow-white sands, turquoise waters, and lush hills that rise on all sides, make it feel miles away from civilization. During the week it's pleasantly uncrowded; on weekends it fills up fast with day-trippers from the mainland. It's the only beach on Culebra with amenities such as camping, restrooms, showers, and kiosks selling simple fare. ✉ *Rte. 251, west of the airport.* ☎ *787/742–0700* ⏲ *Daily dawn–dusk.*

Playa Melones. Just west of Dewey, this is a favorite spot for snorkelers. The reef that runs around the rocky point is easy to reach from shore. Locals swear this is the best place to watch sunsets. To get here, head uphill on the unmarked road behind the church. ✉ *Camino Vecinal, west of Dewey.*

Playa Zoni. On the island's northeastern end, this beach is long and narrow—perfect for afternoon strolls. From the shore you can catch a glimpse of Isla Culebrita, not to mention St. Thomas and St. Croix. Leatherback turtles nest here. ✉ *At the end of Rte. 250, 7 mi (11 km) northeast of Dewey.*

4

Updated by Christopher P. Baker

Although the islands of Vieques and Culebra—known as the "Spanish Virgins"—are only a few miles off the coast of Puerto Rico, they feel like another world. While the rest of the mainland rings with the adrenaline rush of Latin America, this pair of palm-fringed islands has the laid-back vibe of the Caribbean. This is not surprising, as St. Thomas and St. Croix are clearly visible from the eastern edges of Culebra.

Vieques and Culebra are alike in many ways. Neither has much traffic—in fact, you won't find a single traffic light on either island. High-rise hotels haven't cast a shadow on the beaches. And there are no casinos, fast-food chains, strip malls, or most other trappings of modern life. "Barefoot" is often part of the dress code at the casual restaurants, and the hum you hear in your room more likely than not comes from a ceiling fan rather than an air conditioner. Things happen here *poco a poco*—slowly, at the islanders' easy pace.

Beautiful beaches abound on both islands. Many of the best stretches of sand on Vieques—Chiva, Caracas, and Green Beach, to name a few—are on land that was once part of a U.S. naval base. This means that development hasn't reared its ugly head. It also means there are few, if any, amenities, so bring plenty of water and a picnic lunch. The beaches on Culebra are just as unspoiled, as judged by marine turtles, which come ashore to lay eggs.

Wild horses roam Vieques, where two-thirds of the island is a wildlife refuge protecting coastal lagoons, mangrove wetlands, subtropical dry forest, and islands. Ecotourism is a key draw. Fishing in the turquoise flats just offshore is fantastic. And the island is tailor-made for exploring by bicycle and/or kayak, a key draw, too, on Culebra, where several cays delight birders with their colonies of boobies and other seabirds.

Some of the best snorkeling and diving in the Caribbean can be found in the waters surrounding Vieques and Culebra. You can sign up for a half-day or full-day excursion to nearby coral reefs, which are teeming with colorful fish. It's also possible to grab a mask and snorkel, and then simply wade out a few yards to see what you can see. Playa Esperanza, on the southern coast of Vieques, is a good place for beginners. More experienced snorkelers will prefer Blue Beach or Green Beach.

VIEQUES

8 mi (13 km) southeast of Fajardo.

Looking for a place to play Robinson Crusoe? Then head to Vieques, where you can wander along almost any stretch of sand and never see another soul. You can while away the hours underneath coconut palms, wade in the warm water, or get a mask and snorkel and explore the coral reefs that ring the island.

For many years the island was known mostly for the conflict between angry islanders and aloof federal officials. Over the course of six decades, the U.S. Navy used two-thirds of Vieques, mostly on the island's eastern side, as a bombing range, and the western tip as an ammunition dump. After an April 1999 bombing accident took the life of one resident, waves of protests brought the maneuvers to a standstill, and political pressure from the island's governor helped force the military to leave on May 1, 2003.

Ironically, the military's presence helped to keep the island pristine by keeping resort developers away. Today, the military's former holdings have been turned into the Vieques National Wildlife Refuge. The woodsy western end of the island is laced by trails that offer fabulous cycling around the base of Monte Pirata, the island's highest peak. More and more of the eastern part of the island is being opened every year, granting access to stupendous beaches shelving into calm turquoise waters. The park also protects Puerto Mosquito, a flask-shaped bay populated by microscopic organisms that glow when disturbed at night—a thrilling experience for kayakers (*see also Bioluminescent Bays feature in this chapter*).

GETTING HERE AND AROUND

Isabel Segunda is the transportation hub of Vieques. The ferry drops off passengers at the town's dock, and propeller planes deposit passengers at Aeropuerto Antonio Rivera Rodríguez (VQS), which is a 10-minute cab ride from Isabel Segunda or a 15-minute taxi ride from Esperanza. Route 200 leads from the airport to Isabel Segunda, and Route 997 leads from Isabel Segunda to Esperanza. There's also a longer, more scenic route between the two towns: From Isabel Segunda, take Route 200 west to Route 201 south. After about 1 mi (1½ km), take Route 996 to Esperanza.

If you want to rent a car or gas up the one you already have, you need to make a trip to Isabel Segunda. Try Island Car Rental, Maritza Car Rental, or Martineau Car Rental.

You can flag down taxis on the street, but it's faster and safer to have your hotel call one for you. Either way, agree on how much the trip will cost before you get inside the taxi, as many drivers are prone to

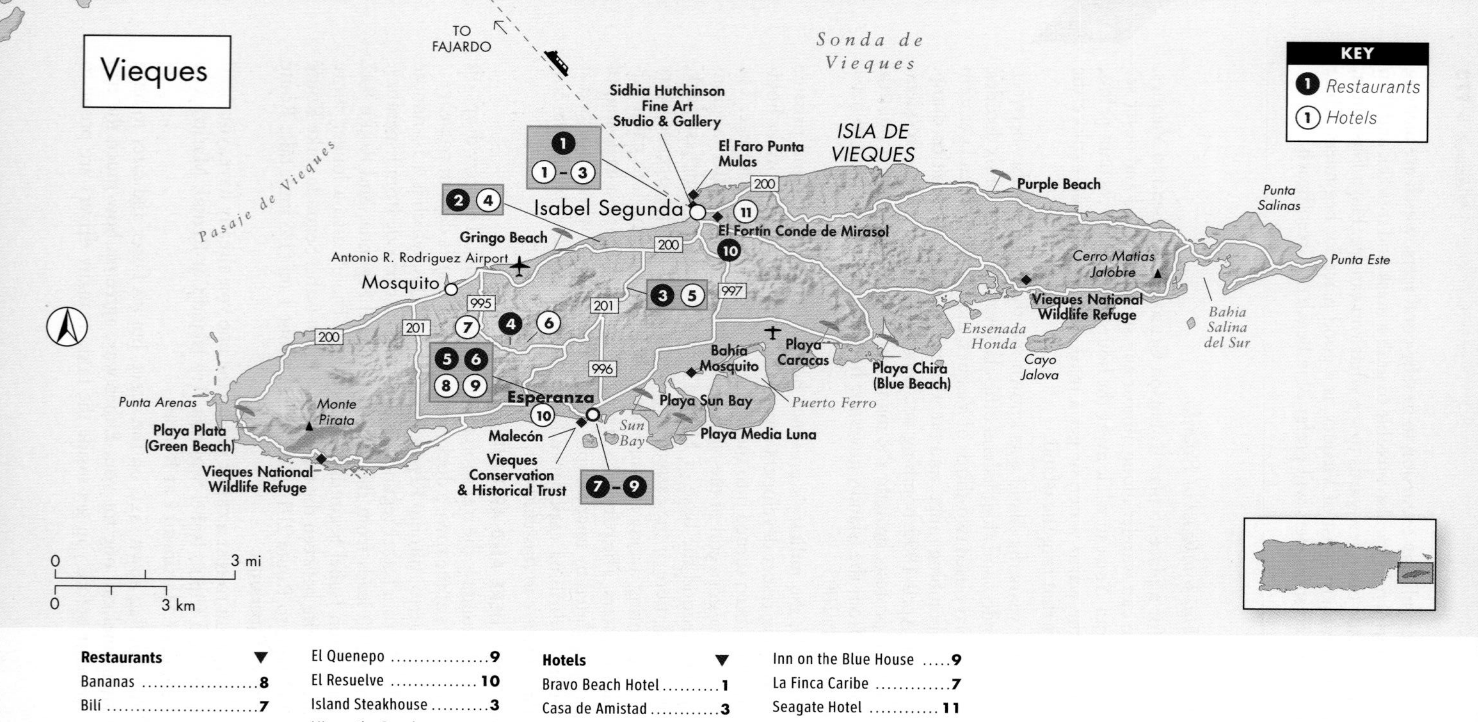

Restaurants	▼
Bananas	8
Bilí	7
Cantina La Reina	1
Carambola	5
Chez Shack	4
Duffy's	6
El Quenepo	9
El Resuelve	10
Island Steakhouse	3
Mix on the Beach	2

Hotels	▼
Bravo Beach Hotel	1
Casa de Amistad	3
Crow's Nest	5
Hacienda Tamarindo	8
Hector's	10
Hix Island House	6
Inn on the Blue House	9
La Finca Caribe	7
Seagate Hotel	11
Trade Winds	2
W Retreat & Spa	4

rip off tourists with exorbitant fares. **TIP→ If you plan to rent a car on Vieques or Culebra, make sure you reserve it in advance, especially when visiting during high season. The rental agencies have a limited number of vehicles, and when they are gone, you're out of luck.**

Airport Information Aeropuerto Antonio Rivera Rodríguez (✉ *Vieques* ☎ *787/741-0515*).

Car Rental Island Car Rental (✉ *Rte. 201, Vieques* ☎ *787/741-1666* 🌐 *www.enchanted-isle.com/islandcar*). **Maritza's Car Rental** (✉ *Rte. 201, Vieques* ☎ *787/741-0078* 🌐 *www.islavieques.com/maritzas.html*). **Martineau Car Rental** (✉ *Rte. 200, Km 3.4, Vieques* ☎ *787/741-0087* 🌐 *www.martineaucarrental.com*).

Ferry Terminal Vieques Terminal (☎ *787/741-4761*).

Taxis Lolo Felix Tours (✉ *Vieques* ☎ *787/485-5447*).

4

EXPLORING VIEQUES

Just because Vieques is sleepy doesn't mean there's nothing to do besides hit the beach. There are two communities—Isabel Segunda and Esperanza—where you can dine at a variety of excellent restaurants, stock up on supplies, or book a trip to the astonishing Puerto Mosquito, perhaps the world's most luminous bioluminescent bay.

ISABEL SEGUNDA

18 mi (29 km) southeast of Fajardo by ferry.

Isabel Segunda (or Isabel II, as it's often labeled on maps) has charms that are not immediately apparent. There's a lovely lighthouse on the coast just east of the ferry dock, and on the hill above town you'll find the last fort the Spanish constructed in the New World. You can also find some of the best restaurants and a great bar here, as well as lodgings ranging from funky to fancy.

El Faro Punta Mulas, a Spanish-built lighthouse above the ferry dock in Isabel Segunda, dates from 1895. It was built to guide vessels into the harbor, which is surrounded by a chain of dangerous reefs. Its red light is rumored to be seen from as far away as St. Croix and St. Thomas. In 1992 the elegant structure was carefully restored and transformed into a maritime museum that traced much of the island's history, including the visit by South American liberation leader Simón Bolívar. The tiny museum is open weekdays, but the lighthouse itself is worth a look on any day. ✉ *At end of Rte. 200* ☎ *787/741-3141* ⏲ *Weekdays 8–3.*

On a hilltop overlooking Isabel Segunda is **El Fortín Conde de Mirasol** *(Count of Mirasol Fort)*, the last military structure built by the Spanish in the New World. It was erected on Vieques's northern coast in 1840 at the order of Count Mirasol, then governor of Puerto Rico. Although it's tiny, it took more than a decade to complete, which meant Mirasol had to repeatedly ask for more money. (Queen Isabel, on being petitioned yet again, asked Mirasol whether the walls were made of gold.) The fort helped solidify Spanish control of the area, keeping British, French, Dutch, and Danish colonists away and dissuading pirates from

GREAT ITINERARIES

IF YOU HAVE 1 DAY

If you are headed to one of the islands for an overnight excursion, your best bet is **Vieques.** Get here by plane, either from San Juan or Fajardo, to maximize your time on the island. Spend the day exploring the beaches, especially the half-moon-shaped Sun Bay. In the evening you can dine at one of the oceanfront restaurants in Esperanza, then head off for an excursion to **Puerto Mosquito,** a bay filled with glow-in-the-dark dinoflagellates. Spend the night in Esperanza or Isabel Segunda.

IF YOU HAVE 3 DAYS

If you have a few days, you can see most of Vieques. Start your first day in Isabel Segunda, where you can take a few snapshots of **El Faro Punta Mulas,** and then explore the hilltop **El Fortín Conde de Mirasol.** Head off for an afternoon by the ocean, perhaps at Green Beach or one of the delightfully deserted beaches on the northern part of the island. Enjoy happy hour at Lazy Jack's, a favorite hangout for expats, in Esperanza. In the cool of the evening, have dinner in one of the chic eateries nearby. On your second day, go for an early morning mountain-bike ride in the western portion of **Vieques National Wildlife Refuge,** a swath of wilderness that was once a naval base. Head for lunch at El Resuelve, or pack a picnic and head off to Playa Media Luna or another of the beautiful beaches along the southern coast. After dinner, make sure to book a tour of **Puerto Mosquito.** Spend your third day kayaking, snorkeling, and/or fishing. In the evening, head to W Retreat & Spa for a spa treatment, cocktails, and fine dining.

IF YOU HAVE 5 DAYS

If you have a few more days, you can see both Vieques and Culebra. After following the itinerary above, head to Culebra on your fourth day. (A 10-minute flight between the islands is the only way to travel between them.) Your destination should be Playa Flamenco, a long, curving beach of talcum-white sands and turquoise waters. The mountains beyond make a striking backdrop. Dine that evening at Susie's in the only town, diminutive Dewey. On your last day, try snorkeling in **Refugio Nacional de Vida Silvestre de Culebra,** the island's lovely nature preserve. One of the best places is **Isla Culebrita,** an islet dominated by a deserted lighthouse.

attacking Isabel Segunda. After sitting empty for several decades, it was transformed into a museum in 1991. The museum has an impressive collection of artifacts from the Taíno Indians and other cultures that thrived on this and nearby islands before the arrival of the Spanish. It also has an impressive collection of small arms, plus exhibits on the island's years as a sugar plantation and its occupation by the U.S. Navy. ✉ *471 Calle Magnolia, Isabel Segunda* ☎ *787/741–1717* 🌐 *www.icp.gobierno.pr* 🎫 *$2* 🕒 *Wed.–Sun. 8:30–4:30.*

El Faro Punta Mulas, a lighthouse built in 1895, is now a small museum exhibiting Vieques historical items.

ESPERANZA

6 mi (10 km) south of Isabel Segunda.

The only time there's a traffic jam in Esperanza is when one of the wild horses frequently seen on the nearby beaches wanders into the road. This community, once a down-at-the-heels fishing village, now hosts a string of budget bars, restaurants, and hotels on the waterfront drag. All of them overlook Playa Esperanza, a shallow stretch of sand made all the more picturesque by the presence of a tiny islet called Cayo Afuera.

In the evening, there's not a better way to enjoy the sunset than a stroll along Esperanza's 200-yard-long **Malecón,** a waterfront walkway running the length of the beach.

The **Vieques Conservation & Historical Trust** was established to help save Puerto Mosquito, one of the last remaining bioluminescent bays in the world. The small museum, located on the main drag in Esperanza, was recently upgraded and has interesting information about the bay, as well as the island's flora and fauna and history. A little pool lets kids get acquainted with starfish, sea urchins, and other denizens of the not-so-deep. There's also a tiny gift shop where the profits are funneled back into the foundation. Call ahead if you're coming at lunchtime, as the place is sometimes closed for an hour or so. ✉ *138 Calle Flamboyán, Esperanza* ☎ *787/741–8850* 🌐 *www.vcht.com* 🎟 *Free* 🕐 *Tues.–Sun. 11–4.*

Popular with local fisherman, the gentle waters of Esperanza Beach are ideal for small boats.

ELSEWHERE ON VIEQUES

Isabel Segunda and Esperanza are just a tiny portion of Vieques. Most of the island—more than two-thirds of it, in fact—was commandeered by the military until 2003. It's now a nature preserve that draws thousands of visitors each year.

Fodor's Choice ★ East of Esperanza, **Puerto Mosquito Bioluminescent Bay** is one of the world's best spots to have a glow-in-the-dark experience with undersea dinoflagellates. Tour operators offer kayak trips or excursions on nonpolluting boats to see the bay's microorganisms, which appear to light up when the water around them is agitated. Look behind your boat, and you'll see a twinkling wake. Even the fish that jump from the water will bear an eerie glow. The high concentration of dinoflagellates sets the bay apart from the other spots (including others in Puerto Rico) that are home to these algae. The bay is at its best when there's little or no moonlight; rainy nights are beautiful, too, because the raindrops splashing in the water produce ricochet sparkles. *See also Bioluminescent Bays feature in this chapter.* ✉ *Reach via unpaved roads off Rte. 997.*

A portion of the west and the entire eastern end of the island is administered by the U.S. Fish & Wildlife Service as the **Vieques National Wildlife Refuge,** comprising 18,000 acres—about 14,900 acres on the eastern end and 3,100 acres on the west—making it the biggest protected natural reserve in Puerto Rico. The 900-acre bombing range is permanently closed off, a consequence of its contamination by the ammunition shot over its 60-year existence. But most of the rest of eastern Vieques is pristine nature, astonishingly beautiful and well forested, with a hilly center region overlooking powder-white sandy beaches and a coral-

CLOSE UP

Vieques Libre

For nearly six decades, the U.S. Navy had a stranglehold on Vieques. It controlled the island's eastern half and western end and exerted enormous influence over the destiny of the civilian area in between. Though long protested, the bombing, shelling, and amphibious landings continued. When an off-target bomb killed a civilian on navy land in April 1999, opposition began to transform the island's placid beaches into political hotbeds.

Protesters camping out on the bombing range kept it shut down from 1999 to 2000. Hundreds of Puerto Rican residents were arrested for trespassing on navy land during war games. They were joined by celebrity protesters from the United States, including environmental lawyer Robert F. Kennedy Jr. (who gave his baby daughter the middle name Vieques), the wife of Reverend Jesse Jackson, and Reverend Al Sharpton, all of whom were arrested for trespassing on the bombing range. For much of 2000 and 2001, protests were so commonplace that there were semipermanent encampments of opponents. Songs such as "Paz Pa' Vieques" ("Peace for Vieques") began to surface, as did bumper stickers and T-shirts with protest slogans. Latin pop celebrities such as singer-songwriter Robie Draco Rosa (who wrote Ricky Martin's "Livin' la Vida Loca"), actor Edward James Olmos, singer Millie Corejter, protest singer Zoraida Santiago, and other actors, painters, doctors, and lawyers added to the fanfare when they joined the activities.

President Bill Clinton finally agreed that residents could vote on whether to continue to host the navy. A nonbinding referendum held in 2001 found that 68% of the island's voters wanted the military to leave immediately. Although some members of Congress argued that the navy should stay indefinitely—their cries grew louder after September 11, 2001, when even local protesters called for a moratorium on civil disobedience—the administration agreed to withdraw the troops. As a result of the protests, the navy finally withdrew from its Atlantic Fleet training grounds in May 2002. In 2003, the naval base was officially closed. By the end of 2005, much of the former military base was transformed into the Vieques National Wildlife Refuge. Today, there are concerns that the sustained bombing activity produced high levels of contamination that are linked to health issues such as higher cancer rates among residents. This is widely regarded as a long-term exposure issue that doesn't affect vacationers, but visitors who may be concerned about potential risks associated with travel to the area should check the Center for Disease Control Web site (🌐 www.cdc.gov) for the latest information.

ringed coastline; it served mainly as a buffer zone between the military maneuvers and civilian population. The vast majority of this acreage remains off-limits to visitors as authorities carry out a search for unexploded munitions and contaminants. Nonetheless, many of the beaches on the northern and southern coasts are open to the public; in 2009 a new asphalt road opened up six southern beaches. 📫 *Box 1527, 00765* ☎ *787/741–2138* 🌐 *www.fws.gov*.

4

WHERE TO EAT

$$ CARIBBEAN ✕ **Bananas.** If you're looking for authentic island cuisine, this ain't it. This longtime open-air favorite, across from the waterfront in Esperanza, is geared almost entirely to gringos. However, that doesn't mean the grub isn't good. Find a spot at one of the curvy concrete tables and order the red-snapper sandwich (popular at lunchtime), or go all out for baby-back ribs or jerk chicken. The salads are excellent, including the *caribeño* (fresh greens with curried chicken) and the *festival* (greens with grilled chicken, blue cheese, and cranberries). When the sun goes down, Bananas is one of the hot spots on this side of the island. ✉ *142 Calle Flamboyán, Esperanza* ☎ *787/741–8700* 🌐 *www.bananasguesthouse.com* 💳 *MC, V.*

$$ CARIBBEAN ✕ **Bilí.** Next door to Bananas, this airy and colorful Mediterranean-style tapas restaurant deserves better than the overflow from its more established neighbor. It has the same view, sleeker decor, and more authentic food, prepared by Eva Bolívar, former private chef to a Puerto Rican governor. For lunch, order a tasty sandwich such as dorado wrap with caramelized onions, plantains, and roasted peppers. For something heartier, try seafood paella—the house specialty. Stop by for a beer in the evening and you won't have to shout to be heard. ✉ *144 Calle Flamboyán, Esperanza* ☎ *787/741–1382* 🌐 *http://enchanted-isle.com/amapola* 💳 *AE, MC, V.*

$$ MEXICAN ✕ **Cantina La Reina.** The former Café Media Luna metamorphosed in June 2009 as a colorful Mexican restaurant and bar decorated with Taxco silver mirrors, sombreros, and prints of Pancho Villa, Freda Kahlo, and other notable *mexicanas*. Very atmospheric! During our visit the menu was limited to light fare, including sizzling gourmet lobster fajitas and tacos. Light eaters can snack on succulent crispy chips, and "snakebites," a house specialty of jalapeño pepper and jack cheese wrapped with bacon, served with roasted corn salsa. The owners were planning on opening a full-service fine-dining restaurant on the third floor. The ground-floor bar is cozy, while the rootop bar serves up great views over town with its margaritas and cocktails. ✉ *351 Calle Antonio Mellado, Isabel Segunda* ☎ *787/741–2700* 🌐 *www.cantina-lareina.com* 💳 *MC, V* ⏲ *Closed Sun.–Mon. No lunch.*

$$$ CARIBBEAN ✕ **Carambola.** It's hard to imagine a more romantic setting than this dining room with unbeatable views of the ocean. Indoors is a long wooden table, surrounded by chairs upholstered in a delectable shade of chocolate brown. Through the open doors are smaller tables scattered around the open-air terrace. The service is formal, and so are the meals. The former five- or seven-course set meals have been replaced by an à la carte menu featuring such main courses as lamb chops with a lentil balsamic salad or the mofongo special with jumbo shrimps. In low season, dining is sometimes restricted to the less elegant terrace. ✉ *Inn on the Blue Horizon, Rte. 996, Km 4.2, Esperanza* ☎ *787/741–3318* 🌐 *www.innonthebluehorizon.com* 💳 *AE, D, MC, V.*

$$–$$$ ECLECTIC ✕ **Chez Shack.** This restaurant is not a shack—but it's close. It's in a delightfully ramshackle wooden building on a one-lane road winding through the hills. The dining room is inches from the pavement, but it's unlikely a single car will pass by while you're enjoying your meal. Chicken, beef, and seafood such as baked crab are prepared to tender perfection, but the

Continued on page 186

BIOLUMINESCENT BAYS

Plankton Pyrotechnics in Puerto Rico

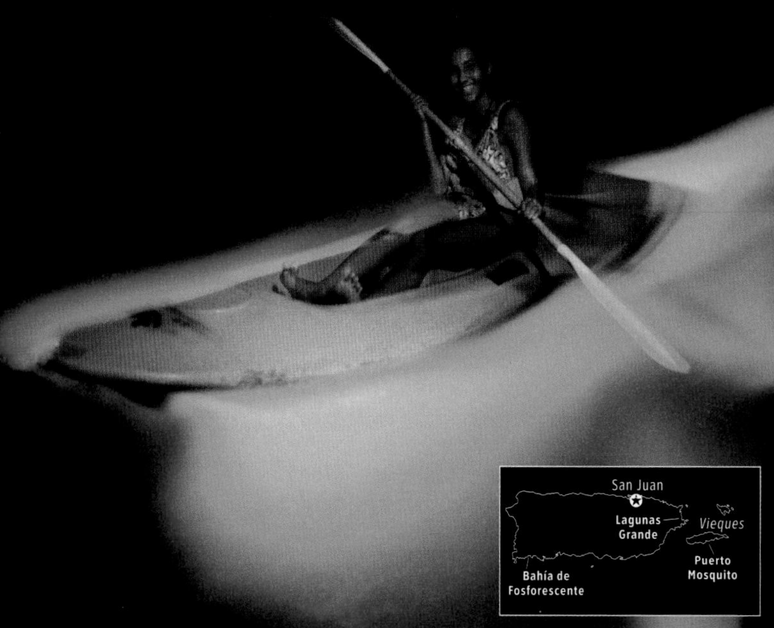

Puerto Rico's bioluminescent bays are beautiful. The slightest stirring of these waters, whether from the swish of a stick or droplets of rain, produces tiny bursts of teal-blue light. The darker the night, the better the bright; a moonless sky affords the most gorgeous marine moments in these wondrous bays.

by Francesca Drago

It's estimated that there are only 12 bio bays in the world, but it's difficult to determine exactly because the phenomenon occurs sporadically in warm seas. Puerto Rico has three. **Puerto Mosquito** in Vieques is the most spectacular bay. It won a Guinness World Record for most outstanding bioluminescent bay in the world. **Lagunas Grande** in Fajardo is not as bright, but convenient to see from San Juan. **Bahía de Fosforescente** in La Parquera's deserves an honorable mention even though water pollution, primarily from gas- and diesel-powered tourist boats, has darkened its luster.

Positively glowing! Puerto Rico's bio bays will literally have you beaming with joy.

WHAT'S IN THE WATER?

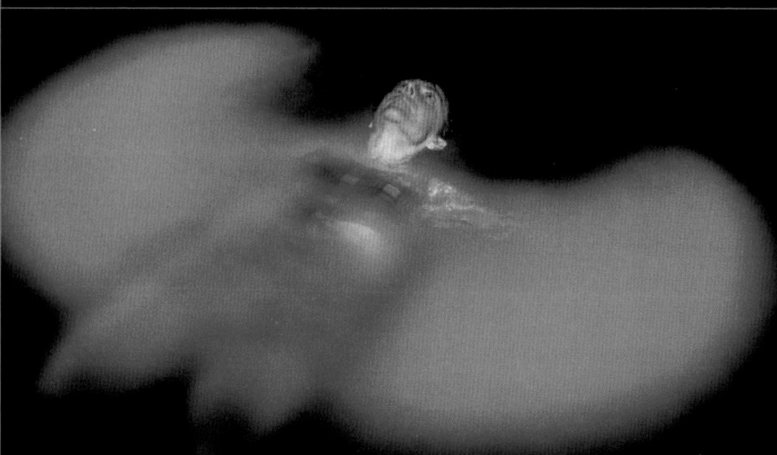

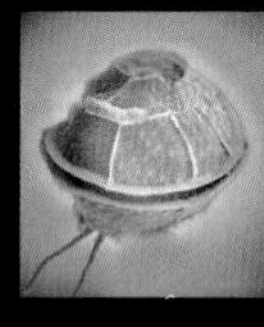

The undersea shooting stars are produced by microscopic algae called dinoflagellates, or "dinos." They convert chemical energy into light energy and emit tiny flashes when the water is disturbed. Scientists have theorized that their sudden sparks are a defense mechanism—a way to startle and disorient a predator and perhaps attract a larger predator to eat the first one.

A bio bay's brightness is a measure of its health. Dinoflagellates use the energy from sunlight to photosynthesize. Their luminescence is influenced by circadian rhythms, meaning their brightness depends on the light-dark conditions over a 24-hour period. One full day of sunshine and no clouds will result in two nights of plankton brilliance—with the second night brighter than the first. A cloudy day may still produce a bright night, but the following night won't be as spectacular. Artificial and ambient light will disrupt the fragile cycles of these "living lanterns" and erase their natural bioluminescence. Preservation of bio-bay brightness depends on public awareness about the harmful effects of light pollution and thoughtful planning for future land development.

(top) "Glow angel:" a swimmer creates water wings in Puerto Mosquito Bay (bottom) The species of dinoflagellate Pyrodinium Bahamenese, found in Puerto Mosquito, is only 1/500 of an inch

NEW MOON

Bioluminescence is best experienced on a cloudy or moonless night. The darkest nights occur during the new moon phase, when its face is in shadow. Ask your tour guide what the moon phase will be and when it will rise, because a full moon may not actually appear in the sky until after your planned excursion.

New Moon Calendar, 2011/2012

- Jan 4/Jan 23
- Feb 3/Feb 21
- Mar 4/Mar 22
- Apr 3/Apr 21
- May 3/May 20
- Jun 1/Jun 19
- Jul 1 & 30/Jul 19
- Aug 29/Aug 17
- Sep 27/Sep 16
- Oct 26/Oct 15
- Nov 25/Nov 13
- Dec 24/Dec 13

PUERTO MOSQUITO: A BAY IN BALANCE

Dinoflagellates occur sporadically in tropical waters around the world, but the highest concentration on earth can be found in Puerto Mosquito Bay in Vieques. Billions of dinos dwell here because their habitat is balanced by a number of ecological features and protections.

"Channel surf:" A kayaker paddles the channel leading to Puerto Mosquito Bay

❶ Puerto Mosquito Bay is a **designated wildlife preserve.** This special zoning prevents rampant development, pollution, and destruction of the surrounding forest, which acts as a natural barrier against strong winds and rain.

❷ Salt-tolerant **mangrove trees** are vital for healthy coastal ecosystems. Their pronged roots stabilize the silt-rich shoreline, helping to filter sediments and reduce erosion, while leaves and bark fall into the water, where they rot and provide food and nutrients essential to the dinos' diet (e.g., vitamin B12). Moreover, the mangroves absorb carbon dioxide and store carbon in their sediments, which makes them a vital resource for reducing greenhouse gasses in the atmosphere.

❸ The long, **narrow channel leading to the ocean** acts as a buffer that minimizes how much seawater flows into the bay daily and limits the amount of dinoflagellates (and nutrients) that are swept out with the tides. This enables the dinos to concentrate in the bay's shallow refuge.

❹ The **channel exit** at the windward end of the bay allows sufficient water exchange with the sea to keep it from overheating or stagnating. The water in Puerto Mosquito remains calm and warm, creating the ideal environment for dinoflagellates to thrive in.

EXPLORING THE BAYS

Kayaks are an environmentally friendly way to explore the bays.

Seeing your oars glow as they blade through the water is a magical experience. Go with an operator that uses glow sticks to illuminate the stern of each kayak (for minimal light interference) and reviews safety practices at the start. Never book a tour with an operator who is unlicensed or uses gas- or diesel-powered boats. Ask your hotel concierge for assistance. On Vieques the **Seagate Hotel** and **Hector's By the Sea** *(see Where to Stay in this chapter)* will help arrange tours of Puerto Mosquito Bay.

RECOMMENDED OUTFITTERS

IN VIEQUES

East Island Excursions runs its Bio Bay tours three weeks per month, which include round-trip transportation from Fajardo to Vieques, dinner, and an educational tour aboard an open-air electric boat. (Prone to motion sickness? Be advised that a 45-minute cruise on a catamaran and 15-minute bus ride on a rough, unpaved road is part of this trip.) **Aqua Frenzy Kayaks** and **Blue Carib Kayaks** both provide sturdy kayaks and knowledgeable guides for day and night trips to Puerto Mosquito.

IN FAJARDO

The two-hour night tour at **Las Cabezas Nature Reserve** *(see Exploring, Fajardo, chapter 3)* takes you on a winding boardwalk through mangroves to the water's edge. Strike the dark lagoon with a stick and marvel at the flashing wakes, or stir the water to "draw" with light.

For more information on recommended outfitters, see Boating & Kayaking in this chapter.

KNOW BEFORE YOU GLOW

- Paddling through the long, dark mangrove channel to reach Mosquito Bay is exciting but also challenging. Kayaking can be strenuous and requires teamwork; book with small groups, if possible, because crowds with varying experience and endurance can lead to exasperation and delay.
- People with little or no kayak experience, or with small children, may prefer a pontoon trip that provides an easy and safe way to swim in luminescent water.
- Puerto Mosquito is aptly named. Wear a hat, water shoes, and nylon pants as protection from bites. A lightweight, waterproof windbreaker worn over a bathing suit is ideal.
- Jellyfish are sometimes present but cannot be seen in the dark water. Look carefully.
- Bring towels and a change of clothes for the ride home.

In the zone: the forest of Puerto Mosquito is protected land

PROTECTING THE BAYS

After the sun sets, the undersea stars shine

Destruction of mangroves, dredging, land development, and overuse of the bays' waters endanger the bio bays. Light pollution is especially harmful, since artificial and ambient light suppress the luminescence of the dinoflagellates. The Vieques Conservation and Historical Trust (VCHT) held its first symposium in the fall of 2008, convening expert scientific and technical authorities to discuss conservation of the bio bays. The goal, said Trust marine expert Mark Martin, was to "involve everybody," including government and the public, and rally commitments and resources to ensure the continuous scientific monitoring of Puerto Mosquito. The VCHT wants to name Puerto Mosquito a UNESCO World Biosphere Reserve to preserve it for future generations.

Here's what you can do to help maintain the pristine condition of this precious natural resource:

- Book with licensed operators who use kayaks or electric boats only.
- Swimming is banned in all the bio bays but Puerto Mosquito. Shun those operators who ignore the law.
- Dinoflagellates absorb basic chemicals directly from the water. Bug repellents containing DEET will kill them. Rinse off any remnants of suntan lotion, perfume, and deodorant before swimming.
- Do not throw any objects in the water or litter in any way.
- Support the conservation efforts of the VCHT.

menu changes according to the chef's whim. The restaurant is justifiably famous for its weekly barbecue night with a steel band on Monday. If you can't make it that evening, good jazz or island rhythms usually flow out of the sound system. The restaurant is a bit off the beaten track on Route 995, off Route 201, and sometimes closes in low season and on Sunday. ✉ *Rte. 995, Km 1.8* ☎ *787/741–2175* 🌐 *www.innonthebluehorizon.com* *Reservations essential* 💳 *MC, V.*

$–$$ CARIBBEAN ✕ **Duffy's.** More than half of the customers crowd around the bar here, which might make you think the food must be pub grub. And that's right, to a point. You have your standard burger and fries, but this popular waterfront restaurant even sells veggie burgers. The rest of the eclectic menu tends toward wraps, sandwiches, and seafood dishes such as delicious crab cakes and salad niçoise with ahi tuna—all a step above your usual beach food. So why do people ignore the dozen or so tables scattered around the open-air dining room in favor of sitting elbow-to-elbow at the bar? Turns out that owner Michael Duffy, son of the owner of Chez Shack, is a real character. Locals love chewing the fat with him, and you will, too. ✉ *140 Calle Flamboyán, Esperanza* ☎ *787/741–7600* 🌐 *www.duffysesperanza.com* 💳 *MC, V.*

$$ Fodor's Choice ★ ECLECTIC ✕ **El Quenepo.** Elegant yet unpretentious, this newcomer was the hottest act in town during our last visit, adding fine dining and a touch of class to the Esperanza waterfront. Local fruits such as *quenepos* and breadfruit find their way into the lively, work-of-art nouvelle dishes that owners Scott and Kate Cole call "fun, funky island food." He plays chef while she plays consummate hostess. Kate likes to wear full-length cocktail dresses but says the dress code is "wet bikinis to wet ball gowns." Start with a grilled Caesar salad followed by sensational seafood such as *mofongo* stuffed with shrimp and lobster in sweet-and-spicy *criollo* sauce. Oenophiles will appreciate the large wine list, heaving on South American labels, and the sangria is delicious. ✉ *148 Calle Flamboyan, Esperanza* ☎ *787/741–1215* 🌐 *http://elquenepovieques.com* *Reservations essential* 💳 *MC, V* ⏲ *Closed Mon. No lunch.*

¢–$ PUERTO RICAN ✕ **El Resuelve.** When you hanker for hearty platters of real local fare with real island-born locals, this is the place to be. Bustling at lunch and by night, this open-air *colmado* (grocery-restaurant) presses up against the main Isabel II–Esperanza road. It's barely more than a shack with a counter and shaded aluminum and plastic seating out back. Service is laid-back to the max, but it's worth the wait for *albondigas* (meatballs), crab empanadas, chicken with rice and beans, barbecue ribs, and—for the daring—boiled pigs' ears. Locals sometimes kick up their heels out back, where there's a pool table and slot machine. ✉ *Route 997, Km 1, Isabel Segunda* ☎ *787/741–1427* 💳 *No credit cards.* ⏲ *Closed Mon.–Tues.*

$$$ STEAK ✕ **Island Steakhouse.** When islanders go out to dinner, they often end up at this spot far away from the beach. But its location on a secluded hilltop doesn't mean fewer crowds, especially since July 2009, when chef PeterBurbela took over with his "gourmet eclectic cuisine," such as flaky margarita pizza appetizer, oven-roasted Thai crab cakes, and a divine lavender crème brûlée. He promises to retain the restaurant's claim to fame: namely, its sizzling steaks, which range in size from petite to hearty—the rib eye, one of the most popular items, weighs in at 20

ounces. The second-floor terrace might remind you of a tree house, as it looks directly into the branches. The restaurant is on Route 201, between Isabel Segunda and Esperanza. ✉ *Crow's Nest, Rte. 201, Km 1.6* ☎ *787/741–0011* 🌐 *www.islandsteakhouse.com* ✍ *Reservations essential* ▭ *AE, MC, V* ⊙ *Closed Wed.–Thurs. No lunch.*

$$$–$$$$ ECLECTIC ✕ **Mix on the Beach.** Opened in spring 2010, the über-hip W Retreat & Spa has taken local dining to divine heights courtesy of celebrated chef Alain Ducasse, who graces Vieques with his luminous presence at the hotel's Mix on the Beach. You'll need a fat wallet to dine here, but you can reliably expect Ducasse's artful French-Caribbean-Latino cuisine to be worth every penny. After all, he was the youngest chef ever to be honored with three Michelin stars and the only chef to earn the honor at three separate restaurants. Food aside, we're enamored of its romantic dining terraces overlooking a sensational swimming pool complex. ✉ *Route 200, Km 3.2, Isabel Segunda* ☎ *787/741–4100* 🌐 *www.whotels.com/vieques* ✍ *Reservations essential* ▭ *AE, D, DC, MC, V.*

4

WHERE TO STAY

$$–$$$ HOTEL **Bravo Beach Hotel.** If this boutique hotel were plopped down into the middle of South Beach, no one would raise an eyebrow. What was once a private residence has been expanded to include four different buildings, all with views of nearby Culebra from their balconies. The guest rooms have a minimalist flair, brightened by splashes of red and yellow. High-tech offerings include an iPod docking station in every room. And if you're traveling with an entourage, the two-bedroom villa has plenty of entertaining space. One of the lap pools is the setting for the Palms, a chic lounge; the other provides a backdrop for the not-to-be-missed tapas bar, for guests only. The hotel is on a pretty stretch of beach, several blocks north of the ferry dock in Isabel Segunda. **Pros:** Gorgeous building; beautiful pools; good dining options. **Cons:** Unattractive neighborhood; new management can be aloof. ✉ *North Shore Rd., Isabel Segunda* ☎ *787/741–1128* 🌐 *www.bravobeachhotel.com* *9 rooms, 1 villa* *In-room: no phone, Wi-Fi. In-hotel: restaurant, bar, pools, no kids under 18* ▭ *AE, MC, V* *BP.*

¢–$ HOTEL **Casa de Amistad.** A groovy vibe permeates this small guesthouse not far from the ferry dock in Isabel Segunda. Citrus colors and wicker furnishings give it a tropical touch. It's hard not to feel at home here, especially when you use the common kitchen to pack a picnic lunch or borrow an umbrella for your trip to the beach. The rooftop terrace is a great place to chill out. An on-site gift shop sells original art by the owners, and several quality restaurants are a short stroll away. **Pros:** Gay-friendly; funky furnishings. **Cons:** On an unattractive block; drive to beaches; some rooms lack en-suite bathrooms; no elevator. ✉ *27 Calle Benito Castaño, Isabel Segunda* ☎ *787/741–3758* 🌐 *www.casadeamistad.com* *7 rooms* *In-hotel: pool, WiFi, public Internet* ▭ *MC* *EP.*

$$ HOTEL **Crow's Nest.** This butter-yellow guesthouse sits on a hilltop and has stunning views of the ocean in the distance. If you want to go to the beaches in or around Esperanza and Isabel Segunda, they are within a few minutes' drive. Or you can relax by the swimming pool. The large rooms have balconies that overlook lovely gardens. Island Steakhouse

Hix Island House

Hacienda Tamarindo

Hector's By the Sea

($$$), housed on a second-floor terrace, is one of the most popular restaurants on Vieques. Less expensive is El Jardín, an Asian-Caribbean eatery on the patio. The hotel is on Route 201, between Isabel Segunda and Esperanza. **Pros:** Hilltop location; good dining options. **Cons:** Far from beach; not the prettiest building; no elevator. ✉ *Rte. 201, Km 1.6,* ☎ *787/741–0033 or 888/484–3783* 🌐 *www.crowsnestvieques.com* *15 rooms, 2 suites* *In-room: kitchen (some), refrigerator, Internet. In-hotel: 2 restaurants, pool, no kids under 12* ▭ *AE, MC, V* *BP.*

$$$ HOTEL Fodor's Choice ★ **Hacienda Tamarindo.** The century-old tamarind tree rising through the center of the main building gives this plantation-style house its name. With its barrel-tile roof and wood-shuttered windows, it's one of the most beautiful hotels on the island. You can easily find a spot all to yourself, whether it's on a shady terrace or beside the spectacular pool. Linda Vail, who runs the place along with her husband, Burr, decorated each guest room individually. "Caribbean chic" may be the best way to describe her effortless way of combining well-chosen antiques, elegant wicker furniture, and vintage travel posters. The nicest room might be Number One, which is in a separate building and has a private terrace overlooking the ocean. If you want more privacy, there's also a nicely furnished villa. The made-to-order breakfasts served on the second-floor terrace are a great reason to get up early. It closes for September. **Pros:** Beautiful views; nicely designed rooms; excellent breakfasts. **Cons:** Drive to beaches; small parking lot; no full-service restaurant; no elevator. ✉ *Rte. 996, Km 4.5, Esperanza* *Box 1569, Vieques 00765* ☎ *787/741–8525* 🌐 *www.haciendatamarindo.com* *16 rooms* *In-room: no phone, no TV, Wi-Fi. In-hotel: pool, public Wi-Fi, no kids under 15* ▭ *AE, MC, V* *BP.*

$–$$ HOTEL **Hector's.** Reached by a steep and denuded dirt road, this endearing little hotel perches on a bluff overlooking a lovely beach. Its two rooms and three self-catering *casitas* sprinkled about breeze-swept lawns are perfect for vacationers who favor extreme privacy and shun frills in favor of clean, comfortable, and simple digs. The sparsely furnished rooms with kitchens are cross-ventilated with screened unglazed windows and feature lofty beamed ceilings and glass-brick bathrooms. Guests who care not to cater for themselves are a 20-minute walk from Esperanza and its many restaurants. Amiable owners Hector and Mary Matos, from New York, live on-site, as do their horses, which munch on fruit from the mango trees. **Pros:** Ceiling fans; hot tub under the stars; marvelous ocean vistas. **Cons:** No credit cards; meager facilities; no maid service. ✉ *Rte. 996, Km 4.3, Esperanza* ☎ *787/741–1178* 🌐 *www.hectorsbythesea.com* *2 rooms, 3 villas* *In-room: no phone, kitchen, refrigerator, no TV. In-hotel: pool, beachfront, laundry facilities, parking (free), no kids under 12.* ▭ *No credit cards.*

$$–$$$ HOTEL Fodor's Choice ★ **Hix Island House.** Constructed entirely of concrete—wait, keep reading!—this award-winning hotel on 13 secluded acres is one of the most striking in Puerto Rico. Architect John Hix set out to echo the gray granite boulders strewn around Vieques, and his success is apparent in the resulting three buildings, which blend beautifully with the environment. A spare aesthetic permeates the rooms, which have dramatic lines and sexy curves. Sunny terraces, vast unglazed windows (actually

4

panoramic open walls), and showers that are open to the stars (yet still very private) keep nature nearby. The resort's embrace of the environment goes beyond form into function, with the use of recycled water and solar-power systems. Even the swimming pool is eco-friendly. The hotel is on Route 995, off Route 201. **Pros:** Eye-popping architecture; secluded setting; friendly staff. **Cons:** No windows means some bugs in the rooms; no elevator; far from restaurants. ✉ *Rte. 995, Km 1.5, Vieques Box 1556* ☎ *787/741–2302* 🌐 *www.hixislandhouse.com* *13 rooms* *In-room: no a/c, no phone, kitchen, refrigerator, no TV. In-hotel: pool* *AE, MC, V* *CP.*

$$$ VILLAS **Inn on the Blue Horizon.** The six Mediterranean-style villas here was the tiny island's first taste of luxury. It's still one of the most sought-after accommodations, to a large extent because of its breathtaking setting on a bluff overlooking the ocean. The mood is plantation-style cozy, from the intimate guest rooms to the open-air lounge. Carambola's, located here, is perhaps the island's most formal restaurant, but many people opt for a meal at the bar, where the staff will make any cocktail you can name—or create a new one and name it after you. Still, this high-priced hotel has lost its edge of late and now struggles to retain its popularity in the face of keen competition. **Pros:** Eye-popping view; elegant accommodations; good dining options. **Cons:** Aloof staff and inattentive management; pricey for what you get; no elevator. ✉ *Rte. 996, Km 4.2, Esperanza, Vieques* *Box 1556, Vieques00765* ☎ *787/741–3318* 🌐 *www.innonthebluehorizon.com* *10 rooms* *In-room: no phone, no TV. In-hotel: restaurant, bar, tennis court, pool, beachfront, bicycles, no kids under 14* *AE, D, MC, V* *BP.*

$ HOTEL **La Finca Caribe.** An edgy, off-beat hotel run along the lines of a Berkeley commune, this hillside getaway seemingly miles from anywhere has an irresistible rustic appeal. It's not for everyone, but convivial, gregarious folks with a taste for barefoot back-to-basics will love it. Edgy and funky, it's even been the setting for a J. Crew catalog shoot. Everyone helps themselves in the common kitchen in the guesthouse made of roughhewn planks splashed with tropical ice cream pastels, with zinc for a roof. Hammocks are slung across the large wooden deck overhanging the veggie garden. While two self-catering casas (one-week minimum rental) dispersed among fruit trees have their own bathrooms, guests in the basic dorm-like rooms shower side by side in roofless outdoor stalls. **Pros:** Communal hibachi; social informality; nature-focused **Cons:** Far from island services. ✉ *Rte. 995, Km 1.2, Vieques* ☎ *787/741–0495* 🌐 *www.lafinca.com* *6 rooms, 3 cabins, 1 house* *In-room: no phone, kitchen (some), refrigerator (some). In-hotel: restaurant, pool, bicycles, laundry facilities, Internet terminal, Wi-Fi, parking (free), some pets allowed, no-smoking rooms.* *MC, V.*

$ HOTEL **Seagate Hotel.** Owner-manager Penny Miller lavishes attention on guests at her spic-and-span hilltop hotel, a 10-minute downhill walk to Isabel Segunda. Tucked into its own leafy compound, with grandstand views over town, the island's oldest—yet still youthful—hotel is a haven of peace and relaxation. The lovely rooms in a gleaming white three-story structure boast lively Caribbean decor and pastels. Each is an individually themed minimuseum of sea corals, old prints, and modern art. Families should opt for the freestanding villa. And there's also a backpackers dorm. Penny offers horseback rides. She also rescues stray dogs and injured horses and other beasts, and animals are a strong presence, although most are discreetly fenced out of sight. **Pros:** Friendly and helpful owner-manager; handy for exploring town. **Cons:** Small rooms; lots of dogs; no restaurant. ✉ *Barrio Fuerte, Isabel Segunda* ☎ *787/741–4661* 🌐 *www.seagatehotel.com* *16* *In-room: no a/c (some), no phone (some), kitchen (some), refrigerator (some), no TV (some), Wi-Fi. In-hotel: bar, tennis courts, pools, gym, spa, bicycles, laundry facilities, laundry service, Wi-Fi, parking (free), some pets allowed, no-smoking rooms.* 💳 *AE, MC, V.*

¢–$ INN **Trade Winds.** The best of a string of inexpensive guesthouses along the main road in Esperanza, this place has an unbeatable location across from the waterfront promenade. The hotel restaurant has a lively bar popular with expats, and a number of eateries are only a stone's throw away. Rooms are basic but more than adequate if you plan on spending most of your time at the beach. They share several terraces, all of which overlook the ocean. **Pros:** Good value; many nearby dining options. **Cons:** Right on the noisy street; no elevator; not the most attractive building. ✉ *142 Calle Flamboyán, Esperanza* *Box 1012, Vieques 00770* ☎ *787/741–8666* 🌐 *www.enchanted-isle.com/tradewinds* *11 rooms* *In-room: refrigerator. In-hotel: restaurant, bar* 💳 *AE, MC, V* *EP.*

$$$$ RESORT ★ **W Retreat & Spa.** Hovering over two gorgeous beaches (one topless), the über-hip, adults-only W Retreat & Spa opened in November 2009 as the island's trendy new hot spot for urbane fashionistas. A $150 million remake of the former colonial-themed Wyndham Martineau Bay & Spa has metamorphosed this beachfront hotel into the very definition of contemporary chic. W's trademark sexy sophistication is reflected in en-vogue white, taupe, and chocolate color schemes. Gourmands will appreciate the dining terrace overlooking a magnificent pool area, with private screened cabañas with flat-screen interactive TVs. The high-tech theme extends to the mammoth guest rooms, featuring retro-style bathtubs floating in their midst. Pampered luxury is a watchword, courtesy of Whatever/Whenever service; the holistic 6,000-square-foot Spa Chakra; and chef Alain Ducasse's Mix restaurant ($$$$), with its fold-back concertina glass doors. **Pros:** Sensational decor; full-service spa; five-minute drive from the airport. **Cons:** High prices even in low season. ✉ *Rte. 200, Km 3.2, Isabel Segunda* ☎ *787/741–4100* 🌐 *www.whotels.com/vieques* *157 rooms* *In-room: kitchen (some), refrigerator (some), DVD, Internet (some). In-hotel: 2 restaurants, room service, bars, tennis courts, pools, gym, spa, beachfront, diving, water sports, bicycles, laundry service, Internet terminal, Wi-Fi, parking (free), some pets allowed, no kids under 21, no-smoking rooms.* 💳 *AE, D, DC, MC, V.* *EP*

4

NIGHTLIFE

Not far from the ferry terminal, **Al's Mar Azul** (✉ *Calle Plinio Peterson, Isabel Segunda* ☎ *787/741–3400*) is where everyone gathers to watch the sunset. The main virtue of this open-air bar is a deck overlooking the ocean. You'll find dart boards, pool tables, and a jukebox.

Bananas (✉ *142 Calle Flamboyán, Esperanza* ☎ *787/741–8700*) is the place for burgers and beer—not necessarily in that order. There's sometimes live music and dancing.

Club Tumby (✉ *Bunkers, Barrio Mosquito* ☎ *787/399–4172* 🌐 *www.clubtumby.com*) causes a double-take when you consider this massive state-of-the-art disco on little, off-the-beaten-path Vieques. Wall-to-wall big screens, a bar stretching to the moon, and a dance floor for 5,000 people? Wow!

Duffy's (✉ *140 Calle Flamboyán, Esperanza* ☎ *787/741–7600*) has become one of the most popular bars on the island, thanks to the jawboning of owner Michael Duffy.

La Nasa (✉ *Calle Flamboyán, Esperanza* ☎ *No phone*) is the only establishment on the waterfront side of the street in Esperanza. This simple wooden shack, decorated with strings of Christmas lights the entire year, serves up cheap beer and rum drinks and draws island-born Viequenses, rather than expats. Locals congregate on plastic chairs out front or stare off into the placid Caribbean from an open-air back room.

PRIVATE VILLA RENTALS

One good way to visit Vieques is to rent one of the beautiful vacation homes that have been built in the hilly interior or along the coasts. These are concentrated in three major areas: Bravos de Boston, Esperanza, and Pilón. Several local real-estate agents deal in short-term rentals of at least a week. A list of properties is available from gay-friendly **Rainbow Realty** (✉ *Rte. 996, Esperanza* ☎ *787/741-4312* 🌐 *www.enchanted-isle.com/rainbow*).

SHOPPING

Most residents do their shopping on the mainland, so there are very few shops on Vieques. You'll find mostly clothing stores that lean toward beach attire, as well as a few art galleries.

Casa Vieja Gallery (✉ *Rte. 201, Esperanza* ☎ *787/741–3078*) is where several local artists show and sell their work.

Diva's Closet (✉ *134 Calle Flamboyán, Esperanza* ☎ *787/741–7595*), which is next door to Kim's Cabin, carries an array of women's clothes. Here you'll find everything you need for the beach or for brunch.

Kim's Cabin (✉ *136 Calle Flamboyán, Esperanza* ☎ *787/741–3145* 🌐 *http://islavieques.com/kimscabin.html*), which has been in business on Vieques since the early 1990s, is a local institution. There's jewelry in the front room and the two other rooms have clothing for men and women.

Vieques has a number of bays and protected coves that provide calm surf perfect for beginners.

★ **Siddhia Hutchinson Fine Art Studio & Gallery** (✉ *15 Calle 3, Isabel Segunda* ☎ *787/741–1343*) is north of the ferry dock. The artist has lived on Vieques since the early 1990s, creating pastel watercolor prints of Caribbean scenes, as well as limited-edition ceramic dinnerware. The gallery is open daily, 9–3.

SPORTS AND THE OUTDOORS

BIKING

Garry Lowe at **Vieques Adventure Company** (☎ *787/692–9162* 🌐 *www.viequesadventures.com*) can set you up with mountain bikes and all the equipment you need starting at $25. They'll even bring the bikes to wherever you happen to be staying. Customized tours of the island—which range from easy rides on country roads to muddy treks into the hills—are $75 half-day to $150 full day.

BOATING AND KAYAKING

Various outfitters offer trips to Puerto Mosquito, the island's celebrated bioluminescent bay. Most are trips in single-person kayaks, which can be a challenge if you lack experience or endurance. A better option for most people is a boat—an electric-powered model is best, as the gas-powered ones harm the environment.

Aqua Frenzy Kayaks (✉ *At dock area below Calle Flamboyán, Esperanza* ☎ *787/741–0913* 🌐 *www.aquafrenzy.com*) rents kayaks and arranges kayak tours of Puerto Mosquito and other areas. Reservations are required for the excursion to the bio bay; the evening kayak trip costs $30. Make reservations at least 24 hours in advance.

Blue Caribe Kayaks (✉ *149 Calle Flamboyán, Esperanza* ☎ *787/741–2522* 🌐 *www.bluecaribekayaks.com*) offers kayak trips to Puerto Mosquito for about $30, as well as trips to deserted parts of the coast and nearby islets. You can also rent a kayak and set off on your own.

★ **East Island Excursions** (✉ *At dock area of Marina Puerto Del Rey* Fajardo ☎ *787/860–3434* 🌐 *www.eastwindcats.com*) can accommodate those who prefer to see Puerto Mosquito and return to the mainland on the same evening. Transportation to Vieques is provided and dinner at a local restaurant included before you board an electrically powered pontoon boat for a tour of Puerto Mosquito. Bring a towel because you can leap into the bio bay, where the outline of your body will be eerily illuminated. Flotation belts are provided. The cost is about $110 per person. Reservations are required. Transportation from your hotel can be arranged for a fee.

Marauder Sailing Charters (☎ *787/435–4858* 🌐 *www.viequessailing.com*) operates the *Marauder,* a 34-foot sailing yacht anchored off Esperanza. It sails around the southern coast, allowing a close-up look at the pristine nature of most of the island. There's a midday stop at a secluded spot for swimming, snorkeling, and sunbathing, followed by a gourmet lunch. The yacht, run by Kris Dynneson and Barbara Berger, has a good sound system and open bar.

DIVING AND SNORKELING

If you want to get your own snorkeling or diving equipment, head to **Black Beard Sports** (✉ *101 Calle Muñoz Rivera, Isabel Segunda* ☎ *787/741–1892* 🌐 *www.blackbeardsports.com*). This little store in downtown Isabel Segunda also arranges diving trips and certification courses.

Blue Caribe Kayaks (✉ *149 Calle Flamboyán, Esperanza* ☎ *787/741–2522* 🌐 *www.bluecaribekayaks.com*) will rent you snorkels, masks, and fins for $12 a day. The efficient staff can also arrange snorkeling trips to nearby islets.

Nan-Sea Charters (☎ *787/741–2390* 🌐 *www.nanseacharters.com*) offers organized dive trips, including shore dives, and snorkeling at Blue Tang Reef and remote offshore isles. The cost for a two-dive trip is $100 per person, not including equipment rental.

FISHING

Vieques Adventure Company (☎ *787/692–9162* 🌐 *www.viequesadventures.com*) will take you on kayak fly-fishing trips for bonefish and tarpon. "It's extreme fishing," says owner and trip leader Garry Lowe. "When you're in a kayak and have a 50-pound tarpon on the line, you're going to go for a ride!"

CULEBRA

17 mi (28 km) east of Fajardo by ferry.

Culebra is known around the world for its curvaceous coastline. Playa Flamenco, the tiny island's most famous stretch of sand, is considered one of the top ten best beaches in the world. If Playa Flamenco gets too crowded, as it often does around Easter or Christmas, many other neighboring beaches will be nearly deserted. And if you crave complete privacy, hire a motorboat to take you to one of the nearby islets such as Isla Culebrita or Cayo Luis Peña. It won't be difficult to find a little cove that you will have all to yourself.

Archaeological evidence shows that Taíno and Carib peoples lived on Culebra long before the arrival of the Spanish in the late 15th century. The Spanish didn't bother laying claim to it until 1886; its dearth of freshwater made it an unattractive location for a settlement. The U.S. Navy and Marine Corps, however, thought it was a very valuable piece of real estate. Although President Theodore Roosevelt created a wildlife refuge in 1909, the military used this island, as well as nearby Vieques, for target practice and amphibious assault training beginning in WWII. Despite their smaller numbers, the residents of Culebra managed to oust the military after staging sit-ins on the beach. The military left Culebra in 1975.

GETTING HERE AND AROUND

Culebra's **Aeropuerto Benjamin Rivera Noriega** (✉ *Culebra* ☎ *787/742–0022*), CPX, is at the intersection of Route 250 and Route 251. The one-room facility has two car-rental agencies and a scooter-rental kiosk. The airport is about three minutes from downtown Dewey. Route 250 leads east and south of the airport. Route 251 leads northeast to Playa Flamenco.

Car Rental **Carlos Jeep Rental** (✉ *Aeropuerto Benjamin Rivera Noriega, Culebra* ☎ *787/742–3514* 🌐 *www.carlosjeeprental.com*).

Ferry Terminal **Culebra Terminal** (☎ *787/742–3161*).

Taxi **Willy's Taxi** (✉ *Culebra* ☎ *787/742–3537*).

EXPLORING CULEBRA

Almost everything about Culebra is diminutive. The island's only community, named in honor of U.S. Admiral George Dewey (island-born locals hate the association and prefer to call the town simply "el pueblo"), is set along a single street leading from the ferry dock. You can explore the few shops along Calle Pedro Márquez in a half hour. The one-room airport is ½ mi (1 km) to the north. Except for one sprawling resort, no hotels have more than a dozen rooms.

Commissioned by President Theodore Roosevelt in 1909, **Refugio Nacional de Vida Silvestre de Culebra** is one of the nation's oldest wildlife refuges. Some 1,500 acres of the island make up a protected area. It's a lure for hikers and bird-watchers: Culebra teems with seabirds, from laughing gulls and roseate terns to red-billed tropic birds and sooty terns. Maps of trails in the refuge are hard to come by, but you can stop by the U.S. Fish & Wildlife Service office east of the airport to find out about trail conditions and determine whether you're headed to an area that requires a permit. The office also can tell you whether the leatherback turtles are nesting. From mid-April to mid-July, volunteers help to monitor and tag these creatures, which nest on nearby beaches, especially Playa Resaca and Playa Brava. If you'd like to volunteer, you must agree to help out for at least three nights. ✉ *Rte. 250, north of*

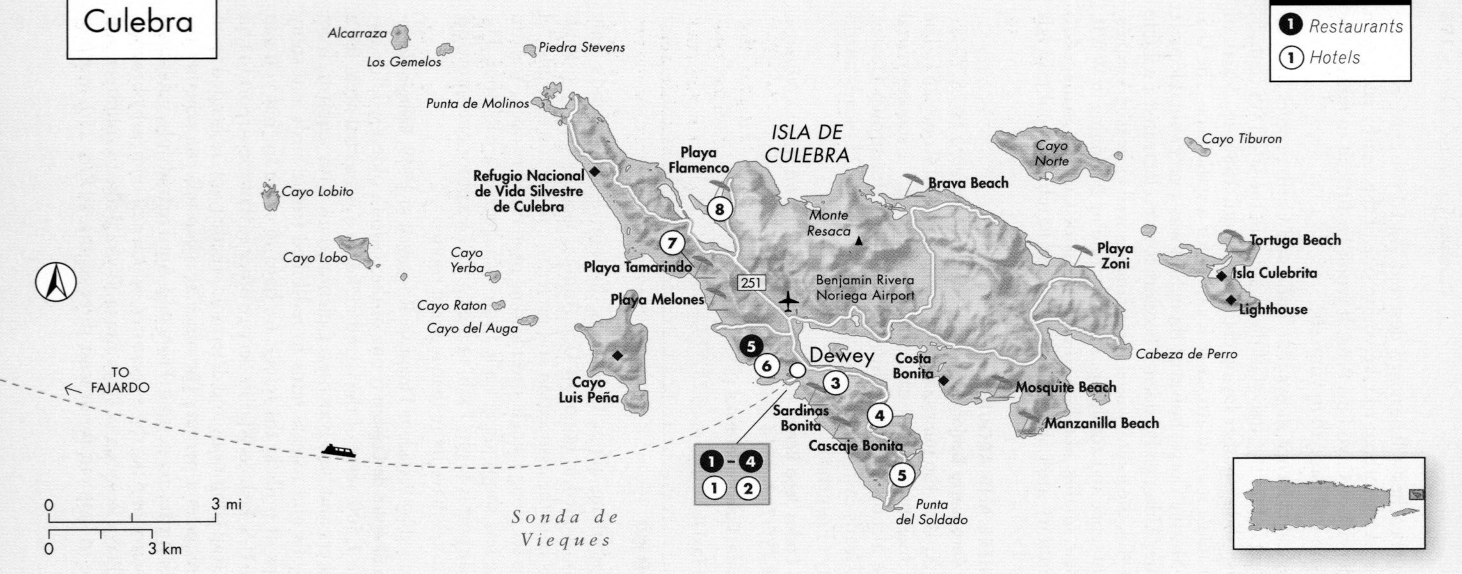

Restaurants	▼
Dinghy Dock	4
Juanita Bananas	5
Mamacita's	3
Pandeli	1
Susie's	2

Hotels	▼
Bahía Marina	5
Club Seaborne	4
Culebra Beach Villas	8
Harbor View Villas	6
Mamacita's	1
Posada La Hamaca	2
Tamarindo Estates	7
Villa Boheme	3

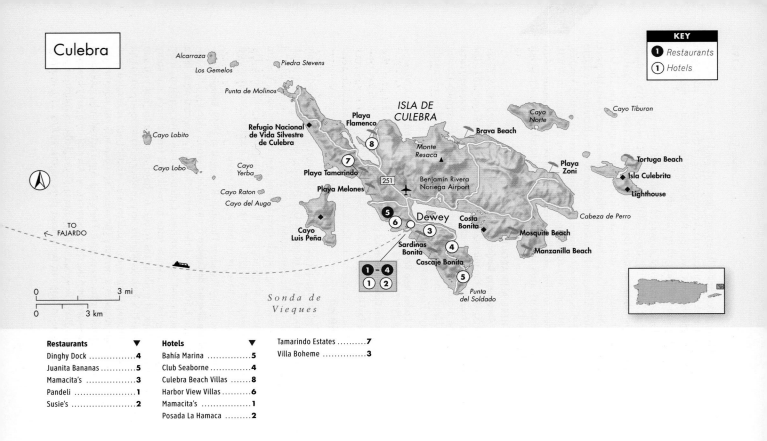

Dewey ☎ *787/742–0115* 🌐 *www.fws.gov/caribbean/Refuges* 🎟 *Free* ⏲ *Daily dawn–dusk.*

WORD OF MOUTH

"Culebra is not for someone looking to be pampered, or someone who wants a golf vacation or shopping vacation. But if you want quiet and solitude and beauty (especially underwater!), this might be for you. I have very fond memories of this island." —cj

Part of the Refugio Nacional de Vida Silvestre de Culebra, uninhabited **Isla Culebrita** is clearly visible from the northeast corner of Culebra. This islet is a favorite destination for sunbathers who want to escape the crowds at Playa Flamenco. On the northern shore there are several tidal pools; snuggling into one of them is like taking a warm bath. Snorkelers and divers love the fact that they can reach the reef from the shore. You can also hike around the island and visit the ruins of an old lighthouse, but it is tumbledown—so don't enter. To get there, take a dive boat or hire a water taxi.

A kayak is a great way to reach **Cayo Luis Peña**, an islet just off the western edge of Culebra. There are a handful of protected beaches where you can soak up the sun and not run into a single soul. Cayo Luis Peña is also part of the Refugio Nacional de Vida Silvestre de Culebra.

4

WHERE TO EAT

$$ CARIBBEAN ✕ **Dinghy Dock.** Culebra's version of heavy traffic—the arrival and departure of the water taxi—takes place around the dock that gives this restaurant its name. The menu leans toward grilled meats, from hamburgers to sirloin steaks. Daily specials often highlight the restaurant's forte: creole-style seafood, including swordfish and yellowtail. The adjacent open-air bar is usually packed with expats. It can get noisy, and the service is anything but doting, so don't expect a quiet dinner for two. ✉ *Calle Fulladoza, Dewey* ☎ *787/742–0233* 💳 *MC, V.*

$$–$$$ CARIBBEAN ✕ **Juanita Bananas.** Trees overflowing with bananas, papayas, and passion fruit line the steep walkway that leads to one of Culebra's best eateries. Chef Jennifer Daubon uses only the freshest local produce—she grows vegetables and herbs on an acre of land on the surrounding hillside. The menu changes with the seasons, but look for dishes like lobster *limonjili* (medallions of lobster in a fresh lime and garlic sauce) and sizzling sushi-grade tuna. Monday is sushi night. The dining room, with its low lights, soft music, and expansive view, is romantic, and you can dine outside beneath an arbor. ✉ *Calle Melones, Km 1* ☎ *787/742–3855* 🌐 *www.juanitabananas.com* ✍ *Reservations essential* 💳 *D, MC, V* ⏲ *Closed Tues.–Thurs. No lunch.*

$–$$ CONTINENTAL ✕ **Mamacita's.** Watching iguanas plodding along the dock is reason enough to dine at this simple open-air, tin-roofed restaurant on a rough-plank deck beside the Dewey canal. Tarpon cruise past in the jade waters below, and the to and fro of boaters also keeps patrons amused. Those are all good reasons why this is the gringo hangout in town, although we suspect that Mamacita's down-home dishes play a part. The menu is heavy on burgers, but seafood dishes include an excellent mahi-mahi. And do try the killer smoothies. You'll dine at tables painted in a rainbow of pastels adorned with floral motifs. ✉ *Calle Castelar, Dewey* ☎ *787/742–0322* 🌐 *www.mamacitasguesthouse.com* 💳 *MC, V.*

¢ CAFE ★ ✕ **Pandeli.** More often than not when locals go out for breakfast or lunch, they head to this little café on Dewey's main street. Beyond the smart red and blue facade is a counter where you can order any number of delicious sandwiches, some of them only a few dollars. The roast beef is the best value for the money. It opens before sunup, but get here early, as the place closes midafternoon. If you are aching to check your e-mail, this eatery has Wi-Fi and is a great place to relax with a gourmet coffee. ✉ *Calle Pedro Márquez at Calle Castelar, Dewey* ☎ *787/742–0296* 💳 *MC, V* ⏲ *No dinner.*

$–$$ ECLECTIC ✕ **Susie's.** Half-expecting Popeye to walk in, you'd never guess that this funky little place hemmed between a gas pump and dry dock could deliver the goods. But what goodies! Sanjuanera owner-chef Susie Hebert learned her culinary skills at San Juan's swank Caribe Hilton and Ritz-Carlton hotels before settling on Culebra and opening her fine-dining restaurant, belied by its locale and simple interior decor. The Caesar salad here excels, and you can't go wrong ordering hummus with pita bread. Follow, perhaps, with sautéed jumbo shrimp in roast garlic and tarragon sauce on a bed of mofongo. Divine! ✉ *Off Calle Escudero, Dewey* ☎ *787/742–0574* 🌐 *www.susiesculebra.com* *Reservations essential* 💳 *MC, V* ⏲ *Closed Mon.–Tues. No lunch.*

WHERE TO STAY

$–$$ VACATION VILLAS **Bahía Marina.** If you're looking for space to spread out, these one- and two-bedroom apartments are for you. Each sleeps four, thanks to a fold-out couch in the living room of the one-bedroom units. Full kitchens are equipped with everything you need to make dinner for the family. Step outside onto your private deck or head out to the swimming pool, and you'll have unobstructed views of the hills surrounding Fulladoza Bay. The hotel recently added 12 two-bedroom villas, bringing the total to 28. The second-floor restaurant, Dakity ($$–$$$), takes full advantage of the island's fresh seafood and hilltop location. Note that there is no elevator. **Pros:** Beautiful setting; good restaurant. **Cons:** Feels like an apartment complex; lots of steps to negotiate. ✉ *Calle Fulladoza, Km 1.5* *Box 807, Culebra 00646* ☎ *787/742–0535* 🌐 *www.bahiamarina.net* *39 apartments* *In-room: kitchen, refrigerator, Wi-Fi. In-hotel: 2 restaurants, room service, bar, pool, public Wi-Fi* 💳 *AE, MC, V* *CP.*

$$–$$$ VACATION VILLAS **Club Seaborne.** The prettiest place to stay in Culebra, this cluster of plantation-style cottages sits on a hilltop overlooking Fulladoza Bay, a five-minute drive south of Dewey. The place feels completely isolated, but it is only a mile or so from the center of town. Opt for one of the rooms surrounding the pool or one of the spacious villas. The largest sleeps five, making it a favorite of families. The plantation-style decor lends a deluxe feel, although it seems out of keeping with the Culebra mood. Specializing in seafood, the terrace restaurant ($$–$$$) is the most elegant on the island. The friendly staff is happy to help you set up snorkeling and diving trips or arrange transportation to the beach. **Pros:** Lovely cottages; well-regarded restaurant;

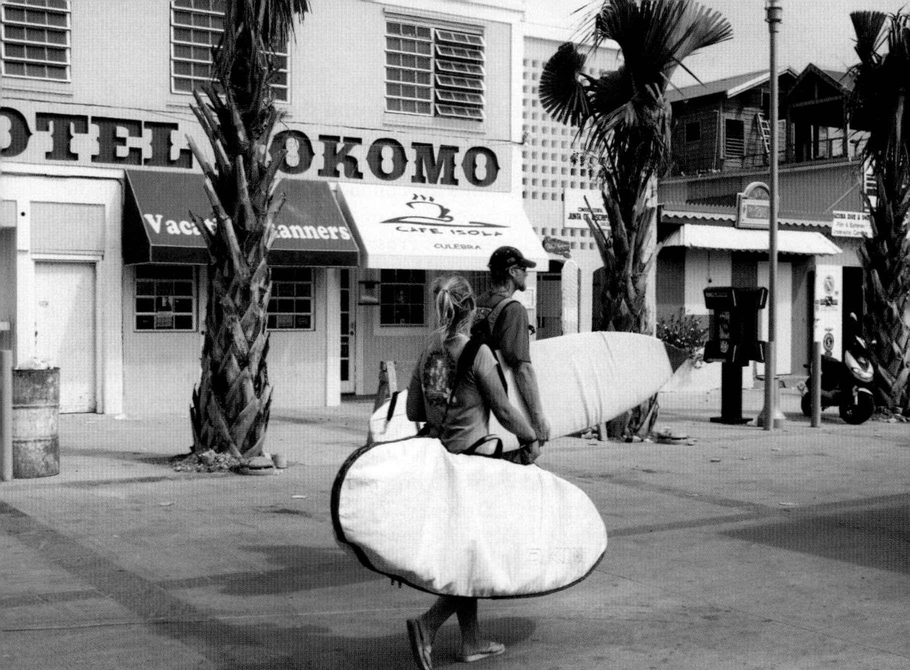

Surfer-crossing is often the extent of traffic flow in the town of Dewey, Culebra.

lush gardens. **Cons:** Staff can seem overworked; some steps to negotiate and no elevator. ✉ *Calle Fulladoza, Km 1.5* 📫 *Box 357, Culebra 00775* ☎ *787/742–3169* 🌐 *www.clubseabourne.com* *3 rooms, 8 villas, 1 cottage* *In-room: kitchen (some). In-hotel: restaurant, bar, pool* 💳 *AE, MC, V* 🍽 *CP.*

$–$$ VACATION VILLAS **Culebra Beach Villas.** There's one main reason to stay here, and that's the beach. In fact, this is the only hotel at Playa Flamingo. The studios (in a three-story beachfront edifice) and cabins here are literally steps from the glorious white sands and turquoise water. The individually owned units vary greatly, so it's worth checking several if possible. All are fairly basic, and although most have kitchens and spacious decks with hammocks, the owners don't invest much time and money for upkeep. Repeat guests know to arrive with groceries in hand, as the nearest grocery is in town. The place is family-friendly—in fact it's ideal for kids. **Pros:** On the best beach in Puerto Rico; secluded. **Cons:** Can get noisy with families; slightly run-down; management not always available. ✉ *Off Rte. 251, Playa Flamingo* ☎ *787/409–2599* 🌐 *www.culebrabeach.com* *rooms & 18 cabins* *In-room: Kitchen, refrigerator. In-hotel: TVs, room service, bar, beachfront, water sports, laundry facilities, Internet terminal, WiFi, parking (free)* 💳 *MC, V* 🍽 *EP.*

$–$$ VACATION VILLAS **Harbor View Villas.** Straddling a ridge that guarantees the breezes, this simple property is also a sure bet for winning views south over the harbor and north over the isle. Both Dewey township and Playa Melones—good for snorkeling—are mere minutes' stroll away. The digs here are free-standing wooden cabins with lofty beamed ceilings, simple kitchenettes, and a bare modicum of furnishings. In fact, it's the antithesis of luxe. But travelers who shun pretension and pampering will appreciate this rustic escape for what it is, in spite of its need of a general sprucing up. Clearly, guests are expected to get out and about, but the balconies are conducive to lazing and savoring the views. The restaurant here is one of the island's best. Owners Jane and Druso Daubon live on site. **Pros:** Spellbinding views; great restaurant. **Cons:** Robinson Crusoe–basic accommodations; a steep uphill climb from the entrance gate; unkempt grounds littered with junk. ✉ *Off Calle Vecinal, Dewey* ☎ *787/742–3855* 🌐 *www.culebrahotel.com* *3 rooms, 3 villas* *In-room: no a/c(some), no phone, kitchen (some), refrigerator (some). In-hotel: restaurant, laundry facilities, laundry service, Internet terminal, parking (free), some pets allowed, no-smoking rooms* *D, MC, V* *EP.*

$ HOTEL **Mamacita's.** PLEASE DON'T FEED THE IGUANAS, reads a sign hanging on the terrace of this longtime favorite. Set beneath lazily turning ceiling fans, the disarmingly charming restaurant ($–$$$) overlooks a canal filled with fishing boats. The bar gets crowded during happy hour, which starts early in these parts. If you like it so much you don't want to leave, there are guest rooms with meager tropical furnishings and kitchenettes upstairs in the venerable wooden mansion. The best have balconies overlooking the canal, but this is decidedly a no-frills establishment befitting travelers who are easy to please. **Pros:** Friendly staff; pickup point for water taxis. **Cons:** Basic furnishings; some noise from restaurant and bar below; no elevator; on a narrow street. ✉ *66 Calle Castelar, Dewey* ☎ *787/742–0090* 🌐 *www.mamacitasguesthouse.com* *10 rooms, 1 suite* *In-room: kitchen (some), refrigerator (some). In-hotel: restaurant, bar* *AE, MC, V* *EP.*

$–$$ HOTEL **Posada La Hamaca.** The shady terrace behind this little lodging adjoining Mamacita's sits on a mangrove-lined canal where owner Al Custer docks his motorboat. The delightful, spic-and-span guest rooms—as simple as they come—have louvered windows and calming color schemes. The inn sits on the edge of Dewey, putting you within walking distance of restaurants, shops, and grocery stores. The staff sends you off to the beach with a little cooler filled with ice. All in all, it offers great value. **Pros:** Walk to shops and restaurants; laid-back atmosphere; cheap rates. **Cons:** Some rooms are small; constant clunking noises from adjacent bridge; no elevator. ✉ *68 Calle Castelar, Dewey* ☎ *787/742–3516* 🌐 *www.posada.com* *10 rooms* *In-room: no phone, kitchen (some). In-hotel: bar, restaurant* *MC, V* *EP.*

$$–$$$ COTTAGES **Tamarindo Estates.** On a 60-acre estate hidden away on the western coast of Culebra, this string of one- and two-bedroom beach-apartment cottages is on a long, sandy beach. Most of the cottages are a bit farther inland, affording great views of the coastline from their covered verandas. Each has a full kitchen. There's a shared beach house with showers and other amenities, including a pool with an oceanfront deck. The waters of nearby Luis Peña Channel are perfect for snorkeling, and it's about a 10-minute drive to Flamenco Beach. **Pros:** Peaceful location; pretty pool area. **Cons:** Short walk to the beach; isolated far from dining options. ✉ *Off Rte. 251* *Box 313, Culebra 00775* ☎ *787/742–3343* 🌐 *www.tamarindoestates.com* *16 cottages* *In-room: kitchen, VCR.*

In-hotel: pool, beachfront ▭ *MC, V* 🍴 *EP.*

$ INN **Villa Boheme.** Colorful and breeze-swept, this Spanish-style guesthouse, painted a particularly pretty shade of apricot, is one of the most distinctive on the island. Its shady terrace, with several hammocks hanging between the palm trees, is a great place to hang out. You may not feel the need to do anything more strenuous than reach for your margarita, but if you do, there are some kayaks that you can rent to explore Ensenada Bay. Apartment rooms are simple, but each one has a view of the water; all share a communal kitchen, but some have kitchens of their own. **Pros:** Expansive view of the bay; walk to restaurants and shops. **Cons:** Basic furnishings; no elevator; room colors tend to be overwhelming. ✉ *Calle Fulladoza, Dewey* ☎ *787/742–3508* 🌐 *www.villaboheme.com* *12 rooms* *In-room: kitchen (some), refrigerator (some)* ▭ *AE, MC, V* 🍴 *EP.*

VILLA RENTALS

Lovely vacation homes are scattered around the island. **Culebra Island Realty** (✉ *Calle Escudero, Dewey* ☎ *787/742–0052* 🌐 *www.culebraislandrealty.com*) has a few dozen properties for rent, ranging from studios to three-bedroom houses.

NIGHTLIFE

Dinghy Dock (✉ *Calle Fulladoza, Dewey* ☎ *787/742–0233*) is the spot where the island's expat community begins piling into the bar around sunset. It can be a raucous scene, especially when there's a band. The party continues into the wee hours, even during the week. **El Batey** (✉ *Calle Escudero, Dewey* ☎ *787/742–3828*) is popular on the weekends, when locals dance to salsa music. It's in a cement-block building halfway between the airport and the town.

SHOPPING

Culebra is smaller than Vieques but has much better shopping. Dewey has several shops on its main drag that sell trendy jewelry, fashionable clothing, and a range of souvenirs from tacky to terrific.

Butiki (✉ *Calle Romero, Dewey* ☎ *787/267–7284* 🌐 *www.butikiculebra.com*) is the cream of the crop. You'll find everything from lovely jewelry to original paintings. And co-owner Stephanie Blake is so helpful that the city should shut down the tourism office and send people here.

La Cava (✉ *138 Calle Escudio, Dewey* ☎ *787/742–0566*) stocks a little bit of everything. Forgot your snorkel? Left your bathing suit at home? This is a good place to find a replacement.

In a wooden shack painted vivid shades of yellow and red, **Fango** (✉ *Calle Castelar, Dewey* ☎ *787/556–9308* 🌐 *www.artefango.com*) is the island's best place for gifts. Jorge Acevedo paints scenes of island life, while Hannah Staiger designs sophisticated jewelry. The shop is no bigger than a walk-in closet, but you could easily spend half an hour browsing among their one-of-a-kind works. £££

On Island (✉ *4 Calle Pedro Marquez, Dewey* ☎ *787/742–0439*) has a selection of black-and-white prints of the island's flora and fauna and a nice display of handmade jewelry.

Paradise (✉ *6 Calle Salisbury, Dewey* ☎ *787/742–3569* 🌐 *www.jill-buckingham.com*) is a good spot for souvenirs ranging from wrought-iron iguanas to hand-carved seagulls to plush baby turtles.

SPORTS AND THE OUTDOORS

BIKING

Since there's very little traffic, biking is a good way to explore the island. You can rent bikes for $20 a day at **Culebra Bike Shop** (✉ *Calle Fulladoza, Dewey* ☎ *787/742–2209* 🌐 *http://culebrabike.com*). The shop is next door to the Dinghy Dock.

BOATING AND KAYAKING

Aquatic Adventures (☎ *787/209–3494* 🌐 *www.diveculebra.com*) Capt. Taz Hamrick will take you out snorkeling, on dolphin trips, or to the surrounding cays. **Kayaking Culebra** (☎ *787/245–4545* 🌐 *www.kayakingpuertorico.com*) has a daytrip from Fajardo, with kayaking, snorkeling, and the round-trip ferry included for $69 per person.

The glass-bottom boat at **Tanamá** (☎ *787/501–0011*) lets you explore the undersea world without even getting wet.

Willy's Water Taxi (✉ *Rte. 251, Dewey* ☎ *787/742–3537*) offers boat trips, including to Culebrita.

DIVING AND SNORKELING

Run by Monica and Walter Rieder, **Culebra Divers** (✉ *4 Calle Pedro Marquez, Dewey* ☎ *787/742–0803* 🌐 *www.culebradivers.com*) caters to people who are new to scuba diving. You travel to dive sites on one of the company's pair of 26-foot cabin cruisers. One-tank dives are $65, and two-tank dives are $95. You can also rent a mask and snorkel to explore on your own. The office is in downtown Dewey, across from the ferry terminal.

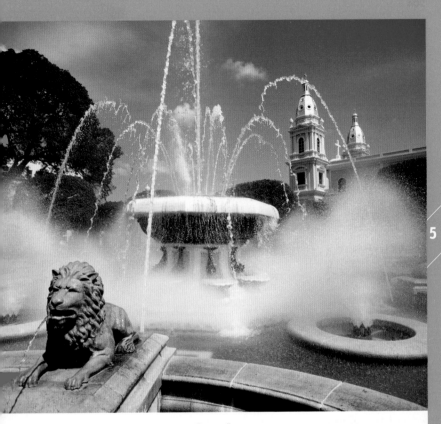

Ponce and the Southern Coast

WORD OF MOUTH

"I love San Germán as it is a mini version of Old San Juan with the small-town atmosphere."

—dariow

WELCOME TO PONCE AND THE SOUTHERN COAST

TOP REASONS TO GO

★ **Parque de Bombas:** Marvel at a century-old firehouse whose red-and-black color scheme has inspired thousands of photographers.

★ **Bosque Estatal de Guánica:** Hike where the cactus may make you think you're in the American Southwest.

★ **Hacienda Buena Vista:** Sample a cup of the local brew at the historic, beautifully restored coffee plantation outside of Ponce.

★ **San Germán:** Stroll cobblestone streets lined with architectural treasures; then dine on Puerto Rican fusion cuisine high above the main plaza.

★ **Casa Cautiño:** Step back in time to a colonial-era residence in the sleepy community of Guayama.

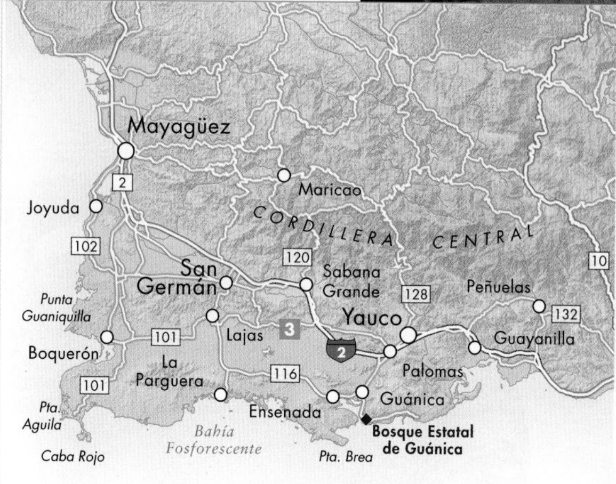

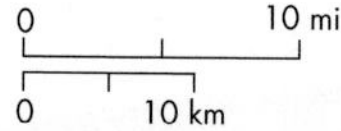

1 Ponce. Reminiscent of Old San Juan before the cruise ships arrived, Ponce has a yesteryear charm and increasingly cosmopolitan vibe that delight many visitors. Take a trolley tour of the colonial past, explore some of the best museums on the island, and at night dine at a six-floor restaurant directly overlooking the famous Parque de Bombas.

2 The Southeastern Coast. Underexplored and untrammeled, the southeast is one of the least-visited parts of the island. Start with a seaside meal in Salinas, where the famous Mojo Isleño sauce was created; then hop into the hills to relax in the Baños de Coamo, a thermal spring used for hundreds of years.

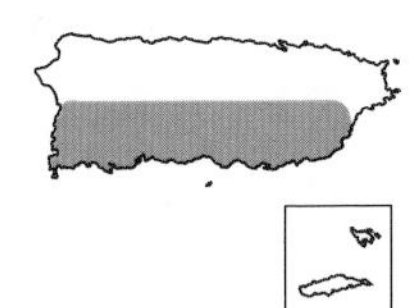

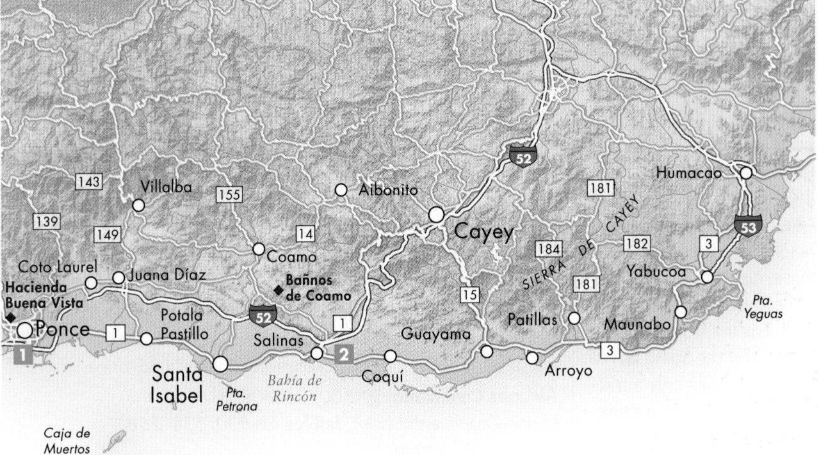

3 The Southwestern Coast. Discover the island's first and most inexpensive bioluminescent bay; the university town of San Germán, whose churches and colonial mansions date back as far as five centuries; and the fascinating dry forest at Guanica.

GETTING ORIENTED

Ponce is the region's dynamic center, with a surrounding metropolitan area that includes a slew of vibrant attractions, sophisticated restaurants, and boutique hotels rivaled only by San Juan. To the southeast the shoreline is rugged and the villages more rural and isolated. Small seaside inns and some of the island's best seafood can be found here. Slightly inland from the coast are the colonial town of Coamo and its thermal baths. In the southwest, dense dry forest, such as the Bosque Estatal de Guánica, and mangroves hide undiscovered bays, inlets, and quaint fishing villages. Here you will also find the beautiful historic city of San Germán, one of Puerto Rico's oldest settlements.

PONCE AND THE SOUTHERN COAST PLANNER

When to Go

The resort towns of Patillas, Guánica, and La Parguera are popular with Puerto Ricans during Easter and Christmas and during the summer, when children are out of school and Ponce's spirited pre-Lenten carnival, held the week before Ash Wednesday, draws many visitors. For the rest of the year much of the South is quiet and receives only a fraction of the number of visitors as other parts of the island, though the weather is equally as superb and facilities remain open. Some *paradores*—small, government-sponsored inns—and hotels require a minimum two- or three-night stay on weekends.

Safety

For the most part, the South is safe. You won't encounter big-city crime, but you should take a few simple precautions. Don't wear flashy jewelry outside of tourist areas. Keep an eye on your belongings at the beach, and don't leave valuables locked in your car for all to see. Avoid out-of-the-way beach areas after dark.

General Emergencies (☎ *911*).

Getting Here and Around

Air Travel. **Aeropuerto Mercedita** (*PSE* ✉ *Rte. 506 off Rte. 52, Ponce* ☎ *787/842–6292*), about 5 mi (8 km) east of Ponce's downtown, is tiny, with very few amenities. The only international flights are on Continental, which shuttles between Ponce and Newark, and JetBlue, which flies between Ponce and Fort Lauderdale and New York–JFK. **Cape Air** (☎ *800/525–0280* 🌐 *www.flycapeair.com*) flies several times a day from San Juan.

Taxis at the airport use meters; expect to pay about $6 to get to downtown Ponce. All hotels have shuttles to and from the airport, but you must make arrangements in advance.

Airlines **Continental** (☎ *800/231–0856* 🌐 *www.continental.com*). **JetBlue** (☎ *800/538–2583* 🌐 *www.jetblue.com*).

Bus Travel. There's no easy network of buses linking the towns in southern Puerto Rico with San Juan or with each other. Some municipalities and private companies operate buses or *públicos* (usually large vans) that make many stops. Call ahead; although reservations aren't usually required, you'll need to check on schedules, which change frequently. The cost of a público from Ponce to San Juan is about $15–$20; agree on a price before hand.

Bus Information **Choferes Unidos de Ponce** (✉ *Terminal de Carros Públicos, Calle Vives and Calle Mendéz Vigo, Ponce Centro, Ponce* ☎ *787/842–1222*). **Línea Sangermeña** (✉ *Terminal de Carros Públicos, Calle Luna at entrance to town, San Germán* ☎ *787/722–3392*).

Car Travel. Getting around southern Puerto Rico without a car can be quite frustrating. You can rent cars at the Luis Muñoz Marín International Airport and other San Juan locations. There are also car-rental agencies in some of the larger cities along the south coast. Rates run about $35–$55 a day. A road map is essential in southern Puerto Rico. So is patience: Allow extra time for twisting mountain roads and wrong turns. Some roads, especially in rural areas, aren't plainly marked.

Taxi. In Ponce you can hail taxis in tourist areas and outside hotels. In smaller towns it's best to call a taxi. You can also hire a car service (make arrangements through your hotel); often you can negotiate a lower rate than a taxi.

About the Restaurants

Not all the culinary hot spots are in San Juan. In fact, people from the capital drive to Ponce or Guánica to see what's new on the horizon. Some of the more ambitious restaurants in this part of Puerto Rico are experimenting with Asian and Latin fusion cuisines, which means you might find pork with tamarind glaze or guava sauce or snapper in a plantain crust. But what you'll mostly find is open-air eateries serving simple, filling fare. The southern coast is known for seafood, particularly Salinas and Ponce, which both have a string of popular seaside restaurants. A 15% –20% tip is customary; most restaurants won't include it in the bill, but it's wise to check.

About the Hotels

Modest, family-oriented establishments near beaches or in small towns and the occasional restored colonial hacienda or mansion are the most typical accommodations. Southern Puerto Rico doesn't have the abundance of luxury hotels and resorts found to the north and east; however, the Hilton Ponce & Casino and the Copamarina Beach Resort are self-contained complexes with a dizzying array of services.

WHAT IT COSTS IN U.S. DOLLARS

	¢	$	$$	$$$	$$$$
Restaurants	under $8	$8–$12	$12–$20	$20–$30	over $30
Hotels	under $80	$80–$150	$150–$250	$250–$350	over $350

Prices are for a double room in high season, excluding 9% tax (11% for hotels with casinos, 7% for paradores) and 5%–12% service charge.

Tour Options

Alelí Tours and Encantos Ecotours Southwest in La Parguera offer ecological tours of the southwestern area, including two- or three-hour kayak trips that cost about $25.

Alelí Tours (✉ *Rte. 304, Km 3.2, La Parguera* ☎ *787/863–5153* 🌐). **Encantos Ecotours Southwest** (✉ *El Muelle Shopping Center, Av. Pescadores, La Parguera* ☎ *787/808–0005*).

Visitor Information

In Ponce the municipal tourist office is open weekdays from 8 to 4:30, as is the small information desk in the Parque de Bombas. The Puerto Rico Tourism Company's office in the Paseo del Sur plaza is open weekdays from 8 to 5. Smaller cities generally have a tourism office in the city hall that are open weekdays from 8 to noon and 1 to 4.

Ponce Municipal Tourist Office (✉ *2nd fl. of Citibank, Plaza de las Delicias, Ponce Centro, Ponce* ☎ *787/841–8160 or 787/841–8044*). **Puerto Rico Tourism Company** (✉ *291 Av. Los Caobos, Sector Vallas Torres, Ponce* ☎ *787/843–0465* 🌐 *welcome.topuertorico.org*).

BEACHES OF PONCE AND THE SOUTHERN COAST

Hop a boat for tiny Gilligan's Island, and enjoy a tranquil day on this uninhabited cay just off of Guánica.

South coast beaches are not the typical resort-lined stretches of sand that Puerto Rico is known for. They're more isolated, smaller, and receive fewer visitors. If you're up for a little bit of exploration, you'll be rewarded with unspoiled Caribbean water that you'll have all to yourself.

On Puerto Rico's southern coast you'll find surfing beaches and calm bays for swimming. Ballena Bay, near Guánica, has oft-deserted sandy stretches. Boat operators make trips to such uninhabited cays as Gilligan's Island off the coast of Guánica and Caja de Muertos off Ponce. After the beach, stick around for the evening in La Parguera for Puerto Rico's most inexpensive and original bioluminescent boat tours in the nearby mangroves.

SEAFOOD BY THE SEA SHORE

What the South Coast lacks in beach facilities, it makes up for with some of the best seafood. The Caribbean warm waters bring everything from mahi mahi and red snapper to arrayao and conch. Open air, waterfront restaurants—many of which are mesone gastronómicos—sit in clusters in places such as Salinas, the Playa de Ponce area, and La Parguera.

PONCE

Caja de Muertos *(Coffin Island)*. This island a few miles off the coast has the best beaches in the Ponce area and is, perhaps, the second-best spot in southern Puerto Rico for snorkeling, after La Parguera. Ask one of the many boatmen at La Guancha to take you out for about $30 round-trip. ✉ *Boats leave from La Guancha, at the end of Rte. 14, Ponce.*

La Guancha. Ponce's public beach isn't anything to write home about, but the shallow water makes it nice for children. There's some shade under thatched umbrellas, but bring sunscreen. ✉ *At the end of Rte. 14, Ponce.*

GUÁNICA

Balneario Caña Gorda. The gentle water at this beach on Route 333 washes onto a wide swath of sand fringed with palm trees. There are picnic tables, restrooms, showers, and changing facilities. ✉ *Rte. 333, west of Copamarina Beach Resort.*

Playa Jaboncillo. Rugged cliffs make a dramatic backdrop for this little cove off Route 333, but the water can be rough. The road down to the beach is extremely rocky, so think twice if you don't have a four-wheel-drive vehicle. ✉ *Rte. 333, west of Copamarina Beach Resort.*

Playa Santa. You can rent canoes, kayaks, and pedal boats at this beach at the end of Route 325 in the Ensenada district. ✉ *Rte. 325, west of Guánica.*

LA PARGUERA

Cayo Caracoles. You can take a boat to and from this island for $5 per person. There are mangroves to explore as well as plenty of places to swim and snorkel. ✉ *Boats leave from marina at La Parguera, off Rte. 304.*

Isla Mata de la Gata. For about $5 per person, boats will transport you to and from this small island just off the coast for a day of swimming and snorkeling. ✉ *Boats leave from marina at La Parguera, off Rte. 304.*

Playita Rosada. The small beach doesn't compare to some of the longer beaches on the southwestern coast, but it's a convenient place for a quick swim. ✉ *At the end of Calle 7.*

5

MASKS OF PUERTO RICO

Red, white, and boo! During festivals vejigante masks frighten and delight spectators along parade routes.

A week before Ash Wednesday, *vejigantes* (pronounced veh-hee-GAN-tays), wearing long, colorful robes and brightly painted horned masks, turn the normally placid city of Ponce into a hotbed of rowdiness. The masked mischief makers prowl city streets, scaring and fascinating anyone in their path.

Puerto Rico's masks are one of the premier expressions of folk art on the island, a tradition that dates back to Spain in the early 17th century. During the Fiestas de Santiago Apóstol (Saint James Festivals), brightly dressed *vejigantes* represented the Devil in a holy battle between good and evil. Their costumes consisted of long robes and grotesque masks and they would wave cow bladders, or *vejigas,* on long sticks at anyone they passed. Parading as devils, their intention was to frighten sinners to compel them to return to church for Lent. Today balloons and plastic bottles have replaced the cow bladders and the now more playful masks have become one of Puerto Rico's most distinguished forms of artistic expression.

ISLAND ART

The best hand-designed masks in Puerto Rico come from three parts of the island: Ponce, Loíza, and Hatillo. Mask making's a family tradition in these towns, and styles are passed down among generations. For a fine souvenir and a memorable experience, head to one of the local artisans' workshops. Small masks cost $20 or $30; larger ones by well-known makers cost more than $1,000.

PONCE

Ponce *vejigantes* masks are made of papier-mâché and are most prominent during the February Carnaval. Many have African and Native American elements; it's even possible to detect influences from ancient Greece and Rome. All masks have at least two horns, but most have several protruding from the forehead, chin, and nose. Some antique masks have more than 100 horns. At the beginning of the 20th century, masks were usually painted red with yellow dots or vice versa, but today they come in every imaginable color and pattern.

Where to Go: One of the best-known mask-making families is the Caraballo family from Playa de Ponce near the El Ancla restaurant (see review in Where to Eat). To purchase a mask, show up at the door to their home, and if someone is there, you'll be allowed to browse their workshop. You're most likely to have success in February leading up to Ponce's Carnaval. ✉ *24 San Tomas, Playa de Ponce* ☎ *No phone.*

LOÍZA

Loíza Aldea, a palm-fringed town east of San Juan founded by freed and escaped African slaves, is known as the island's Capital of Traditions for its bomba music, traditional Taíno and African cuisine, and distinct culture. Loíza's masks are created from coconut husks and the individual shape of each

determines the face and placement of the nose and lips. The teeth are made of bamboo and the tongue is made out of coconut shell.

Where to Go: For generations, the Ayala family, whose workshop sits just east of town, have been the most renowned mask makers in Loíza. Their masks appear during the Saint James Festival of Loíza Aldea each July. ✉ *Artesanias y Folclorica de la Familia Ayala, Barrio Medianía Alta, Carr. 187 Km 6 Hm 6* ☎ *787/886–1655.*

HATILLO

Hatillo was founded in 1823 by settlers from the Canary Islands. These *Islenos,* in honor of King Herod's soldiers, the first Christian martyrs or Holy Innocents, would dress head to toe in costumes with a cape, hat, and mask made of fine metallic screening that is meant to resemble the face of a Spaniard. A parade ensues and the masked performers run through surrounding neighborhoods, joined by children while singing and dancing, eventually ending in the town center. The annual masks festival, Día de las Mascaras, is held every December 28.

Where to Go: ✉ *Puerto Rico Flea Market, Carr. 2, Km 86 Bo. Carrizales* ☎ *787/880–2394.*

Updated by Nicholas Gill

Not as popular as San Juan or Vieques, the South is a region full of underrated attractions, fine food, and a laid-back authentic vibe that is hard to come by elsewhere. From lush tropical mountains to arid seacoast plains, Puerto Rico's southern region lets you sample the island from a local's perspective.

Though rich in history, the area also provides ample opportunities for golf, swimming, hiking, and cave exploration. Snaking roads between major highways reveal a glimpse of how rural Puerto Ricans enjoy life. Every mile or so, you'll see a café or bar, which is the local social center. The only traffic jams you'll likely encounter will be caused by slow-moving farmers taking their goods to the local market.

At the center of everything is Ponce, the "Pearl of the South." Farmers attracted to the rich soil in the area, which was perfect for growing sugarcane, founded Ponce in 1692. Evidence found at the Tibes Indian ceremonial site, just north of the city, suggests that people have been living here since 400 BC. Many residents still carry the last names of the dozens of European pioneer families who settled here during the 19th century. The region's largest city, Ponce is home to some of the island's most interesting architecture, excellent restaurants, and one of its most important art museums. Nearby San Germán, the second-oldest city in Puerto Rico, is known for its two historic main squares, well preserved in a wide variety of architectural styles.

On the coast, Guayama and Patillas show off their splendors as little-known destinations for beachgoers. But the real beach party is at La Parguera, which attracts a young but noisy crowd. If you're willing to explore beyond the casinos, high-rises, and daily traffic congestion of the island's capital, the south is a wise escape from Puerto Rico's usual tourist fare. Don't be surprised by the help many of its residents will offer whether you ask for it or not. Southern *puertorriqueños* are known for their friendliness as well as their hospitality.

IF YOU LIKE

DIVING AND SNORKELING

Southern Puerto Rico is an undiscovered dive destination, which means unspoiled reefs and lots of fish. You can arrange for dive boats at Caribe Playa Beach Resort in the southeast, Ponce's La Guancha, and in La Parguera and the Copamarina Beach Resort in the southwest. Shore diving and snorkeling are best around islands or cays or along the southwestern coast.

HIKING

Vegetation in the region is dramatically different from that of the rest of the island. Near Guánica is the 9,900-acre Bosque Estatal de Guánica, a rare dry tropical forest. With more than 100 species of birds, it's known for its excellent bird-watching. There are good trails throughout the area, but printed guides and trail maps are hard to come by. Ask locals for directions to their favorite paths.

PONCE

21 mi (34 km) southwest of Coamo.

"Ponce is Ponce and the rest is parking space" is the adage used by the residents of Puerto Rico's third-largest city (population 194,000) to express their pride in being a *ponceño*. The rivalry with the island's capital began in the 19th century, when European immigrants from England, France, and Spain settled here. Because the city's limits extend from the Caribbean to the foothills of the Cordillera Central, it's a lot hotter in climate than San Juan. Another contrast is the neoclassical architecture of the elegant homes and public buildings that surround the main square.

Many of the 19th-century buildings in Ponce Centro, the downtown area, have been renovated, and the Museo de Arte de Ponce—endowed by its late native son and former governor Luis A. Ferré—is considered one of the Caribbean's finest art museums. Just as famous is Ponce's pre-Lenten carnival. The colorful costumes and *vejigante* (mischief maker) masks worn during the festivities are famous throughout the world *(see special feature in this chapter)*. The best dining in Ponce is just west of town. Seafood restaurants line the highway in an area known as Las Cucharas, named for the spoon-shape bay you'll overlook as you dine.

GETTING HERE AND AROUND

The fastest route through the region is the Luis A. Ferré Expressway (Route 52), a toll road that runs from San Juan to Ponce, crossing the island's central mountain range. The trip from Condado or Old San Juan takes about 1½ hours. Route 2, also a toll road, connects to San German, Mayagüez, and the western part of the island.

Ponce offers a light tour to its major attractions on its *"chu chu"* train and trolleys for $2. They run daily from 9:00 AM to about 5:00 PM and leave from Plaza de las Delicias. On Sunday, Guayama has a free trolley that runs to many sights. A trolley tour of San Germán is available by appointment. On weekends there are free horse-and-carriage rides around the plaza, or you could just walk. All the downtown sites are within a few blocks of the main square.

Car rental is typical for most visitors to Ponce and makes exploring the surrounding region considerably easier. Most hotels have parking lots, while metered parking is easy to come by in the center.

Car Rental **Avis** (✉ *Mercedita Airport, Ponce* ☎ *787/842–6154*). **Budget** (✉ *Mercedita Airport, Ponce* ☎ *787/848–0907*). **Dollar** (✉ *Av. Los Caobos and Calle Acacia, Ponce* ☎ *787/843–6940*). **Leaseway of Puerto Rico** (✉ *Rte. 3, Km 140.1, Guayama* ☎ *787/864–8149* 🌐 *www.leasewaypr.com* ✉ *Ponce* ☎ *787/843–4330*).

Taxi and Trolley **Borinquen Taxi** (☎ *787/843–6000 in Ponce*). **Ponce Trolley & Chu Chu** (✉ *Plaza de las Delicias, Ponce Centro, Ponce* ☎ *787/841–8160*).

EXPLORING PONCE

Plaza de las Delicias (Plaza of Delights), with its trees, benches, and famous lion fountain, is a perfect people-watching square in which to spend an hour or two on a Sunday afternoon. The old red-and-black firehouse is right on the plaza and has a fire-fighting museum on its second floor. Ponce is known for its museums and has several dedicated to music, art, history, sports, and architecture. Ponceños are proud of their city, nicknamed the Pearl of the South, and offer all visitors a warm welcome.

PONCE CENTRO

At the heart of Ponce Centro is the Plaza de las Delicias, with trees, benches, and the famous lion fountain. Several interesting buildings are on this square or the adjacent streets, making the area perfect for a leisurely morning or afternoon stroll.

Numbers in the margin correspond to the Ponce map.

TOP ATTRACTIONS

7 **Casa Wiechers-Villaronga.** In a city filled with neoclassical confections, this is one of the most elaborate. Alfredo B. Wiechers, who returned to his native Ponce after studying architecture in Paris, designed the house. Though small in scale, it makes a big impression with details like huge arched windows and a massive rooftop gazebo. No wonder that soon after it was completed in 1911 the Villaronga-Mercado family decided to make it their own. Check out the stained-glass windows and other fanciful touches. Inside you'll find original furnishings and exhibits on Wiechers and other Ponce architects of his era. ✉ *Calle Reina and Calle Méndez Vigo, Ponce Centro* ☎ *787/843–3363* 🎟 *Free* ⏲ *Wed.–Sun. 8:30–4:30.*

3 **Parque de Bombas.** After El Morro in Old San Juan, this distinctive red-and-black-striped building may be the second most photographed Fodor's Choice ★ structure in Puerto Rico. Built in 1882 as a pavilion for an agricultural and industrial fair, it was converted the following year into a firehouse. Today it's a museum tracing the history—and glorious feats—of Ponce's fire brigade. Kids love the antique fire truck on the lower level.

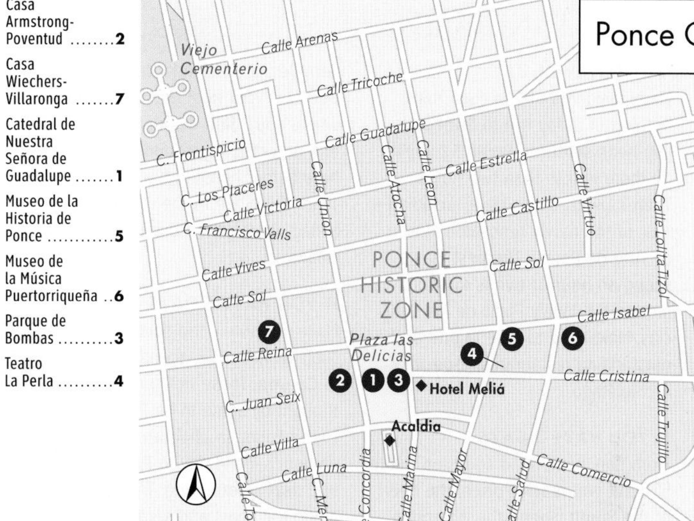

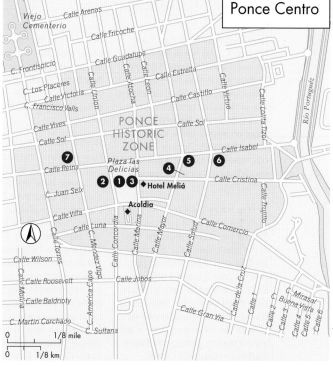

Short tours in English and Spanish are given on the half hour, and you can sign up for trolley tours here. The island's most helpful tourism officials staff a small information desk inside the door. Go ahead—ask them anything. ✉ *Plaza de las Delicias, Ponce Centro* ☎ *787/284–3338* 🎟 *Free* 🕓 *Wed.–Mon. 9–5:30.*

WORTH NOTING

2 **Casa Armstrong-Poventud.** Banker and industrialist Carlos Armstrong and his wife, Eulalia Pou, lived in this neoclassical house designed and built for them in 1901 by Manuel V. Domenech. As this book went to press, the building was in the beginning stages of a top-to-bottom renovation. If it isn't finished when you visit, you can still admire the ornate facade, which is chock-full of columns, statues, and intricate moldings. ✉ *Calle Unión, across from Catedral de Nuestra Señora de Guadalupe, Ponce Centro.*

1 **Catedral de Nuestra Señora de Guadalupe.** This pale blue cathedral has always been one of the city's jewels, but it regained much of its luster after a complete renovation in 2007. Dedicated to the Virgin of Guadalupe, it is built on the site of a 1670 chapel destroyed by earthquakes. Part of the current structure, where mass is still held, dates from 1835. After another earthquake in 1918, new steeples and a roof were put on and neoclassical embellishments were added to the facade. Inside

GREAT ITINERARIES

IF YOU HAVE 1 DAY

Many residents of San Juan think nothing of a day trip to **Ponce**. If you head south on Route 52 you'll be there in less than two hours. There's plenty to do here, including a tour of the newly renovated Museo de Arte de Ponce. The best way to spend an hour or two is to stroll around the lovely Plaza de las Delicias. Make sure to dine in one of the outstanding restaurants, especially Archipiélago.

IF YOU HAVE 3 DAYS

From San Juan, head south on Route 52 until you reach **Ponce**, the Pearl of the South. Spend the afternoon strolling around the Plaza de las Delicias, poking into the beautiful Catedral de Nuestra Señora de Guadalupe and the striking Parque de Bombas. On the following day, visit some of the other attractions in and around the city, perhaps the Museo de Arte de Ponce, the Castillo Serrallés, or Hacienda Buena Vista. Dedicate your final day to **Guánica**, where you'll find wonderful beaches and deserted cays; spend the night here before heading back to San Juan. If you are in the mood for hiking, there's the Bosque Estatal de Guánica.

IF YOU HAVE 5 DAYS

Make a leisurely trip south from San Juan on Route 52, spending a night in **Coamo**. These hot springs were thought by some to be Ponce de León's Fountain of Youth. Continue on your second day to **Ponce** for two days of exploring. Travel west along the coast and settle at a waterfront hotel in **Guánica**. In the evening you can take a boat trip to the bioluminescent bay at **La Parguera**. On your last day explore the beautifully preserved colonial city of **San Germán**, making sure to see the lovely colonial-era chapel known as the Capilla de Porta Coeli.

you'll see stained-glass windows and two alabaster altars. ✉ *Plaza de las Delicias, Ponce Centro* ☎ *787/842–0134* ⏲ *Services daily 6* AM *and 11* AM.

❺ **Museo de la Historia de Ponce.** Housed in two adjoining neoclassical mansions, this museum includes 10 exhibition halls covering the city's residents, from the Taíno Indians to the Spanish settlers to the mix of the present. Hour-long guided tours in English and Spanish give an overview of the city's history. The descriptions are mostly in Spanish, but displays of clothing from different eras still are interesting to see. ✉ *51–53 Calle Isabel, Ponce Centro* ☎ *787/844–7042* 🎟 *Free* ⏲ *Tues.–Sat. 9–5.*

❻ **Museo de la Música Puertorriqueña.** At this museum you'll learn how Puerto Rican music has been influenced by African, Spanish, and Native American cultures. On display are dozens of instruments, such as the *triple* (a small string instrument resembling a banjo), as well as memorabilia of local composers and musicians. The small museum takes up several rooms in a neoclassical former residence, which alone is worth the trip. ✉ *Calle Isabel and Calle Salud, Ponce Centro* ☎ *787/848–7016* 🎟 *Free* ⏲ *Wed.–Sun. 8:30–4:30.*

Today it's a museum, but for more than 100 years Parque de Bombas served as Ponce's main firehouse.

NEED A BREAK?

An institution for more than 40 years, King's Cream Helados (✉ *9223 Calle Marina* ☎ *787/843-8520*), across from Plaza de las Delicias, is *the* place for ice cream in Ponce. It serves 12 varieties, from tamarind and passion fruit to classics chocolate and vanilla. A bench in the tiny storefront seats three, but most folks take their cups and cones across the street and stake out shady benches around the fountain. King's is open daily from 8 AM to midnight.

4 **Teatro La Perla.** This theater was restored in 1941 after an earthquake and fire damaged the original 1864 structure. The striking interior contains seats for 1,047 and has excellent acoustics. It's generally open for a quick peek on weekdays. ✉ *Calle Mayor and Calle Cristina, Ponce Centro* ☎ *787/843-4322* *Free* *Weekdays 8–4:30.*

GREATER PONCE

The greater Ponce area has some of Puerto Rico's most notable cultural attractions, including one of the island's finest art museums and its most important archaeological site.

Numbers in the margin correspond to Greater Ponce map.

TOP ATTRACTIONS

4 **Castillo Serrallés.** This lovely Spanish-style villa—such a massive house that people in the town below referred to it as a castle—was built in the 1930s for Ponce's wealthiest family, the makers of Don Q rum. Guided tours give you a glimpse into the lifestyle of a sugar baron. The dining room is a highlight, with its original hand-carved furnishings.

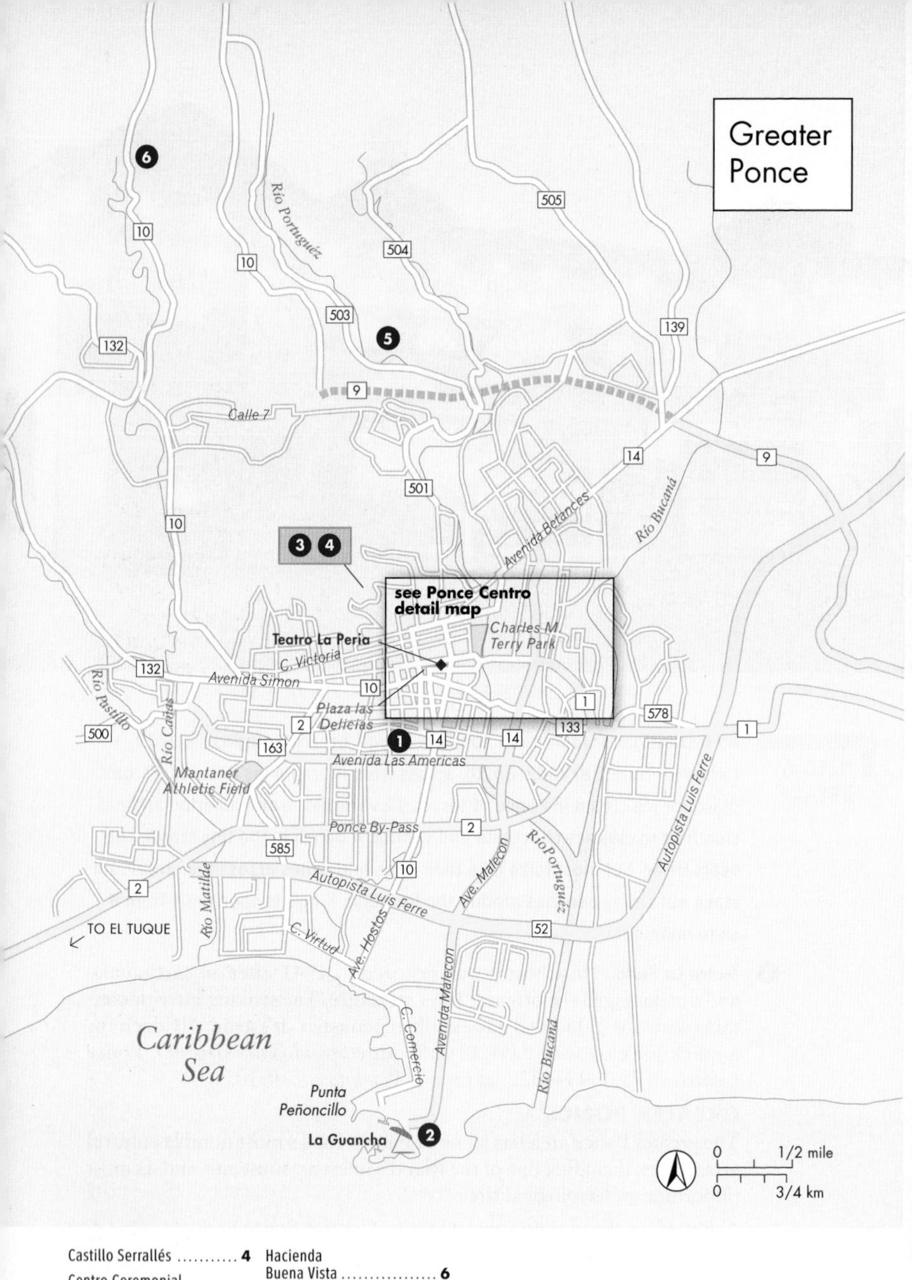

Castillo Serrallés 4

Centro Ceremonial Indígena de Tibes 5

Cruceta El Vigía 3

La Guancha 2

Hacienda Buena Vista 6

Museo de Art de Ponce 1

A GOOD WALK

Start on the tree-lined Plaza de las Delicias. (You'll find parking nearby on Calle Marina, Calle Isabel, and Calle Reina.) Dominating it is the **Catedral Nuestra Señora de Guadalupe,** dating from 1835. Across the street is the **Casa Armstrong-Poventud,** home of the Institute of Culture's Ponce branch. Leaving Armstrong-Poventud, cross back to the plaza, circle south by the Alcaldía, and continue to the plaza's east side to visit the red-and-black-striped fire station, **Parque de Bombas.**

From the intersection of Calles Marina and Cristina, take Calle Cristina a block east to one of the city's first restoration projects, **Teatro La Perla,** at the corner of Cristina and Mayor. One block north of the theater, at Calles Mayor and Isabel, is a former home that's now the **Museo de la Historia de Ponce.** A block east, at the corner of Calles Salud and Isabel, is the **Museo de la Música Puertorriqueña.** Four blocks west (you will go by Plaza de las Delicias again, and Calle Isabel will turn into Calle Reina) is the 1911 architectural masterpiece **Casa Wiechers-Villaronga.** For more early-20th-century architecture, continue west on Calle Reina, where you'll see examples of *casas criollas,* wooden homes with the spacious front balconies that were popular in the Caribbean during the early 1900s.

TIMING

Although it's possible to see Ponce Centro in one morning or afternoon, it's best to devote a full day and evening to it. Explore the streets and museums during daylight, and then head for the plaza at night, when the lion fountain and street lamps are lighted and townspeople stroll the plaza. ■ TIP→ **Several of the city's most popular museums—Casa Wiechers-Villaronga and the Museo de la Música Puertorriqueña—are not air-conditioned, so they close early when the weather is hot. If you want to see these sites, make sure to arrive before 11 am.**

A permanent exhibit explains the area's sugarcane and rum industries. The extensive garden, with sculptured bushes and a shimmering reflection pool, is considered the best kept on the island. ✉ *17 El Vigía, El Vigía* ☎ *787/259–1774* 🌐 *home.coqui.net/castserr* 🎫 *$6, $9 includes admission to Cruceta El Vigía* 🕒 *Tues.–Thurs. 9:30–5, Fri.–Sun. 9:30–5:30.*

6 **Hacienda Buena Vista.** Built by Salvador de Vives in 1838, Buena Vista was one of the area's largest coffee plantations. It's a technological marvel—water from the nearby Río Canas was funneled into narrow brick channels that could be diverted to perform any number of tasks, including turning the waterwheel. (Seeing the two-story wheel slowly begin to turn is fascinating, especially for kids.) Nearby is the two-story manor house, filled with furniture that gives a sense of what it was like to live on a coffee plantation nearly 150 years ago. Make sure to take a look in the kitchen, dominated by a massive hearth. In 1987 the plantation was restored by the Puerto Rican Conservation Trust, which leads four tours a day (one in English). The tours are by reservation only, so make sure to call several days ahead. After seeing the plantation, you

Fodor's Choice ★

can buy coffee beans and other souvenirs at the gift shop. Allow yourself an hour to travel the winding road from Ponce. ✉ *Rte. 123, Km 16.8, Sector Corral Viejo* ☎ *787/722–5882 weekdays, 787/284–7020 weekends* 🎟 *$7.50* ⏲ *Wed.–Sun., by reservation only.*

❷ **La Guancha.** Encircling the cove of a working harbor, the seaside boardwalk features kiosks where vendors sell local food and drink and a small lookout tower. The adjacent park has a large children's area filled with playground equipment and, on weekends, live music. The nearby public beach has restrooms, changing areas, a medical post, and plenty of free parking. ✉ *End of Rte. 14, La Guancha* ☎ *787/844–3995.*

❶ Fodor's Choice ★ **Museo de Arte de Ponce.** This building—designed by Edward Durrell Stone, who also designed the original Museum of Modern Art in New York City and the Kennedy Center in Washington, D.C.—is easily identified by the hexagonal galleries on the second story and underwent a major renovation before reopening in 2010. It has one of the best art collections in Latin America, which is why residents of San Juan frequently make the trip down to Ponce. The 3,000-piece collection includes works by famous Puerto Rican artists such as Francisco Oller, represented by a lovely landscape called *Hacienda Aurora*. There are plenty of European works on display as well, including paintings by Peter Paul Rubens and Thomas Gainsborough. The highlight of the European collection is the Pre-Raphaelite paintings, particularly the mesmerizing *Flaming June*, by Frederick Leighton, which has become the museum's unofficial symbol. Watch for special exhibits, such as a recent one examining the work of Rodin. ✉ *2325 Av. Las Américas, Sector Santa María* ☎ *787/848–0505* 🌐 *www.museoarteponce.org* 🎟 *$5* ⏲ *Daily 10–5.*

WORTH NOTING

❺ **Centro Ceremonial Indígena de Tibes.** This archeological site, discovered after flooding from a tropical storm in 1975, is the most important on the island. The ancient ceremonial center dates from AD 300 to 700 and includes nine playing fields used for a ritual ball game that some think was similar to soccer. The fields are bordered by smooth stones, some of which are engraved with petroglyphs that researchers say might have ceremonial or astronomical significance. The most eye-catching part of the site is the *Plaza de Estrella*, or Plaza of the Star, where the stones are arranged in a pattern that resembles a rising sun. Experts say it might have been used to chart the seasons. A village with several thatched huts has been reconstructed in an original setting. Be sure to visit the small museum before taking a walking tour of the site. ✉ *Tibes Indian Ceremonial Center, Rte. 503, Km 2.8, Barrio Tibes* ☎ *787/840–2255 or 787/840–5685* 🌐 *ponce.inter.edu/tibes/tibes.html* 🎟 *$3* ⏲ *Tues.–Sun. 9–noon and 1–4.*

❸ **Cruceta El Vigía.** At the top of Cerro Vigía—a hill where the Spanish once watched for ships, including those of marauding pirates—is this colossal concrete cross. You can climb the stairs or take an elevator to the top of the 100-foot cross for a panoramic view across the city. Purchase tickets at nearby Castillo Serrallés. ✉ *Across from Castillo Serrallés, El Vigía* ☎ *787/259–3816* 🌐 *home.coqui.net/castserr* 🎟 *$4, $9 includes admission to Castillo Serrallés* ⏲ *Tues.–Sun. 9–5:30.*

A GOOD TOUR

The **Museo de Arte de Ponce** is on Avenida Las Américas, south of Plaza de las Delicias and not far from the Luis A. Ferré Expressway (Route 52). Anyone with a taste for art can happily while away many hours in its galleries. East of the museum you can pick up Route 14 south to the Caribbean and **La Guancha,** a boardwalk with food kiosks, a playground, and a child-friendly public beach. It's a good place to relax and let the younger generation work off energy. From here, if you retrace your path north past downtown you'll be heading to Calle Bertoly and El Vigía (Vigía Hill), where the **Cruceta El Vigía** towers over the city and the **Castillo Serrallés,** a former sugar baron's villa, is a popular attraction.

Farther north on Route 503 is the **Centro Ceremonial Indígena de Tibes,** which displays native artifacts dating back more than 1,500 years. You'll have to backtrack to reach Route 10, then head north to **Hacienda Buena Vista,** a former coffee plantation that's been restored by the Puerto Rican Conservation Trust. (Call ahead to arrange a tour.)

You can drive to all these sights or hop on the free trolleys or "*chu chu*" trains that run from Plaza de las Delicias to the museum, La Guancha, and El Vigía. You'll need a car or a cab to reach the Centro Ceremonial Indígena de Tibes or Hacienda Buena Vista.

TIMING
To visit all the sights mentioned above, you'll need at least two days. If you don't want to devote that much time, visit only the sights that appeal most to you.

5

WHERE TO EAT

$$–$$$ Fodor's Choice ★ LATIN FUSION

Archipiélago. This ambitious restaurant, with perhaps the greatest view in all of Puerto Rico, has stepped in to fill the vacuum left by the closing of Mark's at the Melia. It sits on the sixth and seventh floors of a building that overlooks the Parque de Bombas and Catedral de Nuestra Señora de Guadalupe. New England Culinary Institute–educated chef Alejandro Vélez Blasini's beautifully designed restaurant and lounge have quickly become one of the hottest spots in Puerto Rico. Expect a chic crowd that's dressed to impress dining on Puerto Rican fusion dishes as diverse as pancetta *mofongo* (mashed plantains) stuffed with chicken and Parmesan cream or corn-crusted mahimahi in beurre blanc sauce. A terrace patio has live jazz on the weekends, which pairs well with their renowned mojitos. ✉ *76 Calle Cristina, Ponce Centro* ☎ *787/812–8822* 🌐 *www.archipielagopr.com* 💳 *AE, MC, V.*

$$–$$$ ★ ECLECTIC

Cabuqui. On sweltering hot days, it takes a lot to make *ponceños* leave their homes. Yet they come out in droves to the tree-shaded courtyard of the Cubuqui in the Ponce center. When a breeze shakes the flower-covered branches, things cool down considerably. And if nature doesn't cooperate, there are always the three air-conditioned dining rooms. The menu is extremely well traveled, stopping in Argentina (*churrasco*, or skirt steak, served with homemade chimichurri) and France (veal fillet in a red wine sauce) before heading back to Puerto Rico for such dishes as *masitas de cerdo* (chunks of perfectly seasoned pork). The wine list,

The reflection pool is just one highlight of a guided tour through the gardens and villa of Castillo Serrallés.

which includes many bottles from Spain and Chile, is quite reasonable. There's always live music, whether it's a small band playing jazz or a single accordionist losing himself in a tango. ✉ *32 Calle Isabel, Ponce Centro* ☎ *787/984–5696* ▭ *AE, MC, V.*

$$–$$$ Fodor's Choice ★ MEDITERRANEAN

✕ **Canela Café.** It's a bit out of the town center, but Ponce's newest *Mesón Gastronómico* (a national designation reserved for the highest level of traditional Puerto Rican cuisine) is worth the effort to reach. The intimate second-level restaurant above an X-ray center is one of the South's most creative and reliable. Chef Agnes Toledo-Rivera's menu changes seasonally, focusing on local, organic produce, meats, and seafoods when possible, though global influences are apparent in dishes such as Moroccan-style rib-eye as well as roasted chicken breast with yuca-cilantro mofongo and applewood-smoked bacon. There's a tapas menu for those who opt to sit at the bar and sample the extensive wine list. At this writing there was talk of relocating the restaurant closer to the beach, so give them a call before heading out. ✉ *509 Av. Tito Castro, northeast Ponce, Ponce* ☎ *787/284–6275* ⊕ *www.canela-cafe.com* ▭ *AE, MC, V.*

$–$$$ SEAFOOD

✕ **El Ancla.** Families favor this laid-back restaurant, whose dining room sits at the edge of the sea. The kitchen serves generous and affordable plates of fish, crab, and other fresh seafood with *tostones* (fried plantains), french fries, and garlic bread. Try the shrimp in garlic sauce, salmon fillet with capers, or the delectable mofongo stuffed with seafood. Finish your meal with one of the fantastic flans. The piña coladas—with or without rum—are exceptional. ✉ *9 Av. Hostos Final, Ponce Playa* ☎ *787/840–2450* ▭ *AE, MC, V.*

$$–$$$ SEAFOOD ✕ **Pito's Seafood.** Choose from the waterfront terrace or one of the enclosed dining rooms at this longtime favorite east of Ponce in Las Cucharas. No matter where you sit, you'll have a view of the ocean. The main attraction is the freshly caught seafood, ranging from lobster and crab to salmon and red snapper. To indulge yourself, try the shrimp wrapped in bacon—a specialty of the house. There's also a wide range of chicken and beef dishes. From the expansive wine cellar you can select more than 25 different wines by the glass. There's live music on Friday and Saturday nights. ✉ *Rte. 2, Sector Las Cucharas* ☎ *787/841–4977* ▭ *AE, MC, V.*

$$–$$$ STEAK ✕ **Rincón Argentina.** Housed in a beautifully restored criollo-style house, Rincón Argentina is one of the city's most popular restaurants. Completely unpretentious, this is the kind of steak house you find all over South America. The specialty of the house is *parrilladas,* meaning just about anything that comes off the grill. Don't pass up the skirt steak, served here with lip-smacking chimichurri. On cool evenings, take a table on the terrace. Otherwise, wander through the maze of dining rooms until you find a table you like. ✉ *69 Calle Salud, at Calle Isabel, Ponce Centro, Ponce* ☎ *787/840–3768* ✍ *Reservations essential* ▭ *AE, MC, V.*

5

WHERE TO STAY

¢ HOTEL **Casa del Sol.** This restored colonial home in the heart of Ponce—one block from Plaza Delicias—retains much of the historic architecture and character of the original building. Azulejo tiles adorn many of the walls, and hand-carved woodwork and black iron chandeliers give common areas an elegant antique feel. The rooms, on the other hand, are hit or miss, with some beds being cozier than others, though all amenities are in working order and relatively new. For affordable accommodations, this is a decent option. **Pros:** Nice common areas; Continental breakfast. **Cons:** Rooms lack decor; some employees are unhelpful. ✉ *97 Calle Unión, Ponce Centro* ☎ *787/812–2995* 🌐 *www.casadelsolpr.com* *9 rooms* *In-room: Wi-Fi. In-hotel: laundry service, public, parking (no fee), bar, hot tub, yoga classes* ▭ *MC, V* *EP.*

$–$$$ RESORT **Hilton Ponce Golf & Casino Resort.** The south coast's biggest resort sits on a black-sand beach about 4 mi (6 km) south of Ponce. Everything on this 80-acre property is massive, beginning with the open-air lobby. Constructed of reinforced concrete, like the rest of the hotel, it requires huge signs to point you in the right direction. All its bright, spacious rooms are decorated in a lush, tropical motif and have balconies overlooking the sea. A large pool is surrounded by palm trees and has a spectacular view of the Caribbean. Golf lovers will appreciate the 27-hole course at the adjacent Costa Caribe Resort, which has a clubhouse with its own restaurant and lounge. **Pros:** Good golf; large casino. **Cons:** Not on beach; isolated location; bland rooms. ✉ *1150 Av. Caribe, La Guancha* *Box 7419, Ponce 00732* ☎ *787/259–7676 or 800/445–8667* 🌐 *www.hiltoncaribbean.com* *255 rooms* *In-room: safe, refrigerator, Wi-Fi. In-hotel: 4 restaurants, room service, bars, golf courses, tennis courts, pool, gym, spa, beachfront, bicycles, children's programs (ages 8–12), parking (fee)* ▭ *AE, D, DC, MC, V* *EP.*

¢ HOTEL **Hotel Bélgica.** Near the central square, this hotel is both comfortable and economical. A stairway off the large 1940s-era lobby leads to rather worn yet clean rooms with wrought-iron headboards and other furnishings. Those on the front of the building have balconies with wooden-shutter-style doors. The rooms vary widely in size (Room 3 is one of the largest), and some windows open onto an air shaft, so ask to see a few before you decide. The hotel has no restaurant, but there are plenty of options in the neighborhood. **Pros:** A taste of old Ponce; friendly staff. **Cons:** Front-facing rooms are noisy; very basic rooms; lots of steps to upstairs rooms and no elevator. ✉ *122 Calle Villa, Ponce Centro* ☎ *787/844–3255* 🌐 *www.hotelbelgica.com* *20 rooms* *In-room: Wi-Fi. In-hotel: some pets allowed* 💳 *MC, V* 🍽 *EP.*

$ HOTEL **Hotel Meliá.** In the heart of the city, this family-owned hotel has long been a local landmark. Its neoclassical facade, with flags from a dozen countries waving in the breeze, will remind you of small lodgings in Spain. The lobby, with wood-beamed ceilings and blue-and-beige tile floors, is well worn but very charming. The best rooms have French doors leading out to small balconies; the six suites have terrific views of the main square. Breakfast is served on the rooftop terrace, which overlooks the mountains. A waterfall drops into the beautiful tiled swimming pool. **Pros:** Great location on the main square; walking distance to downtown sites; good dining options near hotel. **Cons:** Rooms are somewhat outdated; front rooms are a bit noisy. ✉ *75 Calle Cristina, Ponce Centro* *Box 1431, Ponce 00733* ☎ *787/842–0260 or 800/448–8355* 🌐 *www.hotelmeliapr.com* *72 rooms, 6 suites* *In-room: Wi-Fi. In-hotel: bar, pool, public Internet, parking (fee)* 💳 *AE, MC, V* 🍽 *CP.*

$ HOTEL **Howard Johnson.** Near the airport, this hotel is a good choice if you have an early morning flight. The rooms are pretty much what you'd expect from a chain hotel, but all have balconies overlooking a palm-shaded pool. There's not much in the way of amenities, but the smiling staff provides little extras like in-room coffeemakers with an unlimited supply of freshly ground beans. ✉ *103 Turpó Industrial Park, Airport* ☎ *787/841–1000* 🌐 *www.hojo.com* *120 rooms* *In-room: refrigerator (some), Wi-Fi. In-hotel: restaurant, room service, bar, pools, gym* 💳 *AE, D, DC, MC, V* 🍽 *EP.*

$ HOTEL **Ramada Inn Ponce.** Opened in mid-2009 in a stunningly restored building that dates to 1882, the Ramada is right on the plaza. It is adjoined by a more modern building as well. The six historic rooms are dazzling and by far the most atmospheric in Ponce. Black and white tiles, hand-carved furniture, and wooden balconies are among many stylish amenities. The other 66 rooms in the more modern part of the hotel, apart from the 12 spacious junior suites, are a bit bland with sterile tile floors. The trendy Lola serves Latin fusion cuisine and cocktails and connects with the small pool area. On weekends there's live music on the patio. **Pros:** Excellent location; lively bar and restaurant. **Cons:** Regular rooms lack charm. ✉ *Calles Reina and Unión, Ponce Centro* ☎ *787/813–5050* 🌐 *www.ramadaponce.com* *70 rooms* *In-room: coffee machine, ironing board, safe, refrigerator, Wi-Fi. In-hotel: restaurant, room service, bar, gym, pool, laundry service, business center, Wi-Fi, parking (fee)* 💳 *AE, D, DC, MC, V* 🍽 *EP.*

DID YOU KNOW?

The vejigante character dates back to medieval Spain and is mentioned in Cervantes' *Don Quixote,* written in 1605. Traditional colors for the vejigante mask are black, red, and yellow, but today it comes in every color imaginable.

NIGHTLIFE AND THE ARTS

NIGHTLIFE

BARS AND CLUBS

AKUA (✉ *Blvd. Miguel Pou, Plaza Nuevo Mundo, NortheastPonce* ☎ *787/601–3425*) is an über-trendy restaurant, wine bar, and lounge that makes you want to order a fancy cocktail. It's open late from Thursday through Saturday, when they feature live music and DJs.Sitting high above the plaza, **Archipiélago** (✉ *76 Calle Cristina, Ponce Centro 787/812–8822* 🌐 *www.archipielagopr.com* 💳 *AE, MC, V.*) has an outdoor terrace and upstairs lounge that lure Ponce's glitterati with hip cocktails, live music, and a dramatic view of the plaza lights below.On the main square, **Café Palermo** (✉ *Calle Unión at Calle Villa, Ponce Centro* ☎ *787/448–8112*) is a hole-in-the-wall. Still, locals crowd around the bar every night of the week.

CASINOS

The casinos in Ponce can't hold a candle to their counterparts in San Juan. **Hilton Ponce Golf & Casino Resort** (✉ *1150 Av. Caribe, Take Rte. 12 to Av. Caribe La Guancha* ☎ *787/259–7676*) has a rather cramped casino that stays open nightly until 4 AM. **Holiday Inn Ponce** (✉ *3315 Ponce Bypass, El Tuque* ☎ *787/844–1200*) has a small casino just off the lobby. It is open nightly until 4 AM.

THE ARTS

The **Museo de Arte de Ponce** (✉ *2325 Av. Las Américas, Sector Santa María* ☎ *787/848–0505*) occasionally sponsors chamber-music concerts and recitals by members of the Puerto Rico Symphony Orchestra. Check for Spanish-language theater productions and concerts at the **Teatro La Perla** (✉ *Calle Mayor and Calle Cristina, Ponce Centro* ☎ *787/843–4322*).

SHOPPING

On holidays and during festivals, artisans sell wares from booths in Plaza de las Delicias. Souvenir and gift shops are plentiful in the area around the plaza, and Paseo Atocha, a pedestrian mall with shops geared to residents, runs north of it.

Den Cayá (✉ *72 Calle Isabel, Ponce Centro* ☎ *787/649–7763*), a fun and funky store, has a wide variety of crafts from around the island as well as from around the world.

Mi Coquí (✉ *9227 Calle Marina, Ponce Centro* ☎ *787/841–0216*) has shelves filled with carnival masks, colorful hammocks, freshly ground coffee, and bottles and bottles of rum.

Plaza del Caribe Mall (✉ *Rte. 2, Km 224.9* ☎ *787/259–8989*), just outside town, is one of the island's largest malls and has such stores as Sears, JCPenney, and Gap.

Ponce Mall (✉ *Rte. 2, Km 225.8* ☎ *787/844–6170*), with more than 25 stores, is an older shopping center, with many local clothing and discount stores.

Utopia (✉ *78 Calle Isabel, Ponce Centro* ☎ *787/848–8742*) sells carnival masks and crafts.

SPORTS AND THE OUTDOORS

DIVING AND SNORKELING

You'll see many varieties of coral, parrotfish, angelfish, and grouper in the reefs around the island of Caja de Muertos. Snorkeling around La Guancha and the beach area of the Ponce Hilton is also fairly good.

Rafi Vega's **Island Venture** (☎ *787/842–8546* 🌐 *www.islandventurepr.com*) offers two-tank dive excursions for $65, as well as snorkeling trips for $35. The company also takes day-trippers from La Guancha to Caja de Muertos—a 45-minute boat ride—for a day of relaxing on the beach.

GOLFING

The **Costa Caribe Golf & Country Club** (✉ *Rte. 14, 1150 Av. Caribe, Take Rte. 12 to Av. Caribe La Guancha* ☎ *787/259–7676* 🏌 *$89 per round, $40 after 4PM*), Ponce's only course, has 18 holes, a driving range, and pro shop adjoining the Ponce Hilton.

5

THE SOUTHEASTERN COAST

As you cross the Cordillera Central, the scenery becomes drier and more rugged. The Caribbean sparkles in the distance, and the plain between the sea and the mountains, once the heart of the sugarcane industry, is now the domain of cattle. Tucked into the foothills is Coamo, a popular hot-springs resort since the early 1900s. Closer to the coast is Guayama, with a tree-lined square surrounded by many historic buildings.

COAMO

21 mi (34 km) northeast of Ponce, 20 mi (33 km) southwest of Cayey, 13 mi (20 km) northwest of Salinas.

Founded by the Spanish in 1579, Coamo was the third city established in Puerto Rico. It dominated the south of the island until the mid-1880s, when political power shifted to Ponce. Coamo town, however, remained an important outpost; several decisive battles were fought here during the Spanish-American War in 1898.

The thermal springs outside Coamo are believed by some to be the Fountain of Youth for which Ponce de León was searching. In the mid-1800s a fashionable resort was built nearby, and people have been coming to soak in the waters ever since. Coamo is also famous for the San Blas Half-Marathon, which brings competitors and spectators from around the world. The race, held in early February, covers 13 mi (18 km) of the city's hilly streets.

GETTING HERE AND AROUND

Coamo sits not far from Luis A. Ferré Expressway (Route 52), the toll road that connects San Juan and Ponce. Coamo is about 20 miles northeast of Ponce. You can take the turn off on to Route 153, though there is also access from several points in the Cordillera. Públicos from Ponce connect with Coamo's town center, though you'll need to flag down a taxi to reach the baths or any of the hotels, which are all a couple of miles away.

EXPLORING

On Coama's main square, the **Iglesia Católica San Blás** has a gorgeous neoclassical facade. Dating from 1563, the whitewashed building is one of the oldest churches on the island. ✉ *Calle Mario Braschetti* ☎ *787/825–1122* ⏲ *Daily 6:30–noon.*

TAKE A WALK

In downtown Ponce, people embrace the Spanish tradition of the *paseo*, an evening stroll with family and friends around Plaza de las Delicias, which is spectacular at night when its old-fashioned street lamps glow and the fountain is lit. The boardwalk at La Guancha is also a lively scene with bands playing on weekends.

Off the main square, the **Museo Histórico de Coamo** is appropriately housed in the former residence of one of the city's illustrious citizens, Clotilde Santiago, a wealthy farmer and merchant born in 1826. The museum is on the second floor of this sprawling, tangerine-colored building, which dates from 1863. Several rooms are decorated with colonial-style furnishings; photographs of the town and the Santiago family line the walls. ✉ *29 Calle José I. Quintón* ☎ *787/825–1150* 🎟 *Free* ⏲ *Weekdays 8–4:30.*

Outside Coamo on Route 546 you can take a dip at the famous **Baños de Coamo,** thermal springs that are said to have curative powers. Parador Baños de Coamo allows day-trippers to bathe in its own warm, modern pool for $5 (parador guests enjoy it on the house). On the weekends families with kids in tow crowd the facilities. There's also a free public bathing area at the end of a path behind the parador. ✉ *Rte. 546, Km 1* ☎ *787/825–2186* 🎟 *$5* ⏲ *Daily 10–5:30.*

WHERE TO EAT AND STAY

¢–$ MEXICAN ✕ **La Ceiba.** The highway leading to Coama is lined by dozens of fast-food restaurants. Luckily, there are a few family-owned eateries worth stopping for, one of the best of which is this open-air cantina. You'll find the usual tacos, burritos, quesadillas, and fajitas, as well as some interesting Puerto Rican dishes like chicken breast stuffed with shrimp. World-class margaritas are served at the bar. ✉ *Rte. 153 at Km. 13* ☎ *787/825–2299* 💳 *MC, V.*

$ INN **Parador Baños de Coamo.** On weekends, musicians wander around the central courtyard of this rustic country inn. Simple, rather worn rooms—in four two-story buildings that date to the mid-1970s—have soaring ceilings and open onto latticed, wooden verandahs. Thermal water flows from natural springs into a swimming pool a few steps up from a cool-water pool, where you can still see walls built for the original resort that date back to 1847. The oldest building still intact is the 19th-century dining room, now a Meson Gastronomico, which serves huge portions of tasty *churrasco* (skirt steak) along with rice and beans. The open-air bar is popular in the afternoons. **Pros:** Relaxing atmosphere; pleasant staff. **Cons:** Uninteresting room decor; no elevator; pools could be cleaner; overpriced. ✉ *Rte. 546, Km 1, Box 1867, Coamo* ☎ *787/825–2186 or 787/825–2239* 🛏 *48 rooms* 👍 *In-hotel: restaurant, 2 bars, 2 pools* 💳 *AE, D, MC, V* 🍽 *EP.*

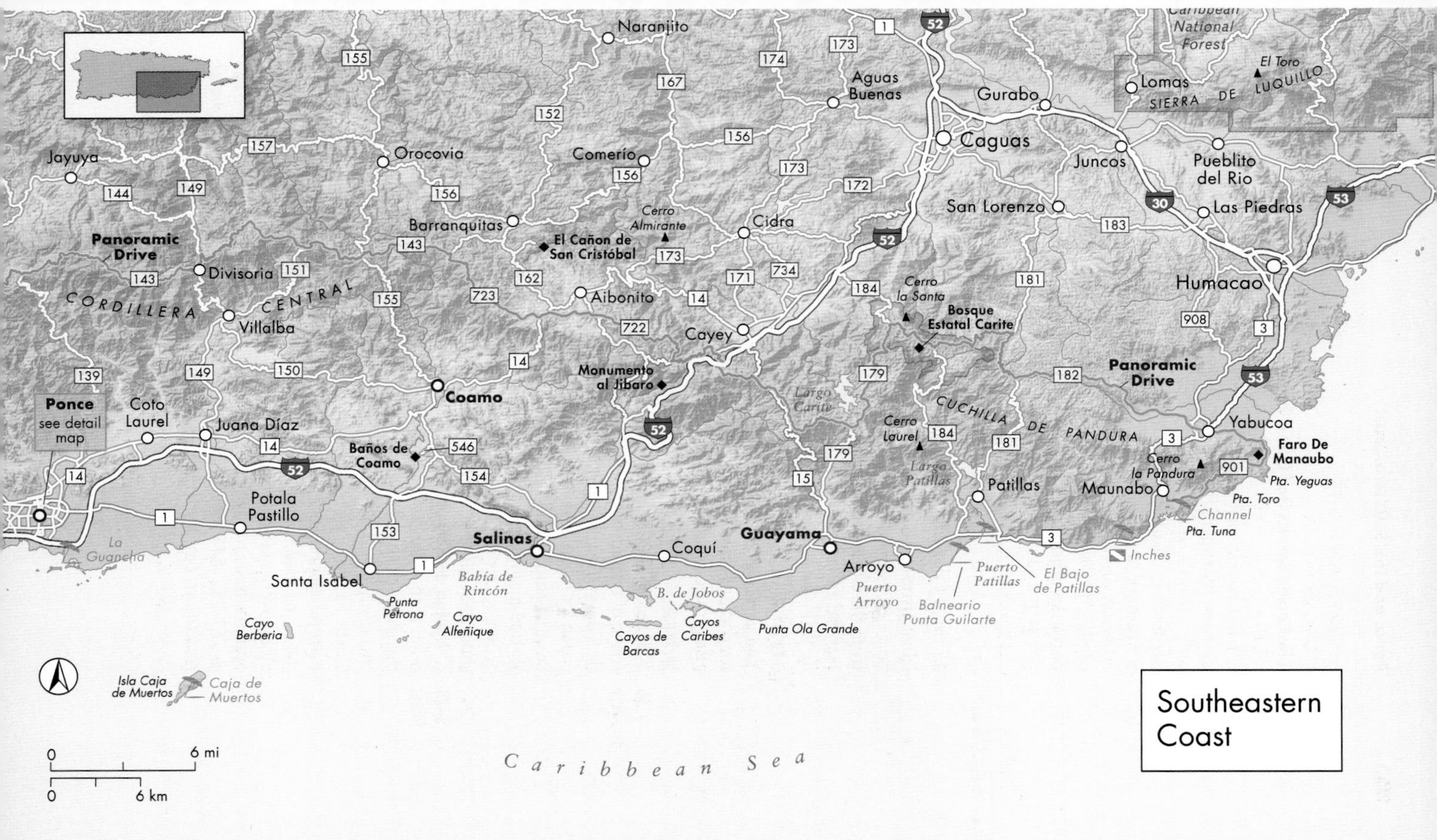
Southeastern Coast
Caribbean National Forest
El Toro
Lomas
Sierra de Luquillo
Naranjito
Aguas Buenas
Gurabo
Caguas
Juncos
Pueblito del Rio
Las Piedras
San Lorenzo
Humacao
Jayuya
Orocovia
Comerío
Barranquitas
Cerro Almirante
Cidra
Panoramic Drive
El Cañon de San Cristóbal
Divisoria
Cordillera Central
Aibonito
Villalba
Cayey
Cerro la Santa
Bosque Estatal Carite
Monumento al Jibaro
Largo Carite
Ponce
see detail map
Coto Laurel
Juana Díaz
Coamo
Baños de Coamo
Cuchilla de Pandura
Cerro Laurel
Largo Patillas
Yabucoa
Faro De Manaubo
Cerro la Pandura
Pta. Yeguas
Pta. Toro
Pta. Tuna
Channel
Maunabo
Patillas
Potala Pastillo
La Guanepia
Salinas
Guayama
Coquí
Arroyo
Santa Isabel
Bahía de Rincón
Punta Petrona
Cayo Alfeñique
Cayo Berberia
B. de Jobos
Cayos de Barcas
Cayos Caribes
Punta Ola Grande
Puerto Arroyo
Puerto Patillas
Balneario Punta Guilarte
El Bajo de Patillas
Inches
Isla Caja de Muertos
Caja de Muertos
Caribbean Sea
0 6 mi
0 6 km

SPORTS AND THE OUTDOORS

GOLF The **Coamo Springs Golf Club & Resort** (✉ *Rte. 546* ☎ *787/825–1370* 🌐 *www.coamosprings.com*) is popular for its rugged beauty. It's the only 18-hole, par-72 course with Bermuda grass on the island. When it's raining in the capital, sanjuaneros may drive down here for a day of play. The 6,647-yard course, designed by Ferdinand Garbin, is open daily. An adjoining thermal-springs resort was under construction at last visit and should be operating by 2011.

SALINAS HAS THE MOJO

When you stop in Salinas—and you should—be sure to try local seafood with *mojo isleño,* a popular sauce made from tomatoes, onions, and spices, which was created here.

SALINAS

27 mi (41 mi) east of Ponce.

Most visitors are familiar with this town only because of seeing its name on an exit sign along Route 52. Islanders, however, know that the road from the expressway exit to Salinas leads to some of Puerto Rico's best seafood restaurants. Most of them are along the seafront in the Playa de Salinas area, reached by heading south on Route 701.

GETTING HERE AND AROUND

You can take either the Luis A. Ferré Expressway (Route 52), the toll road that connects San Juan and Ponce, or the more scenic Route 1 along the coast east from Ponce to reach Salinas.

WHERE TO EAT AND STAY

$$ SEAFOOD ✕ **El Balcón de Capitán.** This *Meson Gastronómico*, hidden among a string of oceanfront seafood restaurants south of the center in the Playa de Salinas area, is one of the most respected on Puerto Rico's southern coast. Sit in either the open-air patio or air-conditioned dining room and bar and sample specialties like *mofongo relleno de mariscos* (seafood-stuffed plantains) or the many preparations of mahimahi, red snapper, arrayao, octopus, lobster, or conch. Be sure to try the local *mojo isleño* sauce. ✉ *Calle 54, Rte. 701* ☎ *787/824–2377AE, MC, V.*

$–$$ HOTEL **Marina de Salinas.** Several different types of mangroves shade this hotel at the Marina de Salinas. Many guests arrive by private yacht, but there's no reason you can't show up in a car. The spacious rooms are cheerfully decorated with tropical colors. Your dining options include Costa Marina, a restaurant that's also in the marina, or a string of seafood restaurants along the road. It's a bit difficult to find; follow the signs leading to the PLAYA DE SALINAS. **Pros:** Off-the-beaten-path vibe, lovely mangrove trees, friendly staff. **Cons:** Far from other dining options, basic rooms, no elevator. ✉ *Calle Chapin G-8* ☎ *787/824–3185 or 787/752–8484* 🌐 *www.marinadesalinas.com* *32 rooms* *In-hotel: restaurant, bar, pool* *AE, MC, V* *EP.*

GUAYAMA

18 mi (29 km) east of Salinas, 17 mi (28 km) southeast of Cayey, 31 mi (49 km) southeast of Barranquitas.

Guayama was founded in 1736, but the city was destroyed by fire in the early 1800s. It quickly recovered when the sugarcane industry grew by leaps and bounds, and the wealth that the surrounding plantations brought to town is evident in the number of striking neoclassical homes on the streets surrounding the main square. Some have been beautifully restored, whereas others are crumbling. One of the finest 19th-century homes, Casa Cautiño, is now a museum.

The nearby countryside is home to Paso Fino horses. Each March at the Marcelino Blondet Stadium you can watch these high-stepping show horses strut their stuff during the Feria Dulce Sueño, a fair named after one of the island's most famous Thoroughbreds. Folk music and crafts are part of the festivities.

GETTING HERE AND AROUND

From the north or west take either Route 53 or the coastal Route 3 to reach Guayama. On Sunday, Guayama has a free trolley that runs to many sights.

Information **Guayama Trolley** (☒ *Acaldía de Guayama, Calle Vicente Pales, Guayama* ☎ *787/864–7765*).

EXPLORING

★ Built for sugar, cattle, and coffee baron Genaro Cautiño Vázquez and his wife, Genoveva Insúa, **Casa Cautiño** is an elegant neoclassical home dating from 1887. The painstakingly restored exterior features a balcony with ornate grillwork. You'll be swept back in time walking through the home's rooms, which are filled with the original Victorian-era furnishings. Don't miss the modern-for-its-time bathroom, complete with a standing shower. The museum is on the main square. ☒ *1 Calle Palmer, at Calle Vicente Palé Matos* ☎ *787/864–9083* *Free* ⏲ *Tues.–Sat. 9–4:30, Sun. 10–4.*

NEED A BREAK?

The fruit-flavored ice cream at Rex Cream (☒ *24 Calle Derkes* ☎ *No phone*) is hard to pass up. Flavors vary, depending on what produce is in season, but often include lime, pineapple, tamarind, and *guanábana* (soursop). You can also get milk shakes—the mango shake is outstanding.

Just a few blocks from the main square, the **Centro de Bellas Artes** is housed in a beautifully restored neoclassical building. Paintings by local artists fill its 11 rooms. ☒ *Calle McArthur and Carr. 3* ☎ *787/864–7765* *Free* ⏲ *Tues.–Fri. 9–4:30, Sat. 10–4:30.*

One of the prettiest churches on the southern coast, **Iglesia San Antonio de Padua** was begun in 1827 but not completed until 40 years later. Don't set your watch by the time on the clock; the hand-painted face forever reads 11:30, the time the church was "baptized." The bells in the tower were cast in gold and bronze in 1835. ☒ *5 Calle Ashford* ☎ *787/864–7765.*

CLOSE UP

A Guide to Puerto Rico's Carved Saints

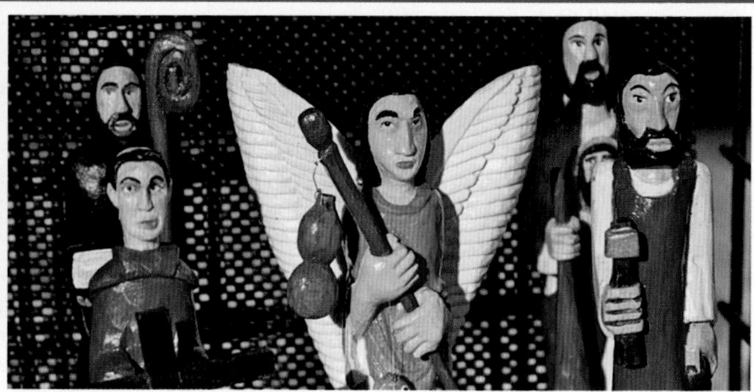

Hand-carved religious figures, or Santos, are an important part of Puerto Rico's cultural history.

Hand carving wooden saints (*santos*), is one of Puerto Rico's oldest traditional art forms, and the practice has survived for centuries. But you wouldn't know it to walk into one of the local souvenir shops, which often lines its shelves with imported pieces. Authentic santos carving thrives today—you just have to know where to find the artisans—and their handiwork.

HISTORY OF THE SANTOS

Influenced by its African, Spanish, and American roots, as well as its Caribbean neighbors and Latin American ties, Puerto Rico has achieved a unique artistic identity through its continual willingness to integrate many traditions. Its artists have worked hard to preserve their culture, and nowhere is their effort more evident than in their hand-carved *santos* statues.

The history of the *santos* is traced back to the arrival of Spanish missionaries in the late 15th and early 16th centuries. The missionaries spread God's word by telling stories animated and illustrated with carved *santos*. According to carver Miguel Diaz, missionaries left *santos* behind with prospective converts so they could pray at home. Churches were few and far between, but *santos* placed on home altars could help keep the spirit of God alive between missionaries' visits. Though missionaries no longer visit homes and churches are more abundant, *santos* still enjoy a place of honor in many Puerto Ricans' homes and have become a popular art form, highly prized by collectors on the island and abroad.

ABOUT THE SAINTS

Santos are not entirely unique to Puerto Rico; just as Spanish missionaries brought them to the island, they also carried them to many other countries. Each country, though, personalized the santos to their own cultures over the years. In Puerto Rico, the most common figures are the Three Kings, Saint Barbara, Saint Francis and The Powerful Hand (*La Mano Poderosa*—a member of the Holy Family tops each finger of a hand bearing the stigma). The santos are typically carved in cedar. Once carved, the santos are brushed with a coat of gesso and then painted. *Santos* can also be found in ceramic.

WHERE TO FIND THEM

Once you stop looking in souvenir shops, it just takes a little scouting to find santos, as well as the artisans who carve them.

The best place to find santos during business hours in Old San Juan is the **Puerto Rican Arts & Crafts** (✉ *204 Calle Fortaleza, Old San Juan* ☎ *787/725–5596* 🌐 *www.puertoricanart-crafts.com*). The store, which ensures that its entire stock comes from the hands of artisans who live on the island, carries the santos of the late, self-taught carver Domingo Orta, and Antonio Aviles Burgos, who was once recognized as artisan of the year and is the third generation of carvers in his family.

After hours, artisans can often be found working wood and selling their santos during craft fairs held along Old San Juan's Plaza Darsena, located between the cruise piers and Paseo de la Princesa. Friday and Saturday evenings are sure bets, as are Sunday afternoons.

The Powerful Hand santos

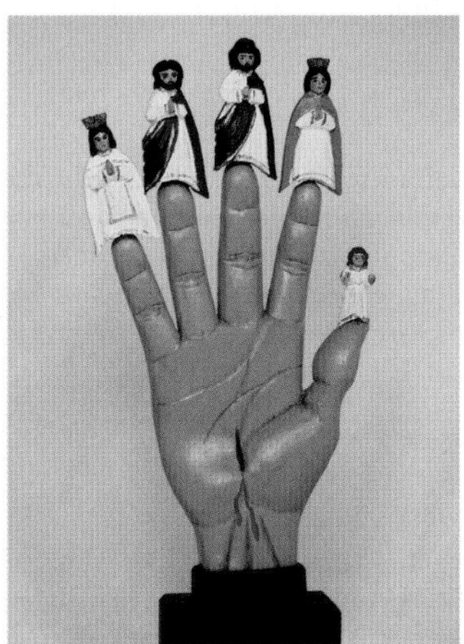

Puerto Rican Arts and Crafts Store

If you're interested in visiting an artisan's workshop, carver **Miguel Diaz** (☎ *787/392–8857* ✉ *tallertabonuco@gmail.com*) hosts visitors in his studio in Carolina.

The **Aviles family** (☎ *787/455–4217*) maintains a museum of their family's generations of craft work. Visits are by appointment only.

PRICES

As with most art and handcrafts, prices depend on several factors, including the carver's history, the quality of craftsmanship, the setting where the pieces are sold, the amount of decoration or elaboration, and the size of the piece. The average size of a santo is 7 to 8 inches, though some are smaller and many carvers produce larger pieces for commissions and other special occasions.

In general, expect prices for santos to begin at $40 and to go up considerably. Some santos fetch as much as several hundred dollars.

Bargaining is not considered as permissible in Puerto Rico as it is in other Spanish-speaking countries. A carver's stated price is likely the lowest he or she is willing to go.

Not far from Guayama, **El Tren del Sur** *(The Train of the South)* takes passengers for one-hour trips along an old rail line beginning in Arroyo. The train carried cane from the fields to the mills from 1915 to 1958; today it's one of the island's few working trains. Call in advance; at last check, the train was shut down until further notice. ✉ *Rte. 3, Km 130.9* ☎ *787/271–1574* *$3.*

WHERE TO EAT AND STAY

¢–$ CARIBBEAN **El Suarito.** You're surrounded by history at this restaurant in a building that dates from 1862. The site has seen life as a repair shop for horse-drawn buggies, a gas station, and—since the mid-1950s—a restaurant. The place is always hopping with townspeople who stop by at all hours for a meal or a drink. You can get eggs and toast for breakfast, sandwiches throughout the day, and roasted chicken or liver and onions for dinner. ✉ *6 Calle Derkes, at Calle Hostos* ☎ *787/864–1820* *MC, V* *Closed Sun.*

$ HOTEL **Molino Inn.** This tidy hotel is on the outskirts of Guayama, near the ruins of a Spanish *molino* (sugar mill). Nine acres of lush, attractive grounds—including flower beds and a large pool—surround its two buildings. In stark contrast, the rooms are plain and provide only the basics. Join the local business crowd for the international and Caribbean cuisines at the restaurant. **Pros:** Convenient location; staff bends over backward to be helpful. **Cons:** Unattractive building; bland rooms. ✉ *Av. Albizu Campos at Rte. 54, Box 2393, Guayama* ☎ *787/866–1515* *molinoinn.net* *20 rooms* *In-hotel: restaurant, bar, tennis court, pool, laundry service* *AE, MC, V* *EP.*

SPORTS AND THE OUTDOORS

GOLF Running through an old sugar plantation, the **Aguirre Golf Club** (✉ *Rte. 705, Km 3, Aguirre* ☎ *787/853–4052*) was built in 1925 for the executives of a local sugar mill. Open daily, the 9-hole course is short but tough. The **El Legado Golf Resort** (✉ *Rte. 153 at intersection 713* ☎ *787/866–8894* *www.ellegadogolfresort.com*), designed by golf legend and native son Chi Chi Rodríguez, is one of the island's best courses. The 7,213-yard, 18-hole course has 12 lakes.

THE SOUTHWESTERN COAST

With sandy coves and palm-lined beaches tucked in the coastline's curves, southwestern Puerto Rico fulfills everyone's fantasy of a tropical paradise. The area is popular with local vacationers on weekends and holidays, but many beaches are nearly deserted on weekdays. Villages along the coast are picturesque places where oysters and fresh fish are sold at roadside stands.

GUÁNICA

24 km (38 km) west of Ponce.

Juan Ponce de León first explored this area in 1508, when he was searching for the elusive Fountain of Youth. Nearly 400 years later, U.S. troops landed first at Guánica during the Spanish-American War in 1898. The event is commemorated with an engraved marker on the city's *malecón*, or jetty. Sugarcane dominated the landscape through much of the 1900s, and the ruins of the old Guánica Central sugar mill, closed in 1980, loom over the town's western area, known as Ensenada. Today most of the action takes place at the beaches and in the forests outside of Guánica.

GETTING HERE AND AROUND

From Ponce Route 2 connects with Guánica via Route 116 and extends to San Germán and Mayagüez. The town hugs Guánica bay and runs almost immediately into the neighboring village of Ensenada.

EXPLORING

The 9,900-acre **Bosque Estatal de Guánica** *(Guánica State Forest)*, a United Nations Biosphere Reserve, is a great place for hiking expeditions. It's an outstanding example of a tropical dry coastal forest, with some 700 species of plants ranging from the prickly-pear cactus to the gumbo limbo tree. It's also one of the best places on the island for bird-watching, since you can spot more than 100 species, including the pearly-eyed thrasher, the lizard cuckoo, and the nightjar.

One of the most popular hikes is the **Ballena Trail,** which begins at the ranger station on Route 334. This easy 1¼-mi (2-km) walk follows a partially paved road and takes you past a mahogany plantation to a dry plain covered with stunted cactus. A sign reading GUAYACÁN CENTENARIO leads you to an extraordinary guayacán tree with a trunk that measures 6 feet across. The moderately difficult **Fuerte Trail** takes you on a 3½-mi (5½-km) hike to an old fort built by the Spanish Armada. It was destroyed during the Spanish-American War in 1898, but you can still see the ruins of the old observatory tower.

In addition to going in the main entrance on Route 334, you can enter on Route 333, which skirts the forest's southwestern quadrant. You can also try the less-explored western section, off Route 325. ✉ *Enter along Rte. 334, 333, or 325* ☎ *787/821–5706* *Free* ⏲ *Daily 9–5.*

Off the southwest coast, near Guánica, is **Gilligan's Island,** a palm-ringed cay skirted by gorgeous beaches. You'll find picnic tables and restrooms but few other signs of civilization on this tiny island, officially part of the Bosque Estatal de Guánica. Wooden boats line up at the small dock in the San Jacinto section of Guánica, off Route 333 just past the Copamarina Beach Resort. Boats depart every hour from 10 to 5 (except Monday, when rangers close the island to visitors). Round-trip passage is $6. The island is often crowded on weekends and around holidays, but during the week you can find a spot to yourself. Nearby **Isla de Ballena,** reached by the same ferry, is much less crowded. ✉ *Rte. 333 or 334* ☎ *787/821–5706* *Free* ⏲ *Daily 9–5.*

WHERE TO EAT

$$$ CARIBBEAN ★ ✕ **Alexandra.** Puerto Ricans drive for miles to reach this restaurant in the Copamarina Beach Resort. You won't find such creative cuisine anywhere else west of Ponce. The kitchen makes traditional dishes into something special; take the free-range chicken with cumin-and-thyme butter, for example, or the grilled pork chops with pineapple chutney. A standout is the risotto, which surrounds tender mussels with rice flavored with saffron, basil, and tomatoes. The elegant dining room

looks out onto well-tended gardens; if you want to get closer to the flora, ask for a table outside on the terrace. The only disappointment may be noisy children, who tend to run in and out. ✉ *Rte. 333, Km 6.5* ☎ *787/821–0505 ext. 766* *Reservations essential* ▭ *AE, MC, V.*

$–$$ CARIBBEAN **San Jacinto.** Popular with day-trippers to Gilligan's Island, this modest restaurant sits right at the ferry terminal. This doesn't mean, however, that the dining room has views of the Caribbean. For those, grab one of the concrete picnic tables outside. The menu is almost entirely seafood, running the gamut from fried snapper to broiled lobster. When it's not high season the menu can be limited to two or three items. Bonus: They also rent kayaks and snorkel gear. ✉ *Off Rte. 333* ☎ *787/821–4941 MC, V.*

WHERE TO STAY

$$$ RESORT **Copamarina Beach Resort.** Without a doubt the most beautiful resort on the southern coast, the Copamarina is set on 16 palm-shaded acres facing the Caribbean Sea. The fruit trees and other plants are meticulously groomed, especially around the pair of swimming pools (one popular with kids, the other mostly left to the adults). All the guest rooms are generously proportioned, especially in the older building. Wood shutters on the windows and other touches lend a tropical feel. A small Asian-influenced spa blends seamlessly with the rest of the hotel. Both the elegant Alexandra and the more casual alfresco Las Palmas Café serve good food. All-inclusive packages are available. **Pros:** Tropical decor; plenty of activities; great dining options. **Cons:** Sand at the beach has a gummy feel; noise from the many kids. ✉ *Rte. 333, Km 6.5, Box 805, Guánica* ☎ *787/821–0505 or 800/468–4553* 🌐 *www.copamarina.com* *104 rooms, 2 villas* *In-room: safe, refrigerator, Wi-Fi. In-hotel: 2 restaurants, room service, bars, tennis courts, pools, gym, spa, beachfront, diving, water sports, laundry facilities* ▭ *AE, MC, V* *EP.*

$–$$ VILLAS Fodor's Choice ★ **Mary Lee's by the Sea.** This meandering cluster of apartments sits upon quiet grounds full of brightly colored flowers. It's home to Mary Lee Alvarez, and she'll make you feel as if it's your home as well. Most units have ocean views; in the others you'll catch a glimpse of the mangroves by the shore as well as the cactus growing in the nearby Bosque Estatal de Guánica. Each of the one-, two-, and three-bedroom units is decorated in bright colors. Every unit is different, but most have terraces hung with hammocks and outfitted with barbecue grills. You can rent kayaks to drift along the coast or hop a boat bound for Gilligan's Island. **Pros:** Feels like a home away from home, warm and friendly owner, near pristine beaches and forests. **Cons:** Weekly maid service unless requested daily, no nightlife options. ✉ *Rte. 333, Km 6.7* *Box 394, Guánica 00653* ☎ *787/821–3600* 🌐 *www.maryleesbythesea.com* *10 apartments* *In-room: no phone, kitchen (some), no TV. In-hotel: laundry facilities, laundry service, some pets allowed* ▭ *MC, V* *EP.*

$ HOTEL **Parador Guanica 1929.** This colonial-style building dates back to 1929, when it housed executives from the nearby sugar plantation. It's very pretty, with lovely arches adding more character than you usually find along the southern coast. There's a lovely view of the ocean, but no beach. The staff members are hospitality students, and

Southwestern Coast
Mani
Mayagüez
Bahía de Mayagüez
Pta. Guanajibo
Joyuda
Playa Joyuda
Buyé
Pta. Caranero
Pta. Guaniquilla
Boquerón
Bahía de Boquerón
Balneario Boquerón
El Combate
Bosque Estatal de Boquerón
Bahía Salinas
La Playuela
Cabo Rojo
Bahía Sucia
Pole Ojea
Refugio de Vida Silvestre
Cabo Rojo
Hormigueros
LAS MESAS
MONTE GRANDE
Lajas
VALLE DE LAJAS
La Parguera
Playita Rosada
Pta. Jorobado
Las Vegas
Maricao
Panoramic Drive
San Germán see detail map
Sabana Grande
Pico Fraile
Largo Luchetti
Ensenada
Guánica
Playa Santa
Punta Jacinto
Pta. Brea
Balneario Caña Gorda
Gilligan's Island
Bahía Ballena
Bosque Estatal de Guánica
Yauco
Palomas
Indiera Rita
Castañer
Largo Guayo
Lares
Cerro Roncador
CORDILLERA CENTRAL
Pico Rodadero
Monte Guilate
Guayanilla
Bahía de Guayanilla
Peñuelas
Tallaboa
El Tuque
Adjuntas
Utuado
Largo Caonillas
Jayuya
La Pica
Cerro Punta
Panoramic Drive
Divisoria
Villalba
Coto Laurel
Juana Díaz
Ponce see detail map
Isla Caja de Muertos
Caribbean Sea
0 6 mi
0 6 km

Fish the waters off La Parguera for blue marlin, tuna, or reef fish.

they try their darnedest to make a good impression. Despite the name, the hotel is actually in Ensenada, just west of Guaníca. **Pros:** Historic setting; hard-working staff; pretty pool area. **Cons:** No beach; slightly off the beaten path. ✉ *Rte. 3116, Km. 2.5, Ensenada* ☎ *787/821–0099* 🌐 *www.guanica1929.com* 29 *rooms* *In room: Wi-Fi. In-hotel: restaurant, pool* 💳 *AE, MC, V* *EP.*

SPORTS AND THE OUTDOORS

DIVING AND SNORKELING

Dramatic walls created by the continental shelf provide great diving off the Guánica coast. Shallow gardens around Gilligan's Island and Cayo de Caña Gorda (off Balneario Caña Gorda) also attract snorkelers and divers. **Dive Copamarina** (✉ *Copamarina Beach Resort, Rte. 333, Km 6.5* ☎ *787/821–0505*) offers instruction and trips.

HORSEBACK RIDING

In nearby Yauco, **Gaby's World** (✉ *Rte. 127, Km 5.1, Yauco* ☎ *787/856–2609* 🌐 *www.gabysworld.net*) is a 204-acre horse ranch that conducts half-hour, one-hour, and two-hour rides through the hills surrounding Yauco. There are also pony rides for children. The on-site steak house serves Yauco's specialty, *chuletas can-can.*

LA PARGUERA

8 mi (13 km) west of Guánica, 15 mi (24 km) southwest of Yauco.

La Parguera is best known for its bioluminescent bay. Although it is not nearly as spectacular as the one of the island of Vieques, it's still a beautiful sight on a moonless night. Glass-bottom boats lined up at the town dock depart several times each evening for 45-minute trips across the bay. During the day, you can explore the nearby mangrove forest.

The town bursts at the seams with vacationers from other parts of the island on long holiday weekends and all during the summer. The town's dock area feels a bit like Coney Island, and not in a good way. Vendors in makeshift stalls hawk cheap souvenirs, and ear-splitting salsa music pours out of the open-air bars. There are signs warning people not to drink alcoholic beverages in the street, but these are cheerfully ignored.

If you're driving through the area between February and April, keep your eyes open for roadside vendors selling the area's famous pineapples, called *piñas cadezonas*. In late June there's the colorful Fiesta de San Pedro, honoring the patron saint of fishermen.

WORD OF MOUTH

"We spent the next night in La Parguera in a little hotel right on the beach. It was a lovely little hotel looking out over the mangroves. There is bioluminescent activity there and you can do a night snorkel trip. We opted not to and really regretted it later. We were there during a new moon, which is the perfect time."

–shillmac

GETTING HERE AND AROUND

You can reach La Parguera from Guánica via Route 116, which turns in to Route 318 when headed to San Germán. Públicos depart from the turnoff at Route 304 and head to Lajas, where connections can be made to San Germán.

EXPLORING

On moonless nights, large and small boats line up along the dock to take visitors out to view the **Bahía de Fosforescente** *(Phosphorescent Bay)*. Microscopic dinoflagellates glow when disturbed by movement, invading the waves with thousands of starlike points of light. The bay's glow has been diminished substantially by pollution—both light pollution from nearby communities and water pollution from toxic chemicals being dumped into the bay. (And, yes, the smoke-belching boats that take tourists to the bay are doing damage, too.) If you've seen the bioluminescent bay in Vieques *(see the feature in Chapter 4)*, give this one a pass. If not, you may find it mildly interesting. There's no need to make arrangements in advance; just show up to the docks around 7:30 pm to find a boat ($6–$7 per person). ✉ *East of La Parguera.*

The eastern section of the **Bosque Estatal de Boquerón** *(Boquerón State Forest)* is made up of miles of mangrove forests that grow at the water's edge. Boats from the dock in La Parguera can take you on cruises through this important breeding ground for seabirds. You can also organize a kayak trip. ✉ *East of La Parguera.*

WHERE TO EAT

$$–$$$ SEAFOOD ✕ **La Casita.** The so-called Little House isn't little at all—it's a sizable establishment that sits smack in the middle of the town's main road. Generous portions make this family-run restaurant one of the town's favorites. Try the *asopao,* which is made with shrimp, lobster, or other types of seafood. You can take a table in the rather bland ground-floor dining room or on the second-floor terrace, which has a view of the water. ✉ *Rte. 304, Km 3.3* ☎ *787/899–1681* *MC, V.*

$$–$$$ CARIBBEAN ✕ **La Pared.** Many restaurants in La Parguera sit beside the bay, but very few have an actual view. This elegant, second-floor dining room at the rear of Posada Porlamar overlooks a lovely stretch of coastline ringed by mangrove trees. The menu is the best in town, going well beyond traditional surf-and-turf offerings. There's the standard rack of lamb, for example, but here you'll find it topped with goat cheese. The lobster tail is as fresh as anywhere else on the strip, but it's topped with a tasty *guanabana* (soursop) sauce. ✉ *Posada Porlamar, Rte. 304, Km 3.3* ☎ *787/899–4015 MC, V.*

WHERE TO STAY

$ HOTEL **Posada Porlamar.** You might not realize it at first, but this small hotel is all about the water. Most of the comfortable rooms have views of the mangrove-ringed bay, as do the restaurant, café, and bar. In the rear you'll find a dock where you can rent a boat to explore the coastline, as well as a full-service dive shop where you can arrange snorkeling and diving excursions. And when you're finished exploring, you can relax by the pretty pool. The hotel is on La Parguera's main drag, but far enough from the action that it's quiet at night. **Pros:** Water views everywhere; excellent dining on the premises and nearby. **Cons:** Bland room décor; a lot of steps to negotiate and no elevator. ✉ *Rte. 304, Km 3.3* *Box 3113, Lajas00667* ☎ *787/899–4343* *38 rooms* *In-hotel: restaurant, bar, pool* *MC, V* *EP.*

$ HOTEL ★ **Villa del Mar.** What sets this family-run property apart is the warmth of the staff, all of whom promise to take care of anything you need. The hotel, painted refreshing shades of lemon and lime, sits on a hill overlooking the boats in the bay. Not all of the squeaky-clean rooms have views, so make sure to specify when you call for reservations. Downstairs you'll find an open-air lounge area near the reception desk and a shimmering pool in the courtyard. There's a breezy restaurant that serves seafood and Puerto Rican staples. To find this hotel, take the first left as you drive into La Parguera. **Pros:** Unbeatable vistas; peace and quiet. **Cons:** Bland room decor; a good number of steps to climb and no elevator. ✉ *3 Av. Albizu Campos* *Box 1297, San Germán* ☎ *787/899–4265* *www.paradorvilladelmar.com* *25 rooms* *In-room: no phone. In-hotel: restaurant, bar, pool* *AE, MC, V* *EP.*

$–$$ HOTEL **Villa Parguera.** The rooms in this gingerbread-trimmed hotel are clustered around small courtyards filled with bright tropical flowers. Many have balconies overlooking the bay, so make sure to look at a few rooms before you decide. A spacious dining room overlooking the pool serves excellent Puerto Rican and international dishes. On Saturday night there's live music and a floor show in the dance club. The staff can be a little brusque at times. **Pros:** Family atmosphere; plenty of entertainment options; walking distance to the marina. **Cons:** Bland rooms; pool area gets crowded; noise from nearby bars; no elevator. ✉ *Rte. 304, Km 3.3* *Box 273, Lajas00667* ☎ *787/899–7777* *www.villaparguera.net* *70 rooms* *In-hotel: restaurant, bar, pool* *AE, D, DC, MC, V* *EP.*

Many of La Parguera's restaurants and shops are situated right on the bay.

NIGHTLIFE AND THE ARTS

La Parguera's dock area heats up after sunset, when crowds come to take excursions to the Bahía de Fosforescente. On weekends **Mar y Tierra** (⊠ *Rte. 304, Km 3.3* ☎ *787/899–4627*) is the most popular place in the strip. The open-air establishment has a couple of pool tables that are always in use. Pay attention to the sign that tells you not to put your feet on the wall.

The live floor show at **Villa Parguera** (⊠ *Rte. 304, Km 2.3* ☎ *787/899–7777 or 787/899–3975*) includes a buffet. The show changes frequently but includes live music, dancing, and comedy of the seltzer-in-your-pants variety.

SHOPPING

Outdoor stands near Bahía Fosforescente sell all kinds of souvenirs, from T-shirts to beaded necklaces. In La Parguera's center, there are several small souvenir shops, including **Nautilus** (⊠ *Rte. 304* ☎ *787/899–4565*), that sell posters, mugs, and trinkets made from shells.

SPORTS AND THE OUTDOORS

DIVING & SNORKELING

Endangered leatherback turtles, eels, and an occasional manatee can be seen from many of the sites that attract divers and snorkelers from all parts. There are more than 50 shore-dive sites off La Parguera. **Paradise Scuba** (⊠ *Hostal Casa Blanca, Rte. 304, Km 3.5* ☎ *787/899–7611*) has classes and trips, including night-snorkeling excursions in phosphorescent waters.

FISHING

You can spend a day or half-day fishing for blue marlin, tuna, or reef fish with Capt. Mickey Amador at **Parguera Fishing Charters** (⊠ *Rte. 304, Km 3.8* ☎ *787/382–4698 or 787/899–4698*). Lunch is included in the price.

SAN GERMÁN

6 mi (10 km) north of La Parguera, 104 mi (166 km) southwest of San Juan.

During its early years, San Germán was a city on the move. Although debate rages about the first settlement's exact founding date and location, the town is believed to have been established in 1510 near Guánica. Plagued by mosquitoes, the settlers moved north along the west coast, where they encountered French pirates and smugglers. In the 1570s they fled inland to the current location, but they were still harassed. Determined and creative, they dug tunnels and moved beneath the city (the tunnels are now part of the water system). Today San Germán has a population of 39,000, and its intellectual and political activity is anything but underground. It's very much a college town, and students and professors from the Inter-American University often fill the bars and cafés.

> **WORD OF MOUTH**
>
> "Loved San Germán—I'd call it quaint. The church museum had some nice art pieces and the town 'rectangle' was very pretty. As someone else mentioned, San Germán dates back to the early 1500s, and part of the original church is preserved. And there is such a gorgeous house right across the street! I could imagine living there."
>
> —shillmac

Around San Germán's two main squares—Plazuela Santo Domingo and Plaza Francisco Mariano Quiñones (named for an abolitionist)—are buildings done in every conceivable style of architecture found on the island, including mission, Victorian, Creole, and Spanish colonial. The city's tourist office offers a free, guided trolley tour. Most of the buildings are private homes; two of them—the Capilla de Porta Coeli and the Museo de Arte y Casa de Estudio—are museums. Strip malls surround the historical center, and the town is hemmed to the south and west by busy seaside resorts.

GETTING HERE AND AROUND

San Germán sits just off Highway 2 between Ponce and Mayagüez on Route 122. Being a university town, it is a transportation hub with públicos departing to nearby villages such as Mayagüez and Lajas from the intersection of Calle Luna and Route 122. A trolley tour of San Germán is available by appointment.

Ojeda Taxi (☎ *787/259–7676 in San Germán*).

San Germán Trolley (✉ *Acaldía de San Germán, 136 Calle Luna, San Germán* ☎ *787/892–3500*).

Numbers in the margin correspond to the "San Germán" map.

TOP ATTRACTIONS

1 ★ **Capilla de Porta Coeli** *(Heaven's Gate Chapel)*. One of the oldest religious buildings in the Americas, this mission-style chapel overlooks the long, rectangular Plazuela de Santo Domingo. It's not a grand building, but its position at the top of a stone stairway gives it a noble

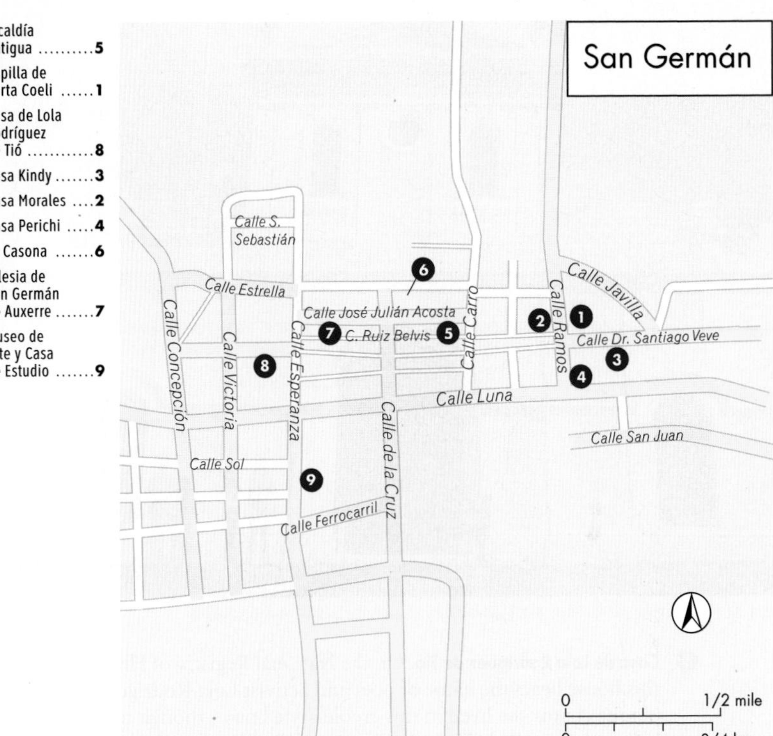

air. Queen Isabel Segunda decreed that the Dominicans should build a church and monastery in San Germán, so a rudimentary building was built in 1609, replaced in 1692 by the structure that can still be seen today. (Sadly, most of the monastery was demolished in 1866, leaving only a vestige of its facade.) The chapel now functions as a museum of religious art, displaying painted wooden statuary by Latin American and Spanish artists. ✉ *East end of Plazuela Santo Domingo* ☎ *787/892–5845* 🌐 *www.icp.gobierno.pr* 🎫 *Free* 🕒 *Wed.–Sun. 8:30–noon and 1–4:15.*

❻ **La Casona.** On the north side of Plaza Francisco Mariano Quiñones, this two-story home was built in 1871 for Tomás Agrait. (If you look closely, you can still see his initials in the wrought-iron decorations.) For many years it served as a center of cultural activities in San Germán. Today it holds several shops. ✉ *Calle José Julien Acosta and Calle Cruz.*

WORTH NOTING

❺ **Alcaldía Antigua** *(Old Municipal Building).* At the eastern end of Plaza Francisco Mariano Quiñones, this Spanish-colonial-style building served as the town's city hall from 1844 to 1950. Once used as a prison, the building is now the headquarters for the police department. ✉ *East end of Plaza Francisco Mariano Quiñones.*

Iglesia de San Germán de Auxerre is a 17th-century church that's still in use today.

8 **Casa de Lola Rodríguez de Tió.** On the National Registry of Historic Places, this house bears the name of poet and activist Lola Rodríguez de Tió. A plaque claims she lived in this creole-style house, though town officials believe it actually belonged to her sister. Rodríguez, whose mother was a descendant of Ponce de León, was deported several times by Spanish authorities for her revolutionary ideas. She lived in Venezuela and then in Cuba, where she died in 1924. The museum, which houses Rodríguez's desk and papers, isn't open regular hours; call ahead to schedule a tour. ✉ *13 Calle Dr. Santiago Veve* ☎ *787/892–3500* *Free* *By appointment only.*

3 **Casa Kindy.** East of the Plazuela de Santo Domingo, this 19th-century home is known for its eclectic architecture, which mixes neoclassical and criollo elements. Note the elegant stained-glass windows over the front windows. It's now a private residence. ✉ *64 Calle Dr. Santiago Veve.*

2 **Casa Morales.** Facing Plazuela de Santo Domingo, this Victorian-style house was designed in 1913 by architect Pedro Vivoni for his brother, Tomás Vivoni. The gleaming white structure has numerous towers and gables. The current owners have kept it in mint condition. It is not open to the public. ✉ *38 Calle Ramos.*

4 **Casa Perichi.** You'll find an excellent example of Puerto Rican ornamental architecture in this elegant mansion, which sits a block south of Plazuela Santo Domingo. This gigantic white home, on the National Register of Historic Places, was built in 1920. Note the sensuous curves of the wraparound balcony and wood trim around the doors. It's not open to the public. ✉ *94 Calle Luna.*

A GOOD TOUR

The best place to start is Plazuela Santo Domingo, the sun-baked park in the center of the historic district. At the eastern edge of the park is the **Capilla de Porta Coeli**, perched at the top of an imposing set of stairs. From the top you get a good view of the rest of the city. Several historic homes, none of them open to the public, are within a block of the Capilla de Porta Coeli. Across the street is the **Casa Morales**, striking for its Victorian-style gables. It would not look out of place in any New England hamlet. Half a block east on Calle Dr. Santiago Veve are two criollo-style houses, **Casa Kindy** and Casa Acosta y Forés. A block south of the Capilla de Porta Coeli is one of the most beautiful homes in San Germán, **Casa Perichi**.

Head west through Plazuela Santo Domingo. The hulking yellow building you see at the northwest corner of the park is the rear of the **Alcaldía Antigua**. It faces the town's other park, the Plaza Francisco Mariano Quiñones. This park is more popular with locals, as the tree-shaded benches are a pleasant place to watch the world go by. On the park's northern edge is **La Casona**, one of the town's best-preserved criollo-style buildings. The most imposing structure on the park, however, is the **Iglesia de San Germán de Auxerre**.

A block and a half west of the church is the **Casa de Lola Rodríguez de Tió**, on Calle Dr. Santiago Veve. It's one of the best examples of criollo-style architecture in the city. Backtrack to Calle Esperanza and head two blocks south to where you'll find the **Museo de Arte y Casa de Estudio**.

TIMING

San Germán's historic district is compact, so you can cover all the sights in about an hour. You'll want to budget a bit more time to stroll around the nearby streets. Be sure to wear comfortable shoes, as there will be a lot of walking uphill and downhill on cobbled streets.

5

7 **Iglesia de San Germán de Auxerre.** Dating from 1739, this neoclassical church has seen many additions over the years. For example, the impressive crystal chandelier was added in 1860. Be sure to take a look at the carved-wood ceiling in the nave. This church is still in use, so the only time you can get a look inside is during services. ✉ *West side of Plaza Francisco Mariano Quiñones* ☎ *787/892–1027* ⏲ *Mass Mon.–Sat. at 7* AM *and 7:30* PM *and Sun. at 7, 8:30, 10* AM*, and 7:30* PM.

9 **Museo de Arte y Casa de Estudio.** This early 20th-century home—built in the criollo style with some obvious neoclassical influences—has been turned into a museum. Displays include colonial furnishings, religious art, and artifacts of the indigenous peoples; there are also changing exhibits by local artists. ✉ *7 Calle Esperanza* ☎ *787/892–8870* 🎟 *Free* ⏲ *Wed.–Sun. 10–noon and 1–3.*

WHERE TO EAT AND STAY

$–$$ MEXICAN ✕ **Chaparritas.** On San Germán's main drag, this place certainly feels like a traditional cantina. The Mexican food here is the real deal. Although you'll find some dishes that are more Tex than Mex, such as the cheesy nachos, the kitchen does best with more authentic tacos, burritos, and enchiladas. For something a bit more off the wall, try the shrimp fried in tequila. ✉ *Calle Luna 171* ☎ *787/892–1078* ▭ *MC, V* ⏲ *Closed Sun.–Wed.*

¢–$ SPANISH ★ ✕ **Tapas Café.** One of the biggest surprises in San Germán is this wonderful little restaurant facing Plaza Santo Domingo. The dining room looks like a Spanish courtyard, complete with blue stars swirling around the ceiling. Don't expect tiny portions just because the eatery serves tapas—several of the dishes, including the medallions of beef topped with a dab of blue cheese, could pass as full entrées anywhere. You'll find old favorites on the menu, including spicy sausage in red wine, but some new creations as well, such as the yam-and-codfish fritters. ✉ *50 Calle Dr. Santiago Veve* ☎ *787/264–0610* ▭ *MC, V* ⏲ *Closed Mon.–Tues. No lunch Wed.–Thurs.*

$ INN **Villa del Rey.** On a quiet country road, Villa del Rey is set among banana and papaya trees. This family-run inn couldn't be simpler, but it's clean and comfortable. The rooms are larger than you'll find in most of the region's lodgings. The patio around the pool is a bit run-down, but the pool itself is refreshing on a hot afternoon. **Pros:** Decent pool and authentic ambiance. **Cons:** Could use an all around face-lift; no elevator. ✉ *Rte. 361, Km 0.8, off Rte. 2* 📫 *Box 3033, San Germán 00667* ☎ *787/264–2542 or 787/642–2627* 🌐 *www.villadelrey.net* 19 *rooms* *In-room: kitchen (some). In-hotel: pool* ▭ *MC, V* 🍽 *EP.*

Rincón and the Porta del Sol

WORD OF MOUTH

"We stayed in Rincón at the Blue Boy Inn. Excellent but not inexpensive. There is a snorkeling place near as well as some good restaurants. From Rincón, there are easy ways to get to the Arecibo Observatory and the Camuy Caves as well as south to Cabo Rojo/Boqueron and perhaps the zoo in Mayaguez."

–OldAnalyst

WELCOME TO RINCÓN AND THE PORTA DEL SOL

TOP REASONS TO GO

★ **Visit El Combate:** Hike to the lighthouse at this peninsula, which juts out into the Caribbean Sea.

★ **Pamper yourself at the Horned Dorset Primavera:** Relax in your private plunge pool at perhaps the most romantic inn in the Caribbean.

★ **Please your palate at the "Golden Mile":** Sample fresh seafood at any of the dozens of oceanfront eateries in Joyuda.

★ **Catch a Wave at Playa Tres Palmas:** Challenge the waves here or at any of Rincón's world-famous surfing spots.

★ **Explore Desecheo Island or Mona Island:** Enjoy snorkeling, diving, or fishing around these spectacular islands.

1 Rincón. The first World Surfing Championships in 1968 put Rincón on the map, and its laid-back vibe and epic waves have kept it there. Paddle out to one of the town's 15 surf spots, or experience horseback riding on the beach and fishing in the crystal Caribbean waters. One of Rincón's greatest attractions is the diving and snorkeling at nearby Desecheo Island.

2 Mayagüez. Stroll the marble-paved square of Plaza Colón, where a statue of Christopher Colombus commemorates the site where he allegedly disembarked. Visit architectural gems such as the Nuestra Señora de la Candelaria Cathedral, built in 1780, or experience an artistic performance at the Teatro Yagüez, which dates back to 1909. Savor the flavor of Mayagüez by sampling traditional *brazo gitano* ("gypsy arm") jelly roll, baked at the century-old Ricomini Bakery.

3 Cabo Rojo. Sample the island's freshest catch at Joyuda's Milla de Oro (Golden Mile), a string of more than 30 waterfront restaurants built on stilts. Slurp fresh oysters and clams from one of the many vendor carts lining the fishing town of Boquerón. Hike to the Cabo Rojo Lighthouse at Puerto Rico's southwestern tip.

4 The Northwestern Coast. The colorful fishing boats that line Playa Crashboat are a photographer's dream. Relax over a rum punch at an oceanfront bar while watching surfers get barreled at Jobos Beach. Explore the hidden waterfalls at El Charco de la Leche ("Puddle of Milk") near San Sebastián.

Isabela
San Antonio
Mora
2
112
Playa Crashboat
4
Aguadilla
110
CORDILLERA JAICOA
Bahía de Aguadilla
Moca
115
Aguada
111
Pta. Higüero
Playa Tres Palmas
110
Rincón
1
← TO DESECHED ISLAND
Córcega
LA CADENA SAN FRANCISCO
2
Pta. Cadena
Añasco
109
108
Mani
MONTAÑAS DE UROYAN
Estación Experimental de Agricultura Tropical
2
Mayagüez
105
Las Vegas
Bahía de Mayagüez
LAS MESAS
Joyuda
2
Hormigueros
119
102
100
114
3
San Germán
Cabo Rojo
102
Pta. Caranero
MONTE GRANDE
Lajas
Pta. Guaniquilla
103
Boquerón
101
Bahía de Boquerón
Refugio de Vida Silvestre
100
Bosque Estatal de Boquerón
Pole Ojea
← TO MONA ISLAND
Bahía Sucia
Bahía Salinas
El Combate
Cabo Rojo
0 4 mi
0 4 km

GETTING ORIENTED

The speedy Highway 22 and the more meandering Highway 2 head west from San Juan and swing around the northwestern part of the island, skirting the beaches of the northern coast. A short 45 minutes from the capital, you'll pass through the resort town of Dorado; after Arecibo, Highway 2 continues along the coast, where the ragged shoreline holds some of the island's best surfing beaches, and a steady contingent of surfers in Aguadilla and Rincón gives the area a laid-back atmosphere. Past Mayagüez, Highway 100 leads to an area known as Cabo Rojo, where you'll find seaside communities like Joyuda, Boquerón, and El Combate.

RINCÓN AND THE PORTA DEL SOL PLANNER

When to Go

Winter weather is the best and it's the height of the surfing season, so you'll need to book well in advance. Between December and February, you might get a glimpse of the humpback whales that winter off the coast. During the summer many family-oriented hotels fill up with *sanjuaneros* escaping the city for the weekend—some hotels require a two-night stay. Larger resorts normally drop their rates in summer by at least 10%. The weather gets hot, especially in August and September.

Safety

Unless you're camping in a recreational area, it's best to go to forest reserves during daylight hours only. Outside metro areas there's little crime, but you should take normal precautions: Remember to lock your car, and don't leave valuables unattended.

For Surfers: The waves in the Rincón area range from gentle, low waves suitable for novice surfers to expert-only breaks. It's a good idea to talk with other surfers about which beaches would be suitable for your skill level. *See also "Surfing" feature later in this chapter.*

Getting Here and Around

Air Travel. Aguadilla is a convenient gateway to western Puerto Rico, thanks to several daily international flights. Continental Airlines flies from Newark to Aguadilla, and JetBlue has daily service from Orlando or New York–JFK to Aguadilla. American Eagle and Cape Air fly between San Juan and Mayagüez.

Information **American Eagle** (☎ *787/749–1747* ⊕ *www.aa.com*). **Cape Air** (☎ *800/525–0280* ⊕ *www.flycapeair.com*). **Continental** (☎ *800/433–7300* ⊕ *www.continental.com*). **JetBlue** (☎ *800/538–2583* ⊕ *www.jetblue.com*).

Bus and Van Travel. No easy network of buses links the towns in the Porta del Sol region of northwestern Puerto Rico. Some municipalities and private companies operate buses and large shared vans *(públicos)* that travel from one city to another, but schedules are loose. But if you're adventurous and not easily frustrated, it's possible to arrange for cheap transportation from San Juan to Aguadilla, Rincón, and Mayagüez, among other towns. Prices from terminal to terminal are set, but drivers may go to another destination if arranged beforehand.

Choferes Unidos travels from San Juan to Aguadilla for about $10 per person. Linea Sultana has vans from San Juan to Mayagüez that also drop off passengers along Highway 2 in Aguada, Quebradillas, and Isabela; the price is about $12 per person. Línea Caborrojeña travels between San Juan and Cabo Rojo.

Information **Choferes Unidos** (☎ *787/751–7622*). **Línea Sultana** (☎ *787/765–9377*). **Línea Caborrojeña** (☎ *787/723–9155*).

Car Travel. You really need a car to see northwestern Puerto Rico, especially the mountain area. The toll road, Highway 22, makes it easy to reach Arecibo from San Juan. Highway 22 turns into Highway 2 just after Arecibo, swings by the northwestern tip of the island, then heads south to Mayagüez. *See also "Ruta Panorámica" feature later in this chapter.*

Taxi Travel. Taxis can be hailed near the main plaza in Mayagüez, but in the smaller towns they may be hard to come by. Check with your hotel or restaurant, and staff there may be able to call one for you.

About the Restaurants

If you like seafood, you're in the right place. Throughout northwestern Puerto Rico you'll find wonderful *criollo* (creole) cuisine. Most local eateries serve deep fried tapas, commonly called *pinchos* (meaning "spike"), because they are served with toothpicks. Offering a break from fried food are dozens of foreign-owned eateries that serve everything from sushi and hamburgers to vegetarian and Thai cuisine. Farther south along the coast, options are limited, so you may want to ask the chef to grill or sauté your fish. A trip to Puerto Rico is not complete without sampling *mofongo relleno*, a seafood mixture served inside a yucca crust. Simply head to where locals from all over the island go for fresh seafood—Joyuda. In Rincón, the Horned Dorset Primavera has a ten-course tasting menu served at one of the most elegant eateries in the Caribbean. When it comes to beverages, locals usually drink rum punch (rum, fruit juice, and grenadine) or Medalla Light, Puerto Rico's most popular and affordable beer. All restaurants are no-smoking. Tips, normally 15%–20%, are usually not included in the bill, but it's always wise to double-check.

About the Hotels

The western part of the island near Rincón has a variety of hotels, from furnished villas geared toward families to beachfront hotels ideal for honeymooners. Interior design leaves much to be desired, however, as most rooms are decorated with faux wood, sun-bleached photographs, floral bedding, and white linoleum flooring. Fortunately, some of the newer accommodations resemble Spanish villas, a refreshing change from the typical 1970s decor. Surprisingly, few hotels in Rincón and the Porta del Sol offer Internet access, and if they do, it is generally limited to the reception area. Smaller beach cottages, especially in Rincón, usually have "adopted" dogs or cats roaming the premises, so guests with allergies may want to inquire ahead.

WHAT IT COSTS IN U.S. DOLLARS

	¢	$	$$	$$$	$$$$
Restaurants	under $8	$8–$12	$12–$20	$20–$30	over $30
Hotels	under $80	$80–$150	$150–$250	$250–$350	over $350

Restaurant prices are per person for a main course at dinner. Hotel prices are for a double room in high season, excluding 9% tax (11% for hotels with casinos, 7% for paradores) and 5%–12% service charge.

Tour Options

The Mayagüez-based **Adven-Tours** (✉ *1102 Calle Uroyán, Mayagüez* ☎ *787/530-8311* 🌐 *www.adventourspr.com*) offers bird-watching, biking, and kayaking trips.

Visitor Information

The Puerto Rico Tourism Company has an office at the Rafael Hernández Airport in Aguadilla. The Cabo Rojo branch is open Monday through Saturday from 8 to 4:30. The town of Rincón has a tourism office on Route 115; it's open weekdays from 9 to 4. Mayagüez has a tourism office in city hall.

Information Isabela Tourism Office (☎ *787/830-1034*). **Mayagüez City Hall** (✉ *8 McKinley St., Mayagüez* ☎ *787/834-8585*). **Puerto Rico Tourism Company** (✉ *Rafael Hernández Airport, Aguadilla* ☎ *787/890-3315*). **Rincón Tourism Office** (✉ *Rte. 115, Rincón* ☎ *787/823-5024 www.rincon.org*).

6

BEACHES OF RINCÓN AND THE PUERTO DEL SOL

Tools of the trade: At nearly all the beaches in Rincón you won't have to look far to find someone with their trusty stick (surfboard) in-hand.

The waves of northwestern Puerto Rico have long served as a siren song for traveling surfers. Spared the trade winds that can limit surf in other areas, the northwest's beaches have some of the best waves in the world, especially in winter. But you don't have to be a big-wave rider to enjoy the beaches of the northwest.

The best beaches north of Rincón are lined up along Route 413 and Route 4413 (the road to the lighthouse). South of town the only beach worth noting is Playa Córcega, off Route 115. As at many other beaches in the Caribbean, there are often urchins, riptides, undertows, and rocky reefs below the surface. Know the area before you head into the water, and never swim alone.

Mayagüez isn't famous for its beaches—you'll find better stretches in Rincón, about 25 minutes north—but Balneario de Añasco, also called Tres Hermanos Beach, is 10 minutes north of town via Highway 2 and Routes 115 and 401. Dotted with palm trees, it's good for swimming and has changing facilities and restrooms.

GOLDEN MILE

Anyone interested in seafood must visit *Milla de Oro del Buen Comer,* aka the Gourmet Golden Mile. In the small fishing village of Joyuda, this string of more than 30 restaurants serves the best fish on the island. It spans from Tony's Restaurant at Km 10.9 to Parada los Flamboyanes at Km 16. The seafood here is the frehsest—caught daily from the Caribbean Sea or from Laguna Joyuda.

RINCÓN

Balneario de Rincón. Swimmers can enjoy the tranquil waters at this beach. The beautiful facility has a playground, changing areas, restrooms, and a clubhouse. It's within walking distance of the center of town. Parking is $2. ✉ *Rte. 115.*

Domes. Named for the eerie green domes on a nearby power plant, this beach is extremely popular with surfers, with its consistent rights and occasional lefts. It's also a great whale-watching spot in winter. To get here, head north on Route 4413. The beach is just north of the lighthouse. ✉ *Rte. 4413, north of the lighthouse.*

Maria's. This surf spot, south of Domes, can get crowded when the waves are high. When waves are small, surf lessons are generally taught here. It's popular with locals, as much for its breaks as for its proximity to the Calypso Café. To get here, look for the street sign reading SURFER CROSSING. ✉ *Rte. 4413, south of the lighthouse.*

Playa Córcega. The long stretch of yellow sand in front of Villa Cofresí is considered one of the best swimming beaches in Rincón. ✉ *Rte. 115, Km 12.0.*

Steps. A set of concrete steps sitting mysteriously at the water's edge gives this beach its name. The waves, breaking on a shallow reef, can get huge. It's hard to find—look for the turnoff at a whale-shaped sign indicating PLAYA ESCALERA.

✉ *Rte. 413, north of turnoff for Black Eagle Marina.*

Tres Palmas. On a handful of days each year, this epic wave is one of the world's best, drawing surfers from around the globe. On calm days, it's an excellent snorkeling spot. It is on the same road as Steps. ✉ *Rte. 413, north of turnoff for Black Eagle Marina.*

BOQUERÓN

Balneario Boquerón. The long stretch of sand at this beach off Route 101 is a favorite with islanders, especially on weekends. You'll find changing facilities, cabins, showers, restrooms, and picnic tables; it costs $3 to enter with a car. ✉ *Off Rte. 101.*

Playa Buyé. The white-sand beach has swaying palm trees and crystal clear water. There is free parking on the side of the road, and a few picnic tables. Bathrooms (although dirty) are available. ✉ *Rte. 307, north of Boquerón.*

EL COMBATE

El Combate Beach. This great beach draws college students to its rustic waterfront eateries. You can rent small boats and kayaks here, and in summer there are often concerts and festivals. ✉ *At the end of Rte. 3301.*

La Playuela. The crescent-shaped strand is the most secluded, and beautiful, of the area's beaches. It's commonly referred to as *Bahía Sucia* ("Dirty Beach") because

of the blankets of seaweed that drift to shore during winter months. The label is rather unfitting for the white sand and turquoise waters that mark the island's southwestern corner, reachable by way of a dirt road lined with mangroves. There are no amenities. ✉ *End of Rte. 301, past the vast salt flats.*

AGUADILLA

Playa Crashboat. Here you'll find the colorful fishing boats that are portrayed on postcards all over the island. The sand is soft and sugary, and the water's smooth as glass. Named after rescue boats used when Ramey Air Force Base was in operation, there are picnic huts, showers, parking, and restrooms. There's a food stand run by locals where the catch of the day is served with cold beer. ✉ *End of Rte. 458, off Rte. 107.*

ISABELA

Playa de Guajataca. Stretching by what is called El Tunel—part of an old tunnel used by a train that ran from San Juan to Ponce from the early to mid-1900s—this beach is lined with kiosks selling local snacks and souvenirs. There's live music on weekends. Just before El Tunel is El Merendero de Guajataca, a picnic area with cliffside trails. ✉ *Off Rte. 113.*

Playa de Jobos. This beach is famous for surfing. On the same stretch there are a couple of restaurants with oceanfront decks. Down the road, the dunes and long stretches of golden sand are gorgeous for walks or running. Route 466 runs parallel, and there are narrow accesses to the beach along the road. ✉ *Rte. 466.*

Playa Montones. Not far from Playa de Jobos, this is a beautiful beach for swimming; it has a protected natural pool perfect for children. ✉ *Rte. 466.*

Playa de Shacks. Known for its surfing and horseback riding, this spot has an area called the Blue Hole that's popular with divers. ✉ *Rte. 4446*

Updated by Marlise Kast

The "Gateway to the Sun" is how tourism officials describe the island's western coast. Although the name calls to mind well-developed, well-traveled vacations spots like Spain's Costa de Sol, the Porta del Sol is neither. Unlike the area around San Juan, the Porta del Sol is relatively undiscovered. Even around Rincón, which has the lion's share of the lodgings, the beaches are delightfully deserted. And in places like Aguadilla and Isabela, two sleepy towns on the northwestern corner of the island, it's easy to find a stretch of shoreline all to yourself.

Adventurers since the time of Christopher Columbus have been drawn to the jagged coastline of northwestern Puerto Rico. Columbus made his first stop here on his second voyage to the Americas in 1493. His exact landing point is the subject of ongoing dispute: Both Aguadilla, on the northernmost tip of the coast, and Aguada, just south of Aguadilla, claim the historic landing, and both have monuments honoring the explorer.

Less than a century ago, western Puerto Rico was still overwhelmingly rural. Some large fruit plantations dotted the coast, while farther inland, coffee was grown on hillside *fincas* (farms). The slow pace of rural life began to change during the mid-20th century. New roads brought development to the once-isolated towns. They also brought international surfers, who were amazed to find some of the world's best waves in Rincón, Isabela, and Aguadilla. Now there are top-notch hotels, interesting natural areas to explore, and almost every kind of water sport imaginable.

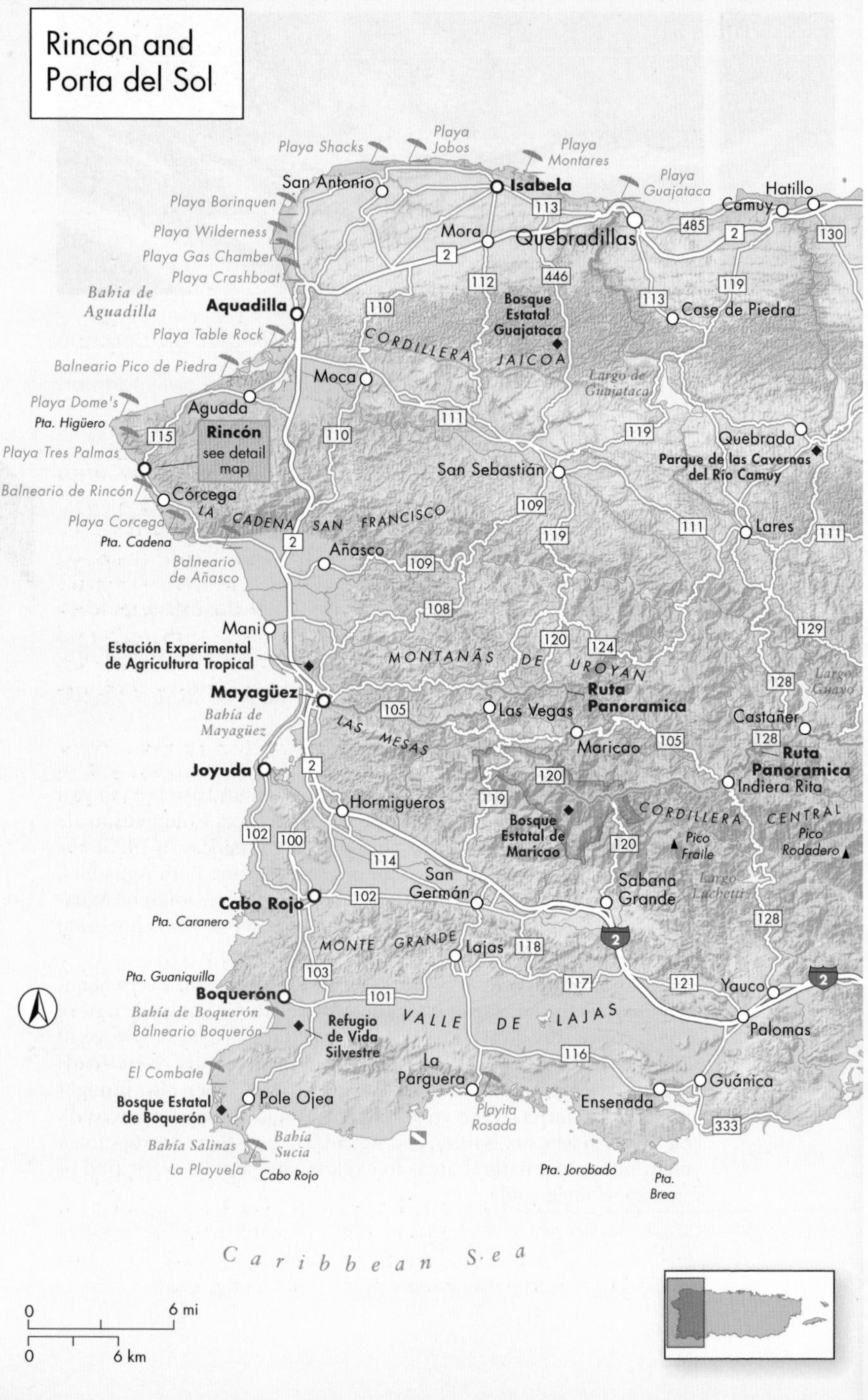

Rincón and Porta del Sol

Playa Shacks
Playa Jobos
Playa Montares
Playa Guajataca
San Antonio
Isabela
Hatillo
Camuy
Playa Borinquen
Playa Wilderness
Playa Gas Chamber
Playa Crashboat
Mora
Quebradillas
Bahía de Aguadilla
Aquadilla
Playa Table Rock
Balneario Pico de Piedra
Playa Dome's
Pta. Higüero
Playa Tres Palmas
Balneario de Rincón
Playa Corcega
Pta. Cadena
Aguada
Rincón see detail map
Córcega
Moca
CORDILLERA JAICOA
Bosque Estatal Guajataca
Largo de Guajataca
Case de Piedra
Quebrada
Parque de las Cavernas del Río Camuy
San Sebastián
LA CADENA SAN FRANCISCO
Balneario de Añasco
Añasco
Lares
Mani
Estación Experimental de Agricultura Tropical
MONTANÃS DE UROYAN
Mayagüez
Bahía de Mayagüez
LAS MESAS
Las Vegas
Ruta Panoramica
Maricao
Castañer
Largo Guayo
Ruta Panoramica
Indiera Rita
Joyuda
Hormigueros
Bosque Estatal de Maricao
CORDILLERA CENTRAL
Pico Fraile
Pico Rodadero
Largo Luchetti
Cabo Rojo
Pta. Caranero
San Germán
Sabana Grande
MONTE GRANDE
Lajas
Pta. Guaniquilla
Boquerón
Bahía de Boquerón
Balneario Boquerón
Refugio de Vida Silvestre
VALLE DE LAJAS
Yauco
Palomas
El Combate
Bosque Estatal de Boquerón
Pole Ojea
La Parguera
Playita Rosada
Ensenada
Guánica
Bahía Salinas
Bahía Sucia
La Playuela
Cabo Rojo
Pta. Jorobado
Pta. Brea

Caribbean Sea

113 485 2 130 112 446 119 110 113 111 119 110 115 109 111 111 119 2 109 108 129 120 124 128 105 105 128 2 120 119 102 100 114 120 102 128 118 103 117 121 101 116 333 2

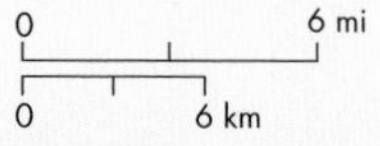

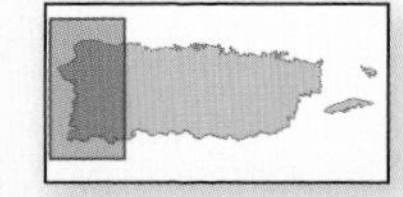

RINCÓN

93 mi (150 km) southwest of San Juan.

Jutting out into the ocean along the rugged western coast, Rincón, meaning "corner" in Spanish, may have gotten its name because it's tucked into a bend of the coastline. Some, however, trace the town's name to Gonzalo Rincón, a 16th-century landowner who let poor families live on his land. Whatever the history, the name suits the town, which is like a little world unto itself.

WORD OF MOUTH

"Rincón is great for all ages. There is a tendency for the younger crowd to stay in the Puntas area, where there are many great beach bars with music and party. Consider the Corcega or Barerro area or just do a seach on Google for "Rincon Puerto Rico Beachfront villas." -luizortiz

The most famous hotel in the region is the Horned Dorset Primavera—the only Relais & Chateaux property in Puerto Rico. It's one of the most luxurious resorts on the island, not to mention in the Caribbean. A couple of larger hotels, including the Rincón of the Seas and Rincón Beach Resort, have been built, but Rincón remains a laid-back place. The town is still a mecca for wave-seekers, particularly surfers from the East Coast of the United States, who often prefer the relatively quick flight to Aguadilla airport direct from New York–area airports instead of the long haul to the Pacific. The town continues to cater to all sorts of travelers, from budget-conscious surfers to families to honeymooners seeking romance.

The pace picks up from October through April, when the waves are the best, but tourists can be found here year-round, and many American mainlanders have settled here. Budget travelers will most likely find discount accommodations during August and September, when tourism is slow. Hurricane season runs from June through November, bringing in occasional swells for the surf crowd.

GETTING HERE AND AROUND

Rincón itself is a spread-out labyrinth of unmarked streets without any apparent logic to its layout. Built on a hillside, most streets are narrow and steep, weaving erratically through the intermingled residential-business zones. There are three main routes to keep in mind; Route 115 cuts through the middle of "downtown" (the administrative center) and connects north to Aguadilla airport and south to Mayagüez airport. Route 413 snakes the hillsides, past villas and local restaurants. The smaller Route 4413 parallels the water, past Punta Higüeras Lighthouse, and ends at the Bonus Thermonuclear Energy Plant.

Air Travel. San Juan's International Airport is the most commonly used on the island and is approximately two hours from Rincón. The closest airports however, are in Mayagüez and in Aguadilla, only 20 minutes' drive in either direction. A taxi from either airport into town costs around $10, but the best option is to rent a car at the airport.

Bus and Van Travel. Amigos Tours & Travel has private transfers from Aguadilla's airport to Rincón and to most hotels in the Porta del Sol for $80 per van (limit five passengers).**Amigos Tours & Travel** (✉ *Carr. 1, AB1, Anasco* ☎ *787/826–6418 or 787/360–9398* 🌐 *www.amigospuertorico.com*).

Car Travel. To reach Rincón from San Juan, take Highway 22, which becomes Highway 2 after Arecibo. Follow it past the northwestern tip of the island, just beyond Aguadilla. Take the 115 southwest past Aguada until you reach Rincón's Route 413, "The Road to Happiness."

TIMING

With a land area of 14 square mi (36 square km), Rincón is easily traversable in an afternoon. However, to fully embrace its laid-back surfer vibe, you'll want to allocate three to five days for surfing, diving, fishing, or just relaxing at the beach.

EXPLORING RINCÓN

Surrounding the Punta Higuera Lighthouse, **Parque Pasivo El Faro** has small kiosks at the water's edge with telescopes you can use to look for whales. (Have patience, though, even during the "season," from December through February; it could take days to spot one.) You can also glimpse the rusting mint-colored dome of the defunct Bonus Thermonuclear Energy Plant from here; it has been closed since 1974. The park—complete with benches, a shop, and a refreshment stand—is a nice place to take in sunsets. The lighthouse is closed to the public, but it's hard to walk away without taking a photo of the stately white structure. ✉ *End of Calle 4413, off Rte. 413* 🎟 *Free* ⏲ *Daily 8 AM–midnight.*

★ For divers, **Desecheo Island,** about 13 mi (20 km) off the coast of Rincón, has abundant reef and fish life. Protected by the U.S. Fish and Wildlife Service, this uninhabited island is home to lizards, rats, and Rhesus monkeys, first introduced in 1967 from Cayo Santiago. In 2008, the monkey population was significantly decreased in an effort to restore the endangered nesting colony of the brown booby. The main draw here is "Candy Cane Lane," a rocky bottom sloping to 120 feet that rims the island. Here, long tunnels and caverns covered with purple hydrocoral distinguish one formation known as Yellow Reef. With visibility of 150 feet, this is also a popular snorkeling spot. There are other sites with plentiful fish and coral in the more shallow water just off Rincón's shores.

OFF THE BEATEN PATH

About 45 minutes east of Rincón, just north of San Sebastian, are the hidden waterfalls of **El Charco de la Leche** (The Pool of Milk). Though difficult to find, these tiered swimming holes are worth the effort it takes to get there. The first of three is generally visited by locals, but a five-minute hike upstream will bring you to a second cascade, where the waters are deep enough for diving. A crude rope swing entices adventurers to mimic Tarzan's antics before plunging into the cool spring. Follow the trail about ½ mi (1 km) farther to reach yet a third oasis. Avoid this area during rainy season, when torrents can quickly cause dangerous flashfloods. ✥ *From Rincón, take Rte. 115 northeast to Rte. 111 east. Near San Sebastian, take the 446 north (left at the gas station) and continue* ½ mi (1 km). *Turn right over the bridge and drive 1 mi (2 km) up hill until you see a white house. Park in the dirt area to the left of the house, across from*

Looking down at Domes Beach from Punta Higuero Lighthouse in El Faro Park.

a row of mailboxes labeled "10813." The trailhead drops down from this point to join a dirt road. Continue on foot past a tin shack beside a murky pond until you reach the river.

WHERE TO EAT

In addition to the restaurants recommended below, the Villa Confresí and the Lazy Parrot hotels also have good restaurants serving fresh seafood.

Use the coordinate (✣ A1) at the end of each listing to locate a site on the corresponding "Where to Eat and Stay in Rincon" map.

¢ CAFE ✕ **Banana Dang.** "Think, Drink, Link" is the motto of this Internet café, where you can check e-mails while drinking one of the specialty coffees. The fruit smoothies are a local favorite, as are the light breakfasts of Eggspresso Paninis and bagels with cream cheese. ✉ *Rte. 413, Km 4.1, Rincón* ☎ *787/823–0963* 🌐 *www.bananadang.com* ▭ *MC, V* ⊗ *Closed Tues.* ✣ *B2*

$ CAFE ✕ **The English Rose.** Specializing in breakfasts only, this quaint bed-and-breakfast is perched above Rincón with a spectacular view of the valley spilling into the sea. House specialties such as the Portabella Stack and the eggs Benedict are served with homemade breads and sausages. If seating is not available on the terrace, inside dining is equally charming with the walls colorfully decorated with the work of local artisans. Adding to the freshness of the dishes are the herbs grown on-site. During high season, you may wait up to an hour for a table, but it's worth every minute.

GREAT ITINERARIES

IF YOU HAVE 1 DAY

If you have only a day to spend in the Porta del Sol, make the drive to **Joyuda** for some of Puerto Rico's freshest seafood. You probably won't be the only ones driving from San Juan for this feast.

IF YOU HAVE 3 DAYS

If you have a few days to explore the region, start in **Rincón,** where you'll find accommodations for every taste, from compact inns to sprawling resorts. There isn't too much to see, other than the lighthouse at Parque Pasivo El Faro, but you will see plenty of beautiful beaches. Most have been discovered, however. If you crave complete solitude, you're more likely to find empty beaches in the communities of **Aguadilla** or **Isabela.** On Day 2 drive south to the coastal communities in the Cabo Rojo. Your first stop should be **Joyuda,** where you can choose from dozens of seaside restaurants. After lunch, continue past **Boquerón** to **El Combate.** This is the end of the line, quite literally. The road ends at the lighthouse that once warned sea captains about the treacherous waters around the island's southwestern tip. On Day 3 you can explore more of this windswept landscape, or head offshore for a look at Mona Island.

IF YOU HAVE 5 DAYS

After spending three days along the western coast, you may be tempted to set sail to one of the islands off the coast. On Day 4, head out on an overnight trip to **Mona Island,** a 14,000-acre paradise known as the "Galápagos of the Caribbean." You'll have to camp on this deserted island, but the view from the 200-foot cliffs on the northern shore makes it all worth it.

✉ *Carr. 413 interior, Km 2.0, Barrio Ensenada* ☎ *787/823–4032* 🌐 *www.larosainglesa.com* 💳 *MC, V* ⏲ *Closed Mon.–Wed. in May–Oct.* ✥ *B2*

$ Fodor's Choice ★ JAPANESE

✕ **The Pool Bar Sushi.** The only sushi restaurant on the west coast, the open-air Pool Bar attracts visitors from as far away as San Juan. The menu rivals that of any high-end Japanese restaurant, offering mango tuna rolls, eel maki, dim sum, and wakame seaweed salads. A house favorite is the Starving Surfer Roll of crunchy shrimp and avocado topped with spicy tuna. The relaxed setting is especially popular with surfers drawn by the nightly surf flicks projected on the movie-screen backdrop. Arrive early on Thursday nights to enjoy live jazz. ✉ *Rte. 413 interior, at Pools Beach, Rincón* ☎ *787/823–2583* 💳 *MC, V* ⏲ *Closed Tues.* ✥ *A1*

$$$$ Fodor's Choice ★ CARIBBEAN

✕ **Restaurant Aaron at the Horned Dorset Primavera.** People come here from all over the island for a meal prepared by chef Aaron Wratten. A pair of stone stairways leads up to the elegant dining room, with black-and-white marble floors, chandeliers with ruby-red shades, and a Steinway piano dating back to 1901. Dessert and after-dinner drinks are often served on the terrace, where you'll hear the constant crash of the waves. The 10-course tasting menu, an extravagant meal with a $110 price tag, might include foie gras with caramelized pear, pan-seared scallops with asparagus risotto, or roasted grouper with pumpkin puree. Adding Caribbean accents to classical French cuisine, the à la carte menu includes roasted rack of lamb and wahoo in a pistachio crust. Dress is formal by island standards, except in the downstairs dining area, where the same menu is served. ✉ *Rte. 429, Km 3, Box 1132, Rincón* ☎ *787/823–4030* 🌐 *www.horneddorset.com* ⚠ *Reservations essential* ▭ *AE, MC, V.* ✥ *C6*

$–$$ CARIBBEAN ✕ **Rincón Tropical.** Don't be scared off by the cheap plastic tables and chairs. What you should notice is that they are almost always full of locals enjoying the area's freshest seafood. The kitchen keeps it simple, preparing dishes with the lightest touch. Highlights include mahimahi with onions and peppers as well as fried red snapper with beans and rice. Fried plantains make a nice accompaniment to almost anything. ✉ *Rte. 115, Km 12, Rincón* ☎ *787/823–2017* 🌐 *www.rinconpr.com/rincontropical* ▭ *AE, MC, V.* ✥ *B4*

$$$ CARIBBEAN ✕ **Shipwreck Bar & Grill.** This pirate-theme restaurant has been voted the most popular eatery in town, and it's easy to see why. It has a laid-back vibe and a friendly staff that's always ready with a smile or a joke. Don't be surprised to see local fishermen making their way to the kitchen with their still-flapping catch, attesting to the freshness of the food. Look for four specials a night, as well as their most requested dishes, such as juicy steaks, grilled mahimahi, homemade pastas, and skewered pork. Although portions are enormous, lighter-fare options include various wraps and seared ahi served on a pyramid of mixed greens. Don't miss the Sunday-afternoon pig roast, available November through April. ✉ *Black Eagle Marina, Black Eagle Rd., off Rte. 413, Rincón* ☎ *787/823–0578* 🌐 *www.rinconspipwreck.com* ▭ *MC, V.* ✥ *B3*

6

$–$$$ CARIBBEAN ✕ **Smilin' Joe's.** This open-air terrace restaurant highlights the impossibly lush greenery that draws so many people to Rincón. The second floor of the Lazy Parrot, it catches a breeze even when the rest of the island is stifling in the heat. It's a convenient stop for lunch if you're on your way to or from the beach. The wonderful wraps are filled with chicken cutlet and garlic-lime sauce or mahimahi and cilantro sour cream. For dinner there are tropical entrées like sesame-ginger steak and pineapple-coconut shrimp. There's also a surprisingly large wine list. This is one of the few places in Rincón with a children's menu. ✉ *The Lazy Parrot, Rte. 413, Km 4.1, Rincón* ☎ *787/823–0101 or 787/823–0103* 🌐 *www.smilinjoes.net/* ▭ *AE, MC, V.* ⊙ *Closed May–Oct.* ✥ *B2*

$$$ CARIBBEAN ✕ **The Spot.** Tiki torches, smooth jazz, and the sound of crashing waves set the scene at this casual waterfront restaurant. Chef Mike Hocko puts a twist on Caribbean cuisine by blending tropical fare with gourmet recipes, such as basil-wrapped shrimp and yellowtail nuggets. The coconut-glazed pork, served with asparagus and sweet potatoes, is very flavorful. Depending on what is in season, the menu changes weekly but will always feature fish, chicken, ribs, and steak. Be sure to arrive in time to watch the surfers catch those final waves at sunset. ✉ *Carr. 413, Km 1.0, Black Eagle Rd., Rincón* ☎ *787/823–3510* ▭ *AE, MC, V.* ✥ *B3*

$–$$ CARIBBEAN ✕ **Tamboo.** Here is a bar and grill that doesn't fall too much into either category. The kitchen prepares any number of unique items, from king-crab sandwiches to baby-back ribs brushed with mango glaze. Despite the laid-back atmosphere, the food presentation is fit for a high-end

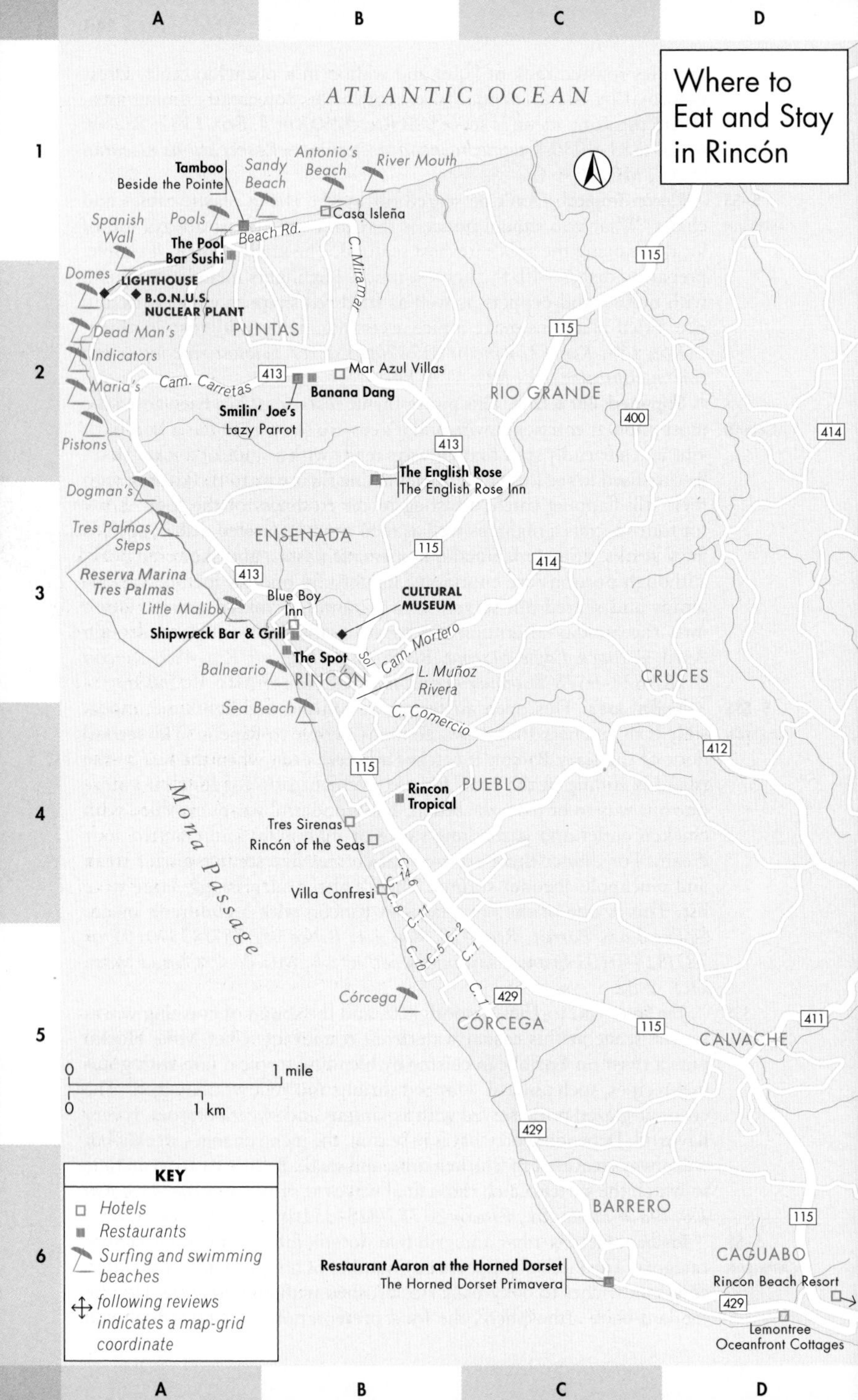
Where to Eat and Stay in Rincón
ATLANTIC OCEAN
Mona Passage
Tamboo
Beside the Pointe
Sandy Beach
Antonio's Beach
River Mouth
Casa Isleña
Spanish Wall
Pools
Beach Rd.
The Pool Bar Sushi
C. Miramar
Domes
LIGHTHOUSE
B.O.N.U.S. NUCLEAR PLANT
PUNTAS
Dead Man's
Indicators
Maria's
Pistons
Cam. Carretas
Mar Azul Villas
Banana Dang
Smilin' Joe's
Lazy Parrot
RIO GRANDE
The English Rose
The English Rose Inn
Dogman's
Tres Palmas/Steps
Reserva Marina Tres Palmas
ENSENADA
Little Malibu
Blue Boy Inn
CULTURAL MUSEUM
Shipwreck Bar & Grill
The Spot
Balneario
RINCÓN
Sol
Cam. Mortero
L. Muñoz Rivera
CRUCES
Sea Beach
C. Comercio
PUEBLO
Rincon Tropical
Tres Sirenas
Rincón of the Seas
Villa Confresi
C. 14
C. 6
C. 8
C. 11
C. 2
C. 5
C. 10
C. 1
Córcega
CÓRCEGA
CALVACHE
BARRERO
CAGUABO
Restaurant Aaron at the Horned Dorset
The Horned Dorset Primavera
Rincon Beach Resort
Lemontree Oceanfront Cottages
115
413
400
414
412
429
411
0
1 mile
0
1 km
KEY
Hotels
Restaurants
Surfing and swimming beaches
following reviews indicates a map-grid coordinate
A
B
C
D
1
2
3
4
5
6

restaurant. The bar, also open to the elements, serves a mean mojito. Happy hour sometimes starts dangerously early—at 10 AM on Saturday. The deck is a great place to watch the novice surfers wipe out on the nearby beach. On weekends, live music is back-dropped by a slide-show of local surfers. ✉ *Beside the Point, Rte. 413, Km 4.4, Rincón* ☎ *787/823–8550* 🌐 *www.besidethepointe.com* 💳 *MC, V.* ✥ *A1*

WHERE TO STAY

Use the coordinate (✥ A1) at the end of each listing to locate a site on the corresponding "Where to Eat and Stay in Rincon" map.

$–$$ HOTEL **Beside the Pointe.** This perennial favorite sits right on Sandy Beach, where the waves are big but not too large for novice surfers. Neutral-tone rooms—ranging from studios to two-bedroom apartments with full kitchens—have gorgeous furnishings and brilliant views. Second-level rooms have private balconies, while all others share a communal sun-deck. Room 8 has the best view, but all guests can enjoy similar scenery from the popular waterfront bar and grill, Tamboo. Sometimes you can spot a whale from the sun deck. **Pros:** Social atmosphere; popular restaurant; great views. **Cons:** Noise from restaurant; not all rooms have ocean views; no elevator. ✉ *Rte. 413, Km 4.4, Rincón* ☎ *787/823–8550* 🌐 *www.besidethepointe.com* *7 rooms, 2 apartments* *In-room: kitchen (some), refrigerator, no phones. In-hotel: restaurant, bar, laundry facilities, public Wi-Fi* 💳 *MC, V* *EP.* ✥ *A1*

$$ INN ★ **Blue Boy Inn.** A walled garden that surrounds this little inn makes you think you're miles away from civilization. The Blue Boy Inn, however, is within walking distance of several bars and restaurants. The rooms come with flat-screen TVs and are individually decorated in a style that might be called "tropical elegant," with dark-wood sleigh beds. The pool area—with an outdoor kitchen and fire pit—is wonderful, especially at night, when it's lit with the inn's trademark blue. A delicious breakfast of French crepes, fruit, and cheeses is included in the rate. **Pros:** Gorgeous gardens; pretty pool; lots of privacy. **Cons:** Not on beach; some noise from nearby restaurant. ✉ *556 Black Eagle Rd., off Rte. 413, Rincón* ☎ *787/823–2593* 🌐 *www.blueboyinn.com* *8 rooms* *In-room: Wi-Fi, kitchenette (some), refrigerator. In-hotel: pool, laundry facilities, public Wi-Fi* 💳 *MC, V* *BP.* ✥ *B3*

$–$$ INN **Casa Isleña.** With its barrel-tiled roofs, wall-enclosed gardens, and open-air dining room, Casa Isleña might remind well-traveled souls of a villa on the coast of Mexico. The secret of its charm is that this little inn retains a simplicity without compromising the romantic flavor of its setting. Several of the terra-cotta-floored rooms have balconies overlooking the pool and the palm-shaded stretch of beach. Others have terraces facing the courtyard. There's also a hot tub and an indoor patio with a soothing, burbling fountain. If it's booked solid—which happens frequently during high season—there's a second building a few minutes away. **Pros:** Secluded setting; beautiful beach; eye-catching architecture. **Cons:** Restaurant closed May through October; books up quickly; management seldom on-site. ✉ *Rte. 413, Km 4.8, Barrio Puntas* ☎ *787/823–1525 or 888/289–7750* 🌐 *www.casa-islena.com* *9 rooms* *In-room:*

6

Fodor's Choice ★

Tres Sirenas

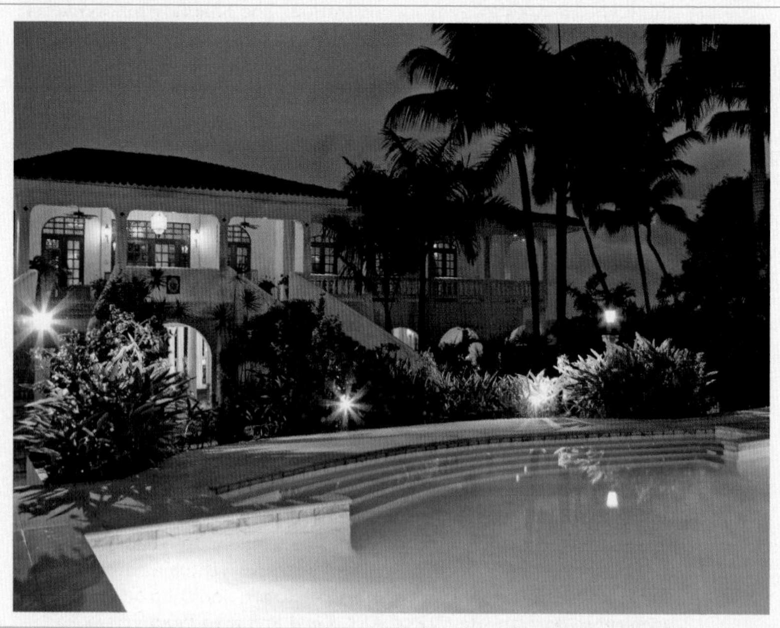

Horned Dorset Primavera

refrigerator, no phone. In-hotel: restaurant, bar, pool, beachfront, public Wi-Fi, parking (no fee) ☰ *MC, V* 🍽 *EP.* ⊕ *B1*

$$$$ **RESORT** **Fodor's Choice** ★ **Horned Dorset Primavera.** This is, without a doubt, the most luxurious hotel in Puerto Rico. The 40 whitewashed villas scattered throughout the tropical gardens are designed so you have complete privacy whether you are relaxing in your private plunge pool or admiring the sunset from one of your balconies. The furnishings in each of the two-story suites are impeccable, from the hand-carved mahogany table in the downstairs dining room to the four-poster beds in the upstairs bedroom. The marble bathroom has a footed porcelain tub that's big enough for two. (There's a second bath downstairs that's perfect for rinsing off after a walk on the beach.) Breakfast is served in your room, and lunch is available on a terrace overlooking the ocean. Dinner in the elegant restaurant is included in the rate. A place to unplug from the rest of the world, the hotel has no radios or televisions and does not allow children younger than 12. **Pros:** Unabashed luxury; unmatched meals; lovely setting. **Cons:** On a very slender beach; staff is sometimes haughty; morning light floods through small shadeless windows near the ceiling. ✉ *Rte. 429, Km 3, Box 1132, Rincón* ☎ *787/823–4030 or 800/633–1857* 🌐 *www.horneddorset.com* *22 villas* *In-room: safe, kitchen, no TV. In-hotel: 2 restaurants, bar, pools, gym, beachfront, no kids under 12* ☰ *AE, MC, V* 🍽 *MAP.* ⊕ *C6*

$–$$ **HOTEL** **Lazy Parrot.** Painted in eye-popping tropical hues, this mountainside hotel doesn't take itself too seriously. Colorful murals of the eponymous bird brighten the open, airy lobby. The accommodations are a bit more subdued, though they continue the tropical theme. Several have colorful fish swimming across the walls, and the family-theme Dolphin Room has—what else?—a stuffed dolphin. Most rooms have a balcony, but if you want to enjoy the view, ask for a room upstairs (do note that there is not an elevator). Smilin' Joe's restaurant serves excellent seafood dishes, and the Rum Shack offers refreshing poolside cocktails. You can browse through the "parrotphernalia" at the small gift shop. **Pros:** Whimsical design; lush setting; friendly staff. **Cons:** Not on the beach; stairs to climb. ✉ *Rte. 413, Km 4.1 Rincón* ☎ *787/823–5654 or 800/294–1752* 🌐 *www.lazyparrot.com* *21 rooms* *In-room: refrigerator, Wi-Fi. In-hotel: 2 restaurants, bars, pool, laundry service, public Wi-Fi* ☰ *AE, D, MC, V* 🍽 *CP.* ⊕ *B2*

$–$$ **HOTEL** **Lemontree Oceanfront Cottages.** Sitting right on the beach, this pair of lemon-yellow buildings holds six apartments named after such fruits as Mango, Cocoa, Banana, and Piña. Choose from one three-bedroom unit, one two-bedroom unit, two one-bedroom units, or two studios. No matter which one you pick, each sleek option has a full kitchen, dining area, small library, and private balcony with views of the coastline. Ted and Jane Davis, who bought the place in 2004, have added uncommon amenities for this price range, such as plasma televisions, DVD players, and free Wi-Fi. The most requested room is Banana, which has a hot tub for two. This is one of the few gay-friendly places in Rincón. **Pros:** Far from the crowds; on-call massage therapist; spacious balconies. **Cons:** Beach is very narrow; must drive to shops and restaurants; no elevator. ✉ *Rte. 429, Km 4.1, Box 200, Rincón* ☎ *787/823–6452* www.lemontreepr.com 6 apartments In-room: kitchen, DVD, Wi-Fi. In-hotel: beachfront, public Wi-Fi MC, V EP. D6

$ VACATION VILLAS **Mar Azul Villas.** Set in a tropical garden behind Mar Azul Surf Shop, these charming villas have all the comforts of home. Each is stark white and comes with a plasma TV, kitchenette, and sitting and dining areas, queen-size bed, and an extra roll-away for children. Private verandas overlook a manicured lawn where you can grill the day's catch or pick mangos and star fruit from the garden. Beach towels, chairs, and umbrellas are included in the rate, and a 50% discount is available on surfboard rentals. The second-floor villa is one of the best places in Rincón to watch the sunset. **Pros:** Spotless rooms; friendly owners; walking distance to restaurants. **Cons:** Limited ocean view; foot traffic from attached surf shop. *Carr. 413, Km 4.4, Rincón 787/214–7224 or 787/823–5692 www.puertoricosurfinginfo.com 2 villas In-room: no phone, kitchenette, refrigerator, Wi-Fi. In-hotel: laundry facilities, parking (free), no-smoking rooms MC, V EP. B2*

$$–$$$ RESORT **Rincón Beach Resort.** It's a bit off the beaten path, but that's part of the allure of this oceanfront resort. The South Seas–style decor begins in the high-ceilinged lobby, where patio chairs invite you to enjoy the view through the almond trees. The rooms continue the theme with rich blue fabrics and dark-wood furnishings. A variety of activities are available, including whale and turtle watching in season. At the end of the infinity pool, a boardwalk leads down to the sand. Unlike the waters at many of the beaches just a few miles north, the waters here are calm—not great for surfing, but perfect for a dip if you're staying here. The resort is tucked away in Añasco, about halfway between Rincón to the north and Mayagüez to the south. **Pros:** Beautiful setting; gorgeous pool area; laid-back vibe. **Cons:** Far from dining options; lacks a Puerto Rican flavor; decor is slightly dated; halls echo. *Rte. 115, Km 5.8, Añasco 787/589–9000 www.rinconbeach.com 112 rooms In-room: safe, kitchen (some), refrigerator, Internet In-hotel: restaurant, room service, bars, pool, gym, beachfront, public Wi-Fi, diving, water sports, laundry service, parking (no fee) AE, MC, V EP. D6*

$$–$$$ HOTEL **Rincón of the Seas.** Tucked at the end of a palm-lined drive, this high-rise hotel feels like it could be in Miami Beach. The gentle curve of the facade and the elegant railings on the balconies give it a vaguely Art Deco feel. (The marble lobby and some of the suites echo this with streamlined furnishings from India.) Of course, the free-form pool has a swim-up bar where you can order drinks with umbrellas. The open-air lobby takes full advantage of the lush foliage in the courtyard, and there is an added botanical garden with a playground for children. A U-shaped design gives every room a wall of windows facing the beach. **Pros:** Lush gardens; gorgeous pool area; on-site babysitting service. **Cons:** On a slender beach; loud music blares from pool area all day. *Rte. 115, Km 12.2, Rincón 787/823–7500 www.rinconoftheseas.com 112 rooms In-room: safe, Inernet. In-hotel: 2 restaurants, room service, bars, gym, pool, beachfront, public Internet, parking (no fee) AE, MC, V EP. B4*

$–$$ BED AND BREAKFAST ★ **The English Rose Inn.** Nestled in the hills of Rincón, this bed-and-breakfast has some of the best views of the Caribbean ocean. The owners, ex-pats from Great Britain, authenticate the English charm enhanced by the pale blue exterior with white plantation shutters. Though varying in size—with accommodations sleeping anywhere from two to six guests––each suite comes with a fully equipped kitchen. The stunning pool, private garden, and extensive movie library make the five-minute drive into town of little consequence. **Pros:** Excellent breakfast; peaceful setting; hospitable owners. **Cons:** Somewhat isolated; no beach; restaurant serves breakfast only. ✉ *Carr. 413 interior, Km 2.0, Barrio Ensenada Rincón* ☎ *787/823–4032* 🌐 *www.larosainglesa.com* *3 apartments* *In-room: no phone, kitchen, refrigerator, DVD, Wi-Fi. In-hotel: restaurant, pool, laundry service, Wi-Fi, parking (free), no-smoking rooms* ▭ *MC, V* *BP.* ✥ *B2*

$$–$$$ INN Fodor's Choice ★ **Tres Sirenas.** Waves gently lap against the shores at this boutique inn named "Three Mermaids" in honor of the owners' daughters. An affordable alternative to the extravagant Horned Dorset, this luxurious two-story villa houses two oceanfront rooms, one pool studio, and one sea-view apartment with a loft. The terra-cotta-tiled rooms are tastefully decorated with teak furniture, chenille coverlets, and fresh flowers cradled in conch shells. Homestyle breakfasts are served promptly at 9 with fare ranging from berry-strewn French toast to sun-dried tomato quiche. The owner can also arrange a candlelit dinner on the beach upon request. **Pros:** In-room massages available; discounted low-season rates; May through October; resident owner. **Cons:** Usually booked; set breakfast hour. ✉ *26 Seabeach Dr., Rincón* ☎ *787/823–0558* 🌐 *www.tressirenas.com* *2 rooms, 1 studio, 1 apartment* *In-room: no phone, kitchen, refrigerator, DVD, Wi-Fi (some). In-hotel: pool, beachfront, water sports, laundry facilities, laundry service, Internet terminal, Wi-Fi, parking (free), some pets allowed, no-smoking rooms* ▭ *MC, V* *BP.* ✥ *B4*

$ HOTEL **Villa Cofresí.** Situated on one of the best swimming beaches in town, Villa Cofresí is Rincón's oldest hotel, making it extremely popular with Puerto Rican families. Parents can keep an eye on the kids while they enjoy the famed "El Pirata" (rum and crème de cacao) at the beachfront bar. The guest rooms are more spacious than most, especially those that have kitchenettes. Rooms on the second floor are preferable, as those surrounding the pool can get a bit noisy; second-floor rooms have better views, too. The restaurant, La Ana De Confresi, serves excellent red snapper and Angus beef. The hotel can arrange a host of water sports. **Pros:** Good on-site restaurant; family-friendly environment. **Cons:** Standard rooms lack ocean views; not enough parking; lots of noise from pool area. ✉ *Rte. 115, Km 12.0, Rincón* ☎ *787/823–2450* 🌐 *www.villacofresi.com* *51 rooms* *In-room: kitchen (some), refrigerator, Wi-Fi. In-hotel: restaurant, bar, pool, beachfront, public Wi-Fi* ▭ *AE, D, MC, V* *CP.* ✥ *B4*

VILLA RENTALS

Villa rentals are becoming more and more popular in Rincón. Because many people come here for a week or more to surf, find a secluded spot on the beach, or just hang out, renting a villa makes perfect sense. Guests can make the place their own, without worrying about the noise from the kids bothering the people in the next room or leaving sandy shoes outside the door. In the long run, it might also be a money saver for those who cook at home rather than dining out. There are several local chefs who will prepare gourmet dinners for large groups in private villas.

A few things to keep in mind: If you're looking for a secluded location, you won't find it on this crowded part of the coast. It's likely that your neighbor will be within shouting distance. In addition, few villas are actually on the ocean, and the ones that are go for a premium price. Many are within walking distance of the water, but some will require that you drive to reach the shore. If a beachfront location is important to you, make sure to specify. And where you stay will depend on whether or not you're a surfer. Those who like to ride the waves favor the northern coast, while those who want to snorkel, scuba dive, or swim prefer the calmer southern shore.

Island West Properties & Beach Rentals (✉ *Rte. 413, Km 0.7, Box 700, Rincón* ☎ *787/823–2323* 🌐 *www.islandwestrentals.com*) can help you rent villas in Rincón by the day, week, or month. The company has been around for years, so it corners the market.

$$$ **Caribbean Paradise.** This two-story house would be great for two families traveling together, as each floor has plenty of room and there is a fenced yard where children can play. There are two bedrooms and two bathrooms upstairs, and two bedrooms and one bathroom downstairs. A spacious dining area is off the full kitchen, but most people prefer taking their meals at the table on the upstairs balcony. From here you can scan the horizon for passing whales (very easy to see from this part of the coast). There's no pool, but just beyond the picket fence is Corsega Beach, one of the area's best swimming beaches. You can cook dinner in the kitchen or outside on the gas grill, or let someone else do the cooking by taking advantage of one of the hotel restaurants down the beach. ✉ *Calle 8, Corsega Beach* ☎ *787/823–2323* 🌐 *www.islandwestrentals.com* *4 rooms, 3 baths* *In-hotel: beachfront, laundry facilities, DVD, kitchen, TV, a/c.* *D, MC, V.*

$$ **Grande Complex.** Located across from Sandy Beach, this small complex includes a two-story house, two pool villas, and two studios. The joint properties sleep up to 24 people, making this one of the area's more affordable options. Bedrooms in the main house have French doors leading out to a pair of wide terraces, where you can catch a glimpse of the ocean above the palm trees. The villas are not on the beach, but you can walk there in a few minutes. Full-size appliances in the kitchens and an outdoor grill make it easy to cook for a crowd, and a couple of restaurants are within walking distance. The complex is in Puntas, on the northern shore. ✉ *Rte. 413, Puntas* ☎ *787/823–2323* 🌐 *www.islandwestrentals.com* *10 bedrooms, 6 baths* *In-hotel: pool, DVD, laundry facilities TV, a/c, kitchen* *D, MC, V.*

$$$$ **Villa Tres Palmas.** Not all beach houses are created equal, as Villas Tres Palmas makes clear. The hand-hewn columns and railings on this gorgeous three-story house might make you think you're in the South Seas. The exotic decor continues inside, where wooden headboards and other furnishings are carved with intricate patterns. The enormous house has

five bathrooms and six bedrooms that look out toward the tropical gardens surrounding the kidney-shaped pool. Beyond the pool, at the foot of the property, is the palm-lined beach. This is Tres Palmas, which has a break that makes it popular with surfers. There's a full kitchen, and the location is near many good restaurants. Only the bedrooms have air-conditioning. ✉ *Off Rte. 413, Playa Tres Palmas* ☎ *787/823–2323* 🌐 *www.islandwestrentals.com* ⇨ *6 bedrooms, 5 baths* ♨ *In-room: no a/c (some rooms), In-hotel: DVD, pool, beachfront, Wi-Fi, laundry facilities* ▭ *D, MC, V.*

NIGHTLIFE

Rincón attracts a younger crowd, so there are plenty of options for fun after dark. On weekends the **Calypso Café** (✉ *Rte. 4413, Maria's Beach* ☎ *787/823–1626*) often has live rock-and-roll bands. The open-air establishment has daily sunset happy hour and is a good place to grab a burger after you've had your fill of the beach. They have the coldest beers in town.

Rock Bottom Bar & Grill (✉ *Carr. 413, Sandy Beach, at Casa Verde Inn, Puntas* ☎ *787/823–3756* 🌐 *www.enrincon.com* ⏲ *Daily 4 pm–2 am*) has an acoustic jam session on Thursday and ladies' night on Wednesday. This circular bar is popular with locals who gather to watch the Sunday surf flicks.**The Rum Shack** (✉ *Lazy Parrot Inn, Carr. 413, Km 4.1, Rincón* ☎ *787/823–0103* 🌐 *www.rumshack.net* ⏲ *11 am–midnight*) serves a mean grapefruit margarita and Kahlúa-banana daiquiri. This poolside bar is the hot spot on Wednesdays, when a live reggae band hits the stage.

6

SHOPPING

Playa Oeste (✉ *Carr. 413, Km 0.5, Rincón* ☎ *787/823–4424* 🌐 *www.playaoeste.com* ⏲ *closed Mon.*) has an eclectic collection of surf art, jewelry, clothing, and pottery. Paintings and photographs can be shipped directly to your home.

SPORTS AND THE OUTDOORS

DIVING AND SNORKELING

Most of the region's dive operators also run fishing charters around Desecheo Island and whale-watching trips in season.

★ **Taíno Divers** (✉ *Black Eagle Marina, Black Eagle Rd., off Rte. 413* ☎ *787/823–6429* 🌐 *www.tainodivers.com*) has daily snorkeling and diving trips that cost $89 and $149, including lunch. It also has daily trips to Desecheo Island, whale-watching trips in winter, and scuba PADI certification courses.

HORSEBACK RIDING

Pintos R Us (✉ *Rte. 413, Km. 4.7, Rincon* ☎ *787/361–3639 or 787/516–7090*) has daily riding along the beach to the lighthouse, as well as full-moon tours and riding lessons. The horses are spirited but gentle enough for newcomers.

SURFING

Desecheo Surf & Dive Shop (✉ *Rte. 413, Km 2.5* ☎ *787/823–0390* 🌐 *www.desecheosurfshop.com*) rents snorkeling equipment ($15 a day), Boogie boards ($15 a day), and a variety of short and long surfboards ($25–$30 a day). The company also organizes diving and snorkeling trips and rents Jet Skis.

Mar Azul (✉ *Carr. 413, Km 4.4, Rincón* ☎ *787/823–5692 or 787/214–7224* 🌐 *www.puertoricosurfinginfo.com*) has Rincón's best selection of performance surfboards and stand-up paddleboards to buy or rent ($25 a day). Two-hour surf lessons ($40) and paddleboard lessons ($65) are also available.

★ **Rincón Surf School** (✉ *Rincón Surf & Board, Rte. 413, Km 4.4* ☎ *787/823–0610* 🌐 *www.rinconsurfschool.com*) offers full-day lessons for $95, which includes board rental and transportation. You can also arrange two-, three-, and five-day surfing seminars for $169–$369. There is also a special five-day surf and yoga school taught by and for women that takes place several times throughout the year.

SAILING Set sail in the morning for a day in the sun, or in the late afternoon for unobstructed sunset views, with **Katarina Sail Charters** (✉ *Black Eagle Marina, off Rte. 413, Km 4.0* ☎ *787/823–7245* 🌐 *www.sailrinconpuertorico.com*). The catamaran sails from Black Eagle Marina, except from August to November during hurricane season.

MAYAGÜEZ

15 mi (24 km) southeast of Rincón.

"Me encanta" is what most people from Puerto Rico say when you ask them about Mayagüez. But you are likely to be less than enchanted by the grungy city, home to 12,000 university students and several casinos. With more charming communities in every direction, there's no real reason to stop in this traffic-clogged area. But if you have some spare time, the city known as the "Sultan of the West" has some worthwhile attractions. Its tree-lined main square, called Plaza Colón, is dominated by a large statue of Christopher Columbus. On the surrounding streets you'll find the domed Teatro Yagüez, which dates from 1902, and a mishmash of buildings that run the gamut from neoclassical to baroque to Art Deco.

GETTING HERE AND AROUND

Air Travel. The small Aeropuerto Eugenio María de Hostos (MAZ), just north of Mayagüez on Highway 2, has flights between San Juan and Mayagüez on American Eagle and Cape Air. If you are not flying into San Juan, you can rent a car at either the Aguadilla or Mayagüez airport. Prices vary from $35 to $65 per day.

Car Travel. Driving in Mayagüez can be complicated, especially in the high-trafficked center of town where one-way streets compose the city grid. Nevertheless, a rental car is your best option to get around town. From Highway 2, you can reach downtown by taking Route 105 (Calle McKinley) or Route 106 (Calle Méndez Vigo). Either route will take you to the heart of the city.

Continued on page 277

SURFING PUERTO RICO

by Marlise Kast

With turquoise waters, sugary sand, hollow barrels, offshore winds, and arching palm trees, it's no wonder the island has been labeled "Hawaii of the Atlantic." This vision of paradise is a magnet for myriad surfers. Whether you're a beginner or a big-wave rider, there's a break to suit your ability—on the northwest coast near Rincón, along the northern beaches, or off the eastern shores.

WAVES OF GLORY

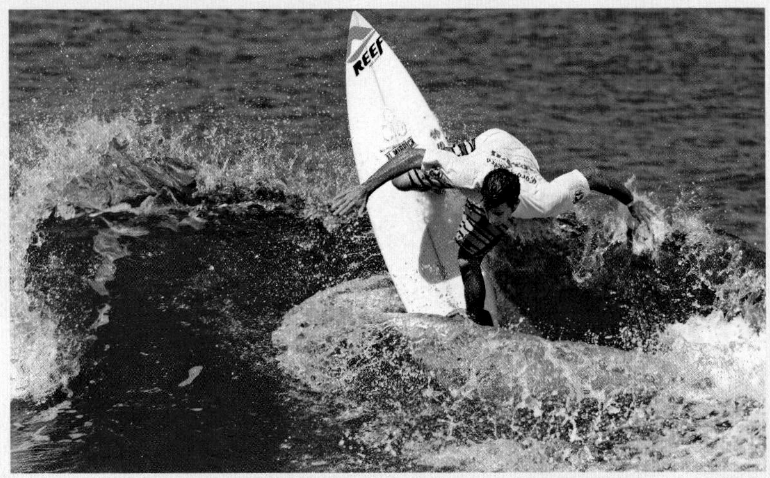

Pro surfer Gabriel Escudero conquers the waves at Domes Beach in Rincón.

Puerto Rico is home to more than 70 surf spots with some of the Caribbean's most consistent waves, breaking anywhere between 3 feet (for beginners) and 20 feet (for advanced/professionals). Along 310 miles of ride-able waters are coral reefs, point breaks, hallow barrels, beach breaks, rights and lefts. The downside of surfing in the tropics are jellyfish and sea urchins that cling onto the rocks. Other dangers include shallow reefs, riptides, and territorialism at some local spots. If you're a beginner, enroll in a surf course and learn from someone who knows the environment. Respect the locals, never surf alone, and remember the unwritten law: never drop in on another surfer.

THE GOOD OLE DAYS

According to local legend, the first surfers to test the northwest waters were Puerto Rico's own Jose Rodriguez, Rafy Viella, and Guille Bermuda. In 1960, American surfer Gary Hoyt opened the island's first surf shop in San Juan. Following in his wake were Johnny Flain and Butch Linden from Malibu, California, who claim that only fifty surfers braved the waters in the mid 60s. It wasn't until 1968, when Rincón hosted the World Surfing Championships, that word spread of epic waves peeling along the north and northwest coasts. Winter waves and a laid-back lifestyle made the island a haven for American surfers and hippies, who took one look at the coastline and never turned back. Since the 1970s, Puerto Rico's roster of talent has featured such legends as Edwin Santos, Juan Ashton, and Pepe Alvarez. Noted for charging monster waves are local big-wave riders like Alberto Lincha, Carlos Cabrero, and Waldo Oliver

Today, the island hosts dozens of competitions and is home to 25,000 surfers and 30 surf shops.

Cresting a wave at the Corona Pro Surfer event

SURF SEASONS

(clockwise from top left) serene paddle-boarding; a crowded wave at Tres Palmas; competing at Middles Beach

Waves peak during winter, but it's possible to catch one during "off season" due to periodic hurricanes and cold fronts that pass Puerto Rico. Summer is generally flat, except when a hurricane passes (season, July–November) off the coast. The fall is when North Atlantic storms create enough swell to make Puerto Rico a world-class destination. This is when the pros take to the waves, providing a spectacle for beachgoers.

BEGINNER

For a light splash in the whitewash, the summer months (late May through August) offer playful waves.

INTERMEDIATE

In springtime (March to mid-May), swells fade but are compensated with offshore winds that hold the wave's barreling shape, averaging between shoulder-to-head high.

ADVANCED

September through May is ideal for experienced surfers. November through February in particular is when top surfers—mostly locals and East Coasters—crowd the line-up for monster waves that can fire as high as 20-feet.

WHERE TO RENT

Puerto Rico has dozens of surf shops renting everything from foam longboards and boogieboards for beginners to high-performance shortboards and paddleboards for experts.

Offering the best quiver on the island is **Mar Azul** (☎ *787/823-5692* 🌐 *www.puertoricosurfinginfo.com*) located on Rincón's Rte 413. **Hang Loose** in Isabela (☎ *787/872-2490* 🌐 *www.hangloosesurfshop.com*) has beginner boards of all shapes and sizes. **WRV** in Aguadilla (☎ *787/890-3351* 🌐 *www.waveridingvehicles.com*) is another top spot for beginner board rentals.

NORTHWEST BREAKS

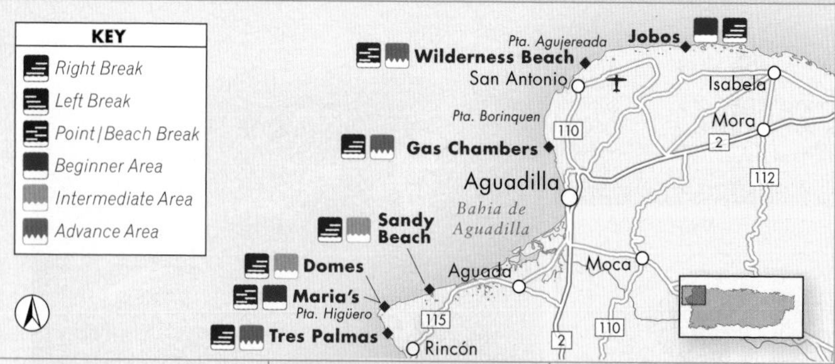

When the surf is on in the northwest, it's on. This is the best place to capture the scene, as some breaks here experience 40-foot swells in winter. Aguadilla and Rincón are ideally stationed for offshore wind conditions, which hold the waves' shape.

ADVANCED

To witness Puerto Rico's true surfing experience, head north of Rincón to Aguadilla's **Wilderness Beach.** Surrounding jungle landscape makes it worth the drive to this local spot where fast, long rights average 8–15 ft.

Considered the "Sunset Beach" of Puerto Rico, **Tres Palmas** is reserved for kamikaze-surfers who take on the 40-foot waves that only break a few days each year. In summer, however, this deep outer reef is surprisingly calm, making it the perfect place to snorkel.

Head to **Gas Chambers** to watch surfers charge Puerto Rico's most powerful wave. Next to Crash Boat Beach, this spot breaks less than 10 times per year, but is labeled world-class due to the 15-foot faces and oblong tubes that crash with unbelievable force.

Corona Pro Surfer event, Rincon

INTERMEDIATE

At **Domes,** a spot named for the nuclear power dome neighboring the parking lot, peaky right-hand waves average 3 to 10 feet. This break is one of the area's most consistent, even on smaller days. Breaking directly in front of Tamboo Restaurant is a sandbar known as **Sandy Beach.** This intermediate spot still delivers on smaller days, but is not as protected from south winds as the neighboring coves. Although generally void of crowds, the rocky shoreline embedded with urchins isn't good for beginners.

BEGINNER

When the waves are between 2 to 4 feet, beginners can head just south of Domes to **Maria's.** This break has some fun right- and left-hand peaks, and offers a pleasant beach for photographing surfers when the swell picks up. Once waves reach head-high (Nov. through Feb.), this spot is best reserved for advanced surfers who can handle the shallow reefs and strong currents.

Popular with beginner and intermediate surfers, **Jobos** in Isabela has 4–10 foot rights that break off a reef in a crescent-shaped bay. This section often connects to the inside waves, making for a nice long ride. Because of the food shacks and shallow waters, this spot is often crowded with beachgoers and beginners learning to surf. Those who prefer to watch the action can photograph surfers from the peninsula on the beach's east side.

NORTH BREAKS

Susceptible to Atlantic storms and their aftermath, the north coast has more than 30 breaks to explore.

ADVANCED

Unless you're quite experienced, you may just want to take photographs from the shores of **Chatarras.** This epic wave breaks on a sharp coral reef, creating hollow left-hand tubes fit for the pros. When the 10+ footers are firing, this spot gets crowded with surfers who will do whatever it takes to claim their wave.

INTERMEDIATE

Near San Juan, **La Ocho**, is a forgiving wave great for intermediate surfers on medium-size days. Working best at 5 feet, this break is long but usually mushy. It's a long paddle to the break so make sure you're in shape before you head to the line-up.

BEGINNER

Near the town of Manati, **Los Tubos** (The Tubes) has a pleasant crowd and is manageable for novices. The best time to come is between September and April, but beware of sea urchins that line the rocky shore. In the town of Luquillo, **La Pared** delivers right and lefts that break on a soft, sandy beach. On a weekday, you may have all the waves to yourself, except after 5 PM when you might be joined by a handful of locals out for a sunset session. This is an excellent beginner's beach, with friendly 3 to 5 foot waves that break 150 days of the year.

SOUTH BREAKS

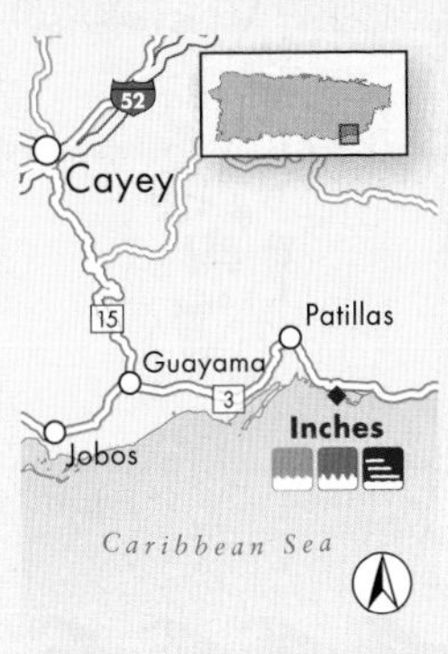

Overshadowed by the north, the south rim of Puerto Rico experiences all types of waves from the Caribbean hurricanes and tropical storms. This is most common between August and October when swells hit the southeastern side from Humacao down to Patillas.

INTERMEDIATE TO ADVANCED

Inches, has the island's longest left-hand barrel. Waves here often peel for 300+ yards. Named for the "inches" separating you from the reef, this spot has powerful waves that spread between three peaks. Trade winds make this the south's most consistent surf break, even in summer when most other spots are flat.

BOARD SHAPES

Longboard: Lengthier (about 2.5—3 m/9–10.5 feet), wider, thicker, and more buoyant than the often-miniscule shortboards. Offers more flotation and speedier paddling, which makes it easier to get into waves. Great for beginners and those with relaxed surf styles. Skill level; Beginner to Intermediate.

Funboard: A little shorter than the longboard with a slightly more acute nose and blunt tail, the Funboard combines the best attributes of the longboards with some similar characteristics of the shorter boards. Good for beginners or surfers looking for a board more maneuverable and faster than a longboard. Skill level; Beginner to Intermediate.

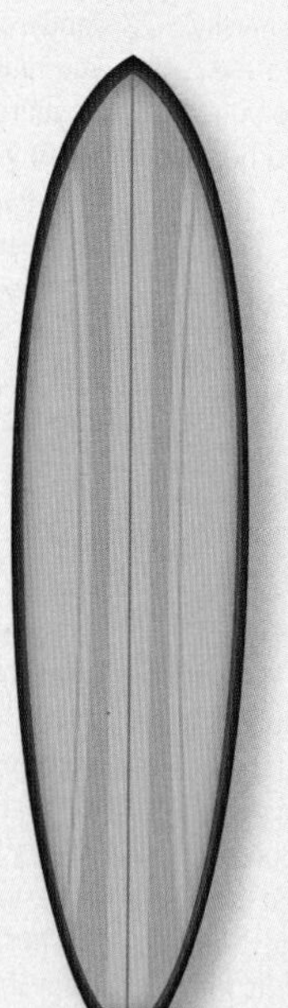

Fishboard: A stumpy, blunt-nosed, twin-finned board that features a "V" tail (giving it a "fish" like look, hence the name) and is fast and maneuverable. Good for catching small, steep slow waves and pulling tricks. At one point this was the world's best-selling surfboard. Skill level; Intermediate to Expert.

Shortboard: Shortboards came on the scene in 1967-70 when the average board length dropped from 9'6" to 6'6" (2.9m to 2m) and changed the wave riding styles in the surf world forever. This board is a short, light, high-performance stick that is designed for carving the wave with a high amount of maneuverability. These boards need a fast steep wave, completely different than a longboard break, which tends to be slower with shallower wave faces. Skill level; Expert.

Beginner **Expert**

Fish

Funboards

Longboards

Shortboards

Shallow wave faces, easiest surfing

Steeper wave faces, difficult surfing

Taxi Travel. In Mayagüez, White Taxi is reliable and charges flat rates—no meters—by location. Fares to or from San Juan are steep: For example, service is $120 from Mayagüez.

Airport Information **Aeropuerto Eugenio María de Hostos** (✉ *Hwy. 2, Km 148.7, Mayagüez* ☎ *787/833–0148 or 787/265–7065*). **Aeropuerto Internacional Rafael Hernández** (✉ *Hwy. 2, Km 148.7, Aguadilla* ☎ *787/891–2286*).

Car Rental **Avis** (☎ *787/832–0406*). **Budget** (☎ *787/823–4570*).
Hertz (☎ *787/832–3314*).**Leaseway of Puerto Rico** (☎ *787/833–1140 in Mayagüez*). **Thrifty** (☎ *787/834–1590*).

Taxi **Arecibo Taxi Cab** (☎ *787/878–2929*).

EXPLORING MAYAGÜEZ

Puerto Rico's only zoo, the 45-acre **Zoológico de Puerto Rico,** is just north of downtown. After $13 million in renovations, it's looking pretty spiffy. New on the scene is a 45-foot-tall aviary, which allows you to walk through a rain-forest environment as tropical birds fly freely above your head. There's also a new butterfly park where you can let brilliant blue morphos land on your hand, and an arthropodarium where you can get up close and personal with spiders and their kin. Video monitors are built into the floor to show off the bugs that normally get trampled underfoot. The older section of the park has undergone an extensive renovation, so most of the cages have been replaced by fairly natural-looking environments. One of the most popular residents is Mundi, a female elephant who arrived as a baby more than two decades ago. There are also plenty of lions, tigers—and even bears. There is a $3 charge for parking. ✉ *Rte. 108, north of Rte. 65* ☎ *787/834–8110* 🌐 *www.parquesnacionalespr.com* 🎟 *$10* ⏲ *Wed.–Sun. 8:30–4.*

Founded in 1901 on a 235-acre farm on the outskirts of Mayagüez, the **Estación Experimental de Agricultura Tropical** *(Tropical Agriculture Research Station)* is run by the U.S. Department of Agriculture and contains a tropical plant collection that has been nurtured for more than a half century. More than 2,000 plant species from all over the tropical world are found here, including teak, mahogany, cinnamon, nutmeg, rubber, and numerous exotic flowers. Free maps are available for self-guided tours. ✉ *Hwy. 2 at Rte. 108* ☎ *787/831–3435* 🎟 *Free* ⏲ *Weekdays 7–4.*

The **Teatro Yagüez** is an extravagant yellow-and-white theater dating from 1902 that's famed throughout the island for its lavish, columned facade and domed roof. The structure, a little over the top, is still the main venue for theater in Mayagüez. ✉ *Calle McKinley at Calle Dr. Basora* ☎ *787/834–0523* 🎟 *Free* ⏲ *Daily, except when rehearsals are scheduled.*

WHERE TO EAT

¢ CAFE **Ricomini Bakery.** This popular bakery, open daily from 5 AM to midnight, is a good spot to try one of the city's trademark delicacies, a *brazo gitano* (literally, "gypsy arm"). These gigantic jellyrolls are filled with anything from guava to lemon to sweet cheese. You can also find another famous local product here, Fido's Sangría, made from the closely guarded secret recipe of Mayagüez resident Wilfredo Aponte Hernández. There are also tasty pastries, freshly baked bread, and a selection of sandwiches. ✉ *101 Calle Méndez Vigo* ☎ *787/833–1444* ▭ *AE, MC, V.*

$ CARIBBEAN ✕ **Siglo XX.** This busy restaurant has an enormous menu of chicken, steak, and seafood prepared every way imaginable. Meals come in a basket with rice, beans, or plantains. Sandwiches, displayed behind the glass counter, are served lightly toasted with the traditional mayo-ketchup "secret sauce." Booths at the diner setting are packed with locals, especially during the midweek lunch hour. This Spanish-speaking eatery is a great place to practice your language skills. ✉ *Calle Peral, No. 9 Norte,* Mayagüez ☎ *787/832–1370 or 787/265–2094* 🌐 *www.sigloxxpr.com* ▭ *AE, MC, V* ⊙ *Closed Sun.*

WHERE TO STAY

$–$$ RESORT **Holiday Inn Mayagüez & Tropical Casino.** Everything seems shoehorned into this big box on the northern edge of Mayagüez. The sound of slot machines is impossible to escape in the extremely popular casino, which is adjacent to the lobby, as well as the bar and restaurant. The rooms are a bit larger than usual but otherwise are nothing special. Holly's Restaurant serves Caribbean cuisine such as fresh fish with fried plantains, rice, and beans. The casino is popular with locals, as is the attached bar, Fat Tuesday, which offers frozen drinks and live music. The easy-to-reach location is about 10 minutes from the downtown historic district and 5 minutes from the airport. **Pros:** Great staff; pretty pool area. **Cons:** Not on the beach; motel-style rooms; free Continental breakfast for executive rooms only. ✉ *2701 Hwy. 2, Km 149.9* ☎ *787/833–1100* 🌐 *www.hidpr.com* *141 rooms* *In-room: Wi-Fi. In-hotel: restaurant, room service, bar, pools, gym, laundry facilities, laundry service, public Internet, public Wi-Fi, parking (free)* ▭ *AE, D, MC, V* *EP.*

$ HOTEL **Howard Johnson Downtown Mayagüez.** Set in a former monastery, this downtown hotel still has stained-glass windows in some rooms and a stone cross on the roof. The rooms are mostly small (they were originally for monks, after all) but more stylish than those in your standard chain hotel. The best are the colorful accommodations designed for families with kids. A Continental breakfast is included in the rate. **Pros:** Interesting building; rooms designed for families and businesspeople. **Cons:** Far from the beach; on an uninteresting block. ✉ *70 Calle Méndez Vigo* ☎ *787/832–9191* 🌐 *www.hojo.com* *39 rooms* *In-room: refrigerator (some), Wi-Fi, safe. In-hotel: pool, laundry service, parking (fee)* ▭ *AE, D, MC, V* *CP.*

$$ RESORT **Mayagüez Resort & Casino.** The center of the city's social life, this old-fashioned hotel is packed with elegantly dressed men and women all weekend. Some are trying their luck in the casino, some are dancing the tango in the lounge, and some are sipping cocktails on the long, sweeping terrace. The nicely decorated guest rooms look out onto 20 acres of lush gardens and an aqua park complete with slides, waterfalls, and rivers. El Castillo specializes in seafood. The public beach in Añasco is 10 minutes away. **Pros:** Lovely pool area; best casino on this coast. **Cons:** Not on the beach; must pay parking even to visit the casino;

guests must wear identity wristbands. ✉ *Rte. 104, Km 0.3, off Hwy. 2, Box 3781* ☎ *787/832–3030 or 888/689–3030* 🌐 *www.mayaguezresort.com* *140 rooms* *In-room: Wi-Fi. In-hotel: restaurant, bar, tennis courts, pool, gym, public Internet, laundry service, parking (fee)* ▭ *AE, D, DC, MC, V* *EP.*

NIGHTLIFE

A block from Plaza Colón, **Dom Pepe** (✉ *56 Calle Méndez Vigo* ☎ *787/834–4941*) has live eclectic music upstairs.

SHOPPING

Small stores and pharmacies dot downtown Mayagüez. For heavy-duty shopping, the **Mayagüez Mall** (✉ *Hwy. 2, Km 159.4* ☎ *787/834–2760*) has local stores, a food court, and stateside chains such as JCPenney, Walmart, Marshalls, and Borders Books.**Western Plaza** (✉ *Hwy. 2, Km 149.7, Mayagüez* ☎ *787/833–0315)* offers fast-food restaurants, Kmart, Sam's Club, and a movie theater showing the latest releases.

CABO ROJO

Named for its pinkish cliffs, "Red Cape" was used in the late-18th century as a port for merchant vessels—and for the smugglers and pirates who inevitably accompanied oceangoing trade. Today the miles of coastline to the west and north of this tiny curl of land jutting into the Atlantic Ocean are a destination for families. Many small, inexpensive hotels can be found in the communities of Joyuda, Boquerón, and El Combate. Outdoor activities are quite popular, from sailing out of Boquerón to hiking to the lighthouse near El Combate.

CABO ROJO TOWN

People often assume that the town of Cabo Rojo is at the southwestern tip of Puerto Rico, where there is a lighthouse by the same name. Cabo Rojo is actually located south of Mayaguez, east of Joyuda, and slightly northwest of Lajas.

GETTING HERE

The area is a good stopping point for those heading from Mayagüez south to El Combate. To get here, take 2 south to 100 south to 102 east. This road will take you directly into the center of Cabo Rojo, approximately 30 minutes from Mayaguez.

EXPLORING

The town itself doesn't have a great deal to offer, other than the **Museo de los Proceres.** (✉ *Rte 312, Km 0.5, Cabo Rojo* ☎ *787/255–1560*), which includes a sculpture exhibition of national leaders and exhibits of local artists.

WHERE TO STAY

$ HOTEL **Villa Vista Puerto.** An adventurer's gem, this secluded retreat on 3 lush acres was hand-built by its owner. Perched on a hillside, the main lodge has a spectacular view of Port Royal and is equipped with a spacious kitchen, bathhouse, and jungle shower. The character-rich smaller cabana is a teepee-like structure crowned with a hexagonal roof that opens for ventilation and light. Though lacking air-conditioning, the building is cooled by fans within the walls that draw air from the adjacent man-made pond. Here, Robinson Crusoe meets eco-lodge with innovative touches like driftwood furnishings, pebble-strewn flooring, sisal matting, and solar-heated showers. Guests have use of the outdoor kitchen with its tree-stump cutting blocks, hand-tooled rocking chairs, and a table fashioned from a cable wheel. Although there is no restaurant on site, the owner can prepare a lobster dinner upon request, and other dining options are only a five-minute drive away. **Pros:** Unique design; eco-friendly; private setting. **Cons:** Mosquitoes during rainy season; cash only; no pool. ✣ *Rte. 100 to Cabo Rojo, right on 308, left on 307, pass the school (Calle Esquela, Km 3.9), right at P.P.V sign., Cabo Rojo* ☎ *787/255–4144* 🌐 *www.caborojovillavista.com* ⇨ *2 cabanas* ♁ *In-room: no a/c, kitchen, refrigerator, Wi-Fi (some). In-hotel: laundry facilities, Wi-Fi, parking (free)* ▭ *No credit cards.* 🍽 *EP.*

JOYUDA

14 mi (21 km) south of Mayagüez.

Known as the *Milla de Oro* (Golden Mile) because of its string of more than 30 seaside restaurants, the community of Joyuda is a must for seafood lovers. The same can't be said for those in search of a beautiful beach, as erosion has taken a terrible toll, leaving in some places only a sliver of sand. But that doesn't stop hordes of local families from making a beeline to the bit of beach that is left.

GETTING HERE AND AROUND

From Mayagüez, take Highway 2 south to Route 100 south toward Cabo Rojo. Head west on Route 102 until you hit the coastal town of Joyuda. Most of the area's restaurants and hotels are staggered along a 2-mi (3-km) stretch on Route 102, making this a convenient town to explore by foot.

EXPLORING

★ About 50 mi (80 km) off the coast of Cabo Rojo, **Mona Island** sits brooding in the Atlantic Ocean. Known as the Galápagos of the Caribbean, the 14,000-acre island has long been a destination for adventurous travelers. It's said to have been settled by the Taíno and visited by both Christopher Columbus and Juan Ponce de León. Pirates were known to use the small island as a hideout, and legend has it that there is still buried treasure to be found here. Today, however, Mona's biggest lure is its distinctive ecosystem. It is home to a number of endangered species, such as the Mona iguana and leatherback sea turtle. A number of seabirds, including red-footed boobies, also inhabit the island. Off its coast are reefs filled with 270 species of tropical fish, black coral, and purple seafans. There are plenty of places to explore, such as the 200-

Surrounded by rugged coastline, the Cabo Rojo Lighthouse is best reached by a 4-wheel drive vehicle.

foot cliffs on the north side of the island or the abandoned lighthouse that once protected ships off the southern coast. Travelers must reach the island by boat—planes aren't permitted to land. Several tour operators in Joyuda and Boquerón, as well as companies in Mayagüez and Rincón, offer overnight camping trips to the island; they will help you with the camping permits from the Department of Natural and Environmental Resources. You need to reserve at least a few weeks ahead for an overnight stay. ☎ *787/724–3724 for Department of Natural and Environmental Resources.*

WHERE TO EAT

$$ SEAFOOD ✕ **El Bohío.** Watch seagulls dive for their food while you dine on a covered deck extending out into the bay. The long list of seafood is prepared in a variety of ways: Shrimp comes breaded, stewed, or skewered; conch is served as a salad or cooked in a butter-and-garlic sauce; and the lobster can be prepared just about any way you can imagine. This restaurant, on stilts above the water, is about the most charming setting in Joyuda. ✉ *Rte. 102, Km 13.9* ☎ *787/851–2755* ▭ *AE, MC, V.*

$$–$$$ SEAFOOD ✕ **Raito's.** Specializing in croquette-encrusted seafood, this waterfront fish house is reminiscent of the '70s with its linoleum speckled floors and clear vinyl table cloths. Mozzarella tops most house favorites, including the baked lobster and snapper. For the seafood-weary, pork chops and filet mignon are on the menu, but be sure to leave room for the mango-, guava-, or coconut-flavored flan. Two inviting gazebos overlook the water, but sadly the view is somewhat obstructed by a chain-

link fence. ✉ *Carr. 102, Km 13.7, Joyuda* ☎ *787/851–4487* ▭ *MC, V* ⊙ *Closed Mon.*

$$–$$$ ★ SEAFOOD ✕ **Tino's.** The colorful neon sign outside this restaurant touts its signature dish: AN EARTHENWARE GOBLET OVERFLOWING WITH MASHED PLANTAINS AND SEAFOOD. It comes in two sizes, but the smaller one is usually enough to satisfy all but the biggest appetites. There are plenty of other seafood dishes on the menu, from red snapper in a spicy sauce to lobster with butter. Although most come here for the fish, the restaurant also serves beef, pork, and chicken. There's no ocean view, but the elegant dining makes up for it. ✉ *Rte. 102, Km 13.6* ☎ *787/851–2976* ▭ *AE, MC, V.*

$$–$$$ SEAFOOD ✕ **Tony's Restaurant.** Serving locals since 1978, this authentic Puerto Rican fish house specializes in lobster, shrimp, and red snapper. The menu features seven varieties of mofongo as well as steak, chicken, and pasta. Every wall is emblazoned with autographed images of Puerto Rican pop stars and politicians. Not for the cholesterol-challenged, this eatery fries nearly everything, including cheese, fish, and vegetables. Sit outside for an ocean view or stop by on weekends for live music and karaoke. ✉ *Carr. 102, Km 10.9, Punta Arenas, Joyuda* ☎ *787/851–2500* 🌐 *www.tonyspr.com* ▭ *AE, MC, V.*

WHERE TO STAY

¢ HOTEL **Joyuda Plaza.** Across the road from the beach, this three-story hotel is one of the best deals in Joyuda. You don't come here for the ambience—the building is little more than a box, and the rooms make only a vague attempt at decor. But if you're on a budget, this place has nice touches you don't always get in this price range, like a pair of kidney-shaped pools sitting side by side in a pretty courtyard. A dozen or so bars and restaurants are within walking distance. **Pros:** Good value; located in the middle of the action. **Cons:** Not much atmosphere; noise from other rooms can be a problem; no elevator. ✉ *Rte. 102, Km 14.7* 📫 *Box 1748, Joyuda 00623* ☎ *787/851–8800* 🌐 *www.joyudaplazapr.com* *57 rooms* *In-hotel: 2 restaurants, laundry service, room service, bar, pools, public Wi-Fi, parking (free)* ▭ *AE, MC, V* *EP.*

$–$$ HOTEL **Parador Joyuda Beach.** Talk about truth in advertising: The beach in question is so close to this place that the water laps against the seawall. Rooms here are spic-and-span, with terra-cotta tile floors. Ask for one of the sunset suites, which have ocean views. There's an open-air restaurant by the beach and a snack bar by the pool. The all-inclusive package is popular with Puerto Ricans who frequent this hotel. **Pros:** Waterfront location; friendly staff. **Cons:** Motel-style rooms; no elevator; ugly white plastic chairs in pool area, bar, and restaurant. ✉ *Rte. 102, Km 11.7* 📫 *Box 18410, Joyuda 00623* ☎ *787/851–5650 or 800/981–5464* 🌐 *www.joyudabeach.com* *41 rooms* *In-hotel: restaurant, bar, pool, beachfront* ▭ *AE, MC, V* *EP, AI.*

SPORTS AND THE OUTDOORS

DIVING AND SNORKELING Several reef-bordered cays lie off the Cabo Rojo area near walls that drop to 100 feet. A mile-long reef along Las Coronas, better known as Cayo Ron, has a variety of hard and soft coral, reef fish, and lobster. You can arrange snorkeling and scuba-diving trips with Capt. Elick Hernández Garciá, who runs **Tour Marine Adventures** (✉ *Rte. 101, Km*

14.1 ☎ *787/375–2625* 🌐 *www.tourmarinepr.com*). They cost between $35 and $75 per person. He'll also arrange trips out to Mona Island for $200 per person.

GOLF Get in 18 holes at the **Club Deportivo del Oeste** (✉ *Rte. 102, Km 15.1* ☎ *787/254–3748* 🌐 *www.clubdeportivodeloeste.com*). Jack Bender incorporated the region's rolling hills in his design to provide golfers with panoramic views. The nicely tended course is open daily, as are the tennis courts on the same property; greens fees are $48.50 and half price after 3 PM.

BOQUERÓN

3 mi (5 km) south of Joyuda.

Once a quiet fishing village, Boquerón still has its share of seaside shanties. Its narrow streets are quiet during the week but come alive on the weekend, when vendors appear with carts full of clams and oysters you can slurp down on the spot—wedges of lemon are provided, of course. Bars and restaurants throw open their doors—if they have any, that is. Many of the establishments here are open to the breeze, making this a Puerto Rican party spot where the music (and the people) plays until 2 in the morning. Boquerón is also a water-sports center; many companies operate from or near the docks of the imposing Club Nautico de Boquerón, which is easy to find at the end of Route 100.

6

GETTING HERE AND AROUND

To reach Boquerón from Mayagüez, head south on Highway 2 to Route 100 south. After bypassing Cabo Rojo, take Route 101 and follow the signs southwest to Boquerón. The small town can easily be explored by foot.

EXPLORING

The **Refugio de Vida Silvestre de Boquerón** *(Boquerón Wildlife Refuge)* encompasses three tracts of land at the island's southern tip. The first is about 1 mi (2 km) south of Boquerón. There is a trail that leads through three different types of mangroves to picnic areas and a dock where you can launch a canoe or kayak. Note: Hunting is allowed in the reserve between November and January, but camping is not. ✉ *Rte. 101, Km 1.1* ☎ *787/851–4795* 🎫 *Free* ⏲ *Weekdays 7:30–4.*

WHERE TO EAT AND STAY

$$–$$$ STEAK ✕ **Brasas Steak House.** Offering a refreshing alternative to seafood, this is Boquerón's most upscale eatery. It's also one of the island's few restaurants serving certified Angus beef, including T-bone, sirloin, Porterhouse, and filet mignon. Equally notable are the grilled chicken, pork, and pastas. Set back from the main strip, this restaurant lacks an ocean view but is quieter and more intimate than others in the area. For a livelier vibe, check out its waterfront sister property, Brasas Beach Pub, just around the corner. ✉ *Calle José de Diego, Suite # 210, Boquerón* ☎ *787/255–1470* 💳 *MC, V* ⏲ *Closed Mon.–Tues.*

$$–$$$ SEAFOOD ✕ **Galloway's.** From a covered deck overlooking Bahía Boquerón, you can catch the sunset while enjoying some seafood—caught fresh from local waters, of course. Steak, ribs, chicken, and pasta are available, but

Locals flock to the pretty beaches of Boquerón on weekends.

the red snapper and dorado—prepared breaded, sautéed, or grilled—are by far the best options. There's a lively happy hour and occasional live music. This place is along the main drag but is set back from the street so you don't have to be a part of the passing parade. One major plus in this traffic-choked town: There's a large free parking lot. ✉ *12 Calle José de Diego* ☎ *787/254–3302* 🌐 *www.gallowaysrestaurant.com* 💳 *AE, MC, V* ⏲ *Closed Wed.*

$$ RESORT 👍 **Aquarius Beach Resort.** As Boquerón's largest property, this high-rise resort offers one-, two-, and three-bedroom suites, each with a private balcony. The entire resort adheres to the blues and greens of the Caribbean palette. Full kitchens, in-suite laundry facilities, arcade games, and an aqua park for children create a family atmosphere. If cooking isn't your thing, enjoy the poolside restaurant or walk across the footbridge leading to the center of town. Be sure to request an ocean-view room from which manatees and humpback whales can be seen cavorting from April to June. Due to the size of the resort, the pool and parking areas tend to be congested. **Pros:** Family-friendly; calm beach; prime location. **Cons:** No Internet; hotel is often full; blocked double parking. ✉ *Carr. 101, Km 18, Acceso Balneario, Boquerón* ☎ *787/254–5400* 🌐 *www.aquariusvacationclub.com* *44 rooms* *In-room: kitchen, refrigerator. In-hotel: restaurant, room service, bar, pools, beachfront, laundry facilities, parking (free), no-smoking rooms* 💳 *AE, D, DC, MC, V* *EP.*

$ HOTEL **Cofresí Beach Hotel.** A favorite with families, this place puts you a few blocks from the hustle and bustle of Boquerón. Its four floors—practically a high-rise in these parts—are filled with one-, two-, and three-bedroom apartments complete with full kitchens. The owners didn't forget a thing, as the cupboards are even stocked with nice china and flatware.

The pool is small but very much appreciated on hot afternoons. **Pros:** Best value in the area; family-friendly environment; walking distance to many restaurants. **Cons:** Not on the beach; some traffic noise; additional $15 daily cleaning fee. ✉ *57 Calle Muñoz Rivera* 📮 *Box 1209, Boquerón 00622* ☎ *787/254–3000* 🌐 *www.cofresibeach.com* *12 apartments* *In-room: kitchen, refrigerator, DVD. In-hotel: Wi-Fi, pool, parking (free)* 💳 *AE, D, DC, MC, V* *EP.*

$ HOTEL **Parador Boquemar.** Even though it's a hike from Balneario Boquerón, families flock to this friendly parador on weekends. Rooms are decorated with bamboo furniture, floral bedding, and hues of blue. Those on the first floor are so cramped that people tend to leave their doors open; for enough room to breathe, ask for a third-floor room with a balcony overlooking the water. The seafood restaurant, La Cascada, has an actual waterfall along one wall. **Pros:** Near plenty of dining and nightlife options; family-friendly environment. **Cons:** Ugly building; rusty tins roofs undermine ocean view; can get very noisy ✉ *Calle Gill Buyé* 📮 *Box 133, Boquerón00622* ☎ *787/851–2158* 🌐 *www.boquemar.com* *75 rooms* *In-room: refrigerator. In-hotel: restaurant, bar, pool, safe, Wi-Fi* 💳 *AE, MC, V* *EP.*

NIGHTLIFE

A curvy bar distinguishes **Boquerón Bay** (✉ *Calle Jose de Diego* ☎ *787/638–5459*) from its straightforward neighbors. The open-air establishment has a second floor where you can catch a glimpse of the sunset, listen to live music, and sample some tapas.

SPORTS AND THE OUTDOORS

DIVING AND SNORKELING Snorkeling and scuba-diving trips are the specialty at **Mona Aquatics** (✉ *Calle Jose de Diego* ☎ *787/851–2185* 🌐 *www.monaaquatics.com*). Night dives are available as well. You'll find the crew in a wooden shack painted an eye-popping shade of blue next to the Club Nautico de Boquerón. The company has weekly trips to Mona Island.

FISHING You can arrange fishing trips with Capt. Francisco "Pochy" Rosario, who runs **Light Tackle Adventure** (☎ *787/849–1430* 🌐 *www.lighttackleadventure.8k.com*). His specialty is tarpon, which are plentiful in these waters.

EL COMBATE

2 mi (3 km) south of Boquerón.

This is the end of the earth—or the end of the island, anyway. El Combate sits on the southwest corner of Puerto Rico, a bit removed from everything. The travel industry hasn't figured out how to market this place, so they've left it mostly to the locals, who have built small but elaborate weekend homes—some with grandiose touches like fountains—along the narrow streets. On the road closest to the beach, which for some reason is called Calle 3, is a cluster of seafood shacks. The more prosperous ones have added second stories.

If you're wondering about the town's odd name, which literally means "The Combat," it seems that long ago some unscrupulous characters were eyeing the salt flats just outside town. But they were repelled by machete-wielding villagers who were to live forever in local lore. Is it a true story? Residents of El Combate swear it is.

GETTING HERE AND AROUND

To reach the costal town of El Combate from the 101, take Route 301 south to km 7.8, where the road intersects with Route 3301. The five-minute drive west on Route 3301 ends at El Combate Beach where a cluster of restaurants and hotels line the main strip, Calle 3. To reach Cabo Rojo Lighthouse and the salt flats, bypass Route 3301 and continue south on Route 301 until the road ends. This paved road soon turns into a bumpy one with potholes dotting the dusty course. The trek is well worth the effort, however, as jutting mangroves and crystal waters welcome travelers to Puerto Rico's southwestern tip.

It's a good idea to rent a four-wheel-drive vehicle from Mayagüez airport if you are heading to Cabo Rojo Lighthouse, as it is reached via a truly terrible dirt road.

EXPLORING

Home to six different ecosystems, the **Refugio de Vida Silvestre de Cabo Rojo** *(Cabo Rojo Wildlife Refuge)* has an interpretive center with exhibits of live freshwater fish and sea turtles. You can see as many as 100 species of birds along the trails, even the elusive yellow-shouldered blackbird. The entrance is about 1 mi (2 km) north of the turnoff for El Combate. ✉ *Rte. 301, Km 1.2* ☎ *787/851–7260* 🎟 *Free* 🕒 *Weekdays 8–4.*

The **Centro Interpretativo Las Salinas de Cabo Rojo** *(Cabo Rojo Sal Flats Interpretive Center)* has two-hour guided tours along the nature trails and a small display about the salt flats. (Remember that the name of the town comes from a battle over control of the salt flats.) The best part of the center is a massive observation tower that lets you scan the outline of Cabo Rojo itself. Next to the main building is an audiovisual center where presentations on marine ecosystems and bird migration are offered. ✉ *Rte. 301, Km 11* ☎ *787/851–2999* 🌐 *proambientepr.org* 🎟 *Center free, tours $3* 🕒 *Thurs.–Sat. 8:30–4:30, Sun. 9:30–5:30, tours at 9:30 and 1:30.*

★ The area's most popular attraction is the neoclassical **Cabo Rojo Lighthouse,** dating from 1881. The magnificent structure is open to the public, and you are free to hike around the rugged terrain or relax on La Playuela or one of the other pink-sand beaches nearby. ✉ *End of Rte. 301, El Combate* ☎ *787/851–7260* 🎟 *Free* 🕒 *Wed.–Sun. 9:30–5.*

WHERE TO EAT AND STAY

$$ SEAFOOD ✕ **Annie's.** A dining room facing the ocean is a fitting place to try some of the southwest coast's best seafood. You can snack on *empanadillas* (deep-fried fritters), then move on to red snapper with rice and beans or mofongo *relleno* (stuffed with seafood). This place, in an unmistakable turquoise building on the main drag, is casual and friendly. ✉ *Rte. 3301, km 3.0, at Calle 3* ☎ *787/254–2353* 🌐 *www.anniesplacepr.com* 💳 *AE, MC, V.*

¢–$ CARIBBEAN ✕ **Los Chapines.** This rustic seaside shack, painted orange and green, sells a variety of fish and chicken dishes. Be sure to try one of the specialty sandwiches, which are made with deep-fried plantains instead of bread.

The dinky deck in back is a perfect place to catch the breeze. ✉ *Rte. 3301, km 3.0, Calle 3* ☎ *787/254–5470* ▭ *MC, V.*

$$ HOTEL Fodor's Choice ★ **Bahía Salinas Beach Hotel.** The Cabo Rojo Lighthouse is this resort's closest neighbor. You can wander along the boardwalk or down the garden paths, bask in the sun on a deck or terrace, or relax in the infinity pool or on a lounge bed draped with silk curtains. Another option is the spa, which offers a wide range of massages and other treatments. The hotel's restaurant serves freshly caught seafood. Spacious guest rooms have antique wood furnishings, but only the villas have ocean views and balconies. Note that on weekends a two-night stay is required. **Pros:** Near interesting sites; good dining options; all-inclusive rate available. **Cons:** Beach at hotel is extremely narrow; staff often seems overworked; no elevator. ✉ *End of Rte. 301* *Box 2356, El Combate 00622* ☎ *787/254–1212 or 877/205–7507* ⊕ *www.bahiasalinas.com* *27 rooms* *In-room: no phone, safe. In-hotel: public Wi-Fi, restaurant, bar, pools, spa* ▭ *AE, MC, V* *BP, AI.*

$ HOTEL **Combate Beach Hotel.** On a quiet side street, this little hotel puts you within walking distance of the main drag. It's not right on the beach, but the second-floor rooms all have views of the water through the palm trees. The downstairs restaurant serves seafood, including tasty *mofongo*. **Pros:** Good value; quiet neighborhood. **Cons:** Not much atmosphere; isolated location; no elevator. ✉ *Rte. 3301, Km 2.7* *Box 1138, El Combate 00622* ☎ *787/254–2358 www.hotelcombatebeach.com* *19 rooms* *In-room: no phone, refrigerator. In-hotel: restaurant, bar, pool* ▭ *MC, V* *EP.*

¢ HOTEL **Combate Guest House.** This simple property—across the street from El Combate Beach—is centrally located just off of Calle 3. The building closest to the ocean sleeps five and comes with a full kitchen and bath. Each unit in the property's adjacent two-story structure can accommodate from one to four people, with one room designed for handicapped guests. Separating the two buildings is a sand-covered courtyard with park benches, lounge chairs, and a communal kitchen with two stoves. Slightly dated, what this property lacks in character is compensated by its affordability and proximity to the beach. **Pros:** Centrally located; good value **Cons:** Noise from beach crowds; cash only. ✉ *Rte. 3301, and Calle 2, across from Combate Beach, Combate* ☎ *787/254–0001* ⊕ *www.combateguesthouse.com* *19 rooms* *In-room: no phone, kitchen (some), refrigerator (some), no TV. In-hotel: beachfront* ▭ *No credit cards* *EP.*

NIGHTLIFE

Check in at **La Nueva Abarca** (✉ *Calle 3* ☎ *787/387–0805*), a lively oceanfront bar with billiard tables, to see whether there's a band playing.

THE NORTHWESTERN COAST

North of Rincón there is a string of beaches that have yet to be discovered. You won't find much large-scale development along this stretch of shoreline. Instead, the area is populated with modest hotels that cater to local families. Many surfers say the waves here are better than those in Rincón itself.

AGUADILLA

12 mi (18 mi) north of Rincón.

Resembling a fishing village, downtown Aguadilla has narrow streets lined with small wooden homes. Weathered but lovely, the faded facades recall the city's long and turbulent past. Officially incorporated as a town in 1775, Aguadilla subsequently suffered a series of catastrophes, including a devastating earthquake in 1918 and strong hurricanes in 1928 and 1932. Determined to survive, the town rebuilt after each disaster, and by World War II it had become known for the sprawling Ramey Air Force Base. The base was an important link in the U.S. defense system throughout the Cold War. Ramey was decommissioned in 1973; today the former base has an airport, a golf course, a university, and some small businesses. As a result of tourism, the north end of town is budding with international restaurants, surf shops, and even an outdoor mall. Additions such as a children's water park and ice-skating rink make Aguadilla a family-friendly destination, too.

Perhaps the town's greatest draw is its surfing at local spots like Wilderness Beach, Table Tops, Playa Crash Boat, and Gas Chamber. Famous for their right-hand barrels, these beaches have hosted a variety of amateur and professional surfing events, including the 1968 and 1988 ISA World Championships.

GETTING HERE AND AROUND

Most people arrive in Aguadilla either by car from San Juan or by flying directly into Aguadilla's Aeropuerto Internacional Rafael Hernandez. Continental Airlines offers daily flights from Newark to Aguadilla, and JetBlue has service from Orlando or New York. Rental cars ($35–$65 per day) are available from companies operating out of the Aguadilla airport, located at the old Ramey Air Force Base. To reach Aguadilla by car from San Juan, head west on toll road Highway 22, which turns into Highway 2. Continue on Highway 2 until it intersects with Route 111, leading to the center of town.

Airport Information **Aeropuerto Internacional Rafael Hernández** (✉ *Hwy. 2, Km 148.7, Aguadilla* ☎ *787/891–2286*).

Car Rental **Avis** (☎ *787/890–3311*). **Budget** (☎ *787/890–1110*). **Hertz** (☎ *787/890–5650*). **L & M Rent a Car** (☎ *787/890–3010*).

EXPLORING

Along Route 107—an unmarked road crossing through a golf course—you'll find the ruins of **La Ponderosa**, an old Spanish lighthouse, as well as its replacement Punta Borinquen at Puerto Rico's northwest point. The original was built in 1889 and destroyed by an earthquake in 1918. The U.S. Coast Guard rebuilt the structure in 1920. Just beyond the ruins is a local surf spot, Playa Wilderness. ✉ *Rte. 107.*

Parque Acuático las Cascadas has a large wave pool, giant slides, and the "Crazy River," a long, free-flowing river pool. It's strictly kid stuff. ✉ *Hwy. 2, Km 126.5* ☎ *787/819–1030* 🌐 *www.parqueacuaticolascascadas.com* ⏱ *Mar.–Aug., weekdays 10–5, weekends 10–6.*

Aguadilla Ice Skating Arena. Commonly referred to as **A.I.S.A.**, it is the only ice-skating complex in the Caribbean. *Rte. 442, Km 4.2., Aguadilla Centro 787/819–5555 www.aguadilla.govierno.com $10 Daily 10 am–11 pm.*

WHERE TO EAT

¢ ECLECTIC **Cocina Creativa.** At first glance, you might mistake this place for a vegetarian restaurant with its organic greens, homemade hummus, and fresh breads. In fact, the menu includes such meat dishes as bacon-wrapped oysters, jerk chicken with mango chutney, and churrasco with caramelized onions. The chalkboard-inscribed menu changes weekly but always features the in-house flan, torte, and cheesecake. With a Bohemian ambience, this is the type of place you could hang out for a while to enjoy the comfy couches, local artwork, and free Internet––while savoring one of their fruit smoothies or specialty coffees. *Carr. 110, Km 9.2, Aguadilla 787/890–1861 MC, V.*

¢ ★ CAFÉ **D'Rose Chocolate Factory.** This truffle treasure camouflaged in a nondescript strip mall is acclaimed for its "best coffee in Puerto Rico." The owner, Jose Rivera, refuses to disclose the secret source of his specialty beans or the technique that produces his mysterious blend. The aroma of chocolate entices passersby into the sweet shop with its candy-striped pink walls and chocolate-toned tables. Rotating glass towers display rich cakes and pastries, while endless rows of candy jars further tempt the palate. Chocolate-covered strawberries and gourmet truffles are all made in-house and are served by adorable grandmothers in their Little Miss Muffet–like uniforms topped with lace bonnets. *Carr. 107, Km 2.1, Borrinquen Aguadilla 787/891–0552 www.drosechocolatefactory.com MC, V.*

$–$$ ★ THAI **One Ten Thai.** Reflecting its location at Carretera 110, this restaurant had its origins in the owner's home where he served takeout to his circle of friends. This unplanned beginning has blossomed into Aguadilla's most popular eatery, today featuring lettuce wraps, curry bowls, and pad Thai noodles with tofu, beef, chicken, or shrimp. The owner's passion for authentic Thai recipes ultimately took him around the world, resulting in such signature dishes as lime-peanut stir-fry with cilantro and chili sauce served over your choice of meat. All herbs are grown on-site, and the beer selection is the largest in Puerto Rico. Seating is limited in this casual setting so expect to wait awhile. *Carr. 110, Km 9.2, Aguadilla 787/890–0113 MC, V Closed Mon.–Wed.*

WHERE TO STAY

$$ HOTEL **Courtyard Marriott.** Formerly a military hospital, this property was renovated in 2008 to cater to business and family clientele. All rooms are uniformly decorated in shades of beige, white, and blue. Amenities include desks with ergonomic chairs, Internet access, complimentary coffee service, and 32" TVs. Although only 10 rooms have a pool view, all guests have access to the on-site casino and aqua park for children. The nearest beach, Playa Crashboat, is a 10-minute drive from the hotel. **Pros:** Near airport; nice pool area. **Cons:** Airplane noise pollution; no beach. *West Parade/Belt Road, Ramey Base, Aguadilla 00603 787/658–8000 www.marriott.com/bqncy 150 rooms In-room:*

6

safe, Internet. In-hotel: restaurant, room service, bars, pools, gym, spa, laundry service, Wi-Fi, parking (paid) ⊟ *AE, D, MC, V* ¶ *EP.*

$ HOTEL **El Faro.** This family-friendly hotel isn't very close to the lighthouse from which it takes its name. But it's a good place to keep in mind if you're driving along the coast and need a place to stop for the night. (Keep a sharp eye out for the PARADOR sign on Route 107, as it's easy to miss.) Cheerfully decorated rooms surround a pair of pools, and there is a game room and basketball court for children to enjoy. The restaurant, Tres Amigos, is one of the most highly regarded in the area. Its specialty is steaks and other meats that come sizzling from the grill. The closest beach is Playa Crashboat, only five minutes by car. **Pros:** Reasonable rates; pretty pool areas. **Cons:** No beach; rather secluded location. ⊠ *Rte. 107, Km 2.1, Box 5148* ☎ *787/882–8000* ⊕ *www.farohotels.net* ⇨ *69 rooms* ♢ *In-hotel: restaurant, tennis court, pools, laundry facilities, public Wi-Fi* ⊟ *AE, D, DC, MC, V* ¶ *EP.*

$ HOTEL **El Pedregal.** Located in what looks like a tropical forest, El Pedregal is a great place to stay on the island's northwestern tip. There's no beach, but several of the best are only a short drive away. In the meantime, the pool can be a refreshing oasis. The rooms, in several two-story buildings, are slightly dated but comfortable with all the basic amenities. Included in the rate is transportation to and from the Aguadilla airport. **Pros:** Family-friendly environment; helpful staff. **Cons:** Noise from nearby housing development; not on beach. ⊠ *Rte. 111, Km. 0.1* ☎ *787/891–6068* ⊕ *www.hotelelpedregal.com* ⇨ *29 rooms* ♢ *In-room: Wi-Fi. In-hotel: restaurant, bar, pool, gym, laundry facilities, airport shuttle* ⊟ *AE, MC, V* ¶ *EP.*

$ HOTEL **Hotel Cielo Mar.** Just north of the town of Aguadilla, this massive hotel is perched on a bluff high above the water. The good news is that nearly every room has a jaw-dropping view of the coastline; the bad news is that the beach is far, far away. The accommodations are comfortable, if a bit old-fashioned. The hotel's restaurant, Terra Mar ($–$$), specializes in lobster, as well as other types of seafood. The open-air dining room is extremely pleasant, especially in the evening. Bring insect repellant especially when you are in the lobby area where mosquitoes tend to congregate. There's a separate kids' pool and a game room. **Pros:** Reasonable rates; great views. **Cons:** No beach; far from other dining options; noise from the game room off the lobby; no elevator. ⊠ *84 Av. Montemar, off Rte. 111* ☎ *787/882–5959 or 787/882–5961* ⊕ *www.cielomar.com* ⇨ *72 rooms* ♢ *In-room: refrigerator, Internet. In-hotel: 2 restaurants, bar, pools, public Wi-Fi* ⊟ *AE, MC, V* ¶ *EP.*

¢–$ HOTEL **JB Hidden Village.** This family-friendly hotel is in Aguada, about halfway between Aguadilla and Rincón. There's plenty here to keep the kids occupied. If you have your heart set on the beach, however, the landlocked location won't be ideal. The rooms and suites all have balconies, most of which overlook the sparkling pool. A well-regarded restaurant and bar are on the premises. **Pros:** Close to several beaches; good base for exploring the area. **Cons:** No beach; bland architecture; difficult to locate. ⊠ *Rte. 4416, Km 9.5 after 416 split, Aguada* ☎ *787/868–8686* ⎙ *787/868–8701* ⇨ *42 rooms* ♢ *In-hotel: restaurant, bar, pool* ⊟ *MC, V, AE* ¶ *EP.*

DID YOU KNOW?

Crash Boat Beach is named for the boats that were used for search and rescue of downed airmen when Ramey Air Force Base was in operation. Now, brightly painted fishing boats line its shore.

SPORTS AND THE OUTDOORS

DIVING AND SNORKELING
Near Gate 5 of the old Ramey Air Force Base, **Aquatica** (✉ *Rte. 110, Km 10* ☎ *787/890–6071 www.aquaticadive-surf.com*) offers scuba-diving certification courses, as well as snorkeling, paddle boarding, and surfing trips. It also rents bikes.

GOLF
The 18-hole **Punta Borinquen Golf Club** (✉ *Rte. 107, Km 2* ☎ *787/890–2987* 🌐 *www.puntaborinquengolf.com*), on the former Ramey Air Force Base, was a favorite of President Dwight D. Eisenhower's. Now a public course, the beachfront course is known for its tough sand traps and strong crosswinds. It is open daily.

SURFING
Surfboard rentals ($30) and two-hour surfing lessons ($65) are offered through **Wave Riding Vehicles** (✉ *Carr. 110, Km 7.3, Augadilla* ☎ *787/890–3351* 🌐 *www.waveridingvehicles.com* 🕑 *Mon.–Sat 10–6*), a surf shop and board factory at the intersection of Route 4416 and Carretera 110.

ISABELA

13 mi (20 km) east of Aguadilla.

Founded in 1819 and named for Spain's Queen Isabella, this small, whitewashed town on the northwesternmost part of the island skirts tall cliffs that overlook the rocky shoreline. Locals have long known of the area's natural beauty, and lately more offshore tourists have begun coming to this niche, which offers secluded hotels, fantastic beaches, excellent surf, and, just inland, hiking through one of the island's forest reserves.

GETTING HERE AND AROUND

Flying into Aguadilla's airport (BQN) is the fastest way to reach Isabela and will eliminate the two-hour drive from San Juan. Direct flights to Aguadilla from Newark are available through Continental Airlines, and from Orlando or New York through JetBlue. Several rental car companies are on-site at Aguadilla's Aeropuerto Internacional Rafael Hernandez, only 15 minutes from Isabela. If you are driving to the town of Isabella from San Juan, take Highway 2 west to Route 112 north. The 1120 will intersect with Route 4466, Isabella's coastal road.

Airport Information Aeropuerto Internacional Rafael Hernández (✉ *Hwy. 2, Km 148.7, Aguadilla* ☎ *787/891–2286*).

Car Rental Avis (☎ *787/890–3311*). **Budget** (☎ *787/890–1110*). **Hertz** (☎ *787/890–5650*). **L & M Rent a Car** (☎ *787/890–3010*).

EXPLORING

Explore karst topography and subtropical vegetation at the 2,357-acre **Bosque Estatal Guajataca** *(Guajataca State Forest)* between the towns of Quebradillas and Isabela. On more than 46 walking trails you can see 186 species of trees, including the royal palm and ironwood, and 45 species of birds—watch for red-tailed hawks and Puerto Rican woodpeckers. Bring a flashlight and descend into the **Cueva del Viento** (Cave of the Wind) to find stalagmites, stalactites, and other strange formations. At the entrance to the forest there's a small ranger station where you can pick up a decent hiking map. (Get here early, as the rangers don't always stay until the official closing time.) A little farther down the road is a recreational area with picnic tables and an observation tower. ✉ *Rte. 446, Km 10* ☎ *787/872–1045* *Free* ⏲ *Ranger station weekdays 8–5.*

OFF THE BEATEN PATH

Palacete Los Moreau. In the fields south of Isabela toward the town of Moca, a French family settled on a coffee and sugar plantation in the 1800s. The grand two-story house, trimmed with gables, columns, and stained-glass windows, was immortalized in the novel *La Llamarada,* written in 1935 by Puerto Rican novelist Enrique A. Laguerre. In Laguerre's novel about conditions in the sugarcane industry, the house belonged to his fictional family, the Moreaus. Although it doesn't have many furnishings, you can walk through the house and also visit Laguerre's personal library in the mansion's basement. On the grounds is an old steam engine once used to transport sugarcane. ✉ *Hwy. 2, Km 115.9* ☎ *787/877–2270* *Free* ⏲ *Tues.–Sat. 8–4:30.*

WHERE TO EAT

In addition to the restaurant listed below, the restaurants at Villa Montaña and Villas del Mar Hau are known for having good food.

$$–$$$ CONTINENTAL

Ocean Front Restaurant. True to its name, this seaside restaurant overlooks Playa de Jobos, the area's most popular surf break. Outdoor seating is appropriately decorated with surfboards hanging from the rafters and a boat-shaped bar in the center of the rough-hewn patio. To take a break from the salty air, step into the air-conditioned comfort of the more formal dining area. Whatever your appetite, you'll find something to please your palate with a menu offering everything from tropical ceviche and salmon wraps to garlic mahimahi and Porterhouse steaks. Drop by on the weekend to enjoy live music on an outdoor stage. ✉ *Rte. 4466, Km 0.1, Playa Jobos, Isabela* ☎ *787/872–3339* *www.oceanfrontpr.com* *AE, MC, V* ⏲ *Closed Mon.–Tues.*

¢ BISTRO

Ola Lola's. Boasting "the friendliest wave on the island," the owners have maximized their residence by converting their garage into overflow seating for their garden bistro. With fairy lights, beach chairs, and Latin music, the no-frills setting complements the simple menu of burgers, sandwiches, and signature dips. Owners John and Elaine Cosbyrefuse to reveal the secret of their rum punch recipe, which draws in a large clientele, as does their great selection of international beers. For an interesting keepsake, buy one of the souvenir T-shirts from each of the island's top surf spots. ✉ *Rte. 4466, Km 2.1, before Villa Montana at Playa Shacks, Isabela* ☎ *787/872–1230* *www.ola-lolas.com* *No credit cards* ⏲ *Closed Tues.–Thurs.*

WHERE TO STAY

$–$$ HOTEL ★

Ocean Blue Villa. Accented with turquoise mosaics, this pristinely white two-story villa is the area's newest hotel. Decorated with modern furnishings, the rooms have chaise longues, leather couches, paper lanterns, and such personal touches as baskets filled with books, DVDs, and beach towels. To cool off, jump in the small pool or walk five minutes to the nearby beach. Only the top-floor suites have kitchens and an ocean view. **Pros:** Clean rooms; modern amenities. **Cons:** Not

CLOSE UP

The Abominable Chupacabra

The Himalayas have their Yeti, Britain has its crop circles, New Jersey has its legendary Jersey Devil—and Puerto Rico has its *Chupacabra.* This "goat sucker" (as its name translates) has been credited with strange attacks on goats, sheep, rabbits, horses, and chickens since the mid-1970s. The attacks happen mostly at night, leaving the animals devoid of blood, with oddly vampire-like punctures in their necks.

Though the first references to these attacks were in the 1970s, the biggest surge of reports dates to the mid-1990s, when the mayor of Canóvanas received international attention and support from local police for his weekly search parties equipped with a caged goat as bait. The police stopped short of fulfilling the mayor's request for a special unit devoted to the creature's capture.

Sightings offer widely differing versions of the Chupacabra; it has gray, scraggly hair and resembles a kangaroo or wolf, or walks upright on three-toed feet. Some swear it hops from tree branch to tree branch and even flies, leaving behind, in the tradition of old Lucifer, the acrid stench of sulphur. It peers through large, oval, sometimes red eyes and "smells like a wet dog" as its reptilian tongue flicks the night air. It has, according to some, attacked humans, ripped through window screens, and jumped family dogs at picnics.

According to a 1995 article in the *San Juan Star,* island lore abounds with monsters predating the Chupacabra. The *comecogollo* was a version of Bigfoot—but smaller and a vegetarian. It was particularly sweet on *cogollo,* a baby plantain that springs up near its parent plant. In the early 1970s the Moca vampire also attacked small animals, but opinion differed on whether it was alien, animal, or really a vampire. The *garadiablo,* a swamp creature that emerged from the ooze at night to wreak havoc on the populace, also struck fear in the early 1970s. This "sea demon" was described as having the face of a bat, the skin of a shark, and the body of a human.

The Chupacabra has also been active in other spots with large Hispanic communities—Mexico, southern Texas, and Miami—and its scope is pretty wide. The list of reported sightings at 🌐 *www.elchupacabra.com* includes such unlikely locales as Maine and Missouri. And the Chupa's coverage on the Web isn't limited to sci-fi fan sites: Princeton University maintains a Web site meant to be a clearinghouse for Chupa information.

What to make of Chupa? Above the clamor of the fringe elements, one hears the more skeptical voice of reason. Zoologists have suggested that the alleged condition of some Chupacabra victims may actually be the result of exaggerated retelling of the work of less mysterious animals, such as a tropical species of bat known to feed on the blood of small mammals. Even some bird species are known to eat warm-blooded animals. Skeletal remains of an alleged Chupacabra found in Chile were determined to be those of a wild dog. This, however, doesn't explain the sightings of the hairy, ravenous beast. Then again, there's no accounting for the Loch Ness monster either.

–Karl Luntta

on the beach; nearby barking dog; no Internet. ✉ *Rte. 4466, Km 5.2, Isabela* ☎ *787/546–8038* 🌐 *www.oceanbluevilla.com* *6rooms* *In-room: kitchen (some), no phone, DVD. In-hotel: pool, parking (free)* *AE, MC, V* *EP.*

$ HOTEL **Pelican Reef.** This is one of the best deals on the coast: studio and one-bedroom apartments for less than you'd pay for a cramped hotel room. The five studios are almost as big as the seven one-bedroom apartments, making them a slightly better value. What they lack, however, are the private balconies overlooking beautiful Playa de Jobos. All have full kitchens and dining areas, and there are plenty of restaurants within walking distance. **Pros:** Great location; good value. **Cons:** Some traffic noise; musty smell in a few of the units. ✉ *Rte. 4466, Km 0* ☎ *787/872–6518 or 866/444–9818* 🌐 *www.pelicanreefapartments.com* *12 apartments* *In-room: kitchen. In-hotel: beachfront* *MC, V* *EP.*

$$$ HOTEL Fodor's Choice ★ **Villa Montaña.** This secluded cluster of villas, situated on a deserted stretch of beach between Isabela and Aguadilla, feels like a little town. You can pull your car into your own garage, then head upstairs to your airy studio or one-, two-, or three-bedroom suite with hand-carved mahogany furniture and canopy beds. Studios have kitchenettes, while the larger suites have full-size kitchens and laundry rooms. Eclipse, the open-air bar and restaurant, serves Caribbean-Asian fusion cuisine prepared with herbs from the hotel garden. Playa de Shacks, a very popular surfer beach, is nearby. An all-inclusive rate is available for an additional $100 per day. **Pros:** An away-from-it-all feel; on a secluded beach; great food. **Cons:** A bit pricey; far from other dining options; airplane noise. ✉ *Rte. 4466, Km 1.9, Box 530, Isabela* ☎ *787/872–9554 or 888/780–9195* 🌐 *www.villamontana.com* *38 rooms, 41 villas* *In-room: DVD. In-hotel: 2 restaurants, tennis courts, safe, pools, water sports, gym, laundry facilities* *AE, D, MC, V* *EP.*

$–$$ HOTEL **Villas de Costa Dorada.** Painted cheerful shades of pink, blue, and yellow, this cluster of buildings certainly gets your attention. The studios and one- and two-bedroom apartments, all with spacious balconies, have a homey feel. Rooms have restricted ocean views, and the complex has a pool and hot tub. **Pros:** Large accommodations; shared amenities with neighboring hotel. **Cons:** Cookie-cutter buildings; some unfortunate fabric selections; mosquitoes in the lobby. ✉ *Rte. 466, Km 0.1* ☎ *787/872–7255 or 800/981–5693* 🌐 *www.costadoradabeach.com* *52 rooms, 34 apartments, 34 studios* *In-hotel: restaurant, Wi-Fi, room service, bar, tennis courts, pools* *AE, MC, V* *EP.*

$–$$ HOTEL ★ **Villas del Mar Hau.** One-, two-, and three-bedroom cottages—painted in cheery pastels and trimmed with gingerbread—are the heart of this beachfront hotel. The accommodations aren't luxurious, but if you're looking for an unpretentious atmosphere, you'll have a hard time doing better. If you are planning on cooking, you should consider one of the studios, all of which have full kitchens. At the end of the private boardwalk paralleling the beach are three new eco-lodges that utilize rainwater and solar. The open-air restaurant, Olas y Arena, is known for its excellent fish and shellfish; the paella is especially good. The hotel also has outdoor grills, as well as basketball and volleyball courts reserved for guests. **Pros:** Laid-back vibe; protected swimming cove great for children; good restaurant. **Cons:** Very basic rooms; may be too kitschy for some. ✉ *Rte. 466, Km 8.9, Box 510* ☎ *787/872–2045* 🌐 *www.hauhotelvillas.com* *40 cottages* *In-room: kitchen (some). In-hotel: restaurant, tennis court, pool, beach front, water sports, laundry facilities* ▭ *AE, MC, V* 🍽 *EP.*

SPORTS AND THE OUTDOORS

HORSEBACK RIDING

Tropical Trail Rides (✉ *Rte. 4466, Km 1.9* ☎ *787/872–9256* 🌐 *www.tropicaltrailrides.com*) has two-hour morning and afternoon rides along the beach and through a forest of almond trees. Groups leave from Playa de Shacks, one of the region's prettiest beaches. At the end you have a chance to take a dip in the ocean. The company also offers hiking trips to the limestone caves at Survival Beach.

DIVING AND SNORKELING

Beginning and advanced divers can explore the submerged caves off Playa de Shacks through **La Cueva Submarina Dive Shop** (✉ *Rte. 466, Km 6.3* ☎ *787/872–1390*), which also offers certification courses and snorkeling trips.

SURFING

For surf lessons **Hang Loose Surf Shop** (✉ *Rte. 446, Km 1.2, Isabela* ☎ *787/872–2490* 🌐 *www.hangloosesurfshop.com* ⏲ *Tues.–Sun. 10–5*) offers a two-hour basic course for $65 and board rentals for $35. Lessons are usually held at Playa de Jobos, a great surfing spot where you can reward yourself with a refreshing drink from one of the beach shacks.

Ruta Panorámica

AN EXHILARATING DRIVE ON THE PANORAMIC ROUTE

WORD OF MOUTH

"The Ruta Panorámica is a drive through the Cordillera Central. The interior mountainous area is my favorite part of Puerto Rico, even more than the beaches. It's generally about 5–10 degrees cooler and so lush. It's where you really here the coquis, at night, too."

–nirosa

DID YOU KNOW?

The Toro Negro State Forest has the island's highest mountain, the 4,398 ft. (1,340 m) Cerro de Punta; the island's highest lake, Lago Guineo; and its most impressive waterfall, the 200 ft. (61 m) Dona Juaña Falls.

The Ruta Panorámica, or Panoramic Route, is an unforgettable overland journey that reveals rugged beauty and tranquil woodlands not found anywhere else on the island. It's an unruly road that clambers its way through the forests of Puerto Rico's mountainous interior. Towering trees create canopies over the narrow roads, and in their shade pink and purple impatiens bloom in profusion. You'll drive through sleepy colonial villages named for their Taíno descendants, discover trails leading to secret waterfalls, and behold one breathtaking vista after another.

The grandiose name may lead you to think that the Ruta Panorámica is a highway, but it's actually a network of mountain roads that snakes through the central region, or Cordillera Central. Some are nicely maintained, others are little more than gravel. But the Panoramic Route certainly lives up to its name, rewarding travelers with sprawling scenery around every bend of the road.

DRIVING THE HIDDEN HEART OF PUERTO RICO

You can explore the Ruta Panorámica in chunks, alternating rural and urban charms. Or you can plan an extended road trip, taking time to fully explore Puerto Rico's interior. Bring your sense of adventure, and on your journey perhaps you'll try *lechon asado,* mouthwatering pork, slow-roasted over open pits. Did we mention that these are whole pigs? You may decide to cool off with a cup of cold mavi, a local drink made of fermented tree bark. The beaches and the city recede from memory here, and you begin to adopt new, unhurried rhythms, allowing serendipity to be your guide. Tropical flora, like birds of paradise, beg to be photographed. On foggy stretches of road umbrella-sized *yagrumo* leaves laden with water brush the roof of your car. Puerto Rico's highest mountain is tucked into the Toro Negro Forest, and look-out points afford views all the way to the ocean.

THREE JOURNEYS

We've divided the Ruta into three discrete trips, each requiring a full day. Trip 1 takes you from Yabucoa to Aibonito; Trip 2, from Aibonito to Adjuntas; and Trip 3 from Adjuntas to Mayaguez. Put them together for the complete journey, which you can start from the east or the west (Yabucoa or San Juan for eastbound journey; Mayaguez for a west coast departure).

RUTA PANORÁMICA DRIVING TIPS

Rent from a nationally recognized rental car agency. Should you break down on the Ruta or need a tire change, the national chains are more able than local agencies to dispatch assistance or a provide a replacement vehicle. Ensure your rental has a spare tire and a jack and have the roadside assistance number handy in the event that you need it.

Fuel up at each opportunity. There are few gas stations on the Ruta; don't wait for a ¼ tank before you fill up.

Avoid driving after dark. The Ruta isn't lit and driving after dark can be dangerous. Occasional patches of washed out road aren't uncommon, and they're sometimes impossible to see at night. Also, there are few, if any, food or gas services available once the sun goes down.

Pack drinks and snacks. Because services are limited along most of the route, your options may be limited when hunger strikes. Be prepared and bring your own drinks and snacks. However this is an agricultural region; bananas, pineapples, and plantains are grown throughout the area. Along your journey you'll encounter roadside stands where men sell just-picked fruits and vegetables from the backs of their trucks. These also make a great snack option, just be sure to wash all produce thoroughly.

Invest in a good map. Most hotels have free maps, courtesy of the tourism board; these are highly detailed maps worth picking up. If you can't find one, invest in a good road map. Although it may not include all the numbered roads that make up the Ruta, it's better than nothing.

San Cristóbol Canyon near Aibonito

YABUCOA TO AIBONITO

> **THE PLAN**
>
> **Distance:** 48 mi (77 km)
>
> **Time:** 6 hours
>
> **Breaks:** Roadside fruit stands and roadside restaurants such as El Tenedor Dorado

To start exploring the Ruta Panorámica from San Juan, make your way south to the town of Yabucoa, picking up Route 901 Oeste (901 West). Don't be discouraged by all the traffic lights, fast-food outlets, pharmacies, and shops you'll first encounter (in fact, you may want to stock up on supplies here). The road will soon give way to the comparative isolation that characterizes the rest of the Ruta. ■ **TIP→ Gas up at the Gulf station less than a mile into Yabucoa at the start of the Ruta; it's the last service station for a while.**

The landscape from Yabucoa to Aibonito is stunning in its variety. From trees typical of the tropics—mango, almonds, palms, and the lush, leafy tree fern—to cedar and bamboo, this stretch offers a preview of the Ruta's diversity.

Don't let your eyes get too carried away by the scenery, though. The Ruta is notorious for its poor signage. Though brown and white RUTA PANORMICA signs are more plentiful on this stretch of the road, they're easy to miss, often covered over by plants or obscured by filmy drippings from the flora. If you're in doubt about your direction, don't hesitate to stop and ask a local. Even if you have road numbers and detailed directions, the Ruta's twists and turns can be puzzling, but going off course and getting back again is all part of the adventure!

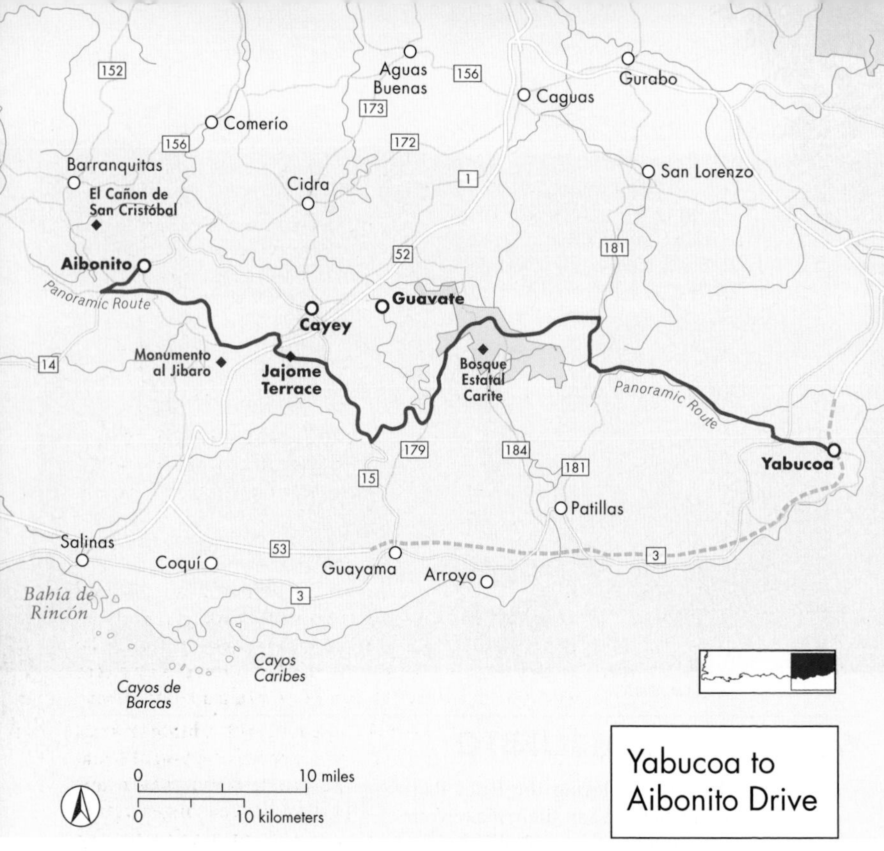

Once you're out of Yabucoa proper, there's little more than the flora to capture your attention—that and the road itself—until you reach Aibonito. Legend has it that Aibonito got its name when a Spaniard exclaimed "*¡Ay, que bonito!*" ("Oh, how pretty!") upon seeing the valley where the town now stands. Puerto Rico's highest city, Aibonito is known as "The Queen of Flowers" because flowering plants thrive in its temperate climate. The city hosts a flower festival every year, usually in late June or July, and gives awards for blossoms and garden design. Live music and craft stalls add to the festivities. A double-steepled cathedral graces the charming town square, which is surrounded by shops and restaurants. Local guides organize outings to nearby Cañon de San Cristóbal.

ROAD WATCH This stretch of the Ruta is demanding of the driver; with no shoulder for most of the way, there's little, if any, opportunity to stop for a rest or pull over to take photos. Be patient; if you tack on trips 2 and 3, you'll find plenty of places to satisfy both needs.

WHERE TO EAT AND STAY

$$ **Jajome Terrace.** This is the only lodging in Cayey, and it nestles itself cozily into its mountain surroundings. An outdoor dining area that offers mountain panoramas is open on weekends. ✉ *Carretera 15 K18.6, Cayey* ☎ *787/738–4016* 🌐 *www.jajometerrace.com* ▬ *AE, MC, V.*

AIBONITO TO ADJUNTAS

THE PLAN

Distance: 46 mi (74 km) direct from Aibonito to Adjuntas; approx 19 mi (30 km) for side trip south to Ponce

Time: 1 day without side visit to Hacienda Buena Vista and Ponce; 2 days for full itinerary

Breaks: Mirador Villalba-Orocovis, Doña Juana Recreational Area of the Toro Negro Forest, Hacienda Buena Vista

Quite possibly the prettiest part of the Ruta Panorámica, the section running from Aibonito to Adjuntas takes you through Puerto Rico's mountain region and the Toro Negro Forest. The views from Aibonito to the midway point of this route open up into sweeping panoramas of valleys; from the vantage point of your high elevation, the houses below look like tiny dots.

Be sure to stop at the **Mirador Villalba-Orocovis** at Km 39.7 for some of the most spectacular views. This state-run overlook has ample parking and is open from 9 AM until 5 PM, Wednesday to Sunday. In addition to the view, there's a playground and sheltered picnic areas. Don't worry if your visit doesn't coincide with the overlook's hours; there's plenty of room to pull over on the side of the road and you can still enjoy the view, surrounded by mountains on either side. It tends to be windy up here at 2,000 feet, so bring an extra layer.

7

After the Mirador, the next stop is the **Toro Negro Forest**. Climbing to an elevation of more than 4,000 feet, the forest has the distinction of being home to the highest point in Puerto Rico, Cerro de Punta, which tops out at 4,390 feet. Outdoor enthusiasts should stop by the ranger station at Km. 32.4 to inquire about trails, request maps, or obtain camping permits. For those who enjoy their scenery within easy reach, pull over at the **Area Recreativa Doña Juana** (the Doña Juana Recreational Area). Just a short walk across from the parking area is a natural pool; feel free to dip your feet in!

From the forest, you can drive through to Adjuntas, picking up either Highway 10 South or Route 123 South. Both will lead you to Ponce, Puerto Rico's second largest city, after San Juan, but 10 is faster and less scenic. It's also newer and somewhat less treacherous than 123.

If time allows, don't miss **Hacienda Buena Vista** (⇨ *above*), one of the historic sites operated by the Fideicomiso de Conservacion de Puerto Rico (the Conservation Trust of Puerto Rico). This 79-acre property was once one of the island's most important agricultural hubs; today, the Fideicomiso maintains the restored hacienda and invites you to explore coffee and cacao production on tours with knowledgeable guides. You'll need to make reservations to visit. Be sure to ask if any special activities—such as the cacao or coffee harvests—coincide with the dates of your visit. Four tours are offered each day: 8:30 AM, 10:30 AM, 1:30 PM, and 3:30 PM.

From Buena Vista, it's just a 20-minute drive to Ponce. Start your visit at the **Plaza de las Delicias** (Plaza of Delights), Ponce's main square. Here, you'll see a historic firehouse, a church, and decorative fountains, all

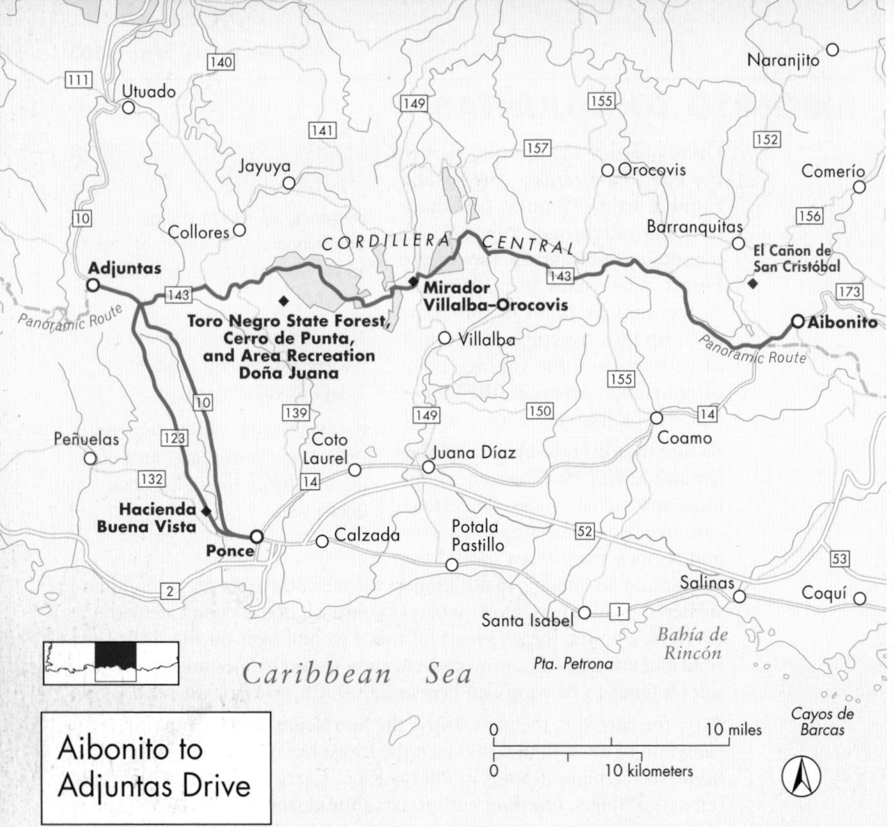

rich with history. Guides and brochures are available at the firehouse. Along the side streets radiating from the square you'll notice Ponce's distinctive architecture, quite different from that of San Juan. If you extend your visit another day, visit the town's cemetery, where many of the island's prominent politicians are buried in elaborate mausoleums. Alternatively, you can scale the hillside for a tour of **Castillo Serralles**, the former home of the Serralles family, Puerto Rico's rum barons, and the Cruceta La Vigia, a cross-shaped observatory that provides views straight to the Caribbean Sea.

WHERE TO EAT AND STAY IN UTUADO

You won't find much food along this stretch of the Ruta, so it's best to time your meal around your arrival in Ponce where dining options are abundant. Unless you plan to camp in the Toro Negro Forest (and if you do, you'll need a permit), you'll have to detour off this section of the Ruta Panorámica to find a place to rest. Ponce offers many places to stay. *For a complete list of our recommended hotels and restaurants in Ponce, see Where to Eat and Where to Stay sections in chapter 5.*

Take Route 10 North out of Adjuntas to get to Utuado.

DID YOU KNOW?

The Panoramic Route is defined by its hilly terrain where each bend in the road brings a new sight

Hiking the Toro Negro Forest

$$–$$$ HOTEL Fodor's Choice ★ **Casa Grande Mountain Retreat.** Here you'll come as close as you can to sleeping in a tree house. Guest rooms are in five wooden buildings on platforms high above the varied vegetation. When you lie in the hammock on your private porch, all you can see are mountains. Furnishings are simple–beds and dressers–but the accommodations lack nothing necessary. Recent improvements include the installation of fans and new bathroom fixtures. Casa Grande also offers a pool, hiking trails, bird-watching opportunities, a book exchange, a restaurant, and yoga classes by request (the owner is a certified Kripalu yoga instructor). **Pros:** Unspoiled setting with spectacular views; accessible for people with disabilities; outdoor activities. **Cons:** No air-conditioning; long drive to other sights/restaurants. ✉ *Rte. 612, Km 0.3, Utuado* ☎ *787/894–3939 or 888/343–2272* 🌐 *www.hotelcasagrande.com* *20 rooms* *In-room: no a/c, no phone, no TV. In-hotel: restaurant, pool, no elevator, no-smoking rooms* 💳 *AE, MC, V.* *EP.*

$$ PUERTO RICAN ✕ **Casa Grande.** The treat of dining here is the view. From the cafe tables on the balcony or deck, you feel as if you've been painted into the landscape. Lunch is served only on weekends, though you can request sandwiches in advance during the week. Dinner consists of typical Puerto Rican dishes, though vegetarians will be pleased to learn that Casa Grande offers viable alternatives to the meat-heavy local diet. Unless you're arriving for breakfast or dinner, you'll need reservations for lunch. ✉ *Rte. 612, Km 0.3, Box 1499, Utuado* ☎ *787/894–3939 or 888/343–2272* 🌐 *wwww.hotelcasagrande.com* *Reservations for lunch required* 💳 *AE, MC, V.*

Tram to Cueva Clara, the cave network of Rio Camuy Cave Park

ADJUNTAS TO MAYAGÜEZ

This is a journey through unspoiled nature. There are few places or reasons to stop from the starting point to the stopping point, but one exception is the **Torre de Piedra** (Stone Tower), an observation tower in Maricao with breathtaking views. On a clear day you can see almost the entire western coast of the island from this vantage point.

THE PLAN

Distance: 69 mi (111 km)

Time: 8–10 hrs without side visits to Camuy Caverns and/or Arecibo Observatory; 2 days for full itinerary

Breaks: Torre de Piedra, Camuy Caverns, Arecibo Observatory

⚠ **This section of the Ruta is perhaps the most treacherous—the road from Adjuntas to Maricao is in bad shape, pocked with potholes and the occasional sink hole that's eaten away part of the road—so take it slow. It's also poorly marked; signage is scarce to nonexistent in some areas.**

If you're looking for something more stimulating than the scenery, veer off the Ruta and steer north on Route 129 toward Lares and Arecibo. This road is no less scenic, but leads through more pueblos until you end up north of Lares at the **Parque de las Cavernas del Rio Camuy** (Rio Camuy Cave Park) and the **Arecibo Observatory.**

Fodor's Choice ★ The 268-acre **Parque de las Cavernas del Rio Camuy** contains one of the world's largest cave networks. After watching an introductory film, a tram takes you down a trail shaded by bamboo and banana trees to Cueva Clara, where the stalactites and stalagmites turn the entrance

DID YOU KNOW?

Arecibo's radio telescope is crucial for identifying NEA's (near-earth asteroids). If a small body is on a collision course for Earth, Arecibo's sensitive radar measurements could detect it.

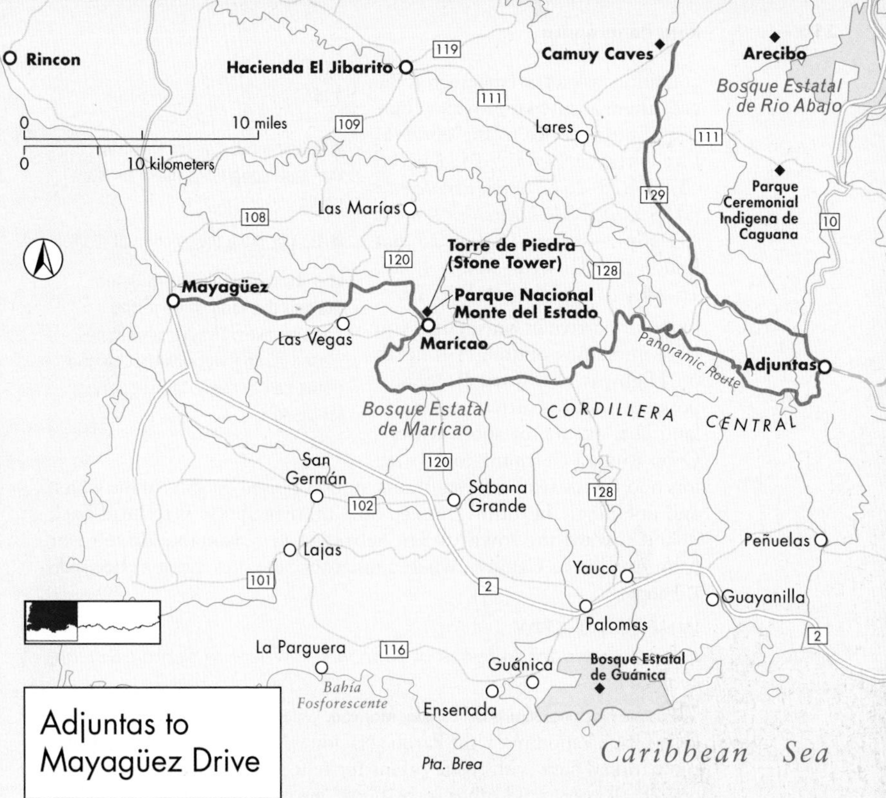

into a toothy grin. Hour-long guided tours in English and Spanish lead you on foot through the 180-high foot cave, which is teeming with wildlife. You're likely to see the blue-eyed river crams and long-legged tarantulas. More elusive are the bats that make their home here. They don't come out until dark, but you can feel the heat they generate at the cave's entrance. The visit ends with a tram ride to the Tres Pueblos sinkhole, where you can see the third longest underground river in the world passing from one cave to another. Tours are first-come, first-served; plan to arrive early on weekends, when locals join the crowds. There's a picnic area, cafeteria, and gift shop. ✉ *Rte. 129, Km 18.9* ☎ *787/898–3100* 💳 *$10* ⏲ *Wed.–Sun. 8–4; last tour at 3:30.*

Fodor's Choice ★ Hidden among pine-covered hills, the **Arecibo Observatory** is home to the world's largest radar-radio telescope. Operated by the National Astronomy and Ionosphere Center of Cornell University, the 20-acre dish lies in a 563-foot deep sinkhole in the karst landscape. If the 600-ton platform hovering eerily over the dish looks familiar, it may be because it was featured in the movie *Contact*. You can walk around the viewing platform and explore two levels of interactive exhibits on planetary systems, meteors and weather phenomena in the visitor center. There's also a gift shop. Note that the trail leading up to the observatory is extremely steep. For those who have difficulty walking or have a medical condition, ask a staff member at the gate about a van that provides courtesy shuttle service to the observatory entrance. ✉ *Rte. 625, Km 3.0* ☎ *787/878–2612* 🌐 *www.naic.edu* 🎫 *$6 adults; $4 children & seniors* ⏲ *Daily 9–4, Dec. 15–Jan. 15 and June 1–July 31; Wed.–Sun. 9–4, Jan. 16–May 31 and Aug. 1–Dec. 14.*

Once you arrive in Mayagüez, you have numerous options. Go north on Highway 2 toward Rincón, a popular town for surfers and mainland U.S. expats, or south toward Cabo Rojo, a charming town with lots of open-air seafood restaurants, houses poised on stilts in the water, and unfailingly beautiful sunsets. Still another option is to head back inland toward the town of San Sebastian (a reasonable drive to or from Arecibo or Camuy), where numerous activities await at **Hacienda El Jibarito.**

TIPS

- Allow a full day for this trip; the road conditions make for slow going.
- Do not drive this section at night.
- If it's rainy, call ahead before making the long drive to the Camuy caves. They're sometimes closed during wet weather, as the paths can become too slippery for visitors.

WHERE TO STAY

For recommended lodgings in Rincón see Where to Stay in Rincón, chapter 6.

¢ CABINS **Parque Nacional Monte del Estado, Maricao.** One of the few lodging options on the Ruta Panorámica, the Parque Nacional Monte del Estado is a state-run national park with rustic cabins for rent. The grounds have a pool, basketball court, and other recreational areas, and the park is in close proximity of the Torre de Piedra. You'll need to bring your own sheets and towels, as these aren't provided. There's no food here, either, and none within driving distance. **Pros:** Affordable lodging in a natural setting; **Cons:** Rustic accommodations; no on-site or nearby dining options. ✉ *Rte. 120, Km 13.2* ☎ *787/873–5632* 🌐 *www.parquesnacionalespr.com/monte_estado_cv.asp* 🎫 *$65.40 per night for cabin.*

$$$ INN **Hacienda El Jibarito, San Sebastian.** Designated the island's first "agrotourism" inn, Hacienda El Jibarito is an attractive parador hidden in the mountains of San Sebastian. It's wildly popular among locals but is virtually unknown to visitors (at least for now). Accommodations are private cabins, equipped with air-conditioning, televisions, coffeemakers, and other basic amenities. Most cabins have at least one porch, decked out with a hammock and/or rocking chairs. When you feel like being around other people, you can take advantage of the indoor and outdoor pools and Jacuzzi. El Jibarito also offers massage services, horseback-riding tours, and coffee-roasting demonstrations. **Restaurant Laurnaga,** on-site, serves excellent meals, its menu inspired by traditional Puerto Rican favorites. **Pros:** Ideal for couples and families; variety of activities; attentive service. **Cons:** Distance from off-site services, including restaurants; quality of food could stand improvement. ✉ *Rte. 445, Km 6.5* ☎ *787/280–4040* 🌐 *http://www.haciendaeljibarito.com.*

Travel Smart Puerto Rico

WORD OF MOUTH

"If you are types who don't mind things a little rustic, PR has wonderful bed-and-breakfasts and paradores. You can Google them. They must meet minimum standards and are government sanctioned family-owned hotels and inns."

—mom23rugrats

www.fodors.com/community

GETTING HERE AND AROUND

■ TIP→ Ask the local tourist board about hotel and local transportation packages that include tickets to major museum exhibits or other special events.

AIR TRAVEL

Nonstop flights to San Juan from New York are 3¾ hours; from Miami, 2½ hours; from Atlanta, 3½ hours; from Boston, 4 hours; from Chicago, 4¾ hours; from Los Angeles, 8 hours; from the United Kingdom, 5 hours; from Germany, 9¾ hours.

There are dozens of daily flights to Puerto Rico from the United States, and connections are particularly good from the East Coast, although there are a few nonstop flights from the Midwest as well. San Juan's international airport is a major regional hub, so many travelers headed elsewhere in the Caribbean make connections here. Because of the number of flights, fares to San Juan are among the most reasonably priced to the region.

Airlines and Airports Airline and Airport Links.com (🌐 *www.airlineandairportlinks.com*) has links to many of the world's airlines and airports.

Airline Security Issues Transportation Security Administration (🌐 *www.tsa.gov*) has answers for almost every question that might come up.

AIRPORTS

The island's main airport is Aeropuerto Internacional Luis Muñoz Marín (SJU), 20 minutes east of Old San Juan in the neighborhood of Isla Verde. San Juan's secondary airport is the small Fernando L. Rivas Dominici Airport (SIG), also called Isla Grande, near the city's Miramar section. From either airport you can catch flights to Culebra, Vieques, and other destinations on Puerto Rico and throughout the Caribbean. (Note that although the Dominici airport was still operating at this writing, its future was uncertain.)

Other Puerto Rican airports include Aeropuerto Internacional Rafael Hernández (BQN) in the northwestern town of Aguadilla, Aeropuerto Eugenio María de Hostos (MAZ) in the west-coast community of Mayagüez, Mercedita (PSE) in the south-coast town of Ponce, Aeropuerto Diego Jiménez Torres (FAJ) in the east-coast city of Fajardo, Antonio Rivera Rodríguez (VQS) on Vieques, and Aeropuerto Benjamin Rivera Noriega (CPX) on Culebra.

Airport Information Aeropuerto Antonio Rivera Rodríguez (✉ *Vieques* ☎ *787/741–8358*). **Aeropuerto Benjamin Rivera Noriega** (✉ *Culebra* ☎ *787/742–0022*). **Aeropuerto Diego Jiménez Torres** (✉ *Fajardo* ☎ *787/860–3110*). **Aeropuerto Eugenio María de Hostos** (✉ *Mayagüez* ☎ *787/265–7065*). **Aeropuerto Fernando L. Rivas Dominici** (✉ *Isla Grande, San Juan* ☎ *787/729–8711*). **Aeropuerto Internacional Luis Muñoz Marín** (✉ *Isla Verde, San Juan* ☎ *787/791–3840*). **Aeropuerto Mercedita** (✉ *Ponce* ☎ *787/842–6292*). **Aeropuerto Rafael Hernández** (✉ *Aguadilla* ☎ *787/891–2286*).

GROUND TRANSPORTATION

Before arriving, check with your hotel about transfers: Some hotels and resorts provide transport from the airport—free or for a fee—to their guests; some larger resorts run regular shuttles. Otherwise, your best bets are *taxis turísticos* (tourist taxis). Uniformed officials at the airport can help you make arrangements. They will give you a slip with your exact fare to hand to the driver. Rates are based on your destination. A taxi turístico to Isla Verde costs $10. It's $15 to Condado and $19 to Old San Juan. There's a 50¢ charge for each bag handled by the driver.

FLIGHTS

San Juan's busy Aeropuerto Internacional Luis Muñoz Marín is the Caribbean hub of American Airlines, which flies nonstop from Boston, Chicago, Dallas, Hartford, Miami, Newark, New York–JFK, and Philadelphia. Continental Airlines flies nonstop from Houston and Newark. Delta flies nonstop from Atlanta, Orlando, New York–LGA, and New York–JFK. JetBlue flies nonstop from Boston, Orlando, and New York–JFK. Spirit Air flies nonstop from Fort Lauderdale and Orlando. United flies nonstop from Chicago, New York–JFK, Philadelphia, and Washington, D.C.–Dulles. US Airways flies nonstop from Baltimore, Boston, Charlotte, Pittsburgh, Philadelphia, and Washington, D.C.–Dulles.

It used to be that travelers arriving at San Juan's international airport had to transfer to nearby Aeropuerto Fernando L. Rivas Dominici (close to Old San Juan and Condado) to take a flight to Vieques or Culebra. This is no longer the case, as all the carriers servicing the islands also have flights from the international airport. Air Flamenco, Isla Nena Air Service, and Vieques Air Link offer daily flights from both airports in San Juan to Vieques and Culebra. Cape Air flies between the international airport and Vieques.

Puerto Rico is also a good spot from which to hop to other Caribbean islands. American Eagle serves many islands in the Caribbean from San Juan; Cape Air connects San Juan to St. Thomas and St. Croix. Seaborne Airlines has seaplanes departing from San Juan Piers 6 and 7 to St. Thomas and St. Croix.

San Juan is no longer the only gateway into Puerto Rico. If you're headed to the western part of the island, you can fly directly into Aguadilla. Continental flies here from Newark, and JetBlue flies here from New York–JFK. If the southern coast is your goal, JetBlue and Continental fly to Ponce from Newark.

Airline Contacts American Airlines (☎ *800/433–7300* 🌐 *www.aa.com*). **Continental Airlines** (☎ *800/523–3273 for U.S. and Mexico reservations, 800/231–0856 for international reservations* 🌐 *www.continental.com*). **Delta Airlines** (☎ *800/221–1212 for U.S. reservations, 800/241–4141 for international reservations* 🌐 *www.delta.com*). **JetBlue** (☎ *800/538–2583* 🌐 *www.jetblue.com*). **Northwest Airlines** (☎ *800/225–2525* 🌐 *www.nwa.com*). **Spirit Airlines** (☎ *800/772–7117* 🌐 *www.spiritair.com*). **United Airlines** (☎ *800/864–8331 for U.S. reservations, 800/538–2929 for international reservations* 🌐 *www.united.com*). **USAirways** (☎ *800/428–4322 for U.S. and Canada reservations, 800/622–1015 for international reservations* 🌐 *www.usairways.com*).

Regional Airlines Air Flamenco (☎ *787/724–1818* 🌐 *www.airflamenco.net*). **Cape Air** (☎ *800/525–0714* 🌐 *www.flycapeair.com*). **Isla Nena Air Service** (☎ *787/741–6362 or 877/812–5144* 🌐 *www.islanena.8m.com*). **Seaborne Airlines** (☎ *888/359–8687* 🌐 *www.seaborneairlines.com*). **Vieques Air Link** (☎ *787/741–8331 or 888/901–9247* 🌐 *www.vieques-island.com/val*).

BUS TRAVEL

The Autoridad Metropolitana de Autobuses (AMA) operates buses that thread through San Juan, running in exclusive lanes on major thoroughfares and stopping at signs marked *parada*. Destinations are indicated above the windshield. Bus B-21 runs through Condado all the way to Plaza Las Américas in Hato Rey. Bus A-5 runs from San Juan through Santurce and the beach area of Isla Verde. Service starts at around 6 am and generally continues until 9 pm. Fares are 75¢ and are paid in exact change upon entering the bus. Most buses are air-conditioned and have wheelchair lifts and lockdowns.

There's no bus system covering the rest of the island. If you do not have a rental car, your best bet is to travel by *públicos,* which are usually shared 17-passenger vans. They have yellow license plates ending in "P" or "PD," and they scoot to towns throughout the island, stopping in each community's main plaza. They operate primarily during the day; routes and fares are fixed by the Public Service Commission, but schedules aren't set, so you have to call ahead.

Bus Information Autoridad Metropolitana de Autobuses (☎ *787/294-0500*).

CAR TRAVEL

Several well-marked, multilane highways link population centers. Route 26 is the main artery through San Juan, connecting Condado and Old San Juan to Isla Verde and the airport. Route 22, which runs east–west between San Juan and Camuy, and Route 52, which runs north–south between San Juan and Ponce, are toll roads. Route 2, a smaller highway, travels west from San Juan toward Rincón, and Route 3 traverses east toward Fajardo. Route 3 can be mind-numbingly slow, so consider taking Route 66, a toll road that bypasses the worst of the traffic.

Five highways are particularly noteworthy for their scenery and vistas. The island's tourism authorities have even given them special names. Ruta Panorámica (Panoramic Route) runs east–west through the central mountains. Ruta Cotorra (Puerto Rican Parrot Route) travels along the north coast. Ruta Paso Fino (Paso Fino Horse Route, after a horse breed) takes you north–south and west along the south coast. Ruta Coquí, named for the famous Puerto Rican tree frog, runs along the east coast. Ruta Flamboyán, named after the island tree, goes from San Juan through the mountains to the east coast.

GASOLINE

All types of fuel—unleaded regular, unleaded super-premium, and diesel—are available by the liter. Most stations have both full- and self-service. Hours vary, but stations generally operate daily from early in the morning until 10 or 11 pm; in metro areas many are open 24 hours. Stations are few and far between in the Cordillera Central and other rural areas, so plan accordingly. In cities you can pay with cash and bank or credit cards; in the hinterlands cash is occasionally your only option.

ROAD CONDITIONS

Puerto Rico has some of the Caribbean's best roads. That said, potholes, sharp turns, speed bumps, sudden gradient changes, and poor lighting can sometimes make driving difficult. Be especially cautious when driving after heavy rains or hurricanes; roads and bridges might be washed out or damaged. Many of the mountain roads are very narrow and steep, with unmarked curves and cliffs. Locals are familiar with such roads and often drive at high speeds, which can give you quite a scare. When traveling on a narrow, curving road, it's best to honk your horn as you take any sharp turn.

Traffic around cities—particularly San Juan, Ponce, and Mayagüez—is heavy at rush hours (weekdays from 7 am to 10 am and 4 pm to 7 pm).

FROM	TO	RTE./ DISTANCE
San Juan	Aguadilla	Rte. 22 81 mi (130 km)
San Juan	El Yunque	Rte. 3 35 mi (55 km)
San Juan	Fajardo	Rte. 3 34 mi (54 km)
San Juan	Mayagüez	Rte. 22 98 mi (160 km)
San Juan	Ponce	Rte. 52 70 mi (112 km)

ROADSIDE EMERGENCIES

In an emergency, dial 911. If your car breaks down, call the rental company for a replacement. Before renting, make sure you investigate the company's policy regarding replacement vehicles and repairs out on the island, and ask about surcharges that might be incurred if you break down in a rural area and need a new car.

RULES OF THE ROAD

U.S. driving laws apply in Puerto Rico, and you'll find no problem with signage or directionals. Street and highway signs are most often in Spanish but use international symbols; brushing up on a few key Spanish terms before your trip will help. The following words and phrases are especially useful: *calle sin salida* (dead-end street), *cruce de peatones* (pedestrian crossing), *cuidado* (caution), *desvío* (detour), *estación de peaje* (tollbooth), *no entre* (do not enter), *prohibido adelantar* (no passing), *salida* (exit), *tránsito* (one way), *zona escolar* (school zone).

Distances are posted in kilometers (1 mi to 1.6 km), whereas speed limits are posted in miles per hour. Speeding and drunk-driving penalties are much the same here as on the mainland. Police cars often travel with their lights flashing, so it's difficult to know when they're trying to pull you over. If the siren is on, move to the right lane to get out of the way. If the lights are on, it's best to pull over—but make sure that the vehicle is a *marked* police car before doing so.

FERRY TRAVEL

The Puerto Rico Ports Authority runs passenger ferries from Fajardo to Culebra and Vieques. Service is from the ferry terminal in Fajardo, about a 90-minute drive from San Juan. Advance reservations are not accepted. There are a limited number of seats on the ferries, so get to the terminal in plenty of time. This means arriving an hour or more ahead of the departure time in Fajardo, somewhat less in Vieques and Culebra. In Fajardo, the ticket counter is in the small building across the street from the actual terminal. In Vieques and Culebra, the ticket counters are at the entrance to the terminals. There are food kiosks at Fajardo and Vieques that are open even for the early morning departures. Culebra doesn't have any eateries nearby.

The Fajardo–Vieques passenger ferry departs from Vieques weekdays at 9 am, 1 pm, 3 pm, 4:30 pm, and 8 pm, returning at 6:30 am, 11 am, 3 pm, and 6 pm. On weekends ferries depart from Vieques at 9 am, 3 pm, and 6 pm, returning at 6:30 am, 1 pm, and 4:30 pm. Tickets for the 90-minute journey are $2 each way. The Fajardo–Culebra ferry leaves Culebra daily at 9 am, 3 pm, and 7 pm, returning at 6:30 am, 1 pm, and 5 pm. The 90-minute trip is $2.25.

Information Puerto Rico Ports Authority (☎ *787/723-2260* 🌐 *www.prpa.gobierno.pr*).

ESSENTIALS

ACCOMMODATIONS

San Juan's high-rise hotels on the Condado and Isla Verde beach strips cater primarily to the cruise-ship and casino crowd, though some also target business travelers. Outside San Juan, particularly on the east coast, you'll find self-contained luxury resorts that cover hundreds of acres. In the west, southwest, and south—as well as on the islands of Vieques and Culebra—smaller inns, villas, condominiums, and government-sponsored *paradores* are the norm.

CATEGORY	COST
$$$$	over $350
$$$	$250–$350
$$	$150–$250
$	$80–$150
¢	under $80

All prices are for a standard double room in high season, based on the European Plan (EP) and excluding tax and service charges.

Most hotels and other lodgings require you to give your credit-card details before they will confirm your reservation. If you don't feel comfortable e-mailing this information, ask if you can fax it (some places even prefer faxes). However you book, get confirmation in writing and have a copy of it handy when you check in.

Be sure you understand the hotel's cancellation policy. Some places allow you to cancel without any kind of penalty—even if you prepaid to secure a discounted rate—if you cancel at least 24 hours in advance. Others require you to cancel a week in advance or penalize you the cost of one night. Small inns and B&Bs are most likely to require you to cancel far in advance. Most hotels allow children under a certain age to stay in their parents' room at no extra charge, but others charge for them as extra adults; find out the cutoff age for discounts.

TIP→ Assume that hotels operate on the European Plan (EP, no meals) unless we specify that they use the Breakfast Plan (BP, with full breakfast), Continental Plan (CP, Continental breakfast), Full American Plan (FAP, all meals), Modified American Plan (MAP, breakfast and dinner), or are all-inclusive (AI, all meals and most activities).

APARTMENT AND HOUSE RENTALS

Local Agents **Island West Properties** (✉ *Box 700, Rincón* ☎ *787/823-2323* 🌐 *www.island-wes.com*) can help you rent condos in Rincón by the week or the month. **Puerto Rico Vacation Apartments** (✉ *Calle Marbella del Caribe Oeste S-5, Isla Verde* ☎ *787/727-1591 or 800/266-3639* 🌐 *www.sanjuanvacations.com*) represents some 200 properties in Condado and Isla Verde. **Rainbow Realty** (✉ *Rte. 996, Esperanza, Vieques* ☎ *787/741-4312* 🌐 *www.enchanted-isle.com/rainbow*) rents condos and villas on Vieques.

HOTELS

In the most expensive hotels your room will be large enough for two to move around comfortably, with two double beds (*camas matrimoniales*) or one queen- or king-size bed, air-conditioning (*aire acondicionado*), a phone (*teléfono*), a private bath (*baño particular*), an in-room safe, cable TV, a hair dryer, iron and ironing board, room service (*servicio de habitación*), shampoo and toiletries, and possibly a view of the water (*vista al mar*). There will be a concierge and at least one hotel restaurant and lounge, a pool, a shop, and an exercise room or spa. In Puerto Rico's smaller inns, rooms will have private baths with hot water (*agua caliente*), air-conditioning or fans, a double to king-size bed, possibly room service, and breakfast (Continental or full) included in the rates. In some smaller hotels, several rooms share baths—it's a good idea to ask before booking. All hotels listed in this guide have private baths unless otherwise noted.

A Puerto Rican law passed in 2007 prohibits smoking in public places including restaurants, bars, cafes, casinos, and hotel common areas.

PARADORES

Some paradores are rural inns offering no-frills apartments, and others are large hotels; all must meet certain standards, such as proximity to an attraction or beach. Most have a small restaurant that serves local cuisine. They're great bargains (usually from $85 to $125 for a double room). You can make reservations by contacting the Puerto Rico Tourism Company. Small Inns of Puerto Rico, a branch of the Puerto Rico Hotel & Tourism Association, is a marketing arm for some 25 small hotels island-wide. The organization occasionally has package deals including casino coupons and LeLoLai (a cultural show) tickets.

Contacts **Puerto Rico Tourism Company** (☎ *787/721–2400 or 800/866–7827* 🌐 *www.gotoparadores.com*). **Small Inns of Puerto Rico** (🌐 *www.prhtasmallhotels.com*).

ADDRESSES

Addresses in Puerto Rico, especially in and around San Juan, can be confusing because Spanish terms like *avenida* and *calle* are used interchangeably with English terms like avenue and street. This means that the shopping strip in Old San Juan may be called Calle Cristo or Cristo Street. (And it might just be called Cristo, as it is on many maps.) A highway is often called an *expreso,* and an alley or pedestrian-only street is labeled a *paseo*.

Outside a metropolitan area, addresses are most often given by the kilometer mark along the road. That means that the address for Parque de las Cavernas del Río Camuy, south of Arecibo, is given as Route 129, Kilometer 18.9.

COMMUNICATIONS

INTERNET

Internet cafés are more common than they once were, but they are still few and far between. As if that weren't bad enough, many hotels have yet to install high-speed Internet access in their rooms. Your best bet is to use your hotel business center.

Contacts **Cyber Net** (✉ *1128 Av. Ashford, Condado* ✉ *5980 Av. Isla Verde,Isla Verde*).

Cybercafes (🌐 *www.cybercafes.com*) lists more than 4,000 Internet cafés worldwide.

PHONES

The good news is that you can now make a direct-dial telephone call from virtually any point on earth. The bad news? You can't always do so cheaply. Calling from a hotel is almost always the most expensive option; hotels usually add huge surcharges to all calls, particularly international ones. In some countries you can phone from call centers or even the post office. Calling cards usually keep costs to a minimum, but only if you purchase them locally. And then there are mobile phones (⇨ *below*), which are sometimes more prevalent—particularly in the developing world—than landlines; as expensive as mobile phone calls can be, they are still usually a much cheaper option than phone calls from your hotel.

All Puerto Rican phone numbers—like those throughout the United States—consist of a three-digit area code and a seven-digit local number. Puerto Rico's area codes are 787 and 939. Toll-free numbers (prefix 800, 888, or 877) are widely used in Puerto Rico, and many can be accessed from North America. You can also access many North American toll-free numbers from the island.

CALLING WITHIN PUERTO RICO

Pay phones, which are abundant in tourist areas, use coins or prepaid phone cards; some accept credit cards. Local calls are 25¢, and on-island, long-distance calls cost about 50¢.

CALLING OUTSIDE PUERTO RICO

The country code for the United States is 1.

Access Codes **AT&T Direct** (☎ *787/725-0300 or 800/331-0500*). **Cellular One** (☎ *800/730-2351*). **Sprint International Access** (☎ *800/298-3266*).

CALLING CARDS

Phone cards are widely available. The Puerto Rico Telephone Company sells its "Ring Card" in various denominations that can be used for both local and international calls. They're available in shops, supermarkets, and drugstores as well as from the phone company.

Information **Ring Cards** (☎ *800/781-1314* 🌐 *www.telefonicapr.com*).

MOBILE PHONES

If you have a multiband phone (some countries use different frequencies than what's used in the United States) and your service provider uses the world-standard GSM network (as do T-Mobile, AT&T, and Verizon), you can probably use your phone abroad. Roaming fees can be steep, however: 99¢ a minute is considered reasonable. And overseas you normally pay the toll charges for incoming calls. It's almost always cheaper to send a text message than to make a call, since text messages have a very low set fee (often less than 5¢).

If you just want to make local calls, consider buying a new SIM card (note that your provider may have to unlock your phone for you to use a different SIM card) and a prepaid service plan in the destination. You'll then have a local number and can make local calls at local rates. If your trip is extensive, you could also simply buy a new cell phone in your destination, as the initial cost will be offset over time.

TIP→ If you travel internationally frequently, save one of your old mobile phones or buy a cheap one on the Internet; ask your cell phone company to unlock it for you, and take it with you as a travel phone, buying a new SIM card with pay-as-you-go service in each destination.

Cell phones are a viable alternative to using local service if you need to keep records of your bills. Call your cell-phone company before departing to get information about activation and roaming charges. Companies that have service on the island include Cellular One, Cingular, and Sprint. Puerto Rico is considered part of the regular nationwide calling area for many cell-phone users; it's considered international for others.

Contacts **Cellular Abroad** (☎ *800/287-5072* 🌐 *www.cellularabroad.com*) rents and sells GMS phones and sells SIM cards that work in many countries. **Mobal** (☎ *888/888-9162* 🌐 *www.mobal.com*) rents mobiles and sells GSM phones (starting at $49) that will operate in 140 countries. Per-call rates vary throughout the world. **Planet Fone** (☎ *888/988-4777* 🌐 *www.planetfone.com*) rents cell phones, but the per-minute rates are expensive.

CUSTOMS AND DUTIES

Puerto Rico is considered a part of the United States for customs purposes, so you will not pass through customs on arrival if you're coming from the mainland. When leaving Puerto Rico, you must pass your bag through a checkpoint of the U.S. Department of Agriculture's (USDA) Animal and Plant Health Inspection Service (APHIS). The list of organic products that can be transported from Puerto Rico to the States includes avocados, bananas, breadfruits, citrus fruits, ginger, papayas, and plantains.

U.S. Information **U.S. Customs and Border Protection** (🌐 *www.cbp.gov*).

EATING OUT

Throughout the island you can find everything from French haute cuisine to sushi bars, as well as superb local eateries serving *comidas criollas*, traditional Caribbean-creole meals. Note that the *mesón gastronómico* label is used by the government to recognize restaurants that preserve culinary traditions. By law, every menu has a written warning about the dangers of consuming raw foods; therefore, if you want something medium rare, you need to be very specific about how you'd like it cooked. *For information on food-related health issues see Health, below.* The restaurants we list are the cream of the crop in each price category.

MEALS AND MEALTIMES

Puerto Ricans' eating habits mirror those of their counterparts on the mainland United States: They eat breakfast, lunch, and dinner, though they don't tend to down coffee all day long. Instead, islanders like a steaming, high-test cup in the morning and another between 2 and 4 pm. They may finish a meal with coffee, but they never drink coffee *during* a meal.

People tend to eat dinner late in Puerto Rico; you may find yourself alone in the restaurant if you eat at 5 pm; at 6, business will pick up a little, and from 7 to 10, it may be quite busy.

Unless otherwise noted, the restaurants listed in this guide are open daily for lunch and dinner.

RESERVATIONS AND DRESS

Regardless of where you are, it's a good idea to make a reservation if you can. In some places, it's expected. We only mention them specifically when reservations are essential (there's no other way you'll ever get a table) or when they are not accepted. For popular restaurants, book as far ahead as you can (often 30 days), and reconfirm as soon as you arrive. (Large parties should always call ahead to check the reservations policy.) We mention dress only when men are required to wear a jacket or a jacket and tie.

Puerto Ricans generally dress up to go out, particularly in the evening. And always remember: Beach attire is only for the beach.

WINES, BEER AND SPIRITS

Puerto Rico isn't a notable producer of wine, but it does make several well-crafted local beers. Legends trace the birthplace of the piña colada to any number of San Juan establishments. Puerto Rican rum is popular mixed with cola (known as a *cuba libre*), soda, tonic, juices, or water, or served on the rocks or even straight up. Rums range from light mixers to dark, aged sipping liqueurs. Look for Bacardí, Don Q, Ron Rico, Palo Viejo, and Barrilito. The drinking age in Puerto Rico is 18.

WORD OF MOUTH

Was the service stellar or not up to snuff? Did the food give you shivers of delight or leave you cold? Did the prices and portions make you happy or sad? Rate restaurants and write your own reviews in Travel Ratings or start a discussion about your favorite places in Travel Talk on *www.fodors.com.* Your comments might even appear in our books. Yes, you, too, can be a correspondent!

ELECTRICITY

Puerto Rico uses the same 110-volt AC (60-cycle), two-prong-outlet electrical system as in North America. Plugs have two flat pins set parallel to each other. European visitors should bring adapters and converters, or call ahead to see whether their hotel has them on hand.

Consider making a small investment in a universal adapter, which has several types of plugs in one lightweight, compact unit. Most laptops and mobile phone chargers are dual voltage (i.e., they operate equally well on 110 and 220 volts), so require only an adapter. These days the same is true of small appliances such as hair dryers. Always check labels and manufacturer instructions to be sure. Don't use 110-volt outlets marked for shavers only for high-wattage appliances such as hair dryers.

EMERGENCIES

Emergencies are handled by dialing 911. You can expect a quick response by police, fire, and medical personnel, most of whom speak at least some English. San Juan's

Tourist Zone Police are particularly helpful to visitors.

General Emergency Contacts **Ambulance, police, and fire** (☎ *911*). **Air Ambulance Service** (☎ *787/756–3424*). **Fire Department** (☎ *787/343–2330*). **Medical Emergency** (☎ *787/754–2222*). **Police** (☎ *787/343–2020*). **Tourist Zone Police** (☎ *787/726–7015 for Condado, 787/728–4770 for Isla Verde*).

HEALTH

The most common types of illnesses are caused by contaminated food and water. Especially in developing countries, drink only bottled, boiled, or purified water and drinks; don't drink from public fountains or use ice. You should even consider using bottled water to brush your teeth. Make sure food has been thoroughly cooked and is served to you fresh and hot; avoid vegetables and fruits that you haven't washed (in bottled or purified water) or peeled yourself. If you have problems, mild cases of traveler's diarrhea may respond to Imodium (known generically as loperamide) or Pepto-Bismol. Be sure to drink plenty of fluids; if you can't keep fluids down, seek medical help immediately.

Infectious diseases can be airborne or passed via mosquitoes and ticks and through direct or indirect physical contact with animals or people. Some, including Norwalk-like viruses that affect your digestive tract, can be passed along through contaminated food. If you are traveling in an area where malaria is prevalent, use a repellant containing DEET and take malaria-prevention medication before, during, and after your trip as directed by your physician. Condoms can help prevent most sexually transmitted diseases, but they aren't absolutely reliable and their quality varies from country to country. Speak with your physician and/or check the CDC or World Health Organization Web sites for health alerts, particularly if you're pregnant, traveling with children, or have a chronic illness.

SPECIFIC ISSUES IN PUERTO RICO

An outbreak of dengue fever, a mosquito-borne disease, hit the island in 2007. Virulent forms of the virus can cause high fever, joint pain, nausea, rashes, and occasionally death, but the strain that spread through the island's urban areas was mild, causing mostly flu-like symptoms. Most cases were reported in urban areas far from the usual tourist destinations. As a precaution, the U.S. Centers for Disease Control and Prevention advises the use of an insect repellent with DEET and clothing that covers the arms and legs.

Health care in Puerto Rico is among the best in the Caribbean, but expect long waits and often a less-than-pleasant bedside manner. At all hospitals and medical centers you can find English-speaking medical staff, and many large hotels have an English-speaking doctor on call.

Tap water on the island is generally fine for drinking, but avoid drinking it after storms (when the water supply can become mixed with sewage). Thoroughly wash or peel produce you buy in markets before eating it.

Do not fly within 24 hours of scuba diving.

OVER-THE-COUNTER REMEDIES

All the U.S. brands of sunscreen and over-the-counter medicines (for example, Tylenol, Advil, Robitussin, and Nyquil) are available in pharmacies, supermarkets, and convenience stores.

HOURS OF OPERATION

Bank hours are generally weekdays from 9 to 5, though a few branches are also open Saturday from 9 to noon or 1. Post offices are open weekdays from 7:30 to 4:30 and Saturday from 8 to noon. Government offices are open weekdays from 9 to 5.

Most gas stations are open daily from early in the morning until 10 or 11 pm. Numerous stations in urban areas are open 24 hours.

As a rule, San Juan–area museums are closed on Monday and, in some cases, Sunday. Hours otherwise are 9 or 10 am to 5 pm, often with an hour off for lunch between noon and 2. Sights managed by the National Parks Service, such as Fuerte San Felipe del Morro and San Cristóbal, are open daily from 9 to 5.

In cities, pharmacies are generally open weekdays and on Saturday from 9 to 6 or 7. Walgreens operates numerous pharmacies around the island; some are open 24 hours.

Street shops are open Monday through Saturday from 9 to 6; mall stores tend to stay open to 9 or sometimes even later. Count on convenience stores staying open late into the night, seven days a week. Supermarkets are often closed on Sunday, although some remain open 24 hours, seven days a week.

MAIL

Puerto Rico uses the U.S. postal system, and all addresses on the island have ZIP codes. The rates to send letters and postcards from Puerto Rico are the same as those everywhere else in the United States. However, mail between Puerto Rico and the U.S. mainland can take more than a week.

Main Branches U.S. Post Office (✉ *100 Paseo Colón, Old San Juan, San Juan* ✉ *113 West Calle Garrido Morales, Fajardo* ✉ *60 Calle McKinley, Mayagüez* ✉ *2340 Av. Eduardo Ruperte, Ponce*).

SHIPPING PACKAGES

Many shops—particularly those in Old San Juan and Condado—will ship purchases for you. Shipping services are especially common at art galleries. Pay by credit card, and save your receipts. Make sure the proprietor insures the package against loss or damage and ships it first-class or by courier. Grab a business card with the proprietor's name and phone number so you can readily follow up with him or her if needed.

Post offices in major Puerto Rican cities offer express mail (next-day) service to the U.S. mainland and to Puerto Rican destinations. In addition, you can send packages via FedEx or UPS. Ask at the concierge desk of your hotel; most have regular courier pickups or can call for one. Hotels that offer business services will take care of the entire ordeal for you. Caveat emptor: Courier delivery and pickup is not available on Saturday, and even "overnight" packages often take two to three days to reach the U.S. mainland.

Express Services FedEx (☎ *800/463-3339*). **UPS** (☎ *787/253-2877 or 800/PICK-UPS*).

MONEY

Puerto Rico, which is a commonwealth of the United States, uses the U.S. dollar as its official currency. Prices for most items are stable and comparable to those in the States, and that includes restaurants and hotel rates. As in many places, city prices tend to be higher than those in rural areas, but you're not going to go broke staying in the city: Soft drinks or a cup of coffee runs about $1; a local beer in a bar, $3; museum admission, $2.

Prices throughout this guide are given for adults. Substantially reduced fees are almost always available for children, students, and senior citizens.

ATMS AND BANKS

Your own bank will probably charge a fee for using ATMs abroad; the foreign bank you use may also charge a fee. Nevertheless, you'll usually get a better rate of exchange at an ATM than you will at a currency-exchange office or even when changing money in a bank. And extracting funds as you need them is a safer option than carrying around a large amount of cash.

TIP→ PIN numbers with more than four digits are not recognized at ATMs in many countries. If yours has five or more, remember to change it before you leave.

Automated Teller Machines (or ATMs, known here as ATHs) are readily available and reliable in the cities; many are attached to banks, but you can also find them in gas stations, drugstores, supermarkets, and larger hotels. Just about every casino has one—to keep people in the game—but these can carry large surcharges, so check the fee before withdrawing money. ATMs are found less frequently in rural areas, but there's usually at least one in even the smallest village. Look to local banks, such as Banco Popular.

CREDIT CARDS

Throughout this guide, the following abbreviations are used: **AE,** American Express; **D,** Discover; **DC,** Diners Club; **MC,** MasterCard; and **V,** Visa.

It's a good idea to inform your credit-card company before you travel, especially if you're going abroad and don't travel internationally very often. Otherwise, the credit-card company might put a hold on your card owing to unusual activity—not a good thing halfway through your trip. Record all your credit-card numbers—as well as the phone numbers to call if your cards are lost or stolen—in a safe place, so you're prepared should something go wrong. Both MasterCard and Visa have general numbers you can call (collect if you're abroad) if your card is lost, but you're better off calling the number of your issuing bank, since MasterCard and Visa usually just transfer you to your bank; your bank's number is usually printed on your card.

Reporting Lost Cards **American Express** (☎ *800/528–4800 in U.S., 336/393–1111 collect from abroad* 🌐 *www.americanexpress.com*). **Diners Club** (☎ *800/234–6377 in U.S., 303/799–1504 collect from abroad* 🌐 *www.dinersclub.com*). **Discover** (☎ *800/347–2683 in U.S., 801/902–3100 collect from abroad* 🌐 *www.discovercard.com*). **MasterCard** (☎ *800/627–8372 in U.S., 636/722–7111 collect from abroad* 🌐 *www.mastercard.com*). **Visa** (☎ *800/847–2911 in U.S., 410/581–9994 collect from abroad* 🌐 *www.visa.com*).

PASSPORTS AND VISAS

U.S. citizens don't need passports to visit Puerto Rico; any government-issued photo ID will do. Nor is there passport control either to or from Puerto Rico; in this respect, flying here is just like traveling on any domestic flight. Nevertheless, it's always wise to carry some form of identification that proves your citizenship, and we still recommend that you carry a valid passport when traveling to Puerto Rico; it's a necessity if you're making any other trips around the Caribbean, except to the U.S. Virgin Islands, where you will pass through customs but not passport control.

SAFETY

San Juan, Mayagüez, and Ponce, like most other big cities, have their share of crime, so guard your wallet or purse in markets, on buses, and in other crowded areas. Avoid beaches at night, when muggings have been known to occur even in Condado and Isla Verde. Don't leave anything unattended on the beach. If you must keep valuables in your vehicle, put them in the trunk. Always lock your car. The exception is at the beaches of Vieques, where rental-car agencies advise you to leave the car unlocked so thieves don't break the windows to search for valuables. This happens extremely rarely, but it does happen.

We recommend that women carry only a handbag that closes completely and wear it bandolier style (across one shoulder and your chest). Open-style bags and those allowed to simply dangle from one shoulder are prime targets for pickpockets and purse snatchers. Avoid walking anywhere alone at night.

TAXES

You must pay a tax on your hotel room rate: For hotels with casinos it's 11%, for other hotels it's 9%, and for government-approved paradores it's 7%. Ask your hotel before booking. The tax, in addition to each hotel's discretionary service charge (which usually ranges from 5% to 12%), can add a hefty 12% to 23% to your bill. There's a 5.5% sales tax in Puerto Rico.

TIPPING

Some hotels automatically add a 5%–12% service charge to your bill. Check ahead to confirm whether this charge is built into the room rate or will be tacked on at checkout. Tips are expected, and appreciated, by restaurant waitstaff (15%–20% if a service charge isn't included), hotel porters ($1 per bag), maids ($1–$2 a day), and taxi drivers (10%–15%).

VISITOR INFORMATION

In addition to the Puerto Rico Tourism Company's *Qué Pasa!*, pick up the Puerto Rico Hotel and Tourism Association's *Bienvenidos* and *Places to Go*. Among them you can find a wealth of information about the island and its activities. All are free and available at tourism offices and hotel desks. The Puerto Rico Tourism Company has information centers at the airport, Old San Juan, Ponce, Aguadilla, and Cabo Rojo. Most island towns also have a tourism office, usually in the city hall.

Contacts Puerto Rico Tourism Company (*Box 902-3960, Old San Juan Station, San Juan 00902-3960 787/721-2400 or 800/866-7827 3575 W. Cahuenga Blvd., Suite 560, Los Angeles, CA 90068 323/874-5991 or 800/874-1230 www.gotopuertorico.com*).

VACATION PACKAGES

Packages *are not* guided excursions. Packages combine airfare, accommodations, and perhaps a rental car or other extras (theater tickets, guided excursions, boat trips, reserved entry to popular museums, transit passes), but they let you do your own thing. During busy periods packages may be your only option, as flights and rooms may be sold out otherwise.

Packages will definitely save you time. They can also save you money, particularly in peak seasons, but—and this is a really big "but"—you should price each part of the package separately to be sure. And be aware that prices advertised on Web sites and in newspapers rarely include service charges or taxes, which can up your costs by hundreds of dollars.

TIP→ Some packages and cruises are sold only through travel agents. Don't always assume that you can get the best deal by booking everything yourself.

Each year consumers are stranded or lose their money when packagers—even large ones with excellent reputations—go out of business. How can you protect yourself?

First, always pay with a credit card; if you have a problem, your credit-card company may help you resolve it. Second, buy trip insurance that covers default. Third, choose a company that belongs to the United States Tour Operators Association, whose members must set aside funds to cover defaults. Finally, choose a company that also participates in the Tour Operator Program of the American Society of Travel Agents (ASTA), which will act as mediator in any disputes.

You can also check on the tour operator's reputation among travelers by posting an inquiry on one of the Fodors.com forums.

Organizations American Society of Travel Agents (*800/965-2782 www.asta.org*). **United States Tour Operators Association** (*USTOA 212/599-6599 www.ustoa.com*).

INDEX

D

E

F

G

H

R

PHOTO CREDITS

1, Katja Kreder / age fotostock. 2, Franz Marc Frei / age fotostock. 5, Franz Marc Frei / age fotostock. **Chapter 1: Experience Puerto Rico:**8, Katja Kreder / age fotostock. 9, Katja Kreder / age fotostock. 10, Christian Wheatley/Starwood Hotels & Resorts. 11 (left), Lori Froeb/Shutterstock. 11(right), John Frink/iStockphoto.14(left), Jacom Stephens/Avid Creative, Inc./iStockphoto. 14 (center), Diueine/Flickr. 14 (right),Ksaraf/wikipedia.org. 14 (bottom), Jorge González. 15 (top left), Nick Hanna /Alamy. 15 (bottom left), Frank Llosa. 15(right), imagebroker / Alamy. 17 (left),Jbermudez/wikipedia.org. 17 (right),MissChatter/wikipedia.org. 18, Danny Lehman/Celebrity Cruises. 19 (left),Tomás Fano/Flickr. 19 (right), Charles Harris/Royal Caribbean International. 20, Hotel El Convento. 21, Hotel El Convento.22, Museo de Arte de Puerto Rico. 23 (left), Museo de Arte de Puerto Rico. 23(right), wikipedia.org. 24, Lynn Watson/Shutterstock. 25 (left), The Ritz-Carlton. 25 (right), The Ritz-Carlton. 27Aleksandar Kolundzija/iStockphoto. 34,Oquendo/Flickr. **Chapter 2: San Juan:** 35, Katja Kreder / age fotostock. 36 (top), John Rodriguez/iStockphoto. 36 (bottom), Lori Froeb/Shutterstock. 37 (left), Miguel A. Alvarez/Shutterstock. 37 (right), Adam Bies/Shutterstock. 40, Katja Kreder / age fotostock. 41 (top right), mysticchildz/Flickr. 41 (bottom left), Stinkie Pinkie/Flickr. 42 (left), DU BOISBERRANGER Jean / age fotostock. 42 (right), DU BOISBERRANGER Jean / age fotostock. 45, Heeb Christian / age fotostock. 47, Tomás Fano/Flickr. 50, George Oze / Alamy. 55 (left), Franz Marc Frei / age fotostock. 55 (top right), Lawrence Roberg/Shutterstock. 55 (bottom right), Franz Marc Frei / age fotostock. 56 (top right), iStockphoto. 56 (bottom left), Oquendo/Flickr. 57 (top left), runneralan2004/Flickr. 57 (top middle), runneralan2004/Flickr. 57 (top left), Franz Marc Frei / age fotostock. 57 (bottom), Prknlot/Flickr. 59, Atlantide S.N.C. / age fotostock. 60, Oliver Gerhard / age fotostock. 64, Greg Vaughn / Alamy. 73, Wendell Metzen / age fotostock. 75, steve bly / Alamy. 82, Wendell Metzen / age fotostock. 86, Ken Welsh / age fotostock. 87, Ken Welsh / age fotostock. 92, DU BOISBERRANGER Jean / age fotostock. 101 (top), Thomas Hart Shelby 2007. 101 (bottom left), The Ritz-Carlton. 101 (bottom right), Hotel El Convento. 105, Lawrence Manning/photolibrary.com. 106, Craig Lovell / Eagle Visions Photography / Alamy. 107 (top middle), Pietro Scozzari / age fotostock. 107 (left), Julie Schwietert. 107 (bottom middle), Julie Schwietert. 107 (bottom right), STEPHANE - FOTODECLIC / age fotostock. 108 (left), Julie Schwietert. 108 (right), Julie Schwietert. 117, Martin Florin Emmanuel / Alamy. 122, Wendell Metzen / age fotostock. **Chapter 3: El Yunque and the Northeast:** 125, Ken Welsh / age fotostock. 126, Diana Lundin/Shutterstock. 127 (left), Joseph/Shutterstock. 127 (right), Thomas Hart Shelby. 130, Robert Fried / Alamy. 131 (bottom left), John Frink/iStockphoto. 131 (top right), iStockphoto. 132, Doug Schneider/iStockphoto. 133, Joseph/Shutterstock. 134, Julie Schwietert. 135 (bottom left), Pavelsteidl/wikipedia.org. 135 (top right), Ryan Bonneau / Alamy. 136, Luis César Tejo/Shutterstock. 141, Kreder Katja / age fotostock. 144, Katja Kreder / age fotostock. 147, Rolf Nussbaumer / age fotostock. 152, Ken Welsh / age fotostock. 153, Ken Welsh / age fotostock. 154, Katja Kreder / age fotostock. 157, Scott Wiseman. 162, Larry Lambrecht. **Chapter 4: Vieques and Culebra:** 165, Katja Kreder / age fotostock. 166 (top), underwhelmer/Flickr. 166 (bottom), underwhelmer/Flickr. 167 (top left), plizzba/Flickr. 167 (top right), Jjankechu/wikipedia.org. 167 (bottom), underwhelmer/Flickr. 170, Katja Kreder / age fotostock. 171 (bottom left), kkaplin/Shutterstock. 171 (top right), blucolt/Flickr. 172 (left), Michele Falzone / age fotostock. 172 (right), Michele Falzone / age fotostock. 177, Michele Falzone / age fotostock. 178, SuperStock/age fotostock. 181, Frank Llosa. 182 (top), Frank Llosa. 182 (bottom), kayakingpuertorico.com. 183, Starwood Hotels & Resorts. 184 (top left), Frank Llosa. 184 (bottom right), Sue Braden. 185, Starwood Hotels & Resorts. 188 (top), Greg Vaughn / Alamy. 188 (bottom left), Natalie Stultz. 188 (bottom right), Hector's By the Sea. 193, jasonsager/Flickr. 199, Kim Karpeles / Alamy. **Chapter 5: Ponce and the Southern Coast:** 203, Ken Welsh / age fotostock. 204 (bottom left), Capricornis Photographic Inc./Shutterstock. 204 (top right), Oquendo/wikipedia.org. 205 (top), Oquendo/Flickr. 205 (bottom), Jmoliver/wikipedia.org. 207, Tony Amador. 208, Oliver Gerhard / Alamy. 209 (bottom left), Oquendo/Flickr. 209 (top right), Greg Vaughn / Alamy. 210, Jim Zuckerman / Alamy. 211 (bottom left), Jim Zuckerman / Alamy. 211 (top right), Nicholas Gill. 212, Oquendo/Flickr. 217, Franz Marc Frei / age fotostock. 222, Eric Fowke / Alamy. 225, Nicholas Gill. 232, Julie Schwietert. 233 (bottom left), Museo de los Santos / Richard Holm. 233 (top right), Tony Amador. 238, DU BOISBERRANGER Jean / age fotostock. 241, giulio andreini / age fotostock. 244, Morales / age fotostock. **Chapter 6: Rincón and the Porta del Sol:** 247, Marlise Kast. 248, Hiram A. Gay/wikipedia.org. 249 (top left), Oquendo/Flickr. 249 (bottom right), Oquendo/Flickr. 251, Israel Pabon/Shutterstock. 252, Katja Kreder / age fotostock. 253 (bottom left), cogito ergo imago/Flickr. 253 (top right), Marlise Kast. 254, BlueMoon Stock / Alamy. 255, SuperStock/age fotostock. 259, Juerg Heinimann / Alamy. 264 (top), Tres Sirenas Beach Inn. 264 (bottom), Horned Dorset Primavera. 271, Marlise Kast.

272 (top), Eric Rivera Vázquez/Shutterstock. 272 (bottom), Eric Rivera Vázquez/Shutterstock. 273 (top left), Marlise Kast. 273 (bottom left), Eric Rivera Vázquez/Shutterstock. 273 (right), Marlise Kast. 274, Eric Rivera Vázquez/Shutterstock. 281, Israel Pabon/Shutterstock. 284, Nicholas Pitt / Alamy. 291, Ken Welsh / age fotostock. **Chapter 7: Ruta Panorámica:** 297, Nick Hanna / Alamy. 298, Michele Falzone / age fotostock. 299, Casa Grande Mountain Retreat. 301, Robert Fried / Alamy. 305, Nick Hanna / Alamy. 306, Oliver Gerhard / Alamy. 307, Jorge González. 308, imagebroker / Alamy.

NOTES

Pack collapsealbe coolers
Grocery store in Fajardo
Flip flops are key
Bring snacks/drinks/cooler to Palomino
sunscreen & pool area
- towels are provided at island free
Dress code - expect to dress up a bit
more than you thought
- volleyball court in Palomino Island
- there are plenty of condom shops
in San Juan & Fajardo
- GPS is a great idea if driving around
San Juan, PR during stay
or having portable GPS system
- ~~$~~ road signs are in Spanish
Backpack
Valet parking v. self-park

Road Kill consist mainly of Iguanas
You will experience the Coqui serenade

* Met couple that drove us to the Blue Iguana
* La Piccola Fontana gave us a bottle of wine
~~Fon~~ Fontana
- he is also an identical twin

NOTES

Travel Times
Cong. to Luquillo - 20 min
Cong. to Rio Grande -
cong to El Yunque 25 min
Cong. to HSA - 35 min
HSA to San Juan - 30 min

ABOUT OUR WRITERS

Travel writer, photographer and Caribbean expert **Christopher P. Baker** has written more than 15 guidebooks to Cuba, Jamaica, The Bahamas, Puerto Rico, and Central America. He is a regular contributor to *Caribbean Travel & Life, National Geographic Traveler* and dozens of other publications worldwide. His many awards include the Caribbean Tourism Organization's 2005 Travel Journalist of the Year and the prestigious Lowell Thomas Award 2008 Travel Journalist of the Year. He promotes himself through his website, www.christopherbaker.com

Julie Schwietert Collazo is a bilingual writer interested in overlooked people and places, especially in Latin America. She has written about Chinese Cubans in Havana, Generation Y in Colombia, workers' and indigenous movements in Mexico City, and environmental issues in Chile. She was one of only a handful of journalists to visit the Joint Detention Facility at Guantanamo Bay in Cuba in 2008. Julie has lived in Mexico City and San Juan, Puerto Rico. She currently calls New York City home. She is the managing editor of Matador Network, an online travel magazine and community.

Lima, Peru, and Brooklyn, New York–based writer and photographer **Nicholas Gill** updated the Ponce and the Southern Coast chapter of this guide. His work appears in publications such as *Conde Nast Traveler, National Geographic Traveler, The New York Times, LA Times,* and *Caribbean Travel & Life.* He also publishes an e-zine on Latin American food & travel, Newworldreview.com. Visit his personal website (www.nicholas-gill.com) for more information.

As a freelance journalist and author, **Marlise Elizabeth Kast** has contributed to over 50 publications including *Forbes, Surfer, San Diego Magazine* and *New York Post.* Her passion for traveling has taken her to 62 countries with short-term residency in Switzerland, Dominican Republic, Spain, and Costa Rica. Following the release of her memoir, *Tabloid Prodigy*, Marlise coauthored *Fodor's Mexico* (2009, 2010, 2011), *San Diego* (2009), *Panama* (2010), and *Corsica & Sardinia* (2010). She has also written *Day & Overnight Hikes on California's Pacific Crest Trail.* Marlise recently completed a 13-month surfing and snowboarding expedition through 28 countries. Now based in San Diego, she is currently working on her next full length manuscript. For more information, visit www.marlisekast.com.

Charyn Pfeuffer has written about food, travel and lifestyle topics for more than a decade and has contributed to more than 80 publications, including *National Geographic Traveler, Seattle Times, Sunset, Destination Weddings & Honeymoons,* the *San Francisco Chronicle* and DailyCandy.com. She'd consider taming her wanderlustful ways (more than 100 flights annually) if she could settle down in an airstream in Latin America, but first needs to perfect her Spanish.

Heather Rodino recently traded the island of Manhattan for the island of Puerto Rico, leaving behind a career in book publishing that included editorial positions at Barnes & Noble's publishing division and the Times Books imprint of Henry Holt. She is now a freelance editor and writer. She lives in the Condado neighborhood of San Juan and doesn't miss those long New York winters.